STUDY GUIDE

Thomas O'Connor
University of New Orleans

Contemporary Marketing PLUS

EIGHTH EDITION

Louis E. Boone
Ernest G. Cleverdon Chair of Business and Management
University of South Alabama

David L. Kurtz
R. A. and Vivian Young Chair of Business Administration
Head, Department of Marketing and Transportation
University of Arkansas

THE DRYDEN PRESS
Harcourt Brace College Publishers

Fort Worth Philadelphia San Diego New York Orlando Austin San Antonio
Toronto Montreal London Sydney Tokyo

Address for Editorial Correspondence
The Dryden Press, 301 Commerce Street, Suite 3700, Fort Worth, TX 76102

Address for Orders
The Dryden Press, 6277 Sea Harbor Drive, Orlando, FL 32887
1-800-782-4479, or 1-800-433-0001 (in Florida)

ISBN: 0-03-003913-4

Printed in the United States of America

4 5 6 7 8 9 0 1 2 3   0 9 5   9 8 7 6 5 4 3 2 1

The Dryden Press
Harcourt Brace College Publishers

Introduction

There have been a number of changes made in the *Study Guide* for *Contemporary Marketing*, Eighth Edition. As always, these were made only when it was felt they would improve the essential purpose of this work—to help the student gain greater understanding of marketing as it is practiced today. The *Study Guide* is coordinated with the textbook and each of its parts is designed as a learning unit exploring a particular area of the discipline of marketing.

Coverage of each chapter of the *Study Guide* begins with an outline of the material in the chapter. The outline, when used in concert with the textbook, is designed to serve as a memory refresher to assist in recalling significant points in the text as you work through the exercises in the guide.

Other features include a **Self Quiz** for each chapter's material; **Experiential Exercises** which let you examine marketing operations firsthand; **Applying Marketing Concepts**, a series of illustrations of how the techniques and principles described in the text are put to use; **Computer Applications** designed to allow you to use some of the more popular analytical tools of the trade in relatively painless fashion; and a **Crossword Puzzle** that relates terms used in the text with their definitions.

In **Creating a Marketing Plan**, you are provided with information you can develop by following the adventures of three young entrepreneurs. This information allows you to create a marketing mix from the ground up.

Each of the parts of this guide contains a brief synopsis of the part as well as several **Cases** that call for problem solving in a marketing context.

As always, I solicit and welcome your comments and those of your teachers. Though every effort has been made to make sure that the answers match the questions and it all makes sense, I'm sure there are errors scattered here and there through the *Study Guide*. For these I apologize and request that if you find them, please tell me about them.

Otherwise, my best wishes to you in your studies and in the use of these materials.

Thomas S. O'Connor

The University of New Orleans

A Few Words of Thanks

As always, it has been a pleasure working with the people at Dryden Press. Paul Stewart has been unfailingly jovial as we worked our way through this revision. My thanks also go to Nancy Carroll for formatting this book. And once again my secretary, Joyce Stall, has ably assisted in keeping other things going while I pursued this project.

My family have tolerated me well while this revision was in progress. I guess they're getting used to it. To them I express my deepest appreciation for that tolerance. Thanks again Val, Brian, and Terry.

Contents

Part 1

The Contemporary Marketing Environment

Marketing is the process of planning and executing the conception, pricing, promotion, and distribution of ideas, goods, and services to create exchanges that satisfy organizational and individual objectives. The marketing process creates time, place, and ownership utility for consumers.

Marketing arises out of the exchange process. The emphasis on marketing activities increases as firms progress through the three eras of: (1) production orientation, (2) sales orientation, and (3) marketing orientation. Long-run success cannot result unless firms adopt a company-wide consumer orientation. This realization has been called the marketing concept.

Marketers plan and coordinate the four strategic areas of product, distribution, promotion, and pricing. A comprehensive marketing mix strategy cannot be set until the needs and wants of the chosen market segment have been determined. For marketing to take place, it is usually necessary that a firm or some combination of firms perform the eight universal functions of: (1) buying, (2) selling, (3) transporting, (4) storing, (5) standardization and grading, (6) financing, (7) risk-taking, and (8) securing marketing information.

In recent years, the marketing concept has been broadened to include the activities of not-for-profit organizations, though their marketing activities often differ significantly from those of for-profit firms.

Quality describes the degree of excellence or superiority of an organization's goods and services, as well as the intangible component of consumer satisfaction. Total quality management is an approach that involves all employees in continually improving products and work processes to achieve customer satisfaction and world-class performance. Applying TQM to marketing involves (1) involving top management, (2) conducting a marketing audit, (3) focusing on customer satisfaction, and (4) working toward continuous improvement in the marketing function. Improvement in the marketing function is achieved by reducing cycle time, reducing variation in work processes, products, and services, and eliminating waste.

Benchmarking is the process in which an organization continuously compares and measures itself against industry leaders to gain information that will improve performance. The three key steps of benchmarking include identifying processes for improvement and companies that implement them best, analyzing internal processes and performance levels compared to those of industry leaders, and implementing changes to improve processes.

Employee involvement in TQM is achieved through internal marketing, employee training, and teamwork. In the marketing mix, TQM may be applied to each element to create a world-class product.

The marketer must be aware of the five interacting environments which affect marketing activities: the competitive, the political-legal, the economic, the technological, and the social-cultural. These environments are complex and are affected by the actions of many persons and organizations.

The competitive environment includes all those organizations competing for the purchasing power of the consumer. A firm chooses its competitive environment when it chooses its markets.

Marketing strategies must be adjusted in response to changes in the political-legal environment. Early antitrust legislation was aimed at maintaining a competitive environment. Later legislation arising out of conditions which existed during the 1930's were designed to protect small competitors from discriminatory practices. Since the 1950's, a number of laws have been designed to protect consumers from harmful marketing practices and unsafe products or services. Beginning in the 1970s, it became common to "deregulate" industries which were formerly under substantial government control.

The rate of inflation, level of unemployment, and availability of critical resources all influence the likelihood of individuals parting with discretionary income. If resources are in short supply it becomes difficult to satisfy consumer demand. Marketers may, in fact, have to engage in "demarketing," encouraging consumers not to buy scarce commodities.

Technology is changing with incredible speed. There are competitors in this environment, too, and technological breakthroughs by others may take market share away from those who don't keep up the pace.

The social-cultural environment is a significant factor to marketers. This area includes all relationships marketers have with society. Rising educational levels and better communications have lead to greater public involvement in this area.

Entering the global market involves understanding the differences in the marketing environment as one moves from culture to culture.

One of the more significant influences on a firm's activities in the global sphere is the trend toward multinational economic integration. Entry into the world market may be by exporting, foreign licensing, or overseas production and marketing. American firms must also recognize that the United States is an attractive market for international entrepreneurs.

Chapter 1

Marketing in Profit and Not-For-Profit Settings

Chapter Outline

You may want to use the following as a guide in taking notes.

   I.   Chapter Overview

       A. All organizations produce and market something

       B. The marketplace is global in scope

       C. Organizations satisfy a commitment to society by creating utility of form, time, place, and possession

   II.   What is Marketing?

       A. Organizations exist, according to Drucker, to "create customers"

       B. Definition of marketing—conception, pricing, distribution, and promotion

  III. The Origins of Marketing Lie in the Need for Exchange of One Valuable Item for Another

       A. Tangible goods and intangible services

       B. Marketing as a process of creating and resolving exchanges

  IV. Three Eras in the History of Marketing

       A. The production era—efficiency on the assembly line in a seller's market

       B. The sales era—output begins to fully meet demand

       C. The marketing era—a new point of view appears

V. Emergence of the Marketing Concept

    A. The buyer's market finally arrives

    B. Consumer orientation

    C. Definition of the concept

VI. Avoiding Marketing Myopia

VII. Broadening the Marketing Concept to Include Not-For-Profit Marketing

    A. Marketing in not-for-profit organizations

    B. Types of not-for-profit marketing

    C. Characteristics of not-for-profit marketing

VIII. Elements of a Marketing Strategy

    A. The target market

    B. The marketing mix variables

    C. The marketing environment

IX. Marketing Costs and Marketing Functions

    A. The exchange functions—buying and selling

    B. The physical distribution functions—transportation and storage

    C. The facilitating functions—standardization and grading, financing, risk-bearing, and securing marketing information

X. The Study of Marketing

Name _____   Instructor _____

Section _____   Date _____

Key Concepts

The purpose of this section is to allow you to determine if you can match key concepts with the definitions of the concepts. It is essential that you know the definitions of the concepts prior to applying the concepts in later exercises in this chapter.

From the list of lettered terms, select the one that best fits each of the numbered statements below. Write the letter of that choice in the space provided.

Key Terms

a. utility
b. marketing
c. exchange process
d. production orientation
e. sales orientation
f. seller's market
g. buyer's market
h. consumer orientation
i. marketing concept
j. marketing myopia
k. broadening concept

l. person marketing
m. place marketing
n. cause marketing
o. organization marketing
p. target market
q. marketing mix
r. product strategy
s. distribution strategy
t. distribution strategy
u. promotional strategy

_____ 1. An example of this would be when states, cities, and countries publicize their tourist attractions to lure vacation travelers.

_____ 2. A blending together of the elements of promotion by marketers to create effective communication with their target market.

_____ 3. Occurs when management fails to recognize the scope of its business.

_____ 4. Expanded view of marketing as a generic function performed by both profit-seeking and not-for-profit organizations.

_____ 5. The blending of marketing strategy elements to fit the needs and preferences of chosen consumer segments.

_____ 6. "The want-satisfying power of a good or service" describes this characteristic.

_____ 7. A market characterized by a shortage of goods and services.

_____ 8. Choosing brand names and trademarks, deciding on package design, and creating the terms of warranties are part of this.

_____ 9. Marketing by mutual-benefit organizations, service organizations, and governments that seek to influence others to accept their goals, receive their services, or contribute to them in some way.

_____ 10. You hear a radio commercial which outlines the plight of the world's children and asks for your help in relieving their difficulty by contributing to the child-oriented charity of your choice. How would you characterize this activity?

_____ 11. This afternoon's mail brings an envelope containing a pamphlet praising a candidate for a local political office. The pamphlet, and the accompanying request for a financial contribution, is typical of this activity.

_____ 12. "The strong buyer's market which appeared in this country after World War II made it necessary for business to realize that it must first market, then sell goods." What new point of view does this phrase describe?

_____ 13. A marketplace characterized by an abundance of goods and services.

_____ 14. The philosophy that if you "build a better mousetrap the world will beat a path to your door."

_____ 15. Assuring that products are shipped to the right destinations is part of this strategy.

_____ 16. The objective of this company-wide consumer orientation is the achievement of long-term success.

_____ 17. The process of planning and executing the conception, pricing, promotion, and distribution of ideas, goods, services, and organizations to create exchanges that will satisfy individual and organizational objectives.

_____ 18. The process of two or more parties trading things of value to satisfy perceived needs.

_____ 19. When a business assumes that consumers do not wish to buy nonessential products and services and relies on creative advertising and personal selling to "push" its offering, it is expressing this philosophy.

_____ 20. A group of people toward whom a firm markets its goods, services, or ideas with a strategy designed to satisfy their specific needs and preferences.

Name _____   Instructor _____

Section _____   Date _____

Self Quiz

You should use these objective questions to test your understanding of the chapter material. You can check your answers with those provided at the end of the chapter.

While these questions cover most of the chapter topics, they are not intended to be the same as the test questions your instructor may use in an examination. A good understanding of all aspects of course material is essential to good performance on any examination.

True/False

Write "T" for True or "F" for False for each of the following statements.

_____ 1. The Bubble Yum Virtuality Tour used new technology to create a unique "immersive" approach to marketing chewing gum.

_____ 2. Marketing does not take place in underdeveloped countries because the traders who sell goods in central marketplaces cannot afford television and radio advertisements.

_____ 3. Marketing has been described as concerned with creating and resolving exchange relationships.

_____ 4. Taylor's book, *Principles of Scientific Management*, through its emphasis on production efficiency, tended to prolong a *production orientation* among management through the early part of this century.

_____ 5. A *sales orientation* is most appropriate for firms in a strong seller's market.

_____ 6. Severe weather such as deep freezes or tornadoes can result in tremendous reductions in fruit crops such as oranges. If the amount of oranges available is less than the number consumers wish to eat, a buyer's market exists.

_____ 7. An example of marketing myopia is when an airline defines its main scope of business activity as providing faster airline service than any other airline.

_____ 8. The marketing concept emerged as the American economy changed from a buyer's market to a seller's market at the end of World War II.

_____ 9. An example of broadening the marketing concept is the American Heart Association using a promotional campaign to encourage people to enroll for courses in cardiopulmonary resuscitation.

_____ 10. If you were in charge of distribution strategy, you would be concerned with transportation, storage, and institutions such as retailers who sell to consumers.

_____ 11. The marketing mix involves blending four types of marketing decisions to satisfy chosen consumer segments.

_____ 12. Until about twenty years ago, marketing was considered to be an activity reserved solely to profit-making organizations.

_____ 13. Trucking companies perform the transportation function; warehouses perform the storage function.

_____ 14. Egg producers who separate their eggs into small, medium, large, and extra-large and package them separately are performing the function of securing marketing information.

_____ 15. Marketing activities should be understood, but it should be remembered that they have little direct impact on job potential because the number of people needed to do them is so small.

_____ 16. The Metropolitan Museum of Art's ads which invited the public to visit the museum and view its vast collection of 19th century paintings and sculptures exemplifies event marketing.

_____ 17. If you should happen to come across a company whose chief marketing executive bore the title of "sales manager," you would have reason to suspect that the company was still in the production, rather than the sales or marketing era.

_____ 18. By focusing on the benefits resulting from the use of products or services, marketing converts wants into needs.

_____ 19. The private sector of the economy has an even more diverse array of not-for-profit organizations than does the public sector.

_____ 20. The definition of marketing that identified it as the performance of business activities that directed the flow of goods and services from producer to consumer proved too broad to be valid in today's markets.

_____ 21. A television commercial sponsored by a citizens' group stressing the necessity for your state to undertake prison reform would be an example of organization marketing.

_____ 22. One characteristic more typical of nonprofit organizations than for-profit organizations is the lack of a clear organization structure.

_____ 23. If you buy a set of tires, you can be sure that if the new set bears the same size markings as the old, it will fit the car. This is because tire sizes are standardized.

_____ 24. If the Alabama Power Company published a statement in which it defined its business as "providing electricity reliably and cheaply" to the geographic area defined in its charter, it would probably be fair to say its management was suffering from marketing myopia.

Multiple Choice

Circle the letter of the word or phrase that best completes the sentence or best answers the question.

Use the following information for Questions 25 - 28:

Assume that you and another student have started a newspaper. The purpose of the paper is to serve as an independent source of campus and community news. You have hired a secretary to type news copy with a personal computer you have bought the firm.

25. The process of changing the information you have collected into a finished product, a newspaper, would create
    a. time utility.
    b. place utility.
    c. form utility.
    d. ownership utility.
    e. marketing utility.

26. If you hire someone to deliver the finished newspapers, instead of requiring your customers to pick them up at your office, you are performing the _____ function and creating _____ utility.
    a. storage, place
    b. buying, time
    c. transportation, time
    d. transportation, place
    e. risk-taking, place

27. You are in charge of contacting potential customers. You talk to students to determine who wants or needs an independent newspaper and how much they are willing to pay. In addition, after a sale is made you assign the title of the paper to the student. The function in which you are involved and the utility you create by helping transfer title are
    a. transporting function; place utility.
    b. buying function; ownership utility.
    c. financing function; time utility.
    d. selling function; ownership utility.
    e. grading function; form utility.

28. The marketing efforts of your firm will not create
    a. form utility.
    b. time utility.
    c. place utility.
    d. ownership utility.
    e. functional utility.

29. "The performance of business activities that direct the flow of goods and services from producer to consumer or user." Which of the following are two major problems with this definition of marketing?
    a. it ignores the marketing functions of transportation and storage
    b. it assumes that marketing creates only form and place utility
    c. it does not recognize marketing's contribution to form utility, nor does it recognize marketing by not-for-profit organizations
    d. it does not consider the importance of production efficiency and quality control
    e. it does not emphasize that the firm must produce output of value to consumers, nor does it mention long-term survival

30. A good marketing strategy should include
    a. seeking high levels of market share regardless of the ethics of the marketing activities necessary to obtain that share.
    b. selecting target segments by analysis of consumer needs prior to production.
    c. establishing the lowest cost marketing program regardless of customer needs.
    d. analyzing consumer needs after the product has been designed and produced.
    e. recognizing that marketing does not apply to nonprofit organizations.

31. Which of the following statements best reflects a firm with a production orientation?
    a. Our company is consumer oriented.
    b. We have a first-rate sales organization which disposes of all the products we can make at a favorable price.
    c. We guarantee our customers complete satisfaction or we will refund their money.
    d. Our basic function is to produce the highest quality product possible.
    e. Selling is only one component of marketing.

32. The marketing concept emphasizes
    a. company-wide consumer orientation.
    b. marketers running the company.
    c. a production orientation.
    d. achievement of short-run success.
    e. building retail stores in the ghettos.

33. Firms facing a buyer's market will tend to be concerned with
    a. producing more goods or services.
    b. convincing consumers to buy their goods and services.
    c. restricting production to meet the level of demand.
    d. hunting for new markets for their goods and services.
    e. offering consumers lower prices than the competitors'

34. Which of the following best exemplifies a firm which has adopted the marketing concept?
    a. Sales must increase 30 percent annually.
    b. We train our sales force to be persuasive so they can wear down consumer resistance.
    c. Our new car was developed to satisfy the needs of young, urban professionals who want a luxurious, quality mode of transportation.
    d. We do not have to worry about competitors because we have a patent on the production process for our products.
    e. Engineers plan our products and marketers sell them.

35. Which of the following would you consider to be an example of marketing myopia?
    a. telephone company—the lowest cost phone service.
    b. railroad company—transportation services to meet customer needs.
    c. perfume company—hope in a bottle.
    d. movie company—entertainment for all ages.
    e. chicken company—nutritional dining enjoyment.

36. The marketing mix includes
    a. planning the product.
    b. blending personal selling, advertising and sales promotion tools.
    c. setting prices.
    d. establishing marketing channels.
    e. all of the above.

37. In order to remain a dealer for a certain brand of computers, a firm must agree with the manufacturer to buy a certain number of units each month. Once bought, the computers can't be returned to the manufacturer. Dealers borrow money from banks and other financial institutions to pay for the computers before they are sold to ultimate users. Some of the functions performed in this example include
    a. dealers: transporting, banks: storing.
    b. dealers: buying, banks: selling.
    c. dealers: securing market information, banks: grading.
    d. dealers: risk-taking, banks: buying.
    e. dealers: risk-taking, banks: financing.

38. Driving to the mall one day, you realize that the commercial you're hearing on the radio isn't trying to convince you to eat at a particular hamburger restaurant, but is trying to convince you to try the "designated driver" (one of the people in your group agrees not to drink so as to be a safe driver for the others) program for holiday revelers who expect to partake of alcoholic beverages at parties and other festive events. The commercial is paid for by a brewing company. This commercial is an example of
    a. place marketing.
    b. organization marketing.
    c. event marketing
    d. person marketing.
    e. cause marketing.

39. Which of the following would be considered an environmental factor which would impact the marketing effort?
    a. doubling the size of the sales force
    b. testing a new product in selected markets
    c. sharing the cost of advertisements with retailers who sell the company's products
    d. Japanese competitors offering higher quality products for the same price
    e. using prime time television advertisements to extol the benefits of the company's products.

40. In which of the following situations would the you expect the utility created by marketing activity to be the greatest?
    a. A physician and his assistants use the facilities of Providence Hospital to study a new surgical technique.
    b. An engineer studies the feasibility of assembling particular integrated circuits, resistors, capacitors, and other electrical and mechanical components into a Sony TV set.
    c. Musicians, sheet music, instruments, and a leader come together in Joe's Bar and Grill after a rehearsal by the Zootsuit Five Plus Two.
    d. Your local Wal-Mart advertises a price reduction on all remaining summer merchandise on an as-is, where-is basis at the end of August.
    e. Delchamps opens a new shopping center built around one of its "super-supermarkets" in a growing suburb

41. A Rolls-Royce executive was once heard to remark, "We have never had to worry about sales or advertising. Our cars are simply the best in the world." The chances are that the automobile division of Rolls Royce is
    a. an active advocate of the marketing concept.
    b. a production oriented company.
    c. a firm with a sales orientation.
    d. unique in its analysis of marketing opportunities and target markets.
    e. operating in a buyer's market.

42. When marketing departments began to emerge during the sales era,
    a. they tended to assume a subordinate position to production, finance, and engineering.
    b. they were often headed by an executive whose background and orientation had nothing to do with sales.
    c. they quickly assumed a position of domination over the firm's other divisions.
    d. marketing to specific target groups of consumers became the rule rather than the exception.
    e. many firms returned to a strong emphasis on product quality and production techniques.

43. Not-for-profit organizations
    a. are prohibited by law from earning a profit on their operations.
    b. are very numerous in the public sector, but are seldom found in the private sector.
    c. have as their primary objective something other than returning a profit to their owners.
    d. seldom deal in tangible goods.
    e. generate over $900 billion in revenues each year.

44. Efforts by not-for-profit institutions to direct the attention, interest, and preferences of a target market toward a person are called
    a. cause marketing.
    b. celebrity marketing.
    c. person marketing.
    d. concept marketing.
    e. personal promotion.

45. Transportation and storage are known as the
    a. exchange functions.
    b. normalizing functions.
    c. delivery functions.
    d. physical distribution functions.
    e. discriminating functions.

46. On the way home from work, John stops at a gasoline station to buy fuel. He buys unleaded regular even though he's never used this brand of gasoline because the sign on the pump says "Minimum Octane Rating = 87" and he knows his car will perform adequately on this fuel. He pays for his purchase with his new oil company credit card. Which of the following marketing functions have most obviously facilitated John's purchase?
    a. risk taking and securing market information
    b. risk taking and financing
    c. standardization/grading and financing
    d. transportation and buying
    e. storing and financing

47. The marketing functions of transportation and storage are most closely related to the utilities of
    a. time and place.
    b. form and time.
    c. ownership and place.
    d. ownership and form.
    e. time and ownership.

48. If they are typical of the average product, about what proportion of the cost of a pair of Nike Air Jordans would you expect represents marketing costs?
    a. About a quarter
    b. About a third
    c. About a half
    d. Well over a half
    e. Almost three-quarters

49. The idea that customers will resist purchasing products and services not deemed essential and that the task of personal selling and advertising is to convince them to buy is typical of the
    a. production-oriented company.
    b. sales-oriented company.
    c. marketing-oriented company.
    d. types of organizations named in (a) or (b) above.
    e. none of the above.

Name _____   Instructor _____

Section _____   Date _____

Applying Marketing Concepts

Dan Fox, a former professional road racer, has opened a bicycle shop located near the campus of Appaloosa State College. The store sells street, mountain, and racing bikes, accessories, and apparel. The brands of equipment Fox's store carries include Fuji, Peugeot, Bianchi, and Raleigh. In addition to sales of new bikes, Mr. Fox provides an extensive repair and service facility capable of restoring even the most sophisticated racing machine to first-class condition.

In a recent interview, Fox explained his business strategy: "I am convinced there is tremendous interest in biking among the students, faculty, and staff of Appaloosa State. I want to satisfy their need for biking-related products and services. Generally, I stock the products and brands that they ask for as long as I can get them and make a profit on the sale. Some manufacturers, like Nishiki, make this a problem. I have had to stop dealing with them because they acted very independently, sometimes not filling orders for up to six months."

"Some of the products I stock are purchased from wholesalers because we order in small quantities. Most of our orders are shipped to us by United Parcel Service (UPS) because this insures we get the product in less than a week after placing the order without incurring an exorbitant freight bill. I do most of my advertising in the school newspaper, *The Old Paint*, where I usually offer students a discount or some free product like a water bottle if they buy more than a certain minimum. My salesforce is myself and two college students. In general, we charge everyone the same price; our prices are comparable to those of our competitors. It's necessary to be competitive because there are several stores nearby that offer comparable products."

"Overall, I am making enough to pay the bills and make a ten percent return on my investment. My major concern is that my marketing costs seem to be too high; they are almost 35 percent of the selling price of my goods."

_____ 1. Dan Fox appears to have adopted the marketing concept.
_____ 2. The Nishiki Company may be production oriented.
_____ 3. Fox's bicycle store faces a seller's market.
_____ 4. Fox's marketing costs are higher than the national average.
_____ 5. Fox's decision to locate his store near his market created time utility for his customers.

6. Repairing bicycles creates
   a. form utility.
   b. place utility.
   c. ownership utility.
   d. time utility.
   e. none of the above.

7. Newspaper advertising and the three-person salesforce are part of Fox's
   a. promotional strategy.
   b. pricing strategy.
   c. product strategy.
   d. distribution strategy.
   e. target market strategy.

8. Fox's distribution strategy includes
   a. UPS.
   b. wholesalers.
   c. student discounts.
   d. free delivery to customers.
   e. UPS and wholesalers.

9. Fox's pricing strategy includes
   a. charging all customers the same price.
   b. prices comparable to competitors' prices.
   c. student discounts.
   d. free products in conjunction with minimum purchases.
   e. all of the above.

10. Fox's product strategy is best described as
    a. stock the lowest cost products available.
    b. sell the highest quality products.
    c. offer customers the products they want.
    d. sell only nationally known brands.
    e. none of the above

M. J. Emerson, who recently graduated from college with a degree in business administration, has returned home to help his father run the company business, Emerson Foundry Company. Begun in 1903, the Emerson Company has long since had a reputation for casting the very finest in American architectural brasses. These brasses, usually used for doorknockers and accent details, typically represent eagles with spread wings, crowing roosters, and other subjects with a traditional motif.

The first thing that M. J. did upon reporting for work was to apply his business training to an analysis of the foundry's financial records. He was surprised to learn that, during the last ten years, there had been a dramatic decline in sales of the company's architectural line. When he asked his father about this, the elder Emerson replied, "Gee, son, I don't really know why that's happening. Our brasses are the very best that can be bought. We are still making them exactly the same way we have for the last eighty-five years, in the same molds and with the same materials. I can't really understand why sales are off so badly. But I have taken steps to do something about it. Just last month, I hired a young man to go out and try and find us some new customers. We really do have to do something to try and increase sales volume."

M. J. was now disturbed. He knew that his father had done what he thought was the right thing, but M. J. thought that more needed to be done. His thinking was that the company needed to look more carefully at the market-place. He felt that Emerson foundry had lost touch with its customers and with architectural fashions. Though he hesitated to do it, he felt that he had to suggest to his father that they invest in some research to find out what was happening in architectural design and to adapt their products to what was currently popular. He thought it might even be possible that the firm would find it desirable to expand or even change the nature of their product line.

11. M. J.'s father, judging from his distress at the decline in his company's fortunes and the fact that he can't understand why the company's brasses aren't selling, is probably a victim of
    a. his inability to produce a product of the required quality.
    b. the "better mousetrap" fallacy.
    c. a general decline in the economy about which nothing can be done.
    d. too much of a commitment to a marketing orientation.

12. Mr. Emerson the elder's retention of a salesman may well be evidence that he has been converted to
    a. a philosophy of company-wide consumer orientation.
    b. an attitude typical of the sales era of marketing history.
    c. a mere figurehead in his son's presence.
    d. a belief that he's in a seller's market.

13. M. J.'s idea of investigating the nature of the market reveals that
    a. he is at least aware of the marketing concept.
    b. he shares his father's attitude toward the changes in the company's sales performance.
    c. his college education has been largely wasted; he should be able to analyze the problem from internal company records.
    d. he, too, is a victim of "marketing myopia".

14. "Marketing myopia" refers to
    a. defining the scope of your business too broadly.
    b. failing to define the scope of your business.
    c. defining the scope of your business too narrowly.
    d. making comparisons between your business and businesses not at all like the one you're in.

Name _____   Instructor _____

Section _____   Date _____

Experiential Exercises

1. The purpose of this exercise is to broaden your understanding by comparing the definitions of marketing provided by managers of organizations which operate near your school or home.

   a. Interview several people to find out how they define marketing. Candidates for interviews include managers of, for example, restaurants, insurance companies, department stores, charitable organizations, city water and sewer departments, manufacturers, financial institutions, and university bookstores. Ask these people how they define marketing. You should also include questions about their organizations, the markets the organizations serve, and their products or services so you can better understand their concepts of marketing.

   b. Use the results of your interviews to complete the table below.

Name of Person Interviewed	Title	Name of Organization	Definition of Marketing

   c.   What are the major points of departure between the definitions you collected and the text definition? Some hints for finding differences in the definitions include examining which marketing mix activities are omitted; the role of the consumer in the marketing process; and the role of production.

2.   The purpose of this exercise is to enhance your understanding of not-for-profit marketing and how not-for-profit organizations conduct marketing activities.

   a.   Select a not-for-profit organization to study. You may choose any such organization you wish; however, try to select one that is accessible, cooperative, and is conducting marketing activities.

   b.   Develop a list of questions that can be used to determine the nature and extent of the organization's marketing involvement. Be sure to include questions about orientation, objectives, and marketing planning activities. Consider questions to extract information about the kind of not-for-profit marketing the organization is doing.

   My list of questions is:

c. Interview several people in the organization you've chosen using the questions you wrote for part b above.

d. Write a brief report on the marketing activities of your chosen organization. Make sure you mention the kind of not-for-profit marketing the organization is doing and make suggestions for improvement where you think appropriate.

3. The purpose of this exercise is to enhance your understanding by comparing the outlook on marketing held by non-business students at your school with what you now know about the subject.

    a. Interview several non-business majors at your school to find out how they define marketing. Ideally, each of your interviewees should be from a different broad field of study such as education, engineering, home economics, liberal arts, and so forth. In addition to your question about the specific definition of the subject, you should also ask them whether they think whatever they have defined as marketing is productive from an economic point of view, whether it benefits society, and whether it should be encouraged or perhaps even prohibited!

        Use the results of your interviews to complete the table below.

Name of Person Interviewed	Major	Definition of Marketing	Outlook on Marketing

Name _____   Instructor _____

Section _____   Date _____

Computer Applications

Review the discussion of the exchange process on page 10 of *Contemporary Marketing*. Then use menu item 1 titled "The Exchange Process" to solve each of the following problems.

1. A group of 76 families living in an isolated region of the Great Sandy Desert has been engaged in decentralized exchange of surplus products for several years. They are considering opening a central market that would operate every Monday in the home of a member family.

    a. How many transactions are involved under the present decentralized exchange system?

    b. How many transactions would be involved if the families decide to establish the central market?

    c. What effect would the central market have on efficiency?

2. Twenty fishing families living in a remote part of Louisiana that process and preserve their catch trade with each other. The oldest son of one of them offers to serve as a marketing intermediar;y among them in order to reduce the time and costs they incur traveling to and from each other's cabins every time they need to trade with each other. He proposes to open a store where they can send their products for sale and from which they can buy each other's specialties. Fifteen of the families readily agree to the proposition, but five refuse, saying they like the travel and visiting that go along with their trading trips. They will neither sell to nor buy from the store.

a. How much will efficiency increase if the intermediary is used by all the families?

b. How much less efficient will the intermediary be if only 15 of the families use the intermediary and the five dissenting families continue to trade individually with each of the other 15 families and themselves?

3. Natives of two adjacent islands of a Pacific Atoll met recently to discuss establishment of a central market. At the present time, the residents are engaged in decentralized exchange, but no trade takes place between the two islands. Namu Raroia, spokesman for the 65 residents of Mokauea Island, proposed that each island establish its own central market. Mako Keanapua, who represents the 35 residents from Mokuoeo Island, has argued that one large central market be established between the two communities. Residents of both Mokauea and Mokuoeo would use this central market and their original decentralized exchange systems would be eliminated.

a. How much will efficiency increase in each community if Namu Raroia's proposal is implemented?

b. How many exchange transactions will be required if Mako Keanapua's suggestion is followed?

c. How much will efficiency increase if Mako Keanapua's proposal is implemented instead of the current decentralized system?

    d. How many transactions would be necessary if each resident traded individually with every other resident of both communities?

Crossword Puzzle for Chapter 1

ACROSS CLUES

1. Blending the four strategy elements—product, price, distribution, promotion—to satisfy need
5. Element of marketing strategy devoted to developing the right good or service for customers
7. Marketplace characterized by shortage of goods and services
9. Element of marketing strategy devoted to getting the right good or service to the customer
13. The want-satisfying power of a good or service
14. Process by which parties give each other value to satisfy perceived needs
15. Marketing by service providers seeking to get people to accept their goals or to contribute
16. Companywide consumer orientation with the objective of achieving long-term success

DOWN CLUES

1. Conceiving of, pricing, promoting, and distribution of goods and services to create exchanges
2. A marketplace characterized by an abundance of goods and services
3. Group toward which a firm markets its goods, services, or ideas to satisfy needs
4. Marketing efforts designed to cultivate attention for, say, a politician or celebrity
6. Marketing of sporting, cultural, and charitable activities to selected markets
8. Element of marketing strategy that blends personal selling, advertising, and sales promotion
10. Orientation that stresses creative advertising and personal selling to overcome resistance
11. Philosophy stressing efficiency in producing a quality product
12. Efforts to attract people to a particular geographic area

WORD LIST:

BUYERSMARKET	MARKETING	PRODUCTION
DISTRIBUTION	ORGANIZATION	SALES
EVENT	PERSON	SELLERSMARKET
EXCHANGEPROCESS	PLACE	TARGETMARKET
MARKETINGMIX	PRODUCT	UTILITY
MARKETINGCONCEPT	PROMOTIONAL	

Chapter 1 Solutions

Key Concepts

1.	m	6.	a	11.	l	16.	i
2.	u	7.	f	12.	h	17.	b
3.	j	8.	r	13.	g	18.	c
4.	k	9.	o	14.	d	19.	e
5.	q	10.	n	15.	t	20.	p

Self Quiz

1.	T	11.	T	21.	F	31.	d	41.	b
2.	F	12.	T	22.	T	32.	a	42.	a
3.	T	13.	T	23.	T	33.	b	43.	c
4.	T	14.	F	24.	T	34.	c	44.	c
5.	F	15.	F	25.	c	35.	a	45.	d
6.	F	16.	F	26.	d	36.	e	46.	c
7.	T	17.	F	27.	d	37.	e	47.	a
8.	F	18.	F	28.	a	38.	a	48.	c
9.	T	19.	T	29.	c	39.	d	49.	b
10.	T	20.	F	30.	b	40.	e		

Applying Marketing Concepts

1.	T	6.	a	11.	b
2.	T	7.	a	12.	b
3.	F	8.	e	13.	a
4.	F	9.	e	14.	c
5.	F	10.	c		

Computer Applications

1. a. If each family desires to trade with every other family, a total of 2,850 transactions would have to occur.

    $$T = [n(n-1)]/2 = [76(75)]/2 = 2,850$$

    b. Establishment of a central market would reduce the number of transactions to 76, one transaction per family with the central market.

    c. Market efficiency would be improved by 3,750% were a central market created.

    $$\text{Increased Eff.}(\%) = (2,850/76)(100) = 3,750\%$$

2. a. If the market remains decentralized, 190 transactions will be required. Using the single intermediary decreases the number to 20. Efficiency increases by a factor of 950% if the intermediary is used.

    $$\text{Increased Eff.}(\%) = (190/20)(100) = 950\%$$

    b. If fifteen families use the intermediary and five trade among themselves and with the others but not through the intermediary, the total number of transactions required will be 100, 15 between the intermediary and its users, ten among the nonusers of the intermediary, and 75 between nonusers and individual users. This system is only 190% as efficient as the original system.

3. a. If each community establishes its own central market, then the number of transactions on Mokauea Island will be reduced from 2,080 to 65, an improvement of 3,200 percent. On Mokuoeo, the number of transactions would be reduced from 595 to 35, an improvement of 1,700 percent.

    Mokauea: $[65(64)]/2$ = 2,080; $(2,080/65)(100)$ = 3,200%
    Mokuoeo: $[35(34)]/2$ = 595; $(595/35)(100)$ = 1,700%

    b. If Mako Keanapu's proposal is accepted and a single market created to serve both islands, 100 residents will now be using that market, and 100 transactions will be required.

    c. Since no trade now takes place between the two islands, a restructuring of the market is taking place, and no true measure of efficiency can be made. However, the total number of transactions will be reduced from 2,675 to 100, so efficiency would theoretically improve by 2,675 percent.

    $$\text{Increased Eff.} = [(2,080+595)/100][100] = 2,675\%$$

    d. If decentralized trade existed between both communities, a total of 4,950 transactions would be required.

    $$\text{Total Transactions} = [100(99)]/2 = 4,950$$

Crossword Puzzle Solution

Chapter 2

Quality and Customer Satisfaction

Chapter Outline

You may want to use the following as a guide in taking notes.

    I.   Chapter Overview—The Importance of Quality and Customer Satisfaction

    II.   History of the Quality Movement

        A. Japanese contribution to quality

        B. Quality programs in Europe

    III.   Total Quality Management (TQM)

    IV.   Applying TQM to Marketing

        A. Involving top management

        B. Conducting a marketing audit

        C. Focusing on customer satisfaction

            1. Obtaining customer feedback

            2. Measuring customer satisfaction

        D. Working toward continuous improvement in marketing

            1. Reducing cycle time

            2. Reducing variation

            3. Eliminating waste

V.   Benchmarking against the best

     A. Analyzing internal processes

     B. Implementing improvements

VI.   Encouraging Employee Involvement

     A. Internal marketing

     B. Employee training

     C. Teamwork

VII.   TQM and the Marketing Mix

     A. TQM and product strategy

     B. TQM and distribution strategy

     C. TQM and promotional strategy

     D. TQM and pricing strategy

VIII.   Quality Opportunities in Global Markets

Name _____   Instructor _____

Section _____   Date _____

Key Concepts

The purpose of this section is to allow you to determine if you can match key concepts with the definitions of the concepts. It is essential that you know the definitions of the concepts prior to applying the concepts in later exercises in this chapter.

From the list of lettered terms, select the one that best fits each of the numbered statements below. Write the letter of that choice in the space provided.

Key Terms

a. quality
b. customer satisfaction
c. statistical quality control
d. ISO 9000
e. total quality management (TQM)
f. marketing audit
g. added value
h. customer satisfaction
    measurement (CSM) program
i. continuous improvement
j. PDCA cycle
k. cycle time

l. cost of quality
m. benchmarking
n. critical success factor
o. employee involvement
p. internal marketing
q. external customer
r. internal customer
s. empowerment
t. quality circle
u. cross-functional team
v. self-managed team

_____ 1. Implementing the concept of continuous improvement through a process of planning, doing, checking, and acting

_____ 2. If we reduce the amount of scrap a process turns out, the need for rework due to defective goods, or loss of customers due to dissatisfaction, we reduce this

_____ 3. When you go to the supermarket to buy food, you are one of these in the eyes of the supermarket operators

_____ 4. The application of statistical techniques to locate and measure quality problems on production lines

_____ 5. A thorough, objective evaluation of an organization's marketing philosophy, goals, policies, tactics, practices and results.

_____ 6. Actions by management, such as memos, posters, and meetings, that outline and stress each employee's role in implementing marketing strategy

_____ 7. Volvo's policy of allowing its employees, working in teams of twelve, to assemble cars in any work arrangement they like, is an example of this.

_____ 8. Procedure for measuring feedback from customers against their satisfaction goals and developing an action plan for improvement

_____ 9. Involves using internal marketing, empowerment, training, and teamwork as motivating forces

_____ 10.   A focus of the benchmarking process, this might be bringing products to the market faster for one firm, keeping customers happy with superior service for another

_____ 11.   When a sales representative makes a sale, he or she should realize that the person who will deliver the goods just bought to the customer who bought them is one of these

_____ 12.   Employees from production, engineering, and purchasing get together to work on a manufacturer's problems with choice of materials for a particular new product. They exemplify this concept

_____ 13.   An approach that involves all employees in continual improvement of products and work processes to achieve customer satisfaction and world-class performance

_____ 14.   A broad term that encompasses both tangible and intangible characteristics, this represents the degree of excellence or superiority of an organization's goods and services

_____ 15.   A small group of employees from one work area or department who meet regularly to identify and solve problems

_____ 16.   Chrysler's offer of a 7-year, 70,000 mile powertrain warranty on some of its products, a warranty several years and many thousands of miles longer than those offered by some of its competitors, represents this to purchasers of its cars

_____ 17.   The ability of a good or service to meet or exceed the buyer's needs and expectations

_____ 18.   Inspired by the discovery that Japanese competitors could *sell* a copier for what it cost them to *make* one, Xerox pioneered this process in the United States in 1979

_____ 19.   The time it takes to complete a work process or activity, like designing an office building or filling a car's tank with gasoline, from beginning to end

_____ 20.   Standards for quality management and assurance developed by the International Standards Organization in Switzerland for the European Community

_____ 21.   Called *kaizan* in Japan, this is the process of constantly studying and making changes in work activities

_____ 22.   Giving employees the authority to make decisions about their work without supervisory approval

Name _____   Instructor _____

Section _____   Date _____

Self Quiz

You should use these objective questions to test your understanding of the chapter material. You can check your answers with those provided at the end of the chapter.

While these questions cover most of the chapter topics, they are not intended to be the same as the test questions your instructor may use in an examination. A good understanding of all aspects of course material is essential to good performance on any examination.

True/False

Write "T" for True or "F" for False for each of the following statements.

_____   1.   Using Total Quality Management, Motorola expects to achieve a defect rate of 20 parts per billion by the year 2000.

_____   2.   The quality of a product depends only on whether it meets the specifications to which it is built, not whether it meets customer needs.

_____   3.   One of the strengths of traditional efforts to improve quality was that defective products were discovered at end-of-the-line inspections.

_____   4.   The implementation of ISO 9000 by the European Community should cause few problems for American producers because our SAE 3661 requirements typically meet or exceed those of ISO 9000

_____   5.   It has proven impossible to conduct a marketing audit of a firm with fewer than 250 employees. Too many people are performing too many tasks to be properly measured.

_____   6.   The Malcolm Baldridge Award is the highest national recognition for quality that a U.S. company can receive.

_____   7.   One of the best-known descriptions of total quality management is "Deming's 14 Points for Quality Improvement."

_____   8.   Men's Wearhouse has based its added value approach to selling men's clothes on the premise that the experience of shopping is as valuable for many men as is receiving value for their money.

_____   9.   A typical step in a customer satisfaction management program would include conducting research to determine the company's performance on the attributes that have been found to be important to customer use of its products or services.

_____   10.   Gaps between customers' expected and perceived quality of a firm's goods and services often exist and may be favorable or unfavorable.

_____   11.   In the PDCA cycle, employees analyze their work, seeking changes that will improve it; make the changes; carry out the changes; and observe the effects of the changes.

_____   12.   GTE discovered that many of its problems with customers' low levels of satisfaction with speed of repair when they called to report trouble on their phone lines was because repair clerks were allowed to try and solve the problem while the customer was on the phone, a time-consuming and usually unsuccessful practice.

_____ 13. Effective work processes build quality into a product by increasing variations in production that could reduce errors.

_____ 14. Total quality organizations apply the PDCA cycle to all marketing processes, from planning long-term strategies to adjusting short-term details of customer service operations.

_____ 15. Boeing believes it will significantly improve customer satisfaction by beginning production of its new 777 aircraft while it is still in the design stage, relying on the ability of its engineering staff to "debug" the design as problems crop up on the factory floor.

_____ 16. Reducing cycle time brings new products to the marketplace more quickly and reduces the time it takes to produce and deliver goods and services to customers.

_____ 17. Quality consultants estimate that for most companies the cost of not doing things right the first time accounts for 15 to 20 percent of sales volume.

_____ 18. The benchmarking process begins with a firm identifying a process or practice it wants to improve.

_____ 19. Competitive benchmarking compares functions of firms in different industries.

_____ 20. An internal marketing program shows employees how their work aids marketing strategy and also promotes customer satisfaction.

_____ 21. Many internal customer satisfaction measures use the same methods as those used for measuring external customer satisfaction.

_____ 22. Some quality analysts believe empowerment may give U. S. firms the opportunity to pass the Japanese in quality by unleashing American workers' potential to innovate—a potential the Japanese worker does not seem to share.

_____ 23. Benchmarking requires two types of analyses: domestic and international.

_____ 24. A self-managed team is made up of employees from different departments, supervised by a member of management, who work on a specific project.

_____ 25. Total quality management challenges organizations to increase the speed with which they deliver goods and services so customers will receive the right amount at the right place at the right time.

Multiple Choice

Circle the letter of the word or phrase that best completes the sentence or best answers the question.

26. A well-phrased conception of the idea of a "defect" in a product from a firm dedicated to total quality management came from John Major at Motorola when he said
    a. "If it doesn't work when we test it, it's a defect."
    b. "If it doesn't meet all the engineering specifications it's supposed to meet, it's a defect."
    c. "If the customer doesn't like it, it's a defect."
    d. "If it doesn't leave this plant in working order, it's a defect."
    e. "If it doesn't reach the customer in good condition, it's a defect."

27. Simplifying work processes, eliminating steps that do not add value to the product, and using cross-functional teams are three specific ways of
    a. redesigning technical processing.
    b. reducing cycle time.
    c. reducing variation.
    d. eliminating waste.
    e. increasing cost of quality.

28. Which of the following was true of traditional end-of-the-production-line inspection of products for manu-facturing defects?
    a. The inspection process was acceptable because it took very little time.
    b. The inspection process was effective because few bad products got through.
    c. The inspection process survived because it was cheaper than alternatives.
    d. The inspection process did nothing to correct the errors that created the problems.
    e. Though more expensive than other methods, the inspection process persisted because it caught more defects.

29. Walter Shewhart, W. Edwards Deming, and A. V. Feigenbaum were pioneers in the field of
    a. writing product specifications that were "human-friendly."
    b. developing product-inspection techniques that caught more defects than other methods could.
    c. creating international standards of quality management such as are now written into ISO 9000.
    d. quality regulation at the national level.
    e. statistical quality control and its uses.

30. The maximum number of Malcolm Baldrige National Quality Awards which can be given in a single year is
    a. twelve: there is a statute that sets this as the limit.
    b. fifty: the committee set up to make the awards has decided on this number.
    c. as many as the Congress chooses to give in a particular year.
    d. three per state: the upper limit is 150.
    e. six: only two awards can be given in each of three categories.

31. ISO 9000 was developed
    a. to ensure consistent quality among products manufactured and sold throughout the nations of the European Community.
    b. to help keep products of the former Soviet nations out of the European Community.
    c. to help keep products of Japanese origin out of the European Community.
    d. to give favored status among European Community imports to products of the former Soviet Union.
    e. to give favored status among European Community imports to products of non-Soviet eastern Euro-pean states like Poland, Hungary, and Rumania.

32. The marketing audit
    a. is a formal process conducted formally.
    b. suffers from being a subjective evaluation of results.
    c. should not examine the philosophy behind marketing activities.
    d. is applicable to any organization, large or small.
    e. provides a foundation on which to build a case against a rival employee.

33. Oversight Computer Company, a fairly large direct marketer of desktop computers, has recently begun offering a three-year on-site parts and service warranty on its units at no increase in price. This is in contrast to the industry standard one year warranty. Oversight is attempting to give its customers
    a. the runaround. Such a warranty is too generous to be taken seriously.
    b. added value. The better warranty makes customer satisfaction more likely.
    c. an incentive to buy their product but at the cost of something else like component durability.
    d. something most of them probably don't want or need.
    e. very little, actually. Few computers cause trouble in the first, second, OR third years of use.

34.   As a first step in boosting customer satisfaction, a company must
   a.   work with its employees to determine the direction it should take.
   b.   set up pilot programs where employees learn how to solve problems.
   c.   compile feedback from customers about its present performance.
   d.   let workers make changes they suggest.
   e.   show willingness to change everything about the company.

35.   The process of constantly making changes in work activities to improve their quality, timeliness, effectiveness, and efficiency is called
   a.   a CSM program.
   b.   sequential development.
   c.   the TQM process.
   d.   KGLA analysis.
   e.   continuous improvement.

36.   Which of the following is the best example of cycle time? The time it takes
   a.   a dentist to begin and complete a dental procedure.
   b.   you to dial a telephone.
   c.   for a filling-station employee to remove a tire for repairs.
   d.   your baby brother to fall out of his high chair once he's in it.
   e.   all of the above.

37.   Any work activity that does not add value for the customer constitutes
   a.   overhead that must be passed on to the customer, anyway.
   b.   variation that can be statistically removed from the process system.
   c.   a necessity in production. Not all processes can be productive.
   d.   waste. Quality companies concentrate on eliminating such waste.
   e.   benchmarking. That's how we get our standard of performance.

38.   The process in which an organization continually compares itself against industry leaders to gain information that will improve performance is called
   a.   PDCA analysis.
   b.   benchmarking.
   c.   appraising the cost of quality.
   d.   process analysis.
   e.   CSM programming.

39.   Which of the following can be a source of variation in a work process, product, or service?
   a.   poor marketing research
   b.   faulty machinery
   c.   inadequately trained employees
   d.   defective parts and materials from suppliers
   e.   all of the above

40.   The process in which an organization compares and measures itself against business leaders that make products the same as or very much like its own is most likely to be
   a.   competitive benchmarking.
   b.   internal benchmarking.
   c.   functional benchmarking.
   d.   miscellaneous benchmarking.
   e.   external benchmarking.

41. Before a company can compare itself with another, it must
    a. analyze the other company's processes to determine strengths and weaknesses.
    b. consult industry standards to provide a benchmark against which both firms can be measured.
    c. analyze its own processes to determine strengths and weaknesses.
    d. recognize that such a comparison can never be wholly meaningful.
    e. do extensive research into the other company's history and development.

42. People or organizations that buy or use another firm's good or service may be classed as its
    a. internal customers.
    b. external customers.
    c. external competitors.
    d. internal competitors.
    e. internal market.

43. A program sponsored by management that showed employees of a firm how their work aided marketing strategy and promoted customer satisfaction would be
    a. an internal marketing program.
    b. a public relations program.
    c. a program to promote sales.
    d. a program aimed at external customers.
    e. less effective than a similar program aimed at employees' families.

44. Empowerment seems to have more of an effect on American workers than on, say, Japanese workers because
    a. most Japanese love their employers while most Americans hate theirs.
    b. American workers are used to having things their own way, anyhow.
    c. American workers, unlike Japanese workers, want to achieve the breakthrough—the impossible dream.
    d. Japanese workers have been empowered for a long time, already.
    e. Japanese workers are far better paid than American workers.

45. As a measure of how important employee training is to American business, the Boston Consulting Group has estimated that each year the cost of training programs and materials bought from outside consultants alone amounts to
    a. $150 million.
    b. $250 million.
    c. $500 million.
    d. $750 million.
    e. $1 billion.

46. A small group of employees from one work area or department who meet regularly to identify and solve problems is
    a. a quality circle.
    b. a cross-functional team.
    c. a self-managed team.
    d. a production-control group.
    e. a project-development task force.

47. The conscious, considered effort to make everyday life manageable and secure now popular in the U. S. is called
a. upsizing.
b. downsizing.
c. downshifting.
d. backing up.
e. dropping out.

48. Baxter Industries' ValueLink Program is an example of the application of TQM to
a. product strategy.
b. distribution strategy.
c. pricing strategy.
d. promotion strategy.
e. budget strategy.

49. TQM can be applied to promotional strategy. An example of this is
a. Bethlehem Steel's partnership arrangement with Ford Motor Company.
b. Dell Computer's "ironclad" warranty of its products.
c. Texas Industries' empowerment of its drivers to make delivery decisions on the spot
d. Compaq Computer's introduction of its less expensive ProLinea line.
e. GM's Saturn Division's low-key, no-haggle sales approach that stresses integrity on the part of the sales representative.

50. Quality may create opportunities in the world market. Americans have had marked success in Russia in recent years because
a. Russians have always been very pro-American, regardless of what you might have heard.
b. producers from other countries have tended to stay out of the Russian market.
c. the Russians are eager to spend the cash they accumulated during all those years of cold war.
d. the shoddy quality of Russian products AND services has created opportunities for American entrepreneurs.
e. American products are so different to Russians, anyway, that they buy them as novelties.

Name _____ Instructor _____

Section _____ Date _____

Applying Marketing Concepts

Willard Catchman works for Harrington Transtar Trucks, a dealership selling and servicing medium to heavy-duty over-the-road tractors and bobtail rigs in Stuttgart, Arkansas. Willard has worked as a mechanic on Diesel and gasoline engines and related components for twenty years, but, to hear him tell it, there's something very different about the Harrington company: "Yep, these people are serious about keeping their customers happy and that makes it very different for the employees, too. We don't get work orders. We get trucks. When a customer brings in a truck for service or repair, it's assigned to a team of us. Each team includes somebody like me that knows engines, transmissions, and so forth, somebody from the suspension side, a body and fender rep, and even someone from the office that's going to handle the paperwork. We go over the truck from stem to stern to see what's wrong or what's needed, and then write up a "recommendation sheet." Then the one that knows the most about what that particular truck needs calls the owner and they talk it over."

"You know, some of the owners of these rigs are very knowledgeable, too, and may WANT some of the things we think of as defects to stay the way they are for one reason or another. If that be the case, that's what we do. After our representative and the owner decide what's to be done, we do it. We decide on the order things are to be done and what they are. When the job's done, we all go over the truck and we don't call the customer till all of us are happy with the overall job. And of course, if the customer isn't happy with any of it, right back it comes, no questions asked. And if we can't make the customer happy, we can decide just to not charge them. Management never says a word. They really believe we know what we're doing."

1. It looks from what Mr. Catchman says that Harrington's has a real commitment to
    a. revenue generation above all else.
    b. management working closely to keep employees active.
    c. customer satisfaction.
    d. union labor and shop rules.
    e. none of the above.

2. In terms of their differing specialties and assignment to work on projects together, Mr. Catchman's workgroup is
    a. a quality circle.
    b. an informal group.
    c. a CSM program.
    d. a cross-functional team.
    e. a task force.

3. Judging from the amount of trouble they get from management, the team must be
    a. intensely managed.
    b. self-managed.
    c. autonomous.
    d. dictatorial.
    e. incompetent.

4. Management believes its use of teams like Mr. Catchman's has improved the quality of its repair work so much that they are going to increase the warranty on such work from 90 days/9000 miles to a full year with no mileage cap at no additional charge. This is
   a. an added value they are able to offer their customers.
   b. an attempt to get customer feedback about their service.
   c. a measure of the satisfaction of their customers.
   d. a kaizen program they're adopting from the Japanese.
   e. a way of reducing cycle time.

5. Over the last year, Mr. Catchman's group met several times to discuss ways they could change what they were doing to improve their performance, made several changes, observed the results, and decided to make some of the changes permanent. This is an example of
   a. a marketing audit.
   b. a strategic orientation toward quality.
   c. implementing a customer satisfaction measurement program
   d. setting up a benchmarking effort.
   e. the workings of the PDCA cycle.

Feldor and Raskin, Inc., manufactures and distributes highway signs for use by road and highway departments and private purchasers across the United States. Despite a reasonable level of success in their field, they recently decided that more effort was needed on their part to create an atmosphere of total commitment to quality for the whole firm. They decided on a three-pronged approach.

First, they began to study intensively the operations of the sign division of the 3-M Company, acknowledged to be the world leader in highway signage. They also began to examine how Federal Printing Company, known masters at screen printing labels on cans, handled their printing processes. (F & R used screen printing on some of its lines of signs.) Finally, they began to look at how their own departments did things, and discovered that the illuminated sign department had developed a really world-class way of handling a difficult fabrication process. The same fabrication process was in use in other departments of F & R.

They decided, as well, to begin a program of employee seminars to tell their own people about what was going on in all these programs and in other ways around the company. They also began a program to encourage production-line workers to take more initiative in improving quality. A "panic button" was installed at each work station that could be used to stop the production line if something seemed to be wrong. Workers were encouraged to fix problems on their own if they thought they could. There was some initial suspicion on the part of employees, but this has been replaced by enthusiasm for the new program.

6. F & R's decision to compare itself to 3-M Company is an example of
   a. obtaining customer feedback about operations.
   b. internal benchmarking.
   c. competitive benchmarking.
   d. quality control planning.
   e. PDCA analysis

7. The relationship between F & R and Federal Printing is most likely to be one of
   a. internal benchmarking.
   b. reducing cycle time.
   c. eliminating variation.
   d. functional benchmarking.
   e. competitive benchmarking.

8. F & R's illuminated sign department is probably in the position of
   a. a customer service center.
   b. an internal benchmark.
   c. a functional benchmark.
   d. a place where wastage can be reduced.
   e. a department with a high cost of quality.

9. F & R's employee seminars fall into the category of
   a. internal marketing.
   b. external marketing.
   c. teamwork.
   d. harassment and aren't permitted under union rules.
   e. none of the above.

10. Encouraging employees to fix assembly-line problems as they occur is
    a. creating a quality circle.
    b. cross-functional; it'll never work.
    c. part of the CSM program.
    d. part of the PDCA cycle.
    e. empowerment.

Name _____   Instructor _____

Section _____   Date _____

Experiential Exercises

1. The purpose of this exercise is to broaden your understanding of the concept by comparing warranties on similar products in the context of the price of those products.

    a. Obtain a copy of a current edition of *Computer Shopper, Modern Photography, Video World,* or a similar periodical carrying advertisements for direct (mail order) sellers of similar products. Decide on a particular product which will be the basis for comparison, such as a computer with a certain processor, a given size of hard drive, a certain amount of Random Access Memory (RAM), and other similar features. For each of several similar units you find, make a note of the price and the warranty offered. Use a table like the one below to record your findings.

	Unit_____	Unit_____	Unit_____	Unit_____
	Price_____	Price_____	Price_____	Price_____
Warranty Features:				
Duration	_____	_____	_____	_____
What's Covered?	_____	_____	_____	_____
On-Site?	_____	_____	_____	_____
Exclusions?	_____	_____	_____	_____

    b. Does the concept of added value appear to be having an effect here? Discuss.

2. The purpose of this exercise is to enhance your understanding of statistical quality control by exposure to the process in operation.

    a. Select a local manufacturing or processing firm; from the processing side, dairies, breweries, canning and meatpacking plants are possibilities. Call them on the telephone and ask to speak to someone who can talk to you about how they maintain quality in their products. (It's best not to ask to talk to the "quality control department" because they may not call it that.) When you've reached a cooperative person, ask them what techniques they use to assure the quality of their output. If possible, make an appointment to visit their facility and have them show you their quality control operation. As always, remember that it is you who are asking the favor! Record below your impressions of your visit.

        i.   Statistical quality control methods used

        ii.   Kinds of products they're applied to

        iii.   How many tests (typical) per product

        iv.   How are failures (products that don't pass) handled?

Name _____ Instructor _____

Section _____ Date _____

Computer Applications

Review the discussion of the exchange process in Chapter 1 of your text. Then use menu item 1, "Exchange Process" to solve each of the following problems.

1. Oshkosh Engine Company makes small gas turbine engines widely used in high-pressure water pumps carried on fire engines. The engines are made in a series of eight processes, each of which results in a component which is then assembled to the next component in an eight-stage process to create the engine. In the past, quality control of individual components was the responsibility of the eight manufacturing departments, but each component was also checked on receipt by the next department in the assembly chain as it became part of an engine. It is proposed to create a central quality testing department which will eliminate the necessity for any of the assembly departments to check previous work.

   a. How many inspections did the old manufacturing process require?

   b. Implementation of the new process will result in how many inspections?

   c. What is the increase in efficiency created by the new quality control system?

2. Tomoratsu Company of Sapporo, Japan, provides security services to businesses on the island of Honshu. The company uses 60 officers on foot patrol, 35 officers in automobiles, and 100 computer sensors. Each of these systems has, as part of its function, checking on the other systems. Management is concerned that this process if very time-consuming and may not have the desired effect of increasing safety of the protected property *and* the officers protecting it. Tomoratsu is considering creating a central communications unit which will handle calls from all of its three information sources.

   a. How many interactions much now take place for all of the firm's security sources to check on each other?

   b. If central communication takes over the checking, how many interactions must take place?

   c. What is the increase in efficiency; under the new system.

3. Every semester, the College of Business at Southwestern State University goes through turmoil. Each of the six departments in the college independently make up a class schecule which it then checks with each of the other departments. Conflict resolution then takes place among the departments. One of the more sensible members of the faculty has suggested that scheduling be turned over to a cross functional team with members from each department which will be charged with creating a coordinated schedule at one meeting.

    a. How many exchanges (minimum) must now take place to create a viable class schedule for Southwestern?

    b. If the committee can come up with a sound schedule in a single meeting, what will be the number of exchanges required?

    c. Enumerate the improvement in efficiency created by the change?

Crossword Puzzle for Chapter 2

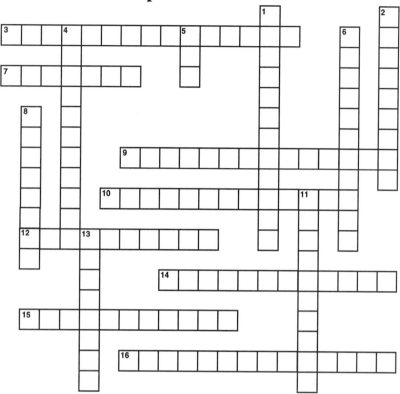

CROSS CLUES

3. Team of employees from different departments who work on a specific project
. Degree of excellence or superiority of an organization's goods or services
. Usually statistical, used to locate and measure quality problems and reduce them
. Group of employees from one department or work area who meet to identify and solve problems
. Increased worth of a good that comes from marketing mix improvements that increase satisfaction
. When an organization compares itself with world leaders to improve its performance
. When continuous, process of constantly studying and changing work activities
. Thorough evaluation of marketing philosophy, goals, policies, tactics, practices, and results

DOWN CLUES

1. Ability of a good or service to meet or exceed the customer's needs and expectations
2. Process of planning, doing, checking, and acting
4. Team of employees who work with little or no supervision
5. Acronym for approach involving all employees in continually improving products and processes
6. Giving employees the right to make decisions about their work without supervisor approval
8. As a customer, employee or department that depends on another employee or department
11. Measuring customer feedback against satisfaction goals and planning for improvement
13. As a customer, person or organization that buys or uses a firm's products or service

WORD LIST:

ADDEDVALUE
BENCHMARKING
CROSSFUNCTIONAL
CSMPROGRAM
EMPOWERMENT
EXTERNAL
IMPROVEMENT
INTERNAL

MARKETINGAUDIT
PDCACYCLE
QUALITY
QUALITYCONTROL
QUALITYCIRCLE
SATISFACTION
SELFMANAGED
TQM

Chapter 2 Solutions

Key Concepts

1.	j	6.	p	11.	r	16.	g	21.	i
2.	l	7.	v	12.	u	17.	b	22.	s
3.	q	8.	h	13.	e	18.	m		
4.	c	9.	o	14.	a	19.	k		
5.	f	10.	n	15.	t	20.	d		

Self Quiz

1.	T	11.	T	21.	T	31.	a	41.	c
2.	F	12.	F	22.	T	32.	d	42.	b
3.	F	13.	F	23.	F	33.	b	43.	a
4.	F	14.	T	24.	F	34.	c	44.	c
5.	F	15.	F	25.	T	35.	e	45.	d
6.	T	16.	T	26.	c	36.	a	46.	a
7.	T	17.	F	27.	b	37.	d	47.	c
8.	F	18.	T	28.	d	38.	b	48.	b
9.	T	19.	F	29.	e	39.	e	49.	e
10.	T	20.	T	30.	e	40.	a	50.	d

Applying Marketing Concepts

1.	c	6.	c
2.	d	7.	d
3.	b	8.	b
4.	a	9.	a
5.	e	10.	e

Computer Applications

1. a.   The current number of inspections required to produce an engine at Oshkosh is

$$T = n(n-1)/2 = 8(7)/2 = 28$$

   b.   The new system reduces the number of inspections to eight.

   c.   The increase in efficiency is $(28/8)(100)$ percent, or 350%.

2. a. Tomoratsu is currently using 195 security units to check on each other. The total number of interactions required for full checking is

$$T = n(n-1)/2 = 195(194)/2 = 18{,}915, \text{ certainly a very large number.}$$

b. Using the central system reduces the required interactions to 195.

c. Efficiency would be increased by (18,915/195)(100) percent, or 9700%.

3. a. Southwestern's present scheduling process calls for

$$T = n(n-1)/2 = 6(5)/2 = 15 \text{ interactions to create a schedule.}$$

b. The single meeting process would require only 6 interactions.

c. Efficiency would be increased by (15/6)(100) percent, or 250%, by the change.

Crossword Puzzle Solution

Chapter 3

Marketing: Its Environment and Role in Society

Chapter Outline

You may want to use the following as a guide in taking notes.

  I. Chapter Overview—Firms and the Impact of External Forces

 II. Environmental Scanning and Environmental Management

III. The Competitive Environment

   A. Types of competition

   B. Developing a competitive strategy

 IV. The Political-Legal Environment

   A. Government regulation

   B. Government regulatory agencies

   C. Other regulatory forces

   D. Controlling the political-legal environment

  V. The Economic Environment

   A. Business cycles

   B. Inflation

   C. Unemployment

   D. Resource availability

   E. Income

VI.   The Technological Environment

A. Applying technology

B. Sources of new technology

VII.   The Social-Cultural Environment

A. Importance in international marketing decisions

B. Consumerism

VIII.   Marketing's Role in Society

A. Evaluating the quality of life

B. Criticisms of the competitive marketing system

IX.   Current Issues in Marketing

A. Marketing ethics

1. Ethical problems in marketing research

2. Ethical problems in product strategy

3. Ethical problems in distribution strategy

4. Ethical problems in promotional strategy

5. Ethical problems in pricing

B. Social responsibility

1. Marketing's responsibilities

2. Marketing and ecology

X.   Controlling the Marketing System

Name _____   Instructor _____

Section _____   Date _____

Key Concepts

The purpose of this section is to allow you to determine if you can match key concepts with the definitions of the concepts. It is essential you know the definitions of the concepts prior to applying them in later exercises in this chapter.

From the list of lettered terms, select the one that best fits each of the numbered statements below. Write the letter of that choice in the space provided.

Key Terms

a. environmental scanning
b. environmental management
c. competitive environment
d. time-based competition
e. political-legal environment
f. economic environment
g. demarketing

h. technological environment
i. social-cultural environment
j. consumerism
k. consumer rights
l. marketing ethics
m. social responsibility
n. green marketing

_____ 1. Marketing philosophies, policies, procedures, and actions that have the enhancement of society's welfare as a primary objective.
_____ 2. Interactive process occurring in the marketplace among marketers of directly competing products, marketers of substitutable products, and marketers competing for consumer purchasing power.
_____ 3. Laws and interpretations of laws that require firms to operate under competitive conditions and serve to protect consumer rights.
_____ 4. Reducing consumer demand for a product or service to a level that the firm can supply.
_____ 5. Application to marketing of knowledge based on discoveries in science, inventions, and innovation.
_____ 6. Attainment of organizational objectives by predicting and influencing the competitive, political/legal, economic, technological, and social/cultural environments.
_____ 7. Collecting information about the external marketing environment to identify and interpret potential trends.
_____ 8. The right to choose freely, to be informed, to be heard, and to be safe.
_____ 9. Standards of conduct and moral values by which marketers operate.
_____ 10. The relationship between the marketer and society and its cultures.
_____ 11. Includes the stage of the business cycle, inflation, unemployment, resource availability, and income.
_____ 12. Aids and protects the consumer by exerting legal, moral, and economic pressure on business and government.
_____ 13. Strategy of developing and distributing goods and services more quickly than competitors.
_____ 14. Producing, marketing, and reclaiming environmentally sensitive products.

Name _____ Instructor _____

Section _____ Date _____

Self Quiz

You should use these questions to test your understanding of the chapter material. Check your answers against those provided at the end of the chapter.

While these questions cover most of the chapter topics, they are not intended to be the same as the test questions your instructor may use in an examination. A good understanding of all aspects of the course material is essential to good performance on any examination.

True/False

Write "T" for True and "F" for False for each of the following statements.

_____ 1. Environmental scanning is the process of collecting information about the firm's internal operations to affect and control resource use.

_____ 2. The firm which uses environmental management does not try to influence the marketing environment.

_____ 3. A major question in competitive strategy is how the firm should compete.

_____ 4. Compact discs by U2 and movies starring Tom Cruise compete with purchases of hip clothes at Bongo's for the discretionary purchasing power of individuals.

_____ 5. The Sherman Act prohibits price discrimination.

_____ 6. Government regulation in the United States has passed through the four phases of: protect competition, protect competitors, protect consumers, deregulate industry.

_____ 7. The Robinson-Patman Act protects consumers from price gouging practices.

_____ 8. Inflation, a rising price level that results in reduced consumer buying power, can occur at any stage in the business cycle.

_____ 9. The Federal Trade Commission cannot do anything to stop firms from using deceptive advertising.

_____ 10. Time-based competition, a strategy used by microprocessor manufacturer Intel Corp., relies on quick development and distribution of goods and services for its success.

_____ 11. Discretionary income is the amount of money people have left to spend after they've paid for food, clothing, housing, and other necessities.

_____ 12. The technological environment may affect the political-legal environment.

_____ 13. The technological environment can be a source of reductions in the cost of producing and marketing products.

_____ 14. The Council of Better Business Bureaus is a national organization devoted to consumer service and to the promotion of increased Federal regulation of business.

_____ 15. To ensure passage of the North American Free Trade Agreement (NAFTA), a number of U.S. based multinational corporations engaged in various activities directed at Congress and promoting the benefits of free trade among the United States, Canada, and Mexico. Such activities are examples of lobbying.

_____ 16. The United States is a mixed society composed of various submarkets, each of which displays unique cultural characteristics.

_____ 17. Consumerism is a radical movement that resists the societal demand that organizations adopt the marketing concept.

_____ 18. President Kennedy's statement of consumer rights includes the "right to be safe." This means that products and services should be designed in such a way that they will be absolutely safe for anyone to use.

_____ 19. Competitive pressures have forced some marketers into packaging practices that may be considered misleading, deceptive, and/or unethical.

_____ 20. Marketing ethics—decisions by individuals and firms to do what is morally right or wrong—is a more easily measured concept than social responsibility.

_____ 21. The billions of tons of packaging materials that the marketing system generates every year—the glass, metal, paper, and plastics—are one example of the ecological problem of planned obsolescence.

_____ 22. The marketing system may be influenced or controlled in four ways: (1) by helping the competitive market system to operate in a self corrective manner; (2) by educating the consumer; (3) by increasing regulation; and (4) by encouraging political action.

_____ 23. "Value-priced" products, typically introduced during the prosperity phase of the business cycle, feature a broad range of premium features a premium prices.

_____ 24. Even modest shifts in the environment can alter the results of marketing decisions.

_____ 25. Utilities such as those providing electricity and cable television service accept considerable regulation of their activities in return for exclusive rights to serve a particular group of customers.

_____ 26. Wal-Mart's commitment to the construction of ecologically sensitive stores that will reduce energy demands and use of natural resources is an example of "green marketing."

_____ 27. When you choose to go to a movie rather than a concert, you are engaging in substitution.

_____ 28. America's single major source of civilian technological innovation is its colleges and universities.

_____ 29. The four phases of government regulation have been: the antimonopoly phase; the phase of protecting competitive conditions; the governmental control phase; and the phase of industry deregulation.

_____ 30. The FCC, the FTC, the FDA, and the Interstate Commerce Commission are all federal regulatory agencies.

_____ 31. Business cycles are characterized by conditions of prosperity followed by recovery, depression, and recession.

_____ 32. Unemployment exists when people who do not have jobs are actively looking for work.

_____ 33. When manufacturers make products so well that they last indefinitely and need never be replaced, they are practicing planned obsolescence.

_____ 34. Despite consumer concerns about privacy, many companies continue to expand their use of databases as a marketing tool.

_____ 35. Pricing is the component of the marketing mix that gives rise to the majority of ethical questions.

Multiple Choice

Circle the letter of the word or phrase that best completes the sentence or best answers the question.

36. The cost of TV advertising is part of which of the following environments of marketing?
    a. the social-cultural environment
    b. the economic environment
    c. the political-legal environment
    d. the technological environment
    e. none of the above

37. Which of the following attitudes should the marketer take toward the marketing environment?
    a. Ignore it.
    b. Realize the need to adjust a firm's marketing mix to fit environmental forces and constraints.
    c. Realize that an individual firm cannot have an effect on the marketing environment.
    d. Do not change marketing strategies until substantial losses result from environmental forces.
    e. Make sure marketing strategies satisfy legal requirements but ignore other aspects of the marketing environment because there are no legal penalties for such behavior.

38. The question of whether an automobile dealership should be coerced into purchasing parts, material, and supplementary services from the parent organization involves an ethical problem in
    a. product strategy.
    b. promotional strategy.
    c. distribution strategy.
    d. pricing strategy.
    e. marketing research.

39. Major reasons why a firm may not choose to compete in a particular market include
    a. inadequate resources.
    b. a lack of fit between the market and the firm's objectives.
    c. insufficient profits.
    d. a, b, and c above.
    e. only a and b above.

40. A correct matchup of a specific law and its objective is
    a. Sherman Act: protect consumers
    b. Robinson-Patman Act: protect competitors
    c. Wheeler-Lea Act: protect competition
    d. Consumer Goods Pricing Act: protect competitors
    e. Consumer Product Safety Act: protect competition

41. All of the following are parts of the economic environment *except*
    a. unemployment.
    b. inflation.
    c. recession.
    d. the business cycle.
    e. consumerism.

42. Firms that have a monopoly position in the market, like public utilities, enjoy, at the cost of considerable regulation, protection from the
    a. economic environment.
    b. competitive environment.
    c. technological environment.
    d. political-legal environment.
    e. social-cultural environment.

43. Which of the following statements correctly matches the law and the primary elements of the marketing mix that the law impacts?
    a. Fair Packaging and Labeling Act: price and distribution
    b. Woll Products Labeling Act: distribution, price
    c. Federal Trade Commission Act: product, price, promotion, distribution
    d. Child Protection Act: promotion, price
    e. Public Health Cigarette Smoking Act: product, distribution

44. Which of the following methods is used by the Federal Trade Commission to protect consumers?
    a. The FTC harasses firms believed to be guilty of violating the law.
    b. A cease and desist order is issued, telling a firm to stop an illegal practice.
    c. Public service announcements identifying all firms which have used deceptive selling practices are broadcast.
    d. The officers of guilty firms are arrested and charged with a criminal act.
    e. A closure order to shut down a guilty firm's operations is issued.

45. An example of an ethical problem related to promotional strategy would be
    a. whether an automobile dealership should be required to purchase parts from the manufacturer of the cars it sells.
    b. the portrayal of women as frivolous or stereotyping them as housewives in advertisements.
    c. the question of whether marketers have an obligation to warn consumers of impending discount or returns policy changes.
    d. whether packages should be kept to some standard size, rather than made extra-large or odd-shaped.
    e. the question of whether there is an obligation to serve areas where there are few users of the firm's product.

46. It is true that the
    a. Sherman Act prohibits tobacco advertising on radio and television.
    b. Clayton Act established the Federal Trade Commission.
    c. Federal Trade Commission Act prohibited price discrimination.
    d. Wheeler-Lea Act bans deceptive or unfair business practices per se.
    e. Consumer Goods Pricing Act allows resale price maintenance in interstate commerce.

47. A correct statement about the economic environment is that
    a. consumers buy more during inflation because prices are lower.
    b. sales may fall during recession because of both high unemployment and declines in consumer purchasing power.
    c. frictional displacement results from recessions.
    d. cyclical unemployment is highest during prosperity.
    e. consumers will not alter their purchasing behavior during recessions.

48. A firm may lose its market share because consumers switch to a new product. The new product introduction is an environmental threat or opportunity from the
    a. economic environment.
    b. technological environment.
    c. political-legal environment.
    d. social-cultural environment.
    e. competitive environment.

49. Which of the following is an example of a demarketing strategy?
   a. Offering a second can of paint for half price if a first can is purchased at full price.
   b. Providing consumers with tips on how to make a product last longer.
   c. Advertising the convenience of owning more than one car.
   d. Telling consumers that there is an abundant supply of the product available.
   e. Making substantial reductions in a firm's advertising budget.

50. Which of the following is an accurate statement about the social-cultural environment?
   a. The social responsibility of business is decreasing.
   b. Income statements are the best way to measure the accomplishment of socially oriented objectives.
   c. Most marketers do not need to take the social environment into consideration.
   d. Marketing strategies that are successful with one cultural segment will also be successful with other cultural segments.
   e. The social-cultural environment changes constantly.

51. H. J. Heinz Company's experience with its ketchup in France illustrates
   a. how powerfully the economic environment can affect sales.
   b. how important social and cultural differences between markets can be in affecting the acceptance of a product.
   c. how different French technology is from that of the rest of Europe.
   d. how the French legal system was used to prevent Heinz from successfully marketing its product.
   e. how effective competition kept Heinz ketchup from dominating the French ketchup market.

52. When a firm engages in lobbying among legislative groups or enters into a joint venture with another firm whose products complement its own, it may be seeking to
   a. avoid prosecution under the Sherman Act.
   b. manage the environment by influencing the technological and competitive environment.
   c. apply environmental management to the political-legal and economic environments.
   d. manage the environment by influencing the political-legal and competitive environments.
   e. more actively apply the marketing concept by expanding its markets.

53. Which of the following situations best reflects the competitive condition of substitution:
   a. the availability of Tide, Cheer, Surf, Oxydol, and Fab in the detergent section of the supermarket
   b. the availability of gypsum board, wood paneling, masonite sheet, and plaster as wall finishing materials
   c. the choice available among rock concerts, videotape rentals, dining out, and listening to stereo tapes for an evening's entertainment
   d. Delta, Continental, and Southwest Airlines all offering cut-rate fares between their major destinations
   e. None of the above are examples of substitution; all represent direct competition.

54. Joint ventures between Imperial Chemical Industries PLC, France's Societé Nationale Elf Aquitaine, Eastman Chemical Company and various Asian chemical producers represent efforts to
   a. practice environment management by improving their competitive positions at home and abroad.
   b. control the supply of basic industrial chemicals and so drive foreign producers out of the market.
   c. to become presences in the Asian market from which they, as westerners, had been frozen out for years.
   d. to enter the global market. Prior to this, none of these firms had ever ventured into the international sphere.
   e. to enter the market for fertilizer, one of Asia's largest uses for basic chemicals.

55. The Robinson-Patman Act and the Miller-Tydings Resale Price Maintenance Act are examples of laws passed during the
    a.   antimonopoly period of government regulation.
    b.   the consumer protection period of government regulation.
    c.   the competitor protection period of government regulation.
    d.   the industry deregulation phase of government regulation.
    e.   the general federal power development phase of government regulation.

56. George, Howard, and Louis are the only three real estate brokers in Milledgeville. They have the habit of getting together for lunch once a month to "talk things over." At their most recent meeting, George proposed that they divide the town up into sections, with each realtor taking one part as his exclusive territory. If they carry out their plan, they can be accused of violating
    a.   the Consumer Goods Pricing Act.
    b.   the Sherman Act.
    c.   the Robinson-Patman Act.
    d.   the Celler-Kefauver Act.
    e.   the Federal Trade Commission Improvement Act.

57. The Federal Regulatory Agency which monitors the rates of interstate rail, bus, truck, and water carriers is
    a.   the Interstate Commerce Commission.
    b.   the Federal Communications Commission.
    c.   the Federal Power Commission.
    d.   the Federal Trade Commission.
    e.   the Transportation Regulatory Commission.

58. Continental Bank of Chicago's decision to relinquish its consumer banking interests and concentrate on the business markets it knows was probably in recognition
    a.   that it could not keep up with the pace of technology in the consumer marketplace.
    b.   of pressure from consumerists who had taken the position that Continental Bank's presence in consumer banking was unethical.
    c.   of competition that spread the company's resources too thin.
    d.   of changes in the cultural environment that made most of its consumer business unprofitable.
    e.   of a legal decision that held that Continental Bank's presence in so many segments of the market was in violation of the Sherman Act.

59. That phase of the business cycle during which consumers frequently shift their buying patterns to basic, functional products with low price tags rather than nonessential products such as convenience foods is
    a.   prosperity.
    b.   depression.
    c.   recovery.
    d.   recession.
    e.   exclusion.

60. During economic recovery,
    a.   consumers' ability to buy increases, but their willingness to buy often lags behind.
    b.   consumer buying power declines and marketers should consider increasing promotional outlays.
    c.   consumer spending is brisk, and demand for premium versions of well-known brands is strong.
    d.   consumer spending readies its lowest level.
    e.   marketers may increase prices or extend their product lines to take advantage of brisk consumer spending.

Name _____   Instructor _____

Section _____   Date _____

Applying Marketing Concepts

Val Cartouche was thinking about her problems with her interior decorating business. They all began when she first decided to go into business for herself. Having found the "perfect location" for her store, she was dismayed when the city wouldn't give her a business license on the grounds that the local zoning ordinances didn't allow a store of that type in that location. After much effort, Val found a new location and was successful in getting a license to operate. She experienced trouble getting some minor renovations to the building done because of a "building boom" the city was experiencing. She also had trouble hiring salespeople and other workers because unemployment was at an all-time low and good people were at a premium.

At long last the renovations were complete, a staff had been hired, and the store was ready to open. But almost the minute the dustsheets were taken off the window displays, Val received a visit from a neighborhood committee objecting to one of her window displays. It seems the display featured a semi-nude mannequin in a rather suggestive pose on a sofa which was the window's central feature. In an effort to be accommodating, Val changed the display.

Soon Val was faced with two new problems. The building she had rented was equipped with an incinerator, which she intended to use to dispose of refuse and excess packing materials from the business. The first time it was lighted, however, the police appeared and presented her with a citation for a violation of a section of the city sanitation code. On top of that, Val discovered that the cost of the goods she was selling was going up so fast that she could barely cover the cost of replacing what she'd sold for what she was able to get for it.

The straw that broke the camel's back, however, was Val's discovery, only sixty days after she'd opened for business, that Interior Industries, a national chain of interior decorating emporiums, was about to open an outlet only two blocks away. Val knew that they could, because of their enormous buying power, undersell her by thirty percent on practically every item in her store.

Realizing that the handwriting was on the wall, Val held a sale to clear out her remaining inventory and closed her store.

_____ 1. Val's difficulty in getting a business license was due to the social/cultural environment.
_____ 2. Val seemed able to adapt her marketing strategy to the constraints of the environment.
_____ 3. Val's problems getting a business license could have been avoided if she had checked the appropriate environmental constraints before she decided on her first location.
_____ 4. The actions of a company like Interior Industries — buying in bulk and selling at low retail prices — are likely a violation of the Robinson-Patman Act.
_____ 5. Val may have been shortsighted in going out of business. It's possible that she may have been able to develop an appeal to a different target market than people who would choose to shop at Interior Industries.

6.   Val had problems with the
    a.   economic environment.
    b.   political-legal environment.
    c.   competitive environment.
    d.   social-cultural environment.
    e.   environments in a through d above.

7.   Val's citation was probably issued by the police because she
    a.   was in violation of an air pollution regulation.
    b.   was destroying valuable recyclable materials.
    c.   used an excessive amount of natural gas firing her incinerator.
    d.   had failed to get a city inspection of her store before opening.
    e.   was a particular target of a "get-tough" administration.

8.   Val's problems in getting her store renovated were probably due to the fact that
    a.   her city was experiencing a period of recession and lots of workers had left town.
    b.   the city was experiencing a prosperous period of the business cycle.
    c.   she was in competition with other employment opportunities for the services of the available labor.
    d.   all of the statements above are true.
    e.   the statements in b and c above are true.

9.   Val's inability to purchase new merchandise for what she'd paid for the old was due to
    a.   her inability to manage her money so as to make sure that she'd have enough to rebuy goods.
    b.   low sales volume and a high proportion of fixed costs in her store's operation.
    c.   inflation which made today's dollar less valuable than yesterday's and drove up merchandise costs.
    d.   unemployment at the national level which increased the cost of government services to merchants like Val.

10.   From Val's point of view, Interior Industries is part of
    a.   the social-cultural environment.
    b.   the competitive environment.
    c.   the political-legal environment.
    d.   the economic environment.
    e.   the ethnic environment.

Lee Ann Palmer was tired, lonely, and a little confused. When she left her home to move to Eisenstadt, she was sure it was the right thing. After all, the job she had been offered had been a real opportunity, and her prospective employer had a fine reputation. But she couldn't seem to get used to Eisenstadt. It was so *different* from Pleasanton, her hometown. For one thing, just getting around town involved fighting traffic which seemed to be totally out of control. Left turns at divided intersections were permitted, and the speed limit was 45 miles an hour—even in residential neighborhoods.

This didn't seem to bother the local population, nor did the fact that their lives revolved around whether or not the tractor plant, Eisenstadt's single major employer, or a Japanese firm which was also bidding for it got the order for those 300 crawler tractors from Industrial Constructors, Incorporated.

Lee Ann couldn't believe how hard it was to make friends in Eisenstadt. It seemed as if everyone she met had been there all their lives and wasn't interested in anything or anyone not an Eisenstadt native. All in all, though, it wasn't so bad for Lee Ann. Her employer was great to work for and her job let her use the latest equipment in her field of acoustical engineering. She felt she was on the very leading edge of scientific thought in her job at Limitech Labs, and that made up a lot for having to live in Eisenstadt. Now if she could only find some friends who didn't think a six-pack of beer and a bug zapper were quality entertainment, she'd be just fine.

11.   Lee Ann's perception of the traffic in Eisenstadt being out of control was very largely due to
       a.   her own rather bad driving habits.
       b.   differences in the political-legal environment between Eisenstadt and Pleasanton.
       c.   her general dissatisfaction with Eisenstadt itself.
       d.   her dislike of her job.

12.   Lee Ann's job appears to have been deeply involved with the
       a.   economic environment.
       b.   social-cultural environment.
       c.   competitive environment.
       d.   technological environment.
       e.   development of military hardware.

13.   Lee Ann's comments about Eisenstadt people being unconcerned with anyone or anything not from Eisenstadt is really a statement relating to the
       a.   social-cultural environment.
       b.   ethnic environment.
       c.   competitive environment.
       d.   political environment.

14.   The relationship between Eisenstadt's tractor plant and the Japanese company which is also bidding on the Industrial Constructors contract is
       a.   part of the legal environment.
       b.   a condition of direct competition.
       c.   a sort of indirect competition
       d.   nonexistent; there is no relationship, direct or indirect, between the two firms.

Name _____ Instructor _____

Section _____ Date _____

Experiential Exercises

1. The purpose of this exercise is to enhance your understanding of the effect of the legal environment on marketing activities of business organizations. In general, the assignment consists of using secondary sources to study a recent legal case involving the marketing efforts of a company or companies.

   a. Select a recent legal case involving the marketing activities of a company or companies. Possible sources to help you locate current legal cases include *Business Periodicals Index, Antitrust and Trade Regulation Report, FTC Reporter, Trade Regulation Reporter, The Antitrust Bulletin,* or the "Legal Developments" section of the *Journal of Marketing.* Try to select a case that has received considerable coverage in the literature.

   b. Using all the published information about the case determine what marketing activities were involved. Was the case related to product strategy? Distribution strategy? Pricing strategy? Promotion strategy?

   c. What laws or rules were being violated by the company?

   d.   Who was being harmed by the actions of the company? Was it competition, consumers, or some other members of the public?

   e.   What remedy, such as fines, imprisonment, corrective advertising, etc. was required in the case?

f.   What impact do you think this case and the remedies required will have on the company or companies involved? Will they conduct business the same as before, alter some of their marketing practices, or go out of business altogether?

2.   The purpose of this exercise is to develop an appreciation for the effect of competition on marketing activities of companies in the scheduled passenger airline industry.
    a.   Go to the reference section of your college or university library and find *U.S. Industrial Outlook* (U. S. Department of Commerce) and Standard and Poor's *Industry Survey.* You may also wish to use other published sources including *Business Week* to gain an understanding of the airline industry.

b. Who are the *major* competitors in this industry?

c. What actions have the major competitors taken in the last year or so that adversely affected the performance of other companies? Which dimensions of the marketing mix have they used? Have they changed product, promotion, distribution, or price?

d. What other firms besides scheduled passenger airlines should also be considered competitors? Remember the text definition of expanded competition suggests all firms competing for the same discretionary spending power should be included as part of the competition. Think of the product from the consumer's point of view: what might consumers consider as a substitute for air travel?

e. Based on what you have learned, do you feel the scheduled airline passenger industry has an expanded view of competition or a myopic one—one that ignores any firms selling different products?

Name _____   Instructor _____

Section _____   Date _____

Computer Applications

Review the discussion of decision tree analysis in Chapter 3 of the text. Then use menu item 2, "Decision Tree Analysis," to solve each of the following problems.

1. Nick Pisani, owner and manager of Nick's salad bowl, a specialty food shop in a college town, is concerned about reports of a new shop opening. In fact, he estimates the likelihood of the new competitor being open for business in time for the beginning of the next school year at 70 percent. If the new shop opens at the location under consideration and Nick takes no competitive moves at this time, Nick estimates that his sales revenue projection for next year would be 40 percent lower than the $800,000 revenue forecast estimated for next year if a new competitor does not open a shop. In addition, projected earnings would probably fall from 20 percent of sales to 10 percent of sales. Nick is contemplating opening a second shop in order to build customer loyalty in case the new competitor materializes. He estimates that if he opens the second shop and the new pizza shop does not materialize, his overall sales revenue would increase to $1,000,000 and earnings would be 14 percent of sales. If he opens a second shop and the new shop does not open, Nick feels that his two shops will generate $600,000 in revenues and earn profits of 12 percent of sales. He would prefer to postpone his decision until he is certain of the plans of his potential competitor, but the need to plan the new shop requires him to make the decision now.

   a. Recommend a course of action for Nick Pisani.

b. Would your recommended course of action change if Pisani estimated the likelihood of a new competitor opening at 50 percent?

2. Rachel Pritchert, vice-president of marketing of Sleepwear, Inc., a manufacturer of children's sleepwear, is concerned about a potential government ban of the fiber material used by her company in its children's sleepwear. Without such a ban, she has projected that next year her company will have sales of 20 million dollars with profits estimated at ten percent of sales. If the government bans the materials, her company will lose about half of their sales and profits will decline to five percent of sales. However, Sleepwear could convert their manufacturing processes to new materials now instead of being forced to switch by the government ban. Immediate conversion would mean the company would not lose any projected sales although its profits would fall to eight percent of sales due to increased material costs. Pritchert feels there is a 40 percent chance that the ban will be enacted.

a. Recommend a course of action for Sleepwear, Inc.

b. Joe Jensen, plant manager for Sleepwear, disagrees with Ms. Pritchert's estimate of immediate conversion costs. He feels that immediate conversion will result in profits of five percent of sales rather than eight percent as projected by Ms. Pritchert. Would your recommended course of action for Sleepwear be different if Joe Jensen is correct?

3. Automobile dealer Melton Nordquist is pleased with next year's ten million dollar revenue forecast and projected earnings of 25 percent of sales. He is concerned, however, about rumors that a competing dealer has been negotiating for a franchise on a hot new car of Korean manufacture that Melton expects to compete directly with his line of Brazilian imports. If the rumor is true and the competitor appears, Melton feels that his sales will be reduced by about 40 percent if he doesn't reduce prices and keeps his percentage earnings the same. He may, on the other hand, reduce prices in hopes of keeping the competitor out. If he reduces prices and the competitor does not appear, he estimates his sales at about $8 million and earnings at 15 percent of that figure. If the competitor does not appear, sales will drop to around $6.5 million, but percentage earnings will stay at 25 percent. Melton figures there's about a 35 percent chance his competitor will receive a franchise for the Korean car

Should Melton reduce his prices?

Crossword Puzzle for Chapter 3

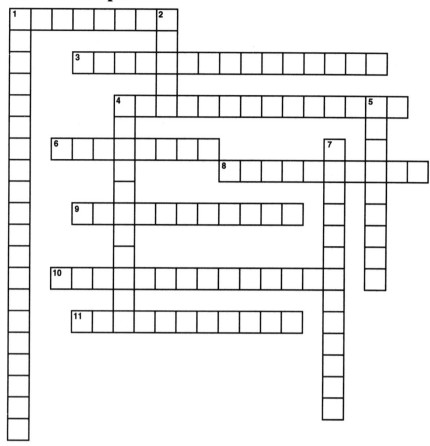

ACROSS CLUES

1. Collecting information about the environment to identify and interpret potential trends
3. Marketing's standards of conduct and moral values
4. Freedom of choice, freedom to be informed, freedom to be heard, freedom to be safe
6. Environmental component dealing with state of the business cycle, inflation, unemployment, and income
8. Attainment of organizational objectives by predicting and influencing environmental factors
9. Efforts to reduce demand for a good or service to a level the firm can supply
10. Environmental factor relating the marketer to society and culture
11. Environment that includes direct competitors, substitute products, and competition for purchases

DOWN CLUES

1. Marketing philosophies and so forth that have society's welfare as an objective
2. Marketing activities having to do with environmentally sensitive products; also a color
4. Social force designed to aid and protect the consumer by pressuring business and government
5. Competition based on developing and distributing goods and services quicker than competition
7. Environmental factor having to do with application to marketing of innovations, inventions, and science

WORD LIST:

CONSUMERRIGHTS
COMPETITIVE
CONSUMERISM
DEMARKETING
ECONOMIC
GREEN
MARKETINGETHICS

MANAGEMENT
SCANNING
SOCIALCULTURAL
SOCIALRESPONSIBILITY
TECHNOLOGICAL
TIMEBASED

Chapter 3 Solutions

Key Concepts

1.	m	6.	b	11.	f
2.	c	7.	a	12.	j
3.	e	8.	k	13.	d
4.	g	9.	l	14.	n
5.	h	10.	i		

Self Quiz

1.	F	11.	T	21.	F	31.	F	41.	e	51.	b
2.	F	12.	T	22.	T	32.	T	42.	b	52.	d
3.	T	13.	T	23.	F	33.	F	43.	c	53.	b
4.	T	14.	F	24.	T	34.	T	44.	b	54.	a
5.	F	15.	T	25.	T	35.	F	45.	b	55.	c
6.	T	16.	T	26.	T	36.	e	46.	d	56.	b
7.	F	17.	F	27.	T	37.	b	47.	b	57.	a
8.	T	18.	F	28.	F	38.	c	48.	e	58.	c
9.	F	19.	T	29.	F	39.	d	49.	b	59.	d
10.	T	20.	F	30.	T	40.	b	50.	e	60.	a

Applying Marketing Concepts

1.	f	6.	e	11.	b
2.	f	7.	a	12.	d
3.	t	8.	e	13.	a
4.	f	9.	c	14.	b
5.	t	10.	b		

Computer Applications

1. a.   Mr. Pisani should open his new location. The logic is as follows: If he does not open a new location, then there is a 70 percent chance that his sales will be reduced from $800,000 to $480,000 with an accompanying reduction in profits from 20 percent to ten. There is a 30 percent chance that he will sell $800,000 worth of salad and make 20 percent profit. If, on the other hand, he does open the new location, there is a 70 percent chance he will gross $600,000 on which he will earn 12 percent and a 30 percent chance he will gross $1,000,000 and net 14 percent. Mathematically,

$$\text{Not open} = \$480,000(.10)(.70) + \$800,000(.20)(.30) =$$
$$\$33,600 + \$48,000 =$$
$$\underline{\$81,600}$$

$$\text{Open} = \$600,000(.12)(.70) + \$1,000,000(.12)(.30) =$$
$$\$50,400 + \$42,000 =$$
$$\underline{\$92,400}$$

The greater expected value of the decision is associated with opening the second store.

   b.   If the probability of his competitor opening were to drop 50 percent, the following would apply:

$$\text{Not open} = \$480,000(.10)(.50) + \$800,000(.20)(.50) =$$
$$\$24,000 + \$80,000 =$$
$$\underline{\$104,000}$$

$$\text{Open} = \$600,000(.10)(.50) + \$1,000,000(.12)(.50) =$$
$$\$30,000 + \$60,000 =$$
$$\underline{\$90,000}$$

The greater expected value would be associated with not opening the second store, which is the appropriate act.

2. a.   Conversion should be undertaken immediately. The facts are: there will either be a ban on this fibre or there won't. The likelihood is <u>40</u> percent that the ban will be enacted. If there is no ban, sales will be <u>20 million dollars</u>, with profits estimated to be <u>ten</u> percent. If there is a ban, sales will be <u>ten million dollars</u> with profits of <u>five</u> percent. If conversion to a new fibre is undertaken now, the company will be unaffected by the ban, but profits will drop to <u>eight</u> percent as the result of increased costs. Mathematically,

$$\text{Wait} = \$20,000,000(.10)(.60) + \$10,000,000(.05)(.40) =$$
$$\underline{\$1,400,000}$$

$$\text{Convert} = \$20,000,000(.08)(1.00) = \underline{\$1,600,000}$$

Conversion offers a $200,000 better expected value.

   b.   If conversion will in fact reduce profits to five percent of sales, then waiting is the best alternative. Again, to wait offers an expected value of <u>$1,400,000</u>, while to convert immediately yields, at five percent profit, only <u>$1,000,000</u> in value.

3. Mr. Nordquist apparently believes this rumor to be true. If that be the case and he does not reduce prices, his expected profit will be $\underline{\$1,890,000}$. If he reduces prices, his expected profit drops to $\underline{\$1,121,250}$. He should maintain his present prices.

$$\text{Value} = \$10,000,000(.25)(.65) +\ \$6,000,000(.25)(.35) =$$
$$\$1,890,000$$

$$\text{Price reduction} = \$8,000,000(.15)(.65) + \$6,500,000(.15)(.35) =$$
$$\$1,121,250$$

Crossword Puzzle Solution

Chapter 4

Global Dimensions of Marketing

Chapter Outline

You may wish to use the outline which follows as a guide in note taking.

  I.   Chapter Overview—The International Market May Be a Source of Considerable Revenue and Other Opportunities

  II.   The Importance of Global Marketing

  III. The International Marketplace—Large and Diverse

     A. Market size

     B. Buyer behavior

  IV. The Environment for International Marketing

     A. Economic factors

     B. Social-Cultural factors

     C. Political-Legal factors

        1. Trade barriers

        2. Dumping

  V.   Multinational Economic Integration and World Marketing

     A. Getting started in global marketing

     B. Strategies for entering international markets.

        1. Exporting

        2. Foreign licensing

        3. Foreign production and marketing

C. From multinational corporation to global marketer

VI.   Developing an International Marketing Strategy

A. Product and promotional strategies

B. Distribution strategy

C. Pricing strategy—countertrading

VII.   The U. S. as a Market for International Marketers

Name _____ Instructor _____

Section _____ Date _____

Key Concepts

The purpose of this section is to allow you to determine if you can match key concepts with the definitions of the concepts. It is essential that you know the definitions of the concepts prior to applying the concepts in later exercises in this chapter.

From the list of lettered terms, select the one that best fits each of the numbered statements below. Write the letter of that choice in the space provided.

Key Terms

a. exporting
b. importing
c. infrastructure
d. exchange rate
e. friendship, commerce, and navigation (FCN) treaties
f. tariff
g. import quota
h. embargo
i. exchange control
j. dumping
k. General Agreement on Tariffs and trade

l. North American Free Trade Agreement (NAFTA)
m. foreign licensing
n. overseas marketing
o. joint venture
p. multinational corporation

q. global marketing strategy
r. multinational marketing strategy
s. straight extension
t. product adaptation
u. promotion adaptation
v. dual adaptation
w. product invention
x. countertrade

_____ 1. The same product marketed in the home market is introduced in the foreign market using the same promotional strategy.
_____ 2. Trade restriction that limits the number of units of certain goods that can enter a country for resale.
_____ 3. Removes trade barriers among the United States, Canada, and Mexico
_____ 4. Purchasing of foreign products and raw materials.
_____ 5. Firm with significant operations and marketing activities outside its home country.
_____ 6. The development of a new product combined with a new promotional strategy to take advantage of unique foreign opportunities.
_____ 7. International agreements that deal with many aspects of commercial relations among nations.
_____ 8. Agreement by which a firm permits a foreign company to produce or distribute goods in a foreign country or gives it the right to use the firm's trademark, patent, or processes in a specified geographical area.
_____ 9. International trade agreement that has helped reduce world tariffs.
_____ 10. International strategy wherein product modifications are made for the foreign market, but the same promotional strategy is used.

_____   11. Price of one nation's currency in terms of another nation's currency.

_____   12. Strategy in which modifications of both product and promotional strategy are used in the foreign market.

_____   13. Firms that maintain a separate marketing or selling operation in a foreign country.

_____   14. Application of market segmentation to foreign markets by tailoring the firm's marketing mix to match specific target markets in each nation.

_____   15. Agreement in which a firm shares the risks, costs, and management of a foreign operation with one or more partners who are citizens of the host country.

_____   16. Complete ban on the import of specific products.

_____   17. Controversial practice of selling a product in a foreign market at a price lower than it receives in the producer's domestic market.

_____   18. Selling of domestically produced goods and services in foreign countries.

_____   19. Standardized marketing mix with minimal modifications that a firm uses in all of its foreign markets.

_____   20. Method used to regulate the privilege of international trade among importing nations by controlling access to foreign currencies.

_____   21. A nation's communications systems (radio, television, print media, telephone), transportation networks (paved roads, railroads, airports), and energy facilities (power plants, gas and electric utilities).

_____   22. Tax levied against imported products.

_____   23. Strategy in which the same product is introduced in a foreign market with a unique promotional strategy for the new market.

_____   24. Form of exporting whereby products and services are bartered rather than sold for cash.

Name _____   Instructor _____

Section _____   Date _____

Self Quiz

You should use these questions to test your understanding of the chapter material. Check your answers against those provided at the end of the chapter.

While these questions cover most of the chapter topics, they are not intended to be the same as the test questions your instructor may use in an examination. A good understanding of all aspects of the course material is essential to good performance on any examination.

True/False

Write "T" for True and "F" for False for each of the following statements.

_____ 1. Many of the most profitable U. S. service exports are business and technical services such as engineering, computing, legal services, and entertainment.

_____ 2. One drawback to global marketing is that involved firms often find it more difficult to hire skilled employees.

_____ 3. The major trading partners of the United States include mainland China, France, and Brazil.

_____ 4. Though many manufacturers are heavily involved in the international market, service firms in general are less involved, not having found the international market attractive enough to induce their entry.

_____ 5. One good reason to become a global marketer is that a firm may be able to meet foreign competition before it becomes a factor in home markets.

_____ 6. In subsistence economies where most people engage in agriculture and per capita income is low, few opportunities for international trade exist.

_____ 7. One-fifth of the world's population lives in China compared with only one-twentieth in the United States.

_____ 8. Mexico City, whose population of 18 million qualifies it for the title "world's largest city," is expected to have a population of 31 million by the year 2000.

_____ 9. Japan's traditional price advantage in the United States over domestic competitors has eroded during the 1990s primarily because of increasingly competitive U. S. companies and the rising value of the yen in comparison to the U. S. dollar.

_____ 10. It should always be possible to determine the precise impact of cultural, social, and economic factors before entering a foreign market.

_____ 11. The newly industrialized nations of the world, though they possess only 15 percent of the world's population, produce more than 50 percent of its output.

_____ 12. The U.K.'s Data Protection Act, which restricts the ways direct marketers can use computer generated lists for promotional campaigns, is an example of the effect of the legal environment on marketing activities.

_____ 13. Revenue tariffs, when applied, are generally higher than protective tariffs.

_____ 14. The United States has used import quotas in regulating trade with foreign nations.

_____   15.   Indirect exporting occurs when a firm sets up a "front" company to handle the majority of its business abroad, thus avoiding government regulation which would otherwise affect it.

_____   16.   The ultimate degree of company involvement in the international marketing arena is overseas marketing.

_____   17.   In Russia, the average worker earns a monthly wage that is twice what the government estimates it takes to make ends meet.

_____   18.   Companies using a global marketing strategy change their approach to the market in each foreign market in which they become involved.

_____   19.   A global marketing perspective and straight extension marketing strategy is appropriate for products with universal appeal such as Coca-Cola.

_____   20.   The marketing of different blends of coffee combined with different promotional programs in the various markets where those products are sold would be an example of a dual adaptation strategy.

_____   21.   Distribution strategy in entering a foreign market is particularly vulnerable to deficiencies in the transportation infrastructure.

_____   22.   The tried and true pricing strategies which have stood the test of time here in the United States seem to work equally well abroad.

_____   23.   Nations with low per capita incomes may be poor markets for expensive industrial machinery but good ones for agricultural hand tools.

_____   24.   Countertrading is a form of exporting where goods are sold "counter to the interests" of one or both of the nations involved in the transaction; in other words, countertrading involves dealing in contraband.

_____   25.   In recent years, the United States has been a favorite target for foreign acquisition; in fact, Columbia Pictures and Universal Studios are both owned in whole or in part by foreign investors.

Multiple Choice

Circle the letter of the phrase or sentence that best completes the sentence or answers the question.

26.   When Howard Furniture Company purchases kiln-dried Spruce or Ash lumber from a Canadian supplier, it is
   a.   acquiring goods to complement its main product line from a foreign supplier.
   b.   taking advantage of a foreign innovation to improve quality of its own products.
   c.   forestalling foreign competition by getting involved in a market abroad.
   d.   buying raw materials from a foreign supplier to use in its domestic operations.
   e.   speculating on the increasing scarcity of Spruce and Ash in the United States by laying in a large supply to beat market fluctuations in the price.

27.   Many eastern European currencies are "soft." This means that
   a.   they cannot readily be converted into Western currencies such as the dollar, the yen, or the Deutsche mark.
   b.   they trade in the open money market and their value fluctuates widely from day to day: their value is "soft."
   c.   their value depends on the nature of the transaction; they may be more or less valuable depending on what's being bought or sold.
   d.   they have unusual names that frequently change (along with their value in exchange) with changes in the government structure of the country.
   e.   currency dealers are reluctant to trade in them until more is known about the political stability of the countries issuing them.

28. Reflecting its newly industrialized status, imports to Mexico
    a. consist mostly of raw materials, heavy industrial equipment, and component parts used in making manufactured goods.
    b. are made up mainly of consumer goods.
    c. consist primarily of agricultural products to feed the population.
    d. are largely services bought from the United States.
    e. are comprised largely of pizzas bought from bordertown Domino's.

29. The 10 percent of the Russian population who have been dubbed the "Cossacks" by an international advertising agency can be described as
    a. highly conservative, narrow-minded, and self-reliant.
    b. overwhelmed by uncertainty, tending to be passive.
    c. strong, independent, patriotic consumers.
    d. motivated by personal gain, pursuing it energetically.
    e. having a broad, cosmopolitan view of the world.

30. A company with production facilities in Great Britain and Italy
    a. may shift production from Britain to Italy when the exchange value of the lira is high relative to the pound.
    b. may shift production from Britain to Italy when the exchange value of the pound is high relative to the lira.
    c. may shift production from Britain to Italy when the exchange value of the dollar is high relative to the pound.
    d. probably won't shift production from one factory to the other regardless of what happens to the exchange value of the lira or the pound.
    e. will first examine the value of other currencies such as the Swiss franc and Polish zloty before shifting production.

31. The fact that there are four times as many food outlets in Europe than in the United States illustrates
    a. the difference in economic conditions; most Europeans don't own cars and shop in their own neighborhoods because they can't afford to travel to supermarkets to shop.
    b. how buyer behavior differs; Europeans traditionally shop for food at many different outlets, often on a daily basis, and are reluctant to change.
    c. how strange Europeans can be; the reason there are so many stores is because many Europeans fear being poisoned by shopkeepers and spread their business around to reduce the risk.
    d. the influence religion has on the average European; the real reason there are so many food stores is because each religion has its own dietary rules and the stores are specialized to appeal to specific religious groups.
    e. how politics can affect even the smallest act; there are so many political parties in Europe that even food stores become identified with the party of their customers and members of other parties won't shop there.

32. A nation's size, its per capita income, and its stage of economic development are characteristics of its
    a. social environment.
    b. cultural environment.
    c. political environment.
    d. legal environment.
    e. economic environment.

33. When one examines the state of a nation's highway and railroad system, the availability and coverage of its radio, TV, and newspaper network, and how much energy is available from its generators, gas pipelines, and other utilities, one is scrutinizing
    a. the social environment of the country from an industrial point of view.
    b. the country's ability to deliver social services at an adequate level.
    c. the likelihood for the country to be subject to a revolutionary takeover.
    d. what has come to be known as the infrastructure provided by that nation's economy.
    e. the possibility of getting caught should the necessity for a fast getaway arise.

34. If the exchange rate of a U. S. dollar went from 200 Japanese Yen to 160 Japanese Yen,
    a. Japanese products should cost only 80 percent of what they cost before the change if paid for in dollars.
    b. American products should cost the Japanese 25 percent more than they did before the change if paid for in Yen.
    c. American products should cost only 80 percent of what they cost before the change if paid for in Yen.
    d. there will be no change in relative prices; money can't be used as a basis for cost in international trade.
    e. the value of the dollar has effectively increased beyond the capacity of the Japanese to buy American products.

35. Components of the cultural environment in international trade include a nation's
    a. size, per capita income, and stage of economic development.
    b. political stability, system of government, number of political parties.
    c. legal system, content of specific laws, operation of the courts system.
    d. participation in such activities as dumping, protective tariffs, and exchange control.
    e. language, educational system, religious attitudes, and value systems.

36. The package of a brand of cookies (biscuits, for the Anglophiles among you) widely distributed in Europe contains on the label a list of the cookies' ingredients in not fewer than seven languages: English, German, French, Italian, Spanish, Dutch, and Danish. The reason for this seeming excess of information
    a. lies in the political environment; the manufacturers of the cookies want all their customers to feel fairly treated.
    b. is a legal one; many countries require that a product's ingredients be listed on the package in the local tongue.
    c. stems from the desire of the cookie baker to impress all its customers with the purity and wholesomeness of its products.
    d. is so that the value of the cookies may be determined for purposes of setting tariff rates.
    e. has been lost in the dimness of the past; even the baker probably is unaware of why this is done.

37. The body of international law may be found
    a. in the United States Statutes and Code of Federal Regulations for citizens of the United States.
    b. in the statutes, laws, and regulations of the appropriate country of jurisdiction.
    c. in the treaties, conventions, and agreements that exist among nations.
    d. in the Codes of the United Nations.
    e. in the Laws and Regulations of the Admiralty.

38. The function of the Webb-Pomerene Export Trade Act of 1918 is to
    a. exempt from the antitrust laws various combinations of U. S. firms acting together to develop foreign markets.
    b. control the shipment of U. S. goods to foreign countries in ships of other than U. S. registry.
    c. empower the United States Coast Guard to board, search, and seize vessels found to have contraband materials aboard regardless of whether inbound or outbound.
    d. encourage export of U. S. products by subsidizing American firms which actively participate in foreign trade.
    e. establish a U. S. foreign trade commission which negotiates with nations abroad for special privileges for U. S. firms.

39. Taxes levied against imported products, whether assessed on the basis of the amount of product being imported or its market value, are called
    a. embargoes.
    b. import quotas.
    c. exchange taxes.
    d. antidumping penalties.
    e. tariffs.

40. A tax levied against imported goods whose purpose is to fund the operations of the government of the importing country is called a(n)
    a. protective tariff.
    b. revenue quota.
    c. exchange control.
    d. general agreement on tariffs and trade.
    e. revenue tariff.

41. Dumping is the practice of
    a. selling outdated, defective, or contaminated goods in the international market rather than in the home market.
    b. escaping from undesirable foreign contracts by simply dumping on the foreign party to the contract and abandoning the agreement.
    c. taking materials which have been seized by the government under the Contraband Products Act out to sea and dumping them overboard.
    d. selling a product in a foreign market for a price lower than that which it brings in the home market.
    e. selling merchandise overseas before it has been introduced in the home market in order to prevent foreign competitors from entering the home market once the goods do become available there.

42. The Common Market, or European Community (EC) as its members now prefer to have it called, is perhaps the world's best example of
    a. a mutual defense organization; like NATO, the members of the EC have agreed to immediately come to each others' aid in the event of war.
    b. an internally self-competitive organization; the natural and political boundaries of Europe have made internal competition among nations fierce and effective.
    c. a multinational economic community, integrated with respect to the abolition of internal tariffs and a uniform tariff policy with respect to nonmembers.
    d. an economic union; since 1948, the EC has operated under a single uniform set of regulations regarding foreign trade by its various members.
    e. how a good idea can have unfortunate consequences; the recent collapse of the EC has demonstrated how fragile any treaty-based organization must be.

43.   The most common form of international marketing is
a.   indirect exporting.
b.   direct exporting.
c.   dumping.
d.   dealing in contraband.
e.   formation of a joint venture with a foreign firm.

44.   When a domestic firm enters into an agreement with a foreign company which allows the foreign company to produce and distribute the domestic company's products or services or to use its trademarks,
patents, or proprietary processes in a specific geographical area, the domestic firm has
a.   issued a license to the foreign firm.
b.   formed a joint venture with the foreign company.
c.   engaged in foreign marketing of its products and services.
d.   laid the groundwork for foreign production and marketing by its own people.
e.   forever lost its rights to those assets which it has allowed the foreign company to use.

45.   A firm which chooses to use a "global marketing strategy" will
a.   use a standardized marketing mix, with minimal modifications, in every market in which it becomes
involved.
b.   alter its products but not its promotional mix as necessary to appeal to the tastes and preferences of its
various markets.
c.   alter its promotional mix but not its products as it enters various foreign markets.
d.   modify both its products and its promotional mix for each of the different markets it enters.
e.   be prepared to take whatever actions are necessary to assure itself of success in each of its different
markets.

46.   A firm which approaches the international market with a product unlike anything it has ever sold in the
domestic market is probably applying the
a.   straight extension strategy for entering the international market.
b.   promotion adaptation strategy for entering that market.
c.   dual adaptation strategy for market entry into a foreign market.
d.   product invention strategy in recognition of unique differences between the domestic and foreign
markets.
e.   product adaptation strategy for entry into foreign markets.

47.   The first decision which must be made concerning distribution strategy for a foreign market is
a.   how the product will be distributed within the foreign market.
b.   the method that will be used to enter the foreign market.
c.   who is going to exercise control over distribution in the foreign market.
d.   what devices will be used to maintain product quality during the distribution process.
e.   whether the product will be packaged differently in the foreign market than at home.

48.   Which of the following would be an example of a countertrade?
a.   Cincinnati-Milacron sells computer controlled milling machines to a West German Company; the
West Germans pay in U. S. dollars.
b.   General Motors sells jet engines to a British firm; the British pay in Pounds Sterling.
c.   Turnbull Cone Baking Company sells ice cream cones to a firm in Bolivia; the Bolivians pay by
shipping tin ingots to the Turnbull people.
d.   Peerless Valve Company sells water valves to the City of Milan, Italy; the city pays in a combination
of U. S. dollars, Italian Lira, and West German bearer bonds.
e.   Rolls-Royce ships nine Silver Cloud convertibles to the Pasha of Ranjipur; the Pasha pays in gold.

49. Pricing decisions in the foreign market
   a. can always be approached the same way they are in the United States; this aspect of marketing never varies.
   b. are seldom subject to political constraints; politicians recognize that without profits, products aren't produced.
   c. are relatively free of competitive implications; most foreign economies are much more highly controlled than is ours, and competition much less active.
   d. must recognize that a pricing strategy that works in the United States doesn't always work abroad; modifications may have to be made to recognize numerous differences between the foreign market and the U.S. one.
   e. are little affected by the actions of commodity marketing organizations like the Organization of Petroleum Exporting Countries.

50. Foreign-owned assets in the United States now exceed
   a. $200 billion.
   b. $450 billion.
   c. $675 billion.
   d. $825 million.
   e. a trillion dollars.

Name _____   Instructor _____

Section _____   Date _____

Applying Marketing Concepts

La Compania por Electrospecialidades de Badajoz (LCEB) is a well-known manufacturer of specialty electrical equipment located in Mérida, Spain. Founded in 1968, the firm made its name in Spain by producing and marketing a line of unitized amplifier-speaker-mixer units specially designed to produce the "fill sound" needed by Spanish acoustical guitar ensembles when they played large halls and stadia. These "Blendadores de Badajoz" are high-quality systems designed to keep output distortion to a minimum (.01 percent) while still delivering respectable output—systems rated at up to 1000 watts of power have been produced. Recently, the company was approached by the Tannoy Company, Ltd., a British manufacturer of electrical equipment, which requested to purchase rights to manufacture some of LCEB's patented antidistortion circuits in Britain, selling them under the Tannoy/LCEB Brand. Tannoy would provide the manufacturing facilities and LCEB the patents, quality control, and marketing expertise.

LCEB has told Tannoy it will consider the arrangement, but in the meantime it is exploring other possibilities. It recognizes that, should it decide to enter the British market on its own, its product would have to be modified to operate on the 220 volt, 50 hertz electrical current used there instead of Spain's 145 volt, 25 hertz supply. There is considerable concern, as well, over whether the British market can be approached the same way as the Spanish market. Data indicate that the British market for products such as LCEB's lies with rock musicians who are seeking brain-jelling output power rather than the low distortion levels on which LCEB has built its reputation. One officer of LCEB has even suggested that the company develop a line of separate Mega-Amps rated at up to 20,000 watts to satisfy this demand.

1. If LCEB enters into the arrangement suggested by Tannoy, it will have created a(n)
   a. export contract.
   b. licensing agreement.
   c. joint venture.
   d. shared-rights consortium.
   e. export trade law standard relationship.

2. If LCEB makes the voltage modifications required by British electrical standards and exports units to that country, promoting them the same way it promotes them in Spain, its strategy will be
   a. straight extension.
   b. dual adaptation.
   c. triple adaptation.
   d. product adaptation.
   e. promotion adaptation.

3. If LCEB accepts the theory that British rock musicians are the target market for their products in that country, modifying its promotional program as well as the equipment's electrical supply standards, it will be adopting a
    a. dual adaptation strategy.
    b. marginal entry strategy.
    c. promotion adaptation strategy.
    d. product invention strategy.
    e. product adaptation strategy.

4. Heeding the advice of the executive who proposes the development of different Mega-Amp units for the different requirements of the British market would result in the adoption of a
    a. dual adaptation strategy.
    b. straight extension strategy.
    c. product invention strategy.
    d. product adaptation strategy.
    e. market development strategy.

Aunt Melba's Natchitoches Pie Corporation, of Natchitoches, Louisiana, has been making and selling for over 50 years its variety of the unique fried meat pies for which that section of the state is justly famous. The company operates more than 30 pie stands and drive-through restaurants in Louisiana, Texas, and Arkansas.

Aunt Melba's recently received an inquiry from an Australian engineer working in nearby Shreveport. The engineer, Walter Christie, has apparently become quite fond of the Natchitoches (pronounced Nack-it-tosh) fried pie and believes that it would be quite a success back home in the land down under, where the inhabitants often eat a quick lunch consisting of the Australian meat pie. The meat pie is a small pot pie eaten from the hands somewhat like a sandwich. Christie has asked Aunt Melba's for the exclusive rights to distribute its fried pies in his homeland.

The company, realizing that a population of some 14 million people is roughly the same size as the one it now serves, countered by offering to bring Walter into the firm. After a brief training period, he would be sent to Australia to introduce the product to the market. He did not reject the offer outright, but did mention that he wanted a proprietary interest in any such venture.

Further investigation of the Australian market by Aunt Melba's officials proved very interesting. While Australians, particularly in heavily populated New South Wales, do like to eat and run, early efforts by U. S. fast food chains specializing in sandwiches met with considerable resistance. Australians simply did not approve of the skimpy portions of meat and poor quality of bread used in the American sandwiches. One U. S. fast food executive was heard to say, "Australians are very fussy about bread; they will put almost anything in a sandwich—beans, spaghetti, even corn—but if the bread isn't up to snuff, that's the end of it." An executive of another firm commented, "They have a sandwich down there they call 'the lot.' It has everything—the lot—on it: pineapple, meat, egg, potato, whatever. We just couldn't compete with that, so we changed our product."

Armed with those observations, Aunt Melba's executives rethought their position. After all, why should they take a financial risk? Since Walter Christie seemed to have financial backing, they decided to let him have the rights to their fried pie in the Australian market for a number of years, provided he paid them a sizable royalty on sales.

5. The level of involvement of the firm under Walter's proposal would be
    a. accidental exporting.
    b. foreign licensing.
    c. overseas marketing.
    d. foreign production and marketing.
    e. direct exporting.

6. The level of involvement of the firm under their original counter to Walter would be
    a. accidental exporting.
    b. foreign licensing.
    c. overseas marketing.
    d. foreign production and marketing.
    e. direct exporting.

7. The major barrier to the introduction of American fast food into Australia, as shown in the testimony of the interviewed executives, was
    a. cultural.
    b. economic.
    c. trade restrictions.
    d. political.
    e. exchange rate controls.

8. Which component of the marketing mix seems to present the greatest challenge for firms entering the Australian fast food market?
    a. distribution
    b. price
    c. product
    d. promotion
    e. none of them do

_____ 9.   It is very likely that Aunt Melba's fried pies will have to be modified to be compatible with Australian tastes.

_____ 10. It is likely that Mr. Christie and Aunt Melba's will be faced with Australian tariffs and import restrictions.

_____ 11. Wealthier countries such as Australia may prove to be prime markets for U. S. products, particularly consumer goods.

_____ 12. If Aunt Melba's and Mr. Christie come to terms, there is a real danger that Aunt Melba's will be guilty of dumping.

_____ 13. Aunt Melba's is following a global marketing strategy.

_____ 14. Mr. Christie's original proposal was in the nature of a request for a joint venture arrangement.

Name _____   Instructor _____

Section _____   Date _____

Experiential Exercises

1. The purpose of this exercise is to familiarize you with the operation of certain special locations all over the United States called "foreign trade zones." There are over 100 of these special areas in the country, set up by the U. S. government.

    a. Contact the nearest office of the United States Department of Commerce and determine the location of the Foreign Trade Zone nearest your home or college. Inquire about the functions it performs and the firms which use it.

    Location:

    Functions performed:

    Companies using it:

    b. Visit the nearest Foreign Trade Zone (if such a visit is feasible) and notice the special arrangements which allow it to function as it does.

    c.   Speak with an official of one of the companies using the FTZ and discuss some of the advantages which its use offers.

2. The purpose of this exercise is to help you understand the importance of imported products to the U. S. market. Visit a local retail store—department store, discount house, specialty store, limited line store, or supermarket.
    a.   Select twenty items at random and check to see the name of the manufacturer or importer and the country where they were produced. List the information in the spaces provided.

	Item	Description	Name of Company	Country of Origin
1.				
2.				
3.				
4.				
5.				
6.				
7.				
8.				
9.				
10.				
11.				
12.				
13.				
14.				
15.				
16.				
17.				
18.				
19.				
20.				

b.   What countries seem to have a competitive advantage in the product lines you surveyed?

c.   How many of the products are manufactured or imported by multinational corporations based in the United States? (You may need to use library resources such as Standard and Poor's *Industry Surveys* to answer this question.)

3.   Determine the location of the nearest consulate of a foreign country. (Foreign consulates are located in most major cities.) Call or write the consulate's commercial representative. Use the materials in your text to formulate a set of questions to ask the consular representative which will reveal the differences between marketing in this country and in the one your contact represents. Be sure to cover the strategic areas of product, pricing, distribution, and promotion. When your questions have been answered, write a brief essay about the major contrasts between the two markets (Use extra paper if needed.)

Name _____   Instructor _____

Section _____   Date _____

Computer Applications

Review the discussion of the *return on investment* (ROI) model in your text. Then use menu item 8 to solve problem 1.

1. Monolith Industries is considering marketing its line of industrial plastics in a developing country. Market research has estimated that it will cost about $4 million to gain the right to do business in the country and establish a modest distribution system. Sales potential is expected to be about $16 million and a beginning sales forecast of $4,800,000 has been made. Monolith executives believe that a profit of 25% of sales can be made the first year.

   a. Assuming accurate forecasts, what will first year ROI be?

   b. If market entry were to cost $12,000,000 rather than the expected $4 million, what would the ROI be?

Review the discussion of the economic order quantity (EOQ) model. Then use menu item 13 titled "Economic Order Quantity" to solve the problem.

2. Hunt Veterinary Labs needs to determine the size of shipments of animal health test units to be shipped to their European warehouse facility. The European warehouse manager has been ordering in lots of 20 and averaging 50 shipments per year. Each test unit costs $50 and the cost of processing each shipment is $50. Inventory carrying costs are 30 percent. Sales in Europe last year were 1,120 units and this year they are expected to be 1,300 units.

   a. What was the EOQ for the European warehouse last year?

b.   What will the EOQ for this year be?

c.   If the warehouse manager desires to keep ordering in multiples of 20 units, what is the appropriate order size for this year?

Crossword Puzzle for Chapter 4

CROSS CLUES

1. Selling domestically produced goods and services in foreign countries
. Form of exporting in which a firm barters goods and services rather than selling them
. Adaptation in which modification of product and promotion strategies are used in foreign markets
. Selling a product in a foreign market for a lower price than it sells in the domestic market
. A nation's communication system, transportation network, and energy facilities
. Price of one nation's currency in terms of currency of another nation
. A trade restriction that limits the amount of a good that can enter a country for resale
. Agreement between a domestic firm and firm(s) in another country to share risks, costs, and management
. A domestic firm allows a foreign firm to use its trademark in the foreign market, for example

DOWN CLUES

2. Adaptation involving developing a brand new product and promotion strategy for a foreign market
3. Purchasing foreign goods and services
4. Adaptation in which the same product is promoted differently in a foreign market
8. A corporation with significant operations and marketing activities outside the home country
10. A tax levied against imported goods
12. A complete ban on the import of a particular product
13. Acronym for treaty that removes trade barriers among Canada, Mexico, and the United States

WORD LIST:

COUNTERTRADE	IMPORTQUOTA	MULTINATIONAL
DUAL	IMPORTING	NAFTA
DUMPING	INFRASTRUCTURE	PRODUCTINVENTION
EMBARGO	JOINTVENTURE	PROMOTION
EXPORTING	LICENSING	TARIFF
EXCHANGERATE		

Chapter 4 Solutions

Key Concepts

1.	s	6.	w	11.	d	16.	h	21.	c
2.	g	7.	e	12.	v	17.	j	22.	f
3.	l	8.	m	13.	n	18.	a	23.	u
4.	b	9.	k	14.	r	19.	q	24.	x
5.	p	10.	t	15.	o	20.	i		

Self Quiz

1.	T	11.	F	21.	T	31.	b	41.	d
2.	F	12.	T	22.	F	32.	e	42.	c
3.	F	13.	F	23.	T	33.	d	43.	b
4.	F	14.	T	24.	F	34.	c	44.	a
5.	T	15.	F	25.	T	35.	e	45.	a
6.	T	16.	F	26.	d	36.	b	46.	d
7.	T	17.	F	27.	a	37.	c	47.	b
8.	T	18.	F	28.	a	38.	a	48.	c
9.	T	19.	T	29.	c	39.	e	49.	d
10.	F	20.	T	30.	b	40.	e	50.	e

Applying Marketing Concepts

1.	c	6.	d	11.	T
2.	d	7.	a	12.	F
3.	a	8.	c	13.	F
4.	c	9.	T	14.	F
5.	a	10.	F		

Computer Applications

1. a.   ROI = Net Profit/Investment = \$1,200,000/\$4,000,000 = 30%,

   or Net Profit/Sales x Sales/Investment =

   \$1,200,000/\$4,800,000 x \$4,800,000/\$4,000,000 = 30%

   b.   ROI = Net Profit/Investment = \$1,200,000/\$12,000,000 = 10%

   or Net Profit/Sales x Sales/Investment =

   \$1,200,000/\$4,800,000 x \$4,800,000/\$12,000,000 = 10%

2. Economic Order Quantity:

Item Cost = $50

Cost to Order = $50

Holding Cost = 30%

Yearly use: Last year = 1,120 units; this year = 1,300 units

a. Last year's EOQ = Square root of (2)(1,120)(50)/(50)(.3)=

$$86.41 = 87 \text{ units}$$

Thirteen orders of 87 units would fill demand.

b. This year's EOQ = Square root of (2)(1,300)(50)/(50)(.3)=

$$93.09 = 94 \text{ units}$$

Fourteen orders of 94 units will do the job.

c. If it is desired to order in even multiples of 20, the correct order quantity for this year would be 100. Thirteen orders would be placed.

Crossword Puzzle Solution

Name _____   Instructor _____

Section _____   Date _____

Cases for Part 1

1. Selectavision: Back After Ten Years?

First introduced in 1981, RCA's SelectaVision laser-readable videodiscs were based on fifteen years and $300 million in scientific research. The firm created a simple disc player which could be attached to any television set. The user inserted the 12" diameter prerecorded disc, flipped a switch, and watched the movie or other performance recorded on the disc.

The video cassette recorder had been introduced in 1976. Its performance in reproducing recorded material was inferior to that of the SelectaVision unit, but it could record, which SelectaVision could not. On the other hand, a SelectaVision unit was initially less expensive than a VCR. Moreover, the VCR market was dominated by units produced in Japan, and SelectaVision was an American product.

By 1984, VCR prices had fallen from an average of $1,000 for a home-quality unit to about $250. A SelectaVision unit sold for $200. SelectaVision discs, at around $20, were much cheaper than prerecorded videotapes, but a tape of a movie could be rented at any of 15,000 tape shops for as little as a dollar.

RCA embarked on a program of rebates and freebies—at one point, the purchase of a SelectaVision player got you a $50 rebate AND a free popcorn popper—but sales remained stagnant. VCRs were outselling laserdisc units by a ratio of fifteen to one. Despite continued promotion and the introduction of newer, cheaper players, retailers ultimately refused to handle SelectaVisions, and RCA abandoned the market in 1984 after losing $200 million.

The laserdisc was not dead, however, and reappeared on the home entertainment scene in 1987 as the compact disc. Vastly superior to the alternatives—the LP phonograph record and tape recording—in sound quality, capacity, and convenience, this product rapidly established itself as the definitive sound source for music recordings played in the home. By 1993, the CD had completely supplanted the LP phonograph record—and RCA, now a division of French electronics giant Thomson-CSF, reintroduced SelectaVision.

Questions

a. Did RCA employ the marketing concept when it introduced SelectaVision?

   b.   What environmental factors affected the original SelectaVision product's failure?

   c.   What changes in the environment do you think argued for the reintroduction of SelectaVision after a ten-year absence?

2. *"Cacao Merivigliao."*[1]

Italian consumers flocked to grocery stores recently to buy "Cacao Merivigliao" (Marvelous Cocoa) only to find that the product didn't exist. The creation of the writers of Italian national TV's "Indietro Tutta" (Everything Backwards) variety show, the mythical Brazilian Cocoa began as a satire of TV sponsorship.

The satire backfired when consumers began to insist on buying the product at their local stores. The question now at issue is whether the product ever will become available. Under Italian law, the person or company who first registers the name of a new product with the trademark office has the rights to it, and several individuals and firms claim to have been first on the scene at the trademark office. The Italian National TV Network (RAI), food marketer Buitoni (through its Perugina candy subsidiary), cocoa importer Toschi Vignola, and film distributor Shlomo Blanga all claim to have registered the "Cacao Merivigliao" name at about the same time.

If Buitoni or Vignola win the rights, Italian consumers will soon be able to buy "Cacao Merivigliao." If, on the other hand, RAI or Mr. Blanga (who claims merely to be a fan of "Indietro Tutta") win the rights, they have sworn that the name will not be allowed to be used on a commercial product. Complicating the issue is the fact that the law states that a trademark can be retained only if it is actively used.

"Indietro Tutta," as a show, pokes fun at other Italian variety TV offerings. The "Cacao Merivigliao" segments feature the show's host, Renzo Arbore, standing in front of a huge product logo—the face of a smiling Brazilian girl—surrounded by Las Vegas style showgirl dancers.

Questions

a. How does this set of conditions relate to the application of the marketing concept in a real world situation?

---

[1]Abstracted from "Italy Is Going Cocoa Loco for Nonexistent Product, *Advertising Age*, February 8, 1988, p. 3 *et seq.*

b. Discuss the ethical considerations behind the actions of the our claimants to the "Cacao Merivigliao" name. Are any of their positions ethically questionable?

c. What changes, if any, would you recommend be made to the Italian trademark law as a result of this event?

3. *Magnano Manufacturing Company*

Betty Schultz got off the plane in Sonno Maggiore, capital of Piulentezza, enthusiastic to get down to business with the local representatives of the National Department of the Post, Telephone, and Telegraph (PTT). Though her plane was three hours late, she didn't consider that a major problem. There are always delays in international travel. She was most surprised to discover that her own firm, Magnano Manufacturing Company, had not sent a car to pick her up. Just as she was getting ready to place a call to them on the airport telephone (there was only one), a vehicle screeched up outside and she heard her name being called. It was a company driver who apologized for not being there when she arrived, but stated that they simply had not expected the plane to get in early! Somewhat taken aback, Betty nonetheless let the man claim her baggage for her and escort her to the company car, a somewhat down-at-the-heels 1969 model. In response to her question about why the company maintained such a disreputable vehicle, his comment was, "Va bene, signorina, it is not good to appear too well off. This is one of the best-maintained cars in all of Sonno Maggiore. Our mechanics keep it in perfect tune and it will outrun any car in the city, either the police or ladros (robbers)." As he said this he ran yet another traffic light and continued on to the Hotel Andare Corsicari, supposedly Sonno Maggiore's best.

Surprisingly, the hotel lived up to its prior billing in every way. Betty's room was large, clean, and beautifully appointed; the service was kindly, considerate, and professional; no one would accept any kind of tip. Dinner that evening was a gastronomic delight, consisting of seven courses of beautifully prepared cuisine, although some of it was a little different from what Betty was used to and she suspected that if she ever found out what it really was, she might become slightly ill.

Betty got a good night's sleep and was up at the crack of dawn, dressed and ready to go to work. But she couldn't seem to get a dial tone from the telephone, and when she went downstairs, the desk clerk told her that the central telephone exchange didn't open until 10 AM. Moreover, she couldn't get a cab to take her to the office because the cabs didn't start running until about 9:30 (more or less). The desk clerk suggested she take breakfast in the dining room while he attempted to satisfy her transportation needs.

Faced with the inevitable, she went into the dining room, which was packed with local businesspeople (most of whom were drinking coffee and carrying on lively conversations). And there, lo and behold, was the manager of the local office of Magnano, who saw Betty enter and waved her over to his table. He was most enthusiastic to see her, and explained that his intention was to meet her in the dining room. He knew she'd show up there because, he laughed, there wasn't anywhere else to go at that hour of the morning.

When Betty stumbled into her room at 1:00 the next morning, she knew she was out of her depth. Sonno Maggiore was a country where telephones only worked ten hours a day and taxicabs didn't come on duty until midmorning. She had been introduced to 20 different and supposedly important people by Magnano's local representative, who seemed more interested in the conditions of their families than in their desire to do business with the company. When she had asked about making appointments with some of these people to talk business, Sr. Bientutti, Magnano's local manager, had muttered something about "Maybe next week or the week after."

Betty was frazzled. She had budgeted four days for this trip, and she could see that whatever was going to happen would take a lot longer than that.

Question

What should Betty Schultz do?

4. *The Lifeline Foundation*

The Lifeline Foundation is a nonsectarian charitable organization that derives the bulk of its revenues from sales in its thrift shops. The foundation is dependent on contributions from businesses and the general public to obtain the merchandise it offers for sale in its stores. Businesses contribute merchandise when it becomes obvious it will not sell or when they are quitting operations. The public contributes its old clothing, furniture, and appliances when they are replaced by new.

Lifeline administration has noticed that there are times when it receives larger donations of resaleable merchandise from businesses than from the general public and other times when the roles are reversed. There are also times when neither is very forthcoming.

Questions

a. What environmental factors influence the sources of contributions to the Lifeline Foundation?

b. Suggest some ways the administration of the Lifeline Foundation can apply the marketing concept to smooth the "hills and valleys" of its contribution stream.

5. *Don Caramel, Assembly-line Worker*

"I thought I was in big trouble when I pulled the wire to stop the line," said Don Caramel, a worker at the Blountville, Arkansas, plant of Earthworm Tractor Company. "The last place I worked, shutting down the line was a major deal, and we were warned that we should never do that unless the union was ready to answer for us in a hearing. At this plant, they thank you when you do something like that. Of course, you do need a reason to pull the wire, but if it has to do with making a good product, no problem!"

"I've never worked for a company that was so education-oriented, either," continued Caramel. "They're forever telling us about the company, our products, even company history. And if we want to trade jobs with another worker, that's fine, too, a long as the other person is willing. We're always showing each other how to do the other one's job."

"I'm in a job group that makes drive wheels for big units. We meet every Monday to talk over how we do our jobs. We've actually improved those wheels a lot by telling management how they could make them better—and easier. And they listened!"

Questions

a.   Which aspects of TQM seem to be having an effect on Mr. Caramel's work experience at Earthworm Tractor?

b.   How do such experiences translate into a quality experience for nonemployees of Earthworm?

Solutions for Cases to Part 1

1. **SelectaVision**
   a. RCA apparently introduced SelectaVision because it had spent so much time and money developing it. There is no mention of marketing research to assess the characteristics of demand (or lack of it) for the product. Moreover, the lack of the ability to record constituted a major disadvantage when the product was compared with its competition, the VCR. One suspects that RCA also failed to conceive of a rental market for prerecorded tapes (or discs, for that matter), and thought its lower priced product would attract people who might otherwise buy VCRs.
   b. The primary factors affecting the market for SelectaVision were competitive, economic, and technological. It was introduced into a market in which an alternative technology had already established itself and over which it did not possess an overwhelming superiority. In addition, considering the types of technology involved, it did not offer a substantial economic advantage in price or cost of materials (given the presence of a rental market which made the cost per viewing using either the disc or tape medium roughly equal).
   c. The arrival of the compact disc (CD) as a medium for reproducing sound and storing computer data (CD-ROM), has created a new window of opportunity (at least in the minds of the people at RCA) for the laserdisc medium. RCA has apparently detected a new perception of disc-read laser technology on the part of the using public. They apparently believe higher video quality is preferred to the capacity to record program material and that the quality known to be present in the audio CD will be seen to carry over into the video version. It is too soon to tell whether the reintroduction of the product will be successful. This depends on whether RCA's perception of the competitive, technological, and economic parameters of the market is better this time than it was last.

2. **"Cacao Merivigliao"**
   a. The various entrepreneurs in this scenario are reacting to having a previously unrecognized market dropped in their laps. What the people want has been found out for them, and they are seeking to satisfy the demand for it. More formally put, a pocket of unfulfilled demand has been discovered, and people are seeking the opportunity to fulfill it.
   b. RAI created the product (as a satire), and may fear that none of the commercial claimants will be able to produce a product that will live up to the claims which have been made for it, in which case RAI could stand to be in somewhat deep legal trouble later for having made the claims in the first place. Secondly, the awarding of the trademark to someone else would foreclose on RAI's ability to produce further "Cacao Merivigliao" satires. Finally, RAI created the concept, and product or no product, undoubtedly feels that it has the right to any benefits which may accrue from production or distribution, should that ever happen (which RAI supposedly seeks to prevent). Both Buitoni and Vignola seek to commercialize the product which RAI has created. Their attempts to trademark the name are certainly opportunistic to the highest degree, but if they are operating in the knowledge that RAI has no intention of commercializing the product, they merely seek to reap the benefit of what could be considered to be the biggest free advertising program in Italy's history.

      Mr. Blanga is the most difficult to understand of all the participants in this little scenario. He seems to have no vested interest in this matter, one way or another—which could make him the most suspect person in the lot. Moreover, his involvement in this situation seems peripheral to that of anyone else, seemingly seeking to deny others the use of something to which he seems to have no rightful claim at all.

      In short, the ethical constructs of all of the participants in this little drama are suspect. RAI could be considered to be unethical for seeking to deny the use of the name to Buitoni or Vignola; after all, they can't, by Italian law, register it or put it to any use. Buitoni and Vignola are certainly attempting to make a profit from someone else's creation, and Blanga seems bent on acting as though he had at least the same claim to this creation as RAI, which he does not. Ethics are relative to the culture and the society under consideration, and Italy is certainly not the United States, but RAI seems the least unethical of the four involved parties, followed by the two candy companies because they might perceive themselves to have a right to produce a product RAI, by definition, has no intention of producing, followed by Mr. Blanga, who shouldn't be involved in this situation at all.

c. If a change in Italian trademark law were to be recommended, it would be a change to allow anyone who could show first use for whatever purpose to register a trademark regardless of whether or not it were ever to be used on a product, perhaps even with a stipulation in the law that the intent was to protect such marks from unauthorized use by a noninnovator. The law would have to be carefully structured so that innovators could reap the benefits of their innovations without fear of ripoff or could choose not to reap such benefits if they so desired.

3. Magano Manufacturing Company

If Betty really wants to do business with the PTT, she has no choice but to "go with the flow" of life in Sonno Maggiore. The culture there is typical of the northern rim of the Mediterranean, only somewhat slower. You should understand that the phones *do* work, it's just that the people of the city (and perhaps the country, as well) only want them to work ten hours a day. The public transportation and the taxicabs may be quite good, they just aren't in service at all hours of the day and night. In short, Ms. Shultz has just experienced the beginnings of culture shock, and is just going to have to live with it or figure out some other way to get the job done. She really has only two choices: (1) settle in and get to know the Piulentezzans and let them get to know her; or (2) go home. One thing is absolutely for sure: the people of Sonno Maggiore are not going to change their way of doing things just to please her. To better understand some of the subtleties of the cultural differences one is likely to encounter, the work of Edward T. Hall is highly recommended. His three books, *The Silent Language* (New York: Doubleday, 1959); *The Hidden Dimension* (New York: Doubleday, 1966); and *Beyond Culture* (Anchor/Doubleday, 1976), are required reading.

4. The Lifeline Foundation

a. When retail sales are up during periods of recovery or prosperity, Lifeline's receipts of merchandise from businesses will decline because their sales are brisk and inventory leftovers and business failures are fewer. Merchandise received from the general public, on the other hand, will increase in volume because their purchases of products from retailers will require the disposal of the goods they replaced. On the other hand, when times become more difficult, as during periods of recession or depression, receipts from the general public decline and those from businesses increase as they dispose of excess inventories or, in some cases, fail. Contributions dry up from both sources when the economy remains stable for a significant period of time.

b. The Lifeline Foundation, by recognizing these phenomena, can shift its solicitation efforts in recognition of which of the two sources are more likely to be productive at a given point in time. Essentially, all charities are susceptible to the condition of the economy. Lifeline is luckier than some in that it has a source of donations available during both up and downswings of the economic activity level. Its worst times for donations are during periods of stability. At such times, solicitations in both markets may need to be intensified if the thrift shops are to be able to function.

5. Don Caramel, Assembly-line Worker

  a. One could say that Don is being impacted by all of the aspects of TQM in that sense that TQM constitutes a philosophy that begins with satisfying the customer. This implies that Don and the firm both perceive that small problems on the assembly line constitute major opportunities for process improvement. Mr. Caramel, more specifically, is being treated as part of Earthworm's internal market. As an employee of the firm, he is learning about it and, apparently, it is learning from him. He is empowered to move from job to job on the line, to stop the line if he detects a problem, and to recommend changes in processes if he feels they will improve the product. He is a member of a quality circle which appears to be substantially self-managed and forwards its recommendations to management, which acts on them.

  b. Mr. Caramel's actions—participating in process and product improvement, feeling free to stop the assembly line if he detects a problem, learning jobs other than his own, being involved in the company as more than just an hourly employee—all create a situation which implies that each Earthworm worker is involved in the quality of the product produced by the company. This involvement inevitably results in a product which is better designed and better made and thus, more likely to satisfy the buyer.

Name _____   Instructor _____

Section _____   Date _____

Creating a Marketing Plan: A Continuing Exercise

Introduction

At this location in each section of this Study Guide, you will be presented with new facts in a continuing narrative designed to give you experience in the gathering of information, relating of abilities to opportunities, and matching of the needs of the marketplace to the desire for success of three young entrepreneurs. You will create for this threesome a marketing plan that will pave their way, if carefully followed, to the realization of their dreams.

The narrative will outline the abilities, aspirations, and strengths of our dynamic trio as well as their shortcomings. You will be given some information about conditions in the real world, but it is expected that you will have sufficient motivation to go beyond what is given, especially when it is presented as an opinion of one of the participants. At the end of each of the narrative parts, questions will be posed to help you stay on the right track. Before beginning this exercise and as you are presented with new facts at the end of each section of this book, you should review the appendix to Chapter 5, "Developing a Marketing Plan," found in *Contemporary Marketing*. The information which you will be given in any one section of this exercise will not necessarily follow the same order as the outline of the marketing plan in your textbook, but will be designed to help you complete a particular section of the plan. By the time you have completed all of the parts of "Creating a Marketing Plan" you will have a document which should serve the needs of the three young people for whom you have prepared it and which will contain all of the essential information required for the entry into the marketplace of their marketing mix.

Meeting the Cast

Brian Patrick and Terrence Michaels were cousins, and with their friend Laura Claire were considering their future. The three had known each other since childhood, but had not thought that their careers might bring them together until recently. After graduating together from Georgia Tech, where Terry had majored in electrical engineering and Brian in Industrial Management (specializing in computer applications), the two young men had decided to attend Data System Corporation's Computing Institute in Chicago to become more familiar with the hands-on side of computers and their applications in business and in the home. They felt that their undergraduate education had given them an excellent preparation for dealing with computer technology, but wanted to know more about how people interacted with the "intelligent machines" of the late twentieth century. Their plan was to use this extra information to get jobs at some computer company where Terry could design new circuits which would enhance the usefulness of computing machinery and Brian could work with software and its applications to make computing systems more "user friendly."

Imagine their surprise when, on reporting with the new class to the Institute, they met their lifelong friend, Laura. She had recently graduated with a degree in Business Administration from the University of Alabama and was attending the Institute because her family used a large number of computers in the operation of their wholesale food distribution business and all of the family members had attended the Institute to learn the details of computer applications for use by the firm. Laura had not yet made a commitment to enter the family firm, and was not being pressured to do so, but her mother had pointed out to her that the information she would receive at the Institute certainly wouldn't hurt her job prospects anywhere, and should she ever decide to join the family firm she would have to attend the Institute, anyway. Looking at the experience as an extension of her college training, Laura enthusiastically decided to go.

The three old friends quickly renewed their acquaintance, and soon recognized that among themselves they possessed a unique combination of talents and interests that might well be put to good use. Brian and Terry had a real desire to improve computing equipment itself, Brian through improvements in software systems and Terry through improvements in the available hardware. Laura, as it turned out really had little interest in distributing fruits and vegetables, and wanted to do something on her own, something interesting, different, and challenging.

All three of the friends did well at the Institute, mastering the details of current thinking on circuit design, software development, and system applications with reasonable facility. Needless to say, each was a bit stronger than the others in his or her own specialty. Terry whizzed through the circuit design part of the course, helping the others when they found themselves in difficulty. Brian found the software logic, even the newest and most esoteric systems, a breeze, and Laura thrived on systems applications, particularly on applications where economy of configuration was important. Soon the course was over, and all of them received the diploma that certified them to be graduates of the DSC Computing Institute.

Now they were sitting around a table in a small neighborhood restaurant they had all come to know and enjoy, relaxing over a friendly repast and discussing their plans for the future. None of them really wanted to break up the set, as they had come to think of themselves, and soon the conversation turned to the possibility of the three starting their own company in a computer related field. Each felt that he or she could raise enough money to support the developmental cost of one-third of a firm in some aspect of the computing industry.

Questions and Instructions

There are no questions for this part. Read the information which appears above two or three times and try and absorb the nature of the strengths and weaknesses of each of the three partners in this venture, whatever its nature turns out to be. After you have completed the material in Part 2 of your text, the development of the marketing plan for Latebri Enterprises will begin in earnest. (Latebri, of course, is the first two letters of Laura and Terry and the first three of Brian strung together.)

Part 2

Marketing Planning and Information

The primary responsibility of the marketing manager is to create plans that will facilitate the achievement of marketing objectives. Marketing management deals with strategic issues in long-range planning and with tactical issues in the planning of shorter-run programs.

Top level managers are responsible for strategic planning; lower levels of management have a greater level of involvement in the development and implementation of tactical plans. Central to marketing planning is the idea of the strategic window—a short period of time when company resources match environmental conditions optimally. The concepts of the Strategic Business Unit, market growth/market share matrix, and market attractiveness/business strength matrix are useful planning tools.

Forecasts of sales can be developed using quantitative or qualitative forecasting methods. Companies using the top-down process for forecasting develop their forecasts of company sales from forecasts of industry sales. Industry forecasts are based on forecasts of Gross National Product and other general economic indicators. Company and product sales forecasts are developed on the basis of past performance and the marketing plan. Grass-roots forecasts begin with sales estimates by each sales representative and are combined and aggregated until an overall projection can be made.

Technology facilitates marketing research. Marketing research projects generate some of the information needed by marketing managers on a day-to-day basis, but a great deal of it should come from a marketing information system (MIS) containing databases appropriate to the needs of marketing managers. Many firms have made and continue to make major resource commitments to the development of marketing information systems. Marketing decision support systems (MDSSs) and Transaction-Based Information Systems (TBISs) help to handle the flow of information needed by every firm.

The purpose of marketing research is to provide useful information for marketing decision making. Marketing research suppliers include syndicated services, full-service research suppliers, and limited-service research suppliers. The marketing research process consists of defining the problem, conducting exploratory research, formulating an hypothesis, designing the research method, collecting data, and interpreting and presenting results.

Generally, secondary data are used first in marketing research because they are less expensive and easier to collect than primary data. Primary data collection must be based on a research design which assures that it is gathered without bias and is truly representative of the population from which it was taken.

Research design involves decisions about how data are to be gathered (observation, experiment, or survey methods), and who is to collect them. These decisions are usually based on the types of information needed and the resources and time available. Related to these decisions is that of how to select the sample from the population. Probability sampling methods such as simple random sampling or nonprobability methods such as convenience sampling may be used.

Presenting research information often requires a meeting of the minds between two very dissimilar people—the researcher and the executive who commissioned the research.

Chapter 5

Marketing Planning and Forecasting

Chapter Outline

You may want to use the following outline as a guide in taking notes.

I. Chapter Overview—Questions About the Future Need Answers in the Present

II. What Is Marketing Planning?

    A. The strategic role of relationship marketing

    B. Strategic planning versus tactical planning

    C. Planning at different organizational levels

III. Steps in the Marketing Planning Process

    A. Defining the organization's mission

    B. Determining organizational objectives

    C. Assessing organizational resources and evaluating risks and opportunities

        1. SWOT analysis

        2. The strategic window

    D. Formulating a marketing strategy

    E. Implementing a marketing plan

IV. Tools Used in Marketing Planning

    A. Strategic business units

    B. The market share/market growth matrix

    C. The market attractiveness/business strength matrix

    D. Spreadsheet analysis

V. Sales Forecasting

    A. Qualitative forecasting techniques

        1. Jury of executive opinion

        2. Delphi technique

        3. Sales force composite

        4. Survey of buyer intentions

    B. Quantitative forecasting techniques

        1. Market tests

        2. Trend analysis

        3. Exponential smoothing

    C. Steps in sales forecasting

        1. Environmental forecasting

        2. Industry sales forecasting

        3. Company and product sales forecasting

        4. Grass-roots forecasting

        5. New-product sales forecasting

Name _____   Instructor _____

Section _____   Date _____

Key Concepts

The purpose of this section is to allow you to determine if you can match key concepts with the definitions of the concepts. It is essential that you know the definitions of the concepts prior to applying the concepts in later exercises in this chapter.

From the list of lettered terms, select the one that best fits in the blank of the numbered statement below. Write the letter of that choice in the space provided.

Key Terms

a. planning
b. marketing planning
c. relationship marketing
d. strategic planning
e. tactical planning
f. mission
g. SWOT analysis
h. strategic window
i. strategic business unit
j. market share/market growth matrix
k. market attractiveness/ business strength matrix

l. spreadsheet analysis
m. sales forecast
n. jury of executive opinion
o. Delphi technique
p. Sales force composite
q. survey of buyer intention
r. market test
s. trend analysis
t. exponential smoothing
u. environmental forecasting

_____ 1. Technique in which a new product, price, promotional campaign, or other marketing variable is introduced in a small location to assess consumer reactions under realistic conditions.

_____ 2. Purpose of the organization.

_____ 3. Anticipating the future and determining the courses of action necessary for achieving marketing objectives.

_____ 4. Limited periods of time during which the "fit" between the key requirements of a market and the particular competencies of a firm are optimal.

_____ 5. Determining an organization's primary objectives, allocating funds, and proceeding on a course of action to achieve those objectives.

_____ 6. Estimate of company sales for a specific future period.

_____ 7. Attempt to develop a long-term cost-effective link with individual customers for mutual benefit.

_____ 8. Estimates of future sales based on the combined estimates of the firm's sales force.

_____ 9. This technique classifies a firm's products in terms of the industry growth rate and their market share relative to competitive products.

_____ 10. Qualitative forecasting method involving several rounds of anonymous forecasting that ends when a consensus of the participants is reached.

_____ 11. Anticipating the future and determining the courses of action necessary to achieve organizational objectives.

_____ 12. Quantitative method of forecasting future sales through statistical analysis of historical sales patterns.

_____ 13. Portfolio analysis technique that rates SBUs according to market attractiveness and the organization's strengths.

_____ 14. Analysis of a firm's strengths, weaknesses, available opportunities, and conditions which threaten it.

_____ 15. In a multiproduct firm, related product groupings of businesses with specific managers, resources, objectives, and competitors

_____ 16. Forecasting that focuses on the impact of external factors on the firm's markets.

_____ 17. Planning tool that uses a decision-oriented computer program to answer "what-if" questions posed by marketing managers.

_____ 18. Qualitative forecasting technique that combines and averages the sales expectations of various executives.

_____ 19. Implementation of activities necessary to achieve the firm's objectives.

_____ 20. Surveying sample groups of present and potential customers concerning their purchase intentions.

_____ 21. Assigns weights to historical sales data, giving greater weight to more recent data

Name _____   Instructor _____

Section _____   Date _____

Self Quiz

You should use these objective questions to test your understanding of the chapter material. You can check your answers with those provided at the end of the chapter.

While these questions cover most of the chapter topics, they are not intended to be the same as the test questions your instructor may use in an examination. A good understanding of all aspects of the course material is essential to good performance on any examination.

True/False

Write "T" for True or "F" for False for each of the following statements.

_____ 1. Strategic plans focus on adoption of courses of action necessary to achieve organizational objectives for fewer than five years.

_____ 2. An example of a tactical plan is when a firm decides to introduce a new product next year so its sales will continue to grow 20 percent annually.

_____ 3. Supervisors should spend at least 50 percent of their time developing strategic plans.

_____ 4. Organizational objectives are the starting point for marketing planning.

_____ 5. Opportunity analysis does not involve any consideration of organizational resources or environmental factors.

_____ 6. The key point of the strategic window concept is that marketing success depends primarily on good production facilities.

_____ 7. Sales forecasts are typically prepared only for the short run.

_____ 8. In a typical firm, middle-level managers, like the advertising director or marketing research manager, would tend to focus their efforts on operational, rather than strategic, planning.

_____ 9. Corporate mission statements provide specific rules on which to base current management actions.

_____ 10. A major reason to organize into SBUs is to help the company make more profitable decisions about which units need additional resources and which ones should be pruned from the company's product portfolio.

_____ 11. Using the market share/market growth matrix, "stars" generate considerable income while requiring little cash flow to provide further growth.

_____ 12. Using the market attractiveness/business strength matrix, financial resources, potential profitability, and the competitive environment are part of the business strengths component.

_____ 13. A survey of buyer intentions is a type of qualitative forecasting technique.

_____ 14. GM's Saturn division invited all 700,000 Saturn owners to a party to keep them happy because it costs five times as much to get a new customer as it does to keep an old one.

_____ 15. An alternative to "top-down" forecasting is "grassroots" forecasting.

_____ 16. Quantitative forecasting techniques are more subjective than qualitative techniques because they are based on opinions rather than exact historical data.

_____ 17. The market share/market growth matrix identifies a firm's businesses as cows, comets, cannibals, and carthorses.

____ 18. The matching of internal strength with external opportunity produces a situation known as leverage for the organization.

____ 19. Southwest Airlines uses a "think small" strategy in competing with larger air lines.

____ 20. NAFTA may not broaden the market for U.S. goods and services.

____ 21. When an organization is unable to capitalize on an opportunity because of internal limitations, it is suffering from constraints.

____ 22. On the market share/market growth matrix, it is much more likely that a question mark will become a star than it is that a dog will become a cash cow.

____ 23. An intermediate sales forecast will typically include a period of up to one year in its projections.

____ 24. Surveys of buyer intentions are limited to situations in which customers are willing to reveal their buying intentions; they are also time-consuming and expensive.

____ 25. The electronic spreadsheet is a rigid grid of columns and rows that enables the manager to organize information in a standardized, easily readable format.

Multiple Choice

Circle the letter of the word or phrase that best completes each sentence.

26. Strategic planning is best described as
    a. decisions on setting the amount of this year's promotional budget.
    b. determining primary objectives of an organization and adopting courses of action.
    c. action based upon review of monthly and quarterly sales data.
    d. planning designed to attack and systematically solve short-term company problems.

27. Which of the following differentiates correctly between strategic and tactical plans?
    a. tactical—10 year plan; strategic—next year
    b. tactical—implementation; strategic—determination of primary objectives
    c. tactical—top management responsibility; strategic—supervisory responsibility
    d. tactical—total company budgets; strategic—unit budgets
    e. tactical—plans for new product development in the next 20 years; strategic—advertising plan for new product to be introduced next year

28. Which of the following is an example of strategic planning?
    a. Southwest Airlines refuses to raise its fares in response to an increase announced by Continental.
    b. The Seattle Seahawks offer the first 25,000 fans into the stadium for their next game a free padded seat cushion.
    c. Ford Motor Company plans to divest itself of its tractor division over the next five years and to purchase small manufacturers of consumer durables to expand its product base.
    d. JC Penney has decided to switch the bulk of this year's advertising from television to newspaper ads.
    e. Panasonic offers a $10 rebate to everyone who purchases a cordless phone of its manufacture during the next month.

29. The Standard Metal Products Company is preparing its strategic plans. Which of the following types of people should be given the greatest responsibility in this planning process?
    a. district sales managers
    b. the marketing research director
    c. the director of advertising
    d. sales representatives
    e. the vice-president of marketing

30. Marketing planning usually includes which of the following?
    a. selection of appropriate manufacturing methods
    b. determining the basic goals or objectives of the firm
    c. making decisions regarding the promotional campaign
    d. deciding whether or not to reorganize the company
    e. determining whether products meet engineering standards

31. Which of the following statements is an example of use of the concept of the strategic window?
    a. Videotapes of the planning meetings of the executive committee are made required viewing for lower level managers.
    b. The Harrison Brothers Hardware Company has decided to sell electric charcoal starters for barbeque pits because it has the resources to produce electric charcoal starters.
    c. Interstate Transportation Company (a bus line) has decided to offer evening bus service to the downtown area because it has done a research study which showed a need for the service. In addition, Interstate has the resources to provide the service.
    d. The Gates Tire and Rubber Company has decided to produce and market hip boots because they feel there is a market for hip boots. The company does not have adequate resources, however, to fund the production and marketing of this new product line.
    e. The Cutrell-Arbison Company has decided to lower the prices of its products by 20 percent across-the-board.

32. Sales forecasts
    a. play no role in new-product decisions.
    b. are important tools for marketing control because they produce standards against which to measure performance.
    c. play a role in setting criteria for success but do not define failure.
    d. are made only in the short run—for a period of one to five years.
    e. may be categorized as inductive and deductive.

33. Qualitative forecasting
    a. relies on objective techniques to prepare its predictions.
    b. is judgmental or subjective in nature.
    c. includes the Delphi technique, jury of executive opinion, and trend analysis.
    d. attempts to eliminate the guesswork found in quantitative forecasting.
    e. may be categorized as reductive or synthetic.

34. Which of the following correctly matches the managerial level of the participant with the type of planning emphasized at that level of the organization.
    a. District sales manager: strategic planning
    b. General sales manager: strategic planning
    c. Chief executive officer: operational planning
    d. Marketing research manager: tactical planning
    e. Divisional vice-presidents: operational planning

35. General Mercantile Company is trying to organize its businesses into Strategic Business Units. Which of the following should be used in deciding on SBUs?
    a. Are the products of the businesses marketed to different customers?
    b. Do the businesses produce mechanically similar products?
    c. Can the businesses use the same production lines?
    d. Do the businesses use the same raw materials?
    e. Do the activities of the businesses use basically the same quality control staff?

36.   If the framework provided by the market growth/market share matrix is used as the guideline, a firm
would be most likely to drop a product which was classed as a
a.   cash cow.
b.   dog.
c.   star.
d.   question mark.
e.   skunk.

37.   You are considering using the market share/market growth matrix approach to adjust your company's
product portfolio. A correct action when using this approach is
a.   eliminate all question marks; they're hopeless, anyway.
b.   delete new products unless they become cash cows within six months after their introduction.
c.   find funds to finance the future growth of stars.
d.   plow money back into your cash cows; they can be made into stars if enough money is invested in
them.
e.   to be prepared to fund the potential growth of dogs into cash cows or maybe even stars.

38.   This forecast focuses on factors external to the firm that affect its markets. It is
a.   a long-term sales forecast.
b.   a sales force composite.
c.   an environmental forecast.
d.   a survey of buyer intentions.
e.   a market test.

39.   Qualitative sales forecasting methods include
a.   trend extensions of past sales results.
b.   sales force composites.
c.   computer simulations of likely consumer reaction to a new product.
d.   levels of sales of product in test markets.
e.   input-output models of relationships between industries.

40.   The Delphi Technique of sales forecasting includes
a.   use of company sales to forecast GDP.
b.   trend extensions of company sales to forecast industry sales.
c.   use of environmental forecasts as the base for industry forecasts.
d.   total reliance on juries of executive opinion for forecasts of product sales.
e.   seeking expert opinion from outside the firm in a manner similar to that used in juries of executive
opinion.

41.   "We seek challenges to create innovative solutions which make statements demonstrating our commitment to excellence." This quote is an example of
a.   a mission statement.
b.   a strategic plan.
c.   an operational plan.
d.   a tactical appraisal of conditions.
e.   wishful thinking: it is obviously not attainable.

42.   Which of the following is one of the Coca-Cola Company's identified strengths?
      a.   extensive experience in the toy and fashion clothing fields
      b.   a long history of success marketing wines and spirits
      c.   the world's best known trademark
      d.   a conservative, noninnovative management team
      e.   a high level of employee turnover

43.   The term that is used to describe the condition that exists when environmental threats attack an organization's weakness is
      a.   leverage.
      b.   a problem.
      c.   vulnerability.
      d.   constraints.
      e.   technoflap.

44.   The term SWOT as used in "SWOT analysis" stands for
      a.   safety without threats.
      b.   standards, work orders, and techniques.
      c.   strengths and weaknesses, opportunities and threats.
      d.   sequences and workovers of organization and territory.
      e.   seasonal, weekly, and orderly transmission (of data).

45.   One of the strategic business units in your company's portfolio is a cash cow. The best set of actions to take with that SBU would be to
      a.   allocate substantial funds for advertising and new equipment to stimulate future growth.
      b.   withdraw from this market by selling or closing this SBU.
      c.   reallocate resources away from this unit if this SBU can't be converted to a star and pursue markets with greater potential; allow this SBU to wither on the vine.
      d.   maintain this status for as long as possible, using the funds generated by this SBU to finance the growth of other SBUs with higher growth potential.
      e.   make a "go" or "no go" decision as soon as possible; then either get out of that market or aggressively pursue development of the SBU.

46.   *LOTUS 1-2-3*, *QuattroProC*, and *Wingz* are examples of
      a.   spreadsheet software for anticipating marketing performance.
      b.   marketing audit systems.
      c.   decision-making tools designed on the basis of the Persian Messenger Rule.
      d.   sales forecasting programs.
      e.   qualitative sales forecasting techniques.

47.   Of the following, which is true of the Delphi technique?
      a.   It is a quick, inexpensive technique to use.
      b.   Inaccurate results may result from low estimates by sales personnel concerned about their influence on quotas.
      c.   Useful in the short and intermediate term for firms with only a few customers.
      d.   It assumes the future is a continuation of the past and does not consider environmental changes.
      e.   It is time-consuming and expensive but can accurately predict long-term events like technological breakthroughs.

48.   Which of the following is a quantitative sales forecasting technique?
   a.   market testing
   b.   Delphi technique
   c.   sales force composite
   d.   jury of executive opinion
   e.   survey of buyer intentions.

49.   An analysis of the historical relationship between sales volume and the passage of time forms the basis of the sales forecasting technique(s)
   a.   called trend analysis and exponential smoothing.
   b.   of market testing.
   c.   used in the Delphi method.
   d.   which are qualitative in nature.
   e.   called Stanforth's Rule.

50.   Of the following, which would typically come first in the marketing planning process?
   a.   the assessment of organizational resources
   b.   evaluation of environmental risks and opportunities
   c.   determination of organizational objectives
   d.   implementing strategy through operational plans
   e.   monitoring and assessing strategy based on feedback

Name _____ Instructor _____

Section _____ Date _____

Applying Marketing Concepts

Arnold Sandifer of Aquasil, Inc., was pleased with his company's prospects. The recent unpleasantness in the Middle East had left a number of cities and towns in coastal areas with damaged or destroyed seawater distillation plants. Aquasil rushed its personnel in to get some of the plants back on line as a humanitarian gesture, but Mr. Sandifer knew that many of the facilities which his personnel had repaired needed to be replaced soon—the repairs made were far from permanent. He knew he had the advantage in competing to sell the replacements over his two closest competitors: Freshwater Corporation, from Great Britain, and Wellco, another U.S. firm.

Freshwater had recently run into some financial difficulties and was unable to send anyone into the area to help out or to solicit business. Wellco, despite making a good product and being financially sound, had only recently gotten into foreign markets and still made products with all U.S. type threads and fasteners—very different from the ISO metric fasteners used in the typical overseas application and hard to interface with existing plants. Aquasil was able to supply either U.S. or ISO fittings and a wide range of special adapters from inventory.

Mr. Sandifer was worried about one thing. He knew that his success in doing business in the Middle East depended on being associated with the right local family—the one with the most power and position. Prior to the war, his firm had worked closely with the al Rashid group and had been quite successful. Rumor had it, though, that the al Rashids, because of some unpopular political positions they had recently taken, might be eased out by the el Harouns, who represented Austrawasser KG, a European manufacturer of saltwater distilleries.

1. Because of its ability to be there when needed and to supply the products to meet local interface needs, Aquasil finds itself
   a. with considerable leverage in the local market.
   b. with a problem doing business in the Middle East.
   c. vulnerable to competitive pressure, particularly from Wellco.
   d. constrained by staff shortages.
   e. lacking a strategic window to develop its opportunity.

2. The Freshwater Corporation
   a. is vulnerable in the Middle East.
   b. suffers from constraints in this market.
   c. has real problems with product quality.
   d. probably has as much leverage as does Aquasil.
   e. has shown more wisdom than any of its competitors so far; it is staying away until the dust settles.

3. Wellco's entry into the Middle Eastern market
   a. is hampered by a problem.
   b. is hampered by constraints.
   c. depends on its leverage in the market.
   d. seems particularly vulnerable.
   e. goes without saying.

4. Aquasil's relationship with the al Rashid group
    a. could never constitute a problem for them.
    b. may make them vulnerable, particularly if the el Harouns accede to power.
    c. places a high level of constraint on them.
    d. has no effect on the amount of leverage they are able to employ.
    e. is irrelevant to their marketing effort.

5. Every town in the region that has access to salt water already uses distillery equipment to produce fresh water from it. If Aquasil succeeds in dominating the market for replacement equipment, it will hold a very large share of the market, but the market probably will not grow very rapidly, if at all. From a market share/market growth matrix point of view, the Middle Eastern saltwater distillation market would appear to be
    a. a question mark.
    b. a cash cow.
    c. a dog.
    d. a star.
    e. a comet.

The Rheinische-Westfalische-Dortmunder Dampfschifflinie (Rhine, Westphalia, and Dortmund Steamship Company—RWD for short) has been involved in an analysis of its operations in the context of the advent of the EC. Despite its name, the firm is a diversified transportation company offering coordinated rail, autobus, and river steamship passenger and cargo service all along the Rhine. Heinz-Helmut Langspiel, the firm's chief executive officer, is concerned about his firm's future. He is, in fact, considering moving his firm's headquarters from Cologne, in Germany, to Rotterdam, in the Netherlands, to take advantage of the more advantageous banking laws there. He is also concerned that the appearance on the lower Rhine of vessels from Switzerland, Austria, and even Hungary may negatively impact his business.

6. If Herr Langspiel polls his ship captains, who serve as the authority over the ship each commands and are like vice-presidents of a landbound firm, concerning their thinking about the future of RWD in the Rhine cargo business, he will be using the forecasting technique known as
    a. a jury of executive opinion.
    b. the Delphi technique.
    c. a sales force composite.
    d. trend analysis.
    e. a survey of buyer intentions.

7. If, on the other hand, Herr Langspiel conducts a survey of potential users of his company's cargo-handling services and asks them about the likelihood of their use of those services in the near future and further asks them about the quantity of cargo they intend to ship, he will be using a
    a. market test.
    b. sales force composite.
    c. survey of buyer intentions.
    d. Delphi technique.
    e. linear retrograde estimate.

8. If a detailed history of sales is used to project sales into the future, the chances are that
    a. a jury of executive opinion will be used.
    b. trend analysis or exponential smoothing will be used.
    c. a qualitative rather than a quantitative tool will be used.
    d. it will be in error; you can't project the past into the future.

The Hawley Robinson Company has been manufacturing a broad line of clothing items for over 100 years. Its product portfolio includes men's work clothing, children's nightwear, women's coats, and even a line of trendy shirts and shorts ensembles aimed a male and female teenagers. The work clothing, which was the first product line the company entered back in 1882, remains a sound, steady performer in the marketplace, with a substantial share of a slowly growing but quite loyal market segment. In recent years, the performance of the women's coat line has been disappointing. Sales have been declining every year despite a determined effort by the company to offer a stylish, well-made product at a reasonable price. A recent analysis by the Hawley marketing team indicates that both market size and Hawley's share of the market are declining in this area.

The children's nightwear line is the company's present pride and joy. The dominant brand in a rapidly growing segment, "H-R Nitees" have proven themselves the company's big profit-producer for the 1990s. The results are still out on the teen ensembles. Only recently introduced, they have not yet captured a large share of the market. Hawley management feels the line is stylish and will ultimately capture a substantial share of this rapidly growing market.

9. According to market share/market growth analysis, the H-R Nitees are
   a. a cash cow.
   b. a star.
   c. a dog.
   d. a question mark.
   e. a duck.

10. Using the market share/market growth matrix as a guide, Hawley's line of men's work clothes would be a
    a. dog.
    b. star.
    c. cash cow.
    d. question mark.

11. Hawley's new line of teen ensembles
    a. is obviously a loser and should be dropped as soon as possible.
    b. shows every evidence of being a question mark offering and should be carefully watched and nurtured.
    c. is undoubtedly a star right now and should be treated as such.
    d. will probably become a cash cow before it becomes a star.

12. If you had to make the decision to drop one of the Hawley lines of products right now, it would be
    a. the teenwear; the market is too uncertain and the risk too great to stay in it.
    b. the men's work clothes; resources could be better allocated to developing the teenwear line.
    c. the children's nightwear; sales have undoubtedly peaked and the end is in sight for this line.
    d. the women's coats; a declining share of a declining market makes this product a dog and a prime candidate for deletion.

Name _____ Instructor _____

Section _____ Date _____

Experiential Exercises

1. The purpose of this exercise is to make you more familiar with sales forecasting techniques as they are applied by marketers.
   a. Pay a visit to one of your local public utilities offices—the power company, gas company, or telephone company, for example. Ask to talk to one of their planning staff and inquire of that person how they project their sales. Request information about projected use of the appropriate product/service for the rest of this year on a monthly basis, and for the next five years in yearly terms. Inquire about how they make their long-term projections.
   b. Visit your local Tourist Office, Convention Bureau, or Chamber of Commerce. If your town has none of these, go to City Hall or to the County Courthouse. Ask an appropriate official about their projections of visitors to your town. Do they know how many people visit there yearly, and how much money each of them spends? What are their expectations for next year? the next three years? What kinds of forecasting techniques do they use to arrive at these projections?
   c. Visit the office of a local retailer, wholesaler, or manufacturer. Ask an appropriate officer of the company about the methods the company uses to project/predict sales. Ask about short-term, mid-range, and long-term projections.

   Be prepared to report to the class on the results of your visits.

2. The purpose of this exercise is to improve your understanding of the market share/market growth matrix. For each of the situations given below, categorize the product offerings as cash cows, stars, dogs, or question marks.
   a. The Universal Electric Products Company sells a portable sweeper for home use. Currently their sweeper has a five percent share of all sweeper sales. Home sweeper sales have been fairly stable over recent years. The Universal Sweeper is a _____.
   b. Scientific Products Company markets self-administered devices that allow people to test for the presence of several blood diseases. The sales of these devices are expected to grow by 50% over the next five years. The Scientific brand has about a 60 percent share of the market. The Scientific devices are

   _____.
   c. The Tomato Products Company markets a line of condiments, soups, and french fries. The company's condiments have been very successful with a market share of about 40 percent. The sale of ketchup and french fries has experienced considerable growth in the past ten years. This growth will probably continue in the near future. Mustard sales have been stable over the past few years. The Tomato Products brand of french fries has about a ten percent share of the market.
   Tomato Products brand of ketchup is a _____
   Tomato Products brand of french fries are_____
   Tomato Products brand of mustard is a _____

3. The purpose of this exercise is to make you more able to identify some of the components of SWOT (strengths and weaknesses, opportunities and threats) analysis.

Using newspapers, recent magazines, and other current printed sources (except your textbook), find at least two examples each of firms which have (a) secured marketplace *leverage* for themselves; (b) have suffered from *constraints* on their seizure of opportunity; (c) have been proven *vulnerable* to environmental conditions; and (d) have experienced *problems* as defined in your text. List each firm and the source from which you got its story below. Be prepared to deliver an oral report on each of them in class.

a.   Firms with leverage:

b.   Constrained firms:

c.   Vulnerable firms:

d.   Firms with problems:

Name _____   Instructor _____

Section _____   Date _____

Computer Applications

Review the discussion of forecasting using trend analysis in chapter 5 of the text. Then use menu item 3 titled "Sales Forecasting" to solve each of the following problems.

1. Francois Oranjello, manager of the South Australia Wombat Ranch (Pty), Ltd., is concerned about the ability of his firm to meet expenses in 1995. The Wombat Ranch was founded to provide a protected habitat for wombats, one of Australia's least offensive and most threatened creatures. Wombats, which are not bats but rather marsupial ground dwellers rather like a large woodchuck, have suffered from the urbanization of their historical breeding grounds in South Australia. Mr. Oranjello derives his operating revenues from donations and from the sale of wombats as pets to particularly caring homes. He believes he will need at least $1,000,000 in revenue for 1995 to break even. Revenues for the past ten years were:

1985	$370,000	1990	$600,000
1986	$406,000	1991	$650,000
1987	$450,000	1992	$720,000
1988	$500,000	1993	$800,000
1989	$540,000	1994	$880,000

a. Forecast revenues for 1995 using the trend extension method.

b. Will projected revenue be enough to meet expenses?

   c. How many years will it be before the trend extension method would project more than $1,000,000 in revenues? More than $1,500,000?

2. William L. Christiana, director of merchandising at Terranova and Sons Supermarket, is trying to forecast total industry food sales in his market area for 1990. Food sales in his markets for the past six years are

1990	$8,000,000	1993	$16,000,000
1991	$10,000,000	1994	$18,000,000
1992	$13,000,000	1995	$20,000,000

  a Use the trend extension method to forecast food sales for 1996.

   b. Bill's boss, the vice president of marketing, argues that Bill should have based his forecasts on eight years rather than six years of past sales data. Yearly sales were $8,000,000 for both 1988 and 1989.

      How much would the sales forecast for 1996 change if it were based on sales for the eight year period 1988-1996?

3. Jane Pepper, director of the Hunting, Fishing, and Outdoor Show, is in charge of making arrangements to handle the crowds who attend this week-long event held every March in Harbor City. Attendance for the past seven years is shown below:

1988	3,000,000		1992	5,000,000
1989	3,500,000		1993	5,000,000
1990	4,000,000		1994	5,000,000
1991	4,500,000			

a. Forecast show attendance for 1995 using the trend extension method.

b. Why might attendance for 1995 differ substantially from the trend extension forecast?

4. Farnsworth Biddle, managing director of Synthfoods, Inc., is trying to decide whether to expand the size of the company's facility that produces synthetic oatmeal. After some consumer resistance, people began to use SynthOats because they were healthier than real oatmeal, cheaper to buy, and easier to prepare. Now they are quite popular and Farnsworth is considering expanding capacity beyond the current 100,000 tons per year. Sales of SynthOats for the last seven years have been:

1989	44,000 tons		1993	78,000 tons
1990	54,000 tons		1994	85,000 tons
1991	62,000 tons		1995	93,000 tons
1992	69,000 tons			

a.   Will the additional capacity be needed for 1996?

b.   If capacity can be expanded in 50,000 ton increments, when will the next expansion be needed?

Crossword Puzzle for Chapter 5

ACROSS CLUES

1. Sales are estimated qualitatively using the combined estimates of the salesforce in this technique
5. Broad-based economic forecast that focuses on the impact of external factors on firm's markets
8. Planning that implements activities necessary for achievement of the firm's objectives
9. Anticipating the future and determining courses of action to achieve organization objectives
10. Quantitative forecasting method in which estimates of future sales are based on past sales
12. Acronym for related product groupings within a multiproduct firm; optimal planning structure
13. Estimate of company sales for a specified future period
14. Limited period during which fit between market requirements and firm competencies is optimal

DOWN CLUES

2. Quantitative forecasting technique that assigns weights to historical data, esp. most recent
3. General enduring statement of organizational purpose
4. Forecasting technique in which a new marketing variable is introduced on a small scale
6. Type of analysis that uses a decision oriented computer program to answer "what if" questions
7. Process of determining organization's primary objectives and acting to achieve them
11. Sales forecasting technique involving anonymous forecasts that ends when consensus is reached

WORD LIST:

COMPOSITE
DELPHI
ENVIRONMENTAL
EXPONENTIALSMOOTHING
MARKETTEST
MISSION
PLANNING

SALESFORECAST
SBU
SPREADSHEET
STRATEGICWINDOW
STRATEGIC
TACTICAL
TRENDANALYSIS

Chapter 5 Solutions

Key Concepts

1.	r	7.	c	13.	k	19.	e
2.	f	8.	p	14.	g	20.	q
3.	b	9.	j	15.	i	21.	t
4.	h	10.	o	16.	u		
5.	d	11.	a	17.	l		
6.	m	12.	s	18.	n		

Self Quiz

1.	F	11.	F	21.	T	31.	c	41.	a
2.	T	12.	F	22.	T	32.	b	42.	c
3.	F	13.	T	23.	F	33.	b	43.	b
4.	T	14.	T	24.	T	34.	d	44.	c
5.	F	15.	T	25.	T	35.	a	45.	d
6.	F	16.	F	26.	b	36.	b	46.	a
7.	F	17.	F	27.	b	37.	c	47.	e
8.	T	18.	T	28.	c	38.	c	48.	a
9.	F	19.	T	29.	e	39.	b	49.	a
10.	T	20.	F	30.	c	40.	e	50.	c

Applying Marketing Concepts

1.	a	5.	b	9.	b
2.	b	6.	a	10.	c
3.	a	7.	c	11.	b
4.	b	8.	b	12.	d

Computer Applications

1. a. Forecast revenues for 1995 are $898,500.

$a = \$5,916,000/10 = \underline{\$591,600}$

$b = \$9,208,000/330 = \underline{\$27,900}$

1995 forecast $= \$5,916,000 + \$27,900(11) = \underline{\$898,500}$

  b. Projected revenues will fall short of expenses by $101,500.

   c.   Projected revenues will exceed $1,000,000 by 1999.

   $591,600 + $27,900(15) = $\underline{1,010,100}$

   Projected revenues will exceed $1,500,000 by 2017.

   $591,600 + $27,900(33) = $\underline{1,512,300}$

2.   a.   Forecast food sales for 1996 are $\underline{23,571,000}$.

   $a = \$85,000,000/6 = \underline{\$14,170,000}$

   $b = \$87,000,000/70 = \underline{\$1,243,000}$

   1996 Forecast = $\$14,170,000 + \$1,243,000(7) = \underline{\$23,571,000}$

   b.   Forecast sales would be $2,324,000 less ($21,247,000 versus $23,571,000) if 8 years of historical data are used.

   $a = \$101,000,000/8 = \underline{\$12,625,000}$

   $b = \$161,000,000/168 = \underline{\$958,000}$

   1996 Forecast = $\$12,625,000 + \$958,000(9) = \underline{\$21,247,000}$

   The question of which of the two periods is the better predictor remains unanswered. Is growth likely to continue or is the market stabilizing and likely to go back to the earlier years' lack of growth?

3.   a.   Forecast attendance for 1995 is 5,730,000 people.

   $a = 30,000,000/7 = \underline{4,290,000}$

   $b = 10,000,000/28 = \underline{360,000}$

   1995 Forecast = $4,290,000 + 360,000(4) = 5,730,000$

   b.   Projecting anything depends on the assumptions on which the projection was based remaining true. Actual attendance for the last three years has remained 5,000,000. Why would it suddenly jump by 730,000 persons. It could very well be that we've accessed the entire market available to us. On the other hand, there may have been bad weather or competing events happening during recent years which may not reoccur. It would probably be a good idea to reexamine the variables which might affect attendance before drawing any conclusions regarding the validity of this prediction. Perhaps we have done something, like raising ticket prices or changing the marketing mix in some way which has adversely affected attendance in recent years. All of these alternatives are possibilities, any of which changes the basic assumptions of the model.

4. a. Yes, as projected sales for 1996 are 101,429 tons of SynthOats.

$a = 485,000/7 = \underline{69,286}$

$b = 225,000/28 = \underline{8,036}$

1996 forecast $= 69,286 + 8,036(4) = \underline{101,429 \text{ tons}}$

b. The next expansion will be needed for the year 2003, when demand will exceed 150,000 tons.

2003 forecast $= 69,286 + 8,036(11) = \underline{157,781 \text{ tons}}$

Crossword Puzzle Solution

Chapter 6

Marketing Research and Information Systems

Chapter Outline

You may want to sue the following outline as a guide in taking notes.

I. Chapter Overview—Quality Decisions Depend on Quality Information

II. The Marketing Research Function

    A. Marketing research activities

    B. Development of the marketing research function

    C. Participants in the marketing research process

        1. Syndicated services

        2. Full-service research suppliers

        3. Limited-service research suppliers

III. Technology and Marketing Research

    A. Marketing information systems (MISs)

        1. Marketing decision support systems (MDSSs)

        2. Transaction based information systems (TBISs)

IV. The Marketing Research Process

V. Defining the Problem

VI.   Conducting Exploratory Research

    A. Using internal data

        1. Sales analysis

        2. Marketing cost analysis

    B. An international perspective

VII. Formulating an Hypothesis

VIII. Creating a Research Design

IX.   Collecting Data

    A. Collecting secondary data

        1. Government data

        2. Private data

    B. Collecting primary data

        1. Observation method

        2. Survey method

        3. Experimental method

X.   Interpreting and Presenting Research Information

XI.   Researching Global Markets

Name _____   Instructor _____

Section _____   Date _____

Key Concepts

The purpose of this section is to allow you to determine if you can match key concepts with the definitions of the concepts. It is essential that you know the definitions of the concepts prior to applying them in later exercises in this chapter.

From the list of lettered terms, select the one that best fits each of the numbered statements below. Write the letter of that choice in the space provided.

Key Terms

a. marketing research
b. marketing information system
c. database
d. marketing decision support system (MDSS)
e. transaction-based information system (TBIS)
f. exploratory research
g. sales analysis
h. sales quota
i. iceberg principle
j. marketing cost analysis
k. hypothesis
l. research design

m. primary data
n. secondary data
o. focus group interview
p. experiment
q. population (universe)
r. probability sample
s. simple random sample
t. stratified sample
u. cluster sample
v. nonprobability sample
w. convenience sample
x. quota sample
y. census

_____ 1. Computerized system that links transactions between a firm's distributors/customers and its suppliers.
_____ 2. In-depth evaluation of a firm's sales.
_____ 3. Arbitrary sample in which most standard statistical tests cannot be applied to the collected data.
_____ 4. Total group the researcher wants to study.
_____ 5. Nonprobability sample based on the selection of readily available respondents.
_____ 6. Series of decisions that, when taken together, comprise a plan for conducting marketing research.
_____ 7. Probability sample constructed so that randomly selected subsamples of different groups are represented in the whole sample.
_____ 8. Sample in which every element of the population has a known chance of being selected.
_____ 9. Collection and use of information for marketing decision making.
_____ 10. Information-gathering procedure in marketing research that typically brings eight to 12 people together to discuss a given subject.
_____ 11. Basic type of probability sample in which every item in the relevant universe has an equal opportunity to be selected.
_____ 12. Previously published data.

_____ 13.   Scientific investigation in which a researcher controls or manipulates a test group and compares these results with those of a group that did not receive the controls or manipulations.

_____ 14.   Probability sample in which geographical areas or clusters are elected and all of or a sample within them become respondents.

_____ 15.   Evaluation of such items as selling costs, billing, and advertising to determine the profitability of particular customers, territories, or product lines.

_____ 16.   Collection of data that are retrievable through a computer.

_____ 17.   Collection of data from all possible sources in a population or universe.

_____ 18.   Statement about the relationship among variables including clear implications for testing it.

_____ 19.   Data collected for the first time during a marketing research study.

_____ 20.   Level of expected sales against which actual results are compared.

_____ 21.   Nonprobability sample that is divided such that diffrent segments or groups are represented in the total sample.

_____ 22.   Theory suggesting that collected data in summary form often obscure important information.

_____ 23.   A planned, computer-based system designed to provide managers with a continuous flow of information relevant to their specific decision areas.

_____ 24.   Discussing a marketing problem with informed sources within the firm as well as outside it and examining information from secondary sources.

_____ 25.   MIS component that links a decision maker with relevant databases.

Name _____ Instructor _____

Section _____ Date _____

Self Quiz

You should use these questions to test your understanding of the material in Chapter 4. You can check your answers with those provided at the end of the chapter.

While these questions cover most of the chapter topics, they are not intended to be the same as the test questions your instructor may use in an examination. A good understanding of all aspects of course material is essential to good performance on an examination.

True/False

Write "T" for True and "F" for False for each of the following statements.

_____ 1. If anyone was the "father of marketing research," it was N. W. Ayer, who conducted the first organized project of this type in 1879.

_____ 2. Charles C. Parlin founded the first commercial marketing research department at Curtis Publishing Company in 1911.

_____ 3. Exploratory research has as its goal the determintion of what data are needed for testing hypotheses.

_____ 4. One of the drawbacks to using secondary data is often the time and expense which must be expended to get it.

_____ 5. A. C. Nielsen, the world's largest marketing research firm, earns more than half its revenues outside the United States.

_____ 6. A check of license plates at a shopping center would be secondary data for the firm that did the study.

_____ 7. Internal secondary data is data which was collected by the U. S. government; external secondary data is data which was collected by foreign governments.

_____ 8. Experimentation is the least-used of the primary data gathering methods because it is so expensive to control all the variables in a real-life situation.

_____ 9. A marketing research organization that provides a standardized set of data on a regular basis to all customers is called a syndicated service.

_____ 10. The step in the marketing research process which we have called "marketing cost analysis" is also known as "situation analysis."

_____ 11. A marketing researcher trying to decide whether to use a telephone survey which will cost $20 per completed interview or a mail questionnaire which will cost $15,000 to print and mail 1,000 should select the mail questionnaire as long as it receives an average response rate.

_____ 12. Stratified and cluster sampling are two types of nonprobability samples.

_____ 13. Stratified sampling assures that members of different groups such as large companies and small companies are included in the sample.

_____ 14. In general, while an MDSS provides raw data, an MIS changes this data into information that is more useful.

____ 15. Marketing information systems can serve as a company's nerve center, monitoring the market-place continually and providing instantaneous information.

____ 16. Despite an increasing recognition of the importance of marketing research as a decision-making tool, less than 50 percent of the nation's leading manufacturing firms have marketing research departments.

____ 17. The use of functional accounts in marketing cost analysis requires that traditional accounts be reallocated to the purpose for which the expenditure was made.

____ 18. A database is any collection of data which is retrievable from public records.

____ 19. The most important source of marketing data in the United States is the Federal government.

____ 20. *Sales and Marketing Management* magazine's annual "Survey of Media Markets" is an excellent source of data on the audiences reached by various advertising media.

____ 21. Mail surveys are among the most unbiased methods of gathering primary data since the respondents know their anonymity will be protected.

____ 22. Telephone surveys may be subject to bias because of the omission of households without telephones and those with unlisted numbers.

____ 23. Focus groups are composed of eight to 12 people brought together to discuss a subject of interest.

____ 24. The FAX survey has come to be looked on as an alternative to the personal interview survey.

____ 25. Of all of the methods of collecting marketing research information, the least used is observation.

Multiple Choice

Circle the letter of the word or phrase that best completes the sentence or best answers the question.

26. Marketing research consists of generating information to
   a. identify and define marketing opportunities.
   b. evaluate marketing actions.
   c. monitor marketing performance.
   d. improve understanding of marketing as a process.
   e. do all of the above.

27. Marketing research efforts commonly center on which of the following activities?
   a. analysis of gross domestic product for various countries
   b. creating budgets for the firm's operating divisions
   c. development of effective advertising copy and layout
   d. gauging the performance of existing products
   e. studying the impact of federal deficits on product sales

28. If a marketing research organization provides a standardized set of data on a regular basis to all customers, it is
   a. a full-service supplier.
   b. a captive data supplier.
   c. a contract research firm.
   d. a syndicated service.
   e. none of the above.

29. The first task of the marketing researcher when conducting a research investigation is to
    a. conduct exploratory research.
    b. go to the library.
    c. define the problem.
    d. do a sales and cost analysis.
    e. plan a research design.

30. Which of the following are sources of secondary data?
    a. company sales records
    b. internal product performance reports
    c. industry sales figures published by a trade organization.
    d. government publications such as the *Census of Retail Trade*
    e. all of the above are sources of secondary data

31. The marketing research process should follow the sequence of
    a. problem definition, research design, hypothesis, exploratory research, data collection, interpretation and presentation.
    b. problem definition, interpretation and presentation, data collection, research design, hypothesis, exploratory research.
    c. problem definition, exploratory research, hypothesis, research design, data collection, interpretation and presentation.
    d. interpretation and presentation, problem definition, exploratory research, research design, data collection, hypothesis.
    e. interpretation and presentation, problem definition, exploratory research, research design, data collection.

32. Compared to secondary data, primary data has the advantage of being
    a. almost always less expensive to collect.
    b. less time-consuming to acquire.
    c. tailored to the specific needs of the marketer.
    d. readily available from the U. S. government.
    e. all of the above.

33. The purpose of a sales analysis is to
    a. eliminate accountants' jobs.
    b. obtain meaningful information from accounting data.
    c. evaluate such items as selling costs, warehousing, advertising, and delivery expenses.
    d. analyze the company's achievement of market share objectives.
    e. acquire external secondary data to make decision-making more successful.

34. It is true that:
    a. the telephone interview method is excellent if the questions to be asked are lengthy and complex.
    b. one of the greatest advantages of the personal interview technique of data gathering is that it is so quick and economical.
    c. test markets are a type of experiment.
    d. focus groups usually include 50 to 60 people.
    e. practically every survey technique used in the United States can be used with equal or greater efficiency in the foreign environment.

35. Which of the follwing correctly matches the type of survey to the reason for choosing it?
    a. focus group—interview many people, one at a time, at very low cost.
    b. mall intercept—wish to contact people where they work.
    c. mail survey—want to receive a response from everyone in the universe.
    d. personal interview—want to contact people living all over the world at the lowest possible cost.
    e. telephone interview—want to gather small quantities of impersonal information cheaply and quickly.

36. Which of the following correctly matches the type of sample with an appropriate example?
    a. cluster sample—interview all residents of six cities which were selected from all U.S. cities.
    b. quota sample—interview 100 students selected randomly from a list of all students.
    c. stratified sample—interview the first 35 men and the first 35 women who enter the Lakeside Shopping Mall.
    d. simple random sample—interview anybody you can find on the street.
    e. convenience sample—call every tenth name in the telephone directory.

37. The focus group interview is an example of
    a. an experimental research technique.
    b. a type of personal interview research technique.
    c. an observational research technique.
    d. a method of collecting secondary personal data.
    e. a method of assuring the accuracy of nonprobabilistic samples.

38. Marketing information systems
    a. provide a continual flow of information.
    b. are subsets of the organization's overall management information system.
    c. deal specifically with marketing data and issues.
    d. provide information relevant to managers' specific decision areas.
    e. do all of the above.

39. A key difference between marketing research and marketing information systems is:
    a. marketing research stores, classifies, and analyzes data.
    b. marketing information systems involve the continuous collection, processing, and production of information relevant to marketing issues.
    c. marketing research focuses daily on the marketplace, providing up to the minute information on market conditions.
    d. marketing research uses more different types of data.
    e. marketing information systems are restricted to providing information about competitors.

40. A simple random sample is
    a. a nonprobability sample designed so that each subgroup in the population will be represented in the sample in proportion to its representation in the population.
    b. a probability sample arranged so that randomly selected subsamples of different groups within the population are represented in the sample.
    c. a probability sample in which every item in the population has an equal chance of being selected.
    d. a nonprobability sample based on the selection of readily available respondents.
    e. a probability sample in which areas are selected from which respondents are drawn.

41.   The critical task of the marketing manager is
    a.   planning and implementing the marketing research function.
    b.   developing a useful and effective marketing information system.
    c.   interpreting research results.
    d.   decision making that involves solving problems as they arise and anticipating and preventing future problems.
    e.   reducing the cost of information-gathering for his/her firm.

42.   It has been said that marketing research
    a.   need not be closely linked with the other elements of the marketing planning process.
    b.   can benefit all marketing decision areas.
    c.   has been an organized marketing activity for so long that there's little new to learn by doing it.
    d.   has benefited little from recent advances in computer technology.
    e.   should only be done by specialists hired from outside the firm that seeks to use the results of the research.

43.   A marketing information system (MIS) consists of
    a.   statistics, opinions, facts, and predictions categorized on some basis for storage and retrieval.
    b.   a compilation of data potentially useful to the marketing manager in making decisions.
    c.   a cardboard box into which the firm's records have been carefully packed so that in the event of the need for a quick getaway, they will be handy.
    d.   a way of writing research reports so that they can be understood by the executives who must use them.
    e.   a planned, computer based system designed to provide managers with a continual flow of information relevant to their decision areas.

44.   A marketing research firm that contracts with a client to conduct a complete marketing research project is called
    a.   a syndicated service.
    b.   a captive research source.
    c.   a limited-service research supplier.
    d.   a full-service research supplier.
    e.   either b or d.

45.   A sudden decline in market share for a popular consumer product would be
    a.   a real problem to be solved as soon as possible.
    b.   typical of situations that happen all the time when the consumer market is involved.
    c.   a symptom that there may have been changes in the target market or in the environment or that changes need to be made in the marketing mix.
    d.   an obvious indication that promotional strategy is not succeeding as expected.
    e.   nothing to worry about; these kinds of things are self-correcting over the long run.

46.   International Strategies, a Boston based company, now offers
    a   *Overseas Business Reports,* an annual synopsis of marketing activity in 100 countries.
    b.   direct access to state trade offices in each state.
    c.   Internet access to many foreign businesses.
    d.   Small Business Development Centers all over the U. S.
    e.   the Export Hotline for 68 nations and 58 industries.

47.   Marketing cost analysis requires a new way of classifying accounting data. This new approach requires that accounts be classified
  a.   arbitrarily.
  b.   functionally.
  c.   traditionally.
  d.   randomly.
  e.   naturally.

48.   Which of the following is an example of an hypothesis?
  a.   We sell 53 percent of the total quantity of this product sold in the world.
  b.   Our sales force consists of 57 people, 14 of whom work in the field; the rest are support staff.
  c.   Our president is an engineer; his brother, who serves as vice-president of finance, is an accountant.
  d.   Gianetti jeans are designed with the active woman in mind.
  e.   When buying a home, families first investigate the neighborhood; then they look for a house in the preferred neighborhood.

49.   Of all of the sources of primary research data, the one which accounts for the majority of all such data is
  a.   observation.
  b.   mail surveys.
  c.   telephone interviews.
  d.   experimentation.
  e.   personal interviews.

50.   If your supervisor in the marketing research department of the Southern States Life, Health, and Accident Insurance Company told you that he wanted you to take a sample such that the members of the sample were equally divided among people under the age of 35, between 35 and 55, and over 55, you would take a
  a.   simple random sample.
  b.   convenience sample.
  c.   stratified sample.
  d.   systematic sample.
  e.   quota sample.

Name _____   Instructor _____

Section _____   Date _____

Applying Marketing Concepts

Helga Whitman, marketing research analyst for Sandusky Sanitary Supply, was told to find out why "Dirtowt," the company's new high-strength floor cleaning compound, wasn't doing as well as it should in the marketplace and to report back to the executive committee in two weeks.

She decided that the first thing to do was to gather primary data from all the 7,500 Sandusky customers who'd bought "Dirtowt" during the past year. Her main concern was to find out why the customers weren't making repeat purchases of the product. After reviewing bids from three outside marketing research suppliers, she chose the Austin Company because its bid was the lowest. Ms. Whitman directed Austin to design and conduct the study of all "Dirtowt" customers without talking to any Sandusky Sanitary management personnel.

After the primary research study was commissioned, Ms. Whitman started talking with Sandusky's sales force and wholesalers to determine the cause of "Dirtowt's" lackluster sales performance. Finally, Helga reviewed the records that were available in the company's marketing information system. These records included breakdowns of sales and marketing costs for "Dirtowt" in each territory. This analysis showed:

Territory

	East Actual*	East Quota*	West Actual*	West Quota*	North Actual*	North Quota*	South Actual*	South Quota*
Sales	$500	$400	$300	$200	$400	$300	$600	$500
Cost of Sales	300		180		120		180	
Gross Margin	200		120		280		420	
Marketing Expenses	400	120	90	60	240	90	500	150
Contribution	($200)		$30		$40		($80)	

*Thousands of dollars

____ 1. Ms. Whitman was collecting primary data before secondary data.
____ 2. A census of customers was taken.
____ 3. Outside marketing research organizations should conduct research projects without talking to the users of the research information.
____ 4. Very few organizations purchase outside marketing research services.
____ 5. Sandusky Sanitary should not need marketing research if its marketing information system is effective.

6. The best way to gather the information Ms. Whitman wanted from customers in two weeks would be by means of
   a. observation.
   b. telephone interviews.
   c. personal interviews.
   d. focus group interviews.
   e. a mail survey.

7. The sales and expense analysis suggests that
   a. sales in all territories were below expectations.
   b. the East territory was the only problem market.
   c. marketing expenses were above expected levels in all territories.
   d. the sales force is incurring excessive travel and entertainment expenses.
   e. customers do not like the products.

8. Ms. Whitman's decision to do primary research before sales and expense analysis was based on the conclusion that answers about the causes of "Dirtowt's" problems could be obtained from
   a. dealers.
   b. customers.
   c. the sales force.
   d. government publications.
   e. company management.

9. The results of her investigation should be
   a. discarded.
   b. reviewed by management and then discarded.
   c. stored in Sandusky's marketing information system for future use.
   d. acted upon immediately.

10. The major reason why Ms. Whitman chose the Austin Company is that
    a. it was the cheapest.
    b. it had the desired expertise.
    c. it was intellectually detached.
    d. it was a subsidiary of the Sandusky Sanitary Supply.
    e. the Austin Company had done many similar projects for other companies.

Janice Albertson, local services director for the Cogburn Cable Communications system, was perturbed. She knew that the government charter under which her company provided cable television service to Mirkheim City required her to provide a "public access" channel to the community. Though the charter said that access to the production facilities and distribution system of Cogburn Cable for purposes of producing and sending out public access programming should be free, there was nothing in the charter which said that the cable company could not sell commercial time on the public access channel. Ms. Albertson wondered if selling commercial time on the public access channel would be worthwhile. Since TV and radio stations and cable channels generally price their commercial time on the basis of the number of people who watch their shows, she knew she would have to get some estimate of how many people watched "Mirkheim at Home," as the public access channel was known. She also felt that she should get the information just as soon as possible, for she knew that Cogburn was soon to have to go before the city council to plead for a renewal of its charter to provide service, and even if didn't prove possible to sell commercial time on the access channel, it would be good to have the information about "watchership" for the council hearings on renewal.

_____   11.   Ms. Albertson's project is in the nature of an exploratory study.
_____   12.   Most of the data for this project must be gathered from primary sources.
_____   13.   A major source of secondary information for this study would be Cogburn's logs of public access
use of its production facilities.

14.   The most appropriate definition of Ms. Albertson's problem is
   a.   Ms. Albertson does not know how many homes are served by Cogburn Cable's system.
   b.   Ms. Albertson does not know the size of the audience which watches "Mirkheim at Home."
   c.   Ms. Albertson does not know who is using the production facilities of Cogburn Cable to produce
shows for "Mirkheim at Home."
   d.   Ms. Albertson is unaware of the legal implications of "public access" television.

15.   Since Ms. Albertson needs her information in a short period of time, the best way to get it would be
   a.   by use of the experimental method.
   b.   through use of a mail survey.
   c.   over the telephone; use telephone interviews.
   d.   by stopping people on the street and asking them questions about "Mirkheim at Home."

16.   Which of the following might be an acceptable hypothesis upon which Ms. Albertson might develop her
research?
   a.   Viewers want to see more entertainment shows and fewer educational offerings on their public access
channel.
   b.   The quality of production for the public access channel is inferior to the quality of production on other
channels.
   c.   Public access television is a waste of time and should be disallowed as a disservice to the viewership.
   d.   Public access television has a sufficiently large audience that advertisers would be willing to pay
enough to use it to make it profitable for the cable company.

17.   If Ms. Albertson does decide to use primary research and to design a sample-based method, which of the
following would you suggest to her as most appropriate?
   a.   Ms. Albertson should randomly sample customers from Cogburn Cable's list of current subscribers.
   b.   Ms. Albertson should conduct depth interviews with highly-placed executives at Cogburn to get the
benefit of their expertise and knowledge about how people watch TV.
   c.   Ms. Albertson should systematically draw a sample from the pages of the local telephone directory.
   d.   Ms. Albertson should carefully analyze the location characteristics of Cogburn's subscribers and assume an audience from what she finds there.

Name   _____   Instructor   _____

Section   _____   Date   _____

Experiential Exercises

1. The purpose of this exercise is to help you understand how marketers can use the marketing research process to gain an understanding of their markets.

    Assume you are considering opening a new business that would be primarily directed toward local college students. Select a type of business—the choice is yours. Some possibilities might be a restaurant, book store, videotape rental store, health spa, or hair care salon.

    a. Determine how many students might be in the market for your product or service. Obtain these numbers from college publications such as admissions brochures or from interviews with records personnel. If there are several schools in your town, get this information for all of them. The number you arrive at may include all students or just a part of the student population depending on your service or product. You may not restrict the market for your product to commuters, members of specific classes, or persons of a particular sex.

    Size of market (persons)_____.

    b. Using a telephone directory, city directory, student newspaper advertisements, or other sources including observation, determine the names and locations of firms currently providing the products or services you plan to market to college students.

Name of Competitor	Location
_____	_____
_____	_____
_____	_____
_____	_____
_____	_____

(If extra space is needed, make your own table like this)

c. What do you think are the marketing strengths and weaknesses of these competitors? For each competitor, prepare a chart like that below:

Competitor:_____

Marketing Mix Element	Strengths	Weaknesses
Product		
Price		
Distribution		
Promotion		

d. Interview at least five students who would be in the market for your product or service to determine where they go to buy the products or services your store will sell; what they like about the places where they now buy; and what they don't like about these competitive businesses.

e. Based on this exploratory research, do you feel that there is sufficient evidence of business potential to support a more formal marketing research project or do you think that your exploratory evidence indicates that there is not need for another business of this type and no more research can be justified?

2. The purpose of this exercise is to show the different types of marketing information available for a retail trade area. It will help you to identify the difference bewteen primary and secondary research and recognize that the value of information in making decisions is sometimes different from the cost.

You are the owner/developer of a chain of women's specialty stores called Career Path. You are interested in the possibility of opening four new stores in a city of 600,000 people that is located 1,000 miles from your current concentration of fourteen stores. You know nothing about the area except that it seems to be a good place for expansion. You contact a market research firm in the area in order to get information about the city, about the competition, and so on. It gives you the information in Table 1, which includes both primary and secondary research and their prices.

a. In the space provided in Table 1, indicate what type of research you feel each point would involve (P = primary; S = secondary). Be able to justify your decisions.

b. Rank the ten types of information listed in the order you think they should be handled when making decisions about the new market area. Rank them in descending order from 1 to 10, with 1 being most important. Be able to justify your ranking.

c. If you were limited to the following dollar amounts in obtaining the market information on the list in Table 1, which of the listed projects would you purchase? Be able to justify your answers.

Dollar Amounts	Which Projects To Do (Write in numbers only)
$4,000 maximum	_____
$8,000 maximum	_____
$12,000 maximum	_____
$16,000 maximum	_____

Table 1

Type	Rank	Cost	
____	____	____	1. List of the gross sales figures of all current women's specialty stores in the area for the last two years (Cost = $400)
____	____	____	2. Map of the area showing major traffic routes, current shopping centers and types of stores, and locations of department and women's specialty stores (Cost = $1,500)
____	____	____	3. Color-coded map of the area showing home and commercial property values (Cost = $1,000)
____	____	____	4. Telephone survey of 500 randomly selected households in the area designed to determine the consumers' familiarity with your store name, interest in specialty stores of this type, and awareness of other specialty stores and their advertising (Cost = $5,000)
____	____	____	5. Demographic breakdown of the area by sex, age, gross income, education, disposable income, family size, and occupation (Cost = $2,000)
____	____	____	6. Mail survey of 300 subscribers to female oriented magazines, questioning about their awareness of styles, need for complete services in specialty women's clothing, amount of money spent on clothing annually, frequency of patronage of specialty shops (Cost = $5,000)
____	____	____	7. Report of fifteen-year summary of economic trends in the area, shopping centers, occupations, disposable income, clothing sales, and specialty shops (Cost = $1,800)
____	____	____	8. Focus group report of twelve people concerning attitudes toward prices of clothing and specialty shops, services expected, appropriate atmosphere, type of salespersons, and seasonal changes (Cost = $2,800)
____	____	____	9. List of all organizations, clubs, and restaurants that cater to the in-crowd and their manager's names (Cost = $800)
____	____	____	10. List of all current retail space openings in the area with price per square foot, turnover rate for that spot and shopping centers, population within one square mile with income ranges, housing values, occupations, ages and family sizes (Cost = $2,400)

3. The purpose of this exercise is to familiarize you with the process of sample selection. It will help you to understand some of the practical problems faced by the sample designer.

You have been approached by the owner of a large local automobile dealership. She is concerned because sales have recently begun to decline and is wondering if perhaps the dealership has an "image problem." She feels that a survey of people who own the make of car she sells will help her get a better "handle" on the true state of affairs, and knowing of your interest in sampling theory, she has asked you to help in the process of sample design.

a. Design a process for selecting a simple random sample of owners of a particular make of automobile registered in your county. CAUTION! Remember that each member of the population must have an exactly equal chance of being chosen for the sample to be truly random.

b. How might a cluster sample be chosen from among the same population?

c. Discuss some of the ways you might sample the automobile owners in a nonprobabilistic fashion. What are the drawbacks to this type of sampling scheme?

Name _____   Instructor _____

Section _____   Date _____

Computer Applications

Review the discussion of sales analysis in Chapter 6 of the text. Then use menu item 4 titled "Sales Analysis" to solve each of the following problems.

1. Northwestern Business Supply Company uses outside sales representatives to sell its broad line of business forms in the States of Washington, Oregon, Idaho, Utah, and Montana. Each State is a sales territory and has its own sales representative. Last year's salaries and expenses for each of the five representatives were:

State	Salaries	Expenses
Washington	$45,000	$15,000
Oregon	75,000	15,000
Idaho	60,000	30,000
Utah	52,500	7,500
Montana	90,000	45,000

All were assigned sales quotas twenty times their salaries; the representative servicing Idaho, for example, is expected to sell $1,200,000.

Actual sales of Northwestern's products were:

Washington	$ 750,000
Oregon	1,450,000
Idaho	1,275,000
Utah	795,000
Montana	2,250.000

a. Calculate the cost/sales ratio for each of the five States.

b. Calculate the performance to quota ratio for each of Northwestern's sales representatives.

c. Overall, what is the performance to quota ratio for all of Northwestern's sales force?

2. Debbie Gibson, a marketing consultant, has been hired to analyze the sales of Eastern Shore Industries of Daphne, Alabama. The company sells fiberglass boats nationally, and is organized into four sales regions: the Northwest, Southwest, Northeast, and Southeast. Average salaries of sales representatives in these regions are $90,000, $70,000, $85,000, and $110,000, respectively. Average levels of sales are $1,800,000 in the Northwest, $2,000,000 in the Southwest, $1,400,000 in the Northeast, and $2,400,000 in the Southeast.

a.   Calculate the cost/sales ratio for each of the four regions.

b.   Following Ms. Gibson's recommendation, Eastern Shore has decided to examine the sales performance of the four sales representatives in the Northeast. Each sales representative is assigned a $400,000 quota. Their actual sales are:

Aubert $600,000

Kidd $250,000

Lambert $400,000

Nicholls $150,000

Calculate the performance to quota ratio for the Northeast region and each of the sales representatives in the region.

Crossword Puzzle for Chapter 6

ROSS CLUES

Level of expected sales against which actual results are compared

Arbitrary sample in which most standard statistical tests cannot be applied to the data

Total group that the researcher wishes to study

Collection and use of information for marketing decision making

In-depth evaluation of a firm's sales

Marketing information system component linking a decision maker with relevant databases (Abbr.)

Probability sample constructed so that randomly selected subsamples comprise the total sample

Probability sample in which geographical areas are selected and all/part become part of sample

Principle suggesting that collected data in summary form often obscures important information

Nonprobability sample based on the selection of readily available respondents

DOWN CLUES

2. Nonprobability sample divided so that different segments are represented in the total sample

3. Technique in which a researcher controls a test group and compares results with a control

5. Collection of data on all possible members of a population

7. Collection of data retrievable through a computer

8. Computer-based system designed to provide managers with a constant flow of decision information

9. Research in which secondary sources and informed people within the firm are consulted

11. Probability sample in which every item in the universe has an equal chance of being selected

12. Tentative explanation for some specific event

RD LIST:

CENSUS	HYPOTHESIS	POPULATION
CLUSTER	ICEBERG	QUOTA
CONVENIENCE	MARKETINGRESEARCH	SALESQUOTA
DATABASE	MDSS	SALESANALYSIS
EXPERIMENT	MIS	SIMPLERANDOM
EXPLORATORY	NONPROBABILITY	STRATIFIED

Chapter 6 Solutions

Key Concepts

1.	e	6.	l	11.	s	16.	c	21.	x
2.	g	7.	t	12.	n	17.	y	22.	i
3.	v	8.	r	13.	p	18.	k	23.	b
4.	q	9.	a	14.	u	19.	m	24.	f
5.	w	10.	o	15.	j	20.	h	25.	d

Self Quiz

1.	T	11.	F	21.	F	31.	c	41.	d
2.	T	12.	F	22.	T	32.	c	42.	b
3.	F	13.	T	23.	T	33.	b	43.	e
4.	F	14.	F	24.	F	34.	c	44.	d
5.	T	15.	T	25.	F	35.	e	45.	c
6.	F	16.	F	26.	e	36.	a	46.	e
7.	F	17.	T	27.	d	37.	b	47.	b
8.	T	18.	F	28.	d	38.	e	48.	e
9.	T	19.	T	29.	c	39.	b	49.	c
10.	F	20.	F	30.	e	40.	c	50.	e

Applying Marketing Concepts

1.	F	6.	b	11.	F	16.	d
2.	T	7.	c	12.	T	17.	a
3.	F	8.	b	13.	F		
4.	F	9.	c	14.	b		
5.	F	10.	a	15.	c		

Computer Applications

1. a.   Cost/Sales Ratios (Costs/Sales)

Washington:	$60,000/$500,000 =	12.0%
Oregon:	$90,000/$900,000 =	10.0%
Idaho:	$90,000/$850,000 =	10.6%
Utah:	$60,000/$650,000 =	9.2%
Montana:	$135,000/$1,500,000 =	9.0%

    b.   Performance to Quota (Sales/Quota) = [Sales/(Salary x 20)]

Washington:	$500,000/$600,000 =	83.3%
Oregon:	$900,000/$1,000,000 =	90.0%
Idaho:	$850,000/$800,000 =	106.25%
Utah:	$650,000/$700,000 =	92.86%
Montana:	$1,500,000/$1,200,000 =	125.0%

    c.   Overall performance to quota = $4,400,000/$4,300,000 = 102.3%

2. a.   Cost/Sales Ratios (Costs/Sales)

Northwest:	$90,000/$1,800,000 =	5.0%
Southwest:	$70,000/$2,000,000 =	3.5%
Northeast:	$85,000/$1,400,000 =	6.1%
Southeast:	$110,000/$2,400,000 =	4.6%

    b.   Performance to Quota (Sales/Quota)

Aubert:	$600,000/$400,000 =	150.0%
Kidd:	$250,000/$400,000 =	62.5%
Lambert:	$400,000/$400,000 =	100.0%
Nicholls:	$150,000/$400,000 =	37.5%

    Northeastern region: $1,400,000/$1,600,000 = 87.5%

Crossword Puzzle Solution

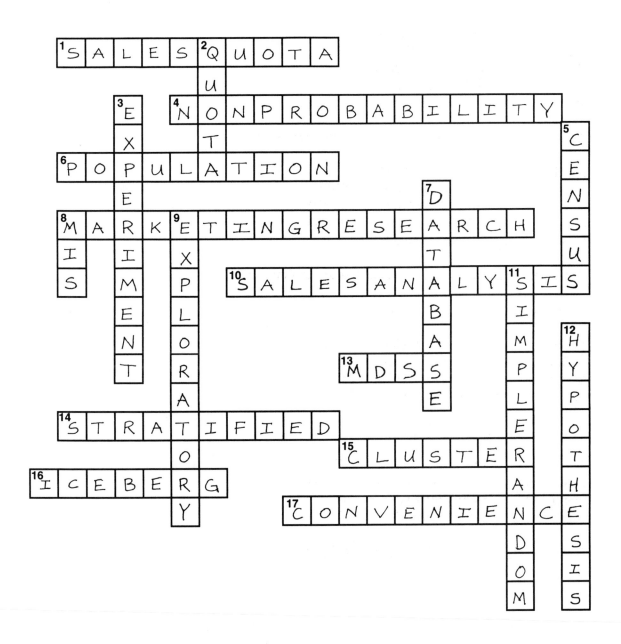

Name _____ Instructor _____

Section _____ Date _____

Cases for Part 2

1. The Manustat Corporation

The Manustat Corporation is a medium-sized producer of ball-point, roller-tip, and hard felt-tipped pens located in Squamus, New Jersey. Management has recently become concerned because sales have declined from $2,000,000 last year to $1,600,000 this year. In an effort to find the source of the decline in sales, they have performed a sales and costs analysis of company field operations. The firm maintains three regional sales forces: the northern force, the middle force, and the southern force, each of which calls on sixteen of the contiguous United States. The northern force also handles Alaska and the Aleutian Islands, the middle force represents the company in the Hawaiian Islands and other U. S. Pacific territories such as Guam and American Samoa, and the southern force handles Puerto Rico and the Virgin Islands. The results of the Company's sales and cost analysis appear in Table P2-1.

Table P2-1: The Manustat Corporation

Sales Performance By Sales Force Area: Last Year versus This

Area:	Northern		Middle		Southern		Total	
Year:	Last	This	Last	This	Last	This	Last	This
Sales*	$1000	$1160	$600	$200	$400	$240	$2000	$1600
Cost of Sales	600	920	360	120	240	120	1200	1080
Gross Margin	400	240	240	80	160	120	800	440
Marketing Expenses	280	200	200	20	120	20	600	240
Area Contrib.	$120	$40	$40	$60	$40	$100	$200	$200
Product Sales by Area								
Ball Pens	$300	$500	$100	$100	$100	$100	$500	$700
Roller Pens	200	600	300	80	0	120	500	800
Felt-Tips	500	60	200	20	300	20	1000	100
Totals	$1000	$1160	$600	$200	$400	$240	$2000	$1600

*All numerical values are in thousands (x 000)

Having examined the information contained in Table P2-1, answer the following questions.

Questions:

a.   What are the problems facing the Manustat Corporation?

b.   What other information, if any, would you need prior to suggesting action to correct the problems?

2. *The Four Wise Men*[1]

Once upon a time, in a faraway land, there lived four wise and learned men who were, unfortunately, blind. And one day there came to them a traveler who had been to an even more distant land where he had acquired a handsome elephant. Now this stranger knew that the four wise men had the ear of the king and if they were to go to his majesty and extol the virtues of his wondrous beast, his fortune would assuredly be made. Accordingly, he appealed to the wise men to come and examine his new acquisition so they could go forth and tell the king what they found the animal to be like. The wise men agreed, but being wise, they did not wish to hear a sales talk from the elephant's owner. He was allowed to leave with the elephant only a voiceless mahout to hold the animal's rein while the wise men conducted their examination. The wise men, meanwhile, had agreed to keep their own counsel (mouths shut) about their opinions of the new animal, even among themselves.

---

[1]This story, in one or another of its many forms, appears either in the *Rubyiat of Omar Khayam* or the *Tales of a Thousand and One Nights*, or possibly in both.

The first wise man approached the elephant, and, feeling about, encountered the animal's facile and active trunk. Grasping it and feeling it writhe about in his hands, he thought, "A-ha; this animal is very like a snake." And so thinking, he withdrew and allowed the second wise man to approach the animal. The second wise man promptly collided with one of the elephant's massive legs. Feeling the rough, craggy skin of the animal and the huge girth of its leg, this wise man thought, "So! This animal is very like a tree." The third wise man, after nearly being knocked from his feet by the movement of the elephant's ear and feeling its leathery yet plastic texture, concluded that elephants must be some species of giant bat, and the fourth, encountering the tail of the animal, concluded that "This animal must surely be some kind of giant horse."

And each wise man, thinking his own thoughts, left the elephant's stall to report to the king.

Questions:

a.   If the elephant as a whole described the population the four wise men were to sample, how representative of that population do you suppose their four samples are?

b.   What sort of sample did each wise man take? Answer in the context of the descriptions of sampling methods in your text.

c. What changes in the method of sampling and the analysis of the information gained from the samples would you advise the wise men to use the next time they are called upon to describe some innovation to the king (provided their credibility and their heads survive this experience).

3. *Wheat Shipments to Europe: The Data Looks Good But How About the Interpretation?*

As part of a Federal Faculty Fellowship[2] assignment with the Foreign Agricultural Service (FAS) of the U.S. Department of Agriculture (USDA), a marketing researcher interviewed officials of grain importing and processing firms in several European countries. These interviews, which were completed during the late-middle 1980's, were designed to field-test two survey questionnaires which it was hoped would improve the process of evaluation of FAS foreign market development programs.

The FAS is a USDA agency with the responsibility of promoting the export sales of U.S. agricultural commodities, including both animal feeds and foodstuffs for humans. With a network of agricultural attaches and assistants in over 60 foreign service posts around the world—in addition to a support and administrative staff in Washington—FAS cooperates with major U. S. trade and commodity organizations to develop these foreign markets.[3]

Many of the European officials with whom the Federal Faculty Fellow discussed the questionnaires took advantage of the opportunity to bring up a problem with which they were concerned. They lamented what they reported was the deteriorating quality of U. S. grain shipments to their part of the world. Their specific complaints were that the shipments contained excessive quantities of dirt and other foreign matter. The researcher was urged to report this problem to USDA officials in order to reinforce the foreign officials' previous requests that grain shipments be brought up to U. S. domestic standards.

---

[2]The Federal Faculty Fellowship Program is jointly sponsored by the Sears Roebuck Foundation and the American Assembly of Collegiate Schools of Business.

[3]See *What Is the Foreign Agricultural Service?*, Foreign Agricultural Service, United States Department of Agriculture, July, 1970, p. 2.

Before departing for home, the researcher discussed the problem with an official at the U. S. Embassy in the country from which he was leaving. The embassy staff member replied, "Oh, you've got to watch out for these buyers; they're shrewd. The grain they're receiving now was bought under cash grain contracts for future delivery at prices that are higher than the spot market price today. These guys are just looking for an excuse to get out of these costly contracts. Don't worry about their complaints. It happens often that when grains have been contracted for future delivery at a high price and the market falls, we get lots of complaints about quality. We have to be careful to separate *real* quality problems from attempts to deal with market fluctuations."

Not long after the researcher's return to the United States, newspapers broke the first story about the bribery of federal grain inspectors at the port of Houston; two months later, a similar situation was reported in New Orleans. It should be noted, however, that grain inspectors would be well aware that the likelihood of detection of substandard shipments would be much higher at ports in advanced, industrialized countries than would be the case in a developing nation. It would be much more risky to take a bribe for upgrading shipments to Europe than to some third world countries.

Questions:

a. Is this a common type of problem—field-level interpretation and filtering of information affecting the adequacy of the home office data base?

b. What might have been done by the embassy official in Europe to determine whether the problem was real or the European buyers were trying to take advantage of a situation affecting primarily third-world destinations?

c.   What control measures might be incorporated into a marketing information system to protect against the possibility of field-level misinterpretation and excessive filtering of data flows?

4. *Norsk Magasins A/S*

Jens Pedersen, Managing Director of Norsk Magasins A/S, a major Norwegian department store chain, is examining the performance of several of his firm's branches. Oslo Main, the company's flagship store, remains one of its best and most consistent performers, increasing its share of the growing Oslo market at a rate greater than that of the competition. It now holds 44 percent of downtown department store sales, up from 41 percent two years ago. Given that Oslo trade is up by 14 percent during the same period, Jens feels very good about the store. Jens is not so comfortable about the stores in Narvik and Trondheim, though. Opened with much fanfare just a year ago, the store in Trondheim, Norway's third largest city and a growing tourist and manufacturing center, is off to a slow start. Jens realizes it faces competition from two well-established locally-owned stores, but feels that ultimately it will move ahead of them and become dominant in the market. In Narvik, things don't look so hopeful. The once thriving fishing port has been suffering for years from the depression in sardine prices caused by intense competition from Oriental products. Population is down, incomes are down, and the NM store is losing trade to Gundersen's—the Norwegian version of Wal-Mart. Finally, Jens looks at the figures for the store in Bergen. The firm's oldest store, the Bergen store still has on the tips of its third-floor dormers the bronze models of the sailing ships that used to bring it the goods that it sold. A solid, steady performer, thought Jens. It's true that Bergen isn't growing very fast, but its people are very loyal to NM. The store there continues to hold onto its comfortable market share.

Question

Using the market growth/market share matrix, characterize each of the four Norsk Magasins stores discussed, and advise Mr. Pedersen concerning how they should be treated. Which should receive substantial resource commitments, and which not, and why?

Name _____   Instructor _____

Section _____   Date _____

Creating a Marketing Plan: Getting Started

The information you will receive in this part will help you to complete Parts I.A. and I.B. of your marketing plan for Latebri Industries.

Episode Two

In episode one, we learned of the decision by Laura, Terry, and Brian to get together and start a company called Latebri Industries. For reasons of simplicity, and because of their families, the three ultimately decided to return to their home town, a city of some 1.3 million people located in the Southeast. After careful consideration of their resources, they decided that they could not possibly afford to enter the highly competitive computer sales market, as there were already over 160 vendors in the local market. They also discovered that custom software was available from not fewer than 75 local sources. Having absorbed the marketing concept and wishing still to match their abilities and resources with some untapped pool of demand, they cast about a little further and discovered that, though 160 firms sold computers and 75 developed software for them, only 42 companies were equipped to repair them. A few hours in the library revealed that the market for repair of computers was expected to reach $46 billion in potential for the current year [1], increasing at a rate of some 14 percent per year into the forseeable future. Of the $46 billion current potential in the computer repair market, some $3.5 billion was expected to be derived from repair of personal computers, with the remainder coming from business repairs[2]. It was further predicted that the market for service of office automation equipment, mainly PCs used for word processing and spreadsheet analysis, would grow at a rate of 33% per year, leading all other computer-related service fields.

Environmentally, analysis revealed that a computer service company faced no special inhibitions in law; a business license would be needed and a sales tax account would have to be opened (sales taxes were collected on physical goods sold, but not on pure services). There was, of course, competition in the local market, but it seemed to be divided along very specific lines: some firms serviced large-scale mainframes and others the lines of computers which they sold; the local economy was simply a miniature of the national economy. Projections made for the national scene could be scaled down to fit the local. The influence of the social environment on the firm would be minimal, except of course that people who use computers and own them for business or pleasure tend to be the more affluent and leaders of the community. Finally, the technological environment offers perhaps the greatest risk and complication to Latebri Industries. Changes in computer technology could conceivably lead to the "disposable computer." In other words, the pace of change in this industry has been such that it may soon become more cost-effective to replace a computer that breaks down, rather than repair it; mitigating this possibility, however, is the fact that the computer industry has for some years been building their machines with the capacity for internal upgrades at minimal expense.

---

[1]"Makers' Share of Service Mart Seen Shrinking," *Computer World*, 1 October 1984, p.83.
[2]"A New Industry is Fixing to Fix Your Personal Computer," *Fortune*, 18 March 1985, pp. 150-156.

A research project conducted by the partners acquired additional information about the local market. This information is summarized in Table P2-2.

Table P2-2: Characteristics of the Local Market

Total Population: 1,300,000
Proportion of National Population: 0.52%
Number of households: 335,000
Proportion of households owning computers: (Est.) 35.5%

Businesses in the Market:

	Total	1-4	By Number of Employees 5-9	10-19	20-49	50 up
Central Area	23,521	12,597	4,548	2,976	2,059	1,341
Suburbs	2,374	1,294	481	278	186	135
Total	25,895	13,891	5,029	3,254	2,245	1,476
Percent Using PCs (Est.)	95	93	97	99	99	100
Avg. No. Per Firm (Est.)	3	1	2	3	9	15

The partners, who, by the way, are going to incorporate their firm for reasons of taxation and personal liability, have on hand at present $150,000 in cash. $60,000 of this is their own, the remaining having been borrowed from various friends and relatives.

Guidelines:

a. In the context of part I.A. of the outline of the marketing plan in the Appendix to Chapter 3 of your text, how would you characterize the likely nature of this firm?

b. On the basis of the information presented, complete part I.B. of the marketing plan. Basically, the points to be considered should relate, first, to the segments available for penetration, which segments may appear feasible for these people, and which you think they should choose.

Solutions for Cases to Part 2

1. The Manustat Corporation

a. The cause of falling sales can't be explicitly determined solely from the type of data given in this case, though some definition of the area in which the problem has developed may be undertaken. Both Middle and Southern Sales Force Areas have shown declining sales performance. Only the Northern Area managed to improve its performance this period over last, though cost of sales went up, reflecting the change in sales mix this period. On the other hand, marketing expenses in the North did not decline as a proportion of sales as was the case in the other two areas, leading one to wonder what might have happened in that regard. As a result, the Northern sales force actually contributed less to the bottom line than did either middle or southern groups.

If one seeks something to look at more closely, sales in the middle and southern areas seem to be appropriate for closer scrutiny, as does the level of marketing expenses in the North. It is possible that they are scrimping too much in the southern and middle areas and not enough in the north. In any event, sales have declined for some reason. That reason may be hinted at in these reports, but it may be beyond the control of the field sales force.

b. Other information needed include:

Industry sales trend figures;

Information on actions by competitors;

General economic information;

Specific economic conditions in the sales force areas;

Sales and cost quotas used by the sales forces as guidelines;

Overall cost of sales figures for each product.

2. The Four Wise Men

a. The four samples represent a limited view of only a part of the population. They are biased samples because they were not taken across the whole sampling space. They certainly aren't representative of the population called "this elephant."

b. Each wise man took a nonprobabilistic sample of the convenience type. Each simply acquired data from whatever part of the population he happened to encounter first. Suffice it to say, none of the samples represented the whole population.

c. A redesign of the sample such that the wise men would gather data from all parts of the elephant is certainly in order. The best way to assure that this will be the case is by taking a simple, random sample of points scattered all over the body of the elephant. The wise men should, in addition, pool their knowledge. The idea of going off to the king to report individually had the effect of reducing the sample acquired by each to one-fourth its potential size. In the analytical phase, data should be culled of incongruities and if there is persistent conflict between one description and another, a resampling undertaken.

3. Wheat Shipments to Europe: The Data Looks Good But How About the Interpretation?

a. The whole concept of managerial span of control is based on the premise that decisions are made at every level of an organization. This implies that a certain amount of informational filtering takes place as data finds its way up through the chain of command. A problem which is perceived to be within the scope of one's authority to solve is not made known to one's superiors, but is instead solved at one's own level. The problem, of course, is that middle managers may unilaterally decide to act like upper-level managers, and entry level personnel like middle managers. In many cases, such actions place people beyond the scope of their experience and competence, and bad decisions result.

b.   Had the U. S. agricultural officials in Europe made reinspections of the questioned grain shipments or had them made by qualified grain inspectors familiar with U. S. standards instead of turning a deaf ear to the complaints of their European counterparts, it is likely that much of this situation could have been avoided.

c.   As was already discussed, field level filtering of information flows is a necessary part of organizational behavior. Real problems arise when too much information is filtered out or if filtration is selective, removing from the information stream bits of data which might make some particular person or office appear in a negative light. One way of assuring that information is passed along in something resembling its original configuration is by rotation of individuals through the organization so that entrenchment of the communications channel cannot take place. It is, of course, costly to move people about like this, so it is not often done domestically and is even less often done in the international sphere, thus increasing the level of danger that the system will come to serve the vested interests of those who function within it rather than those who pay its bills. For a superb illustration of exactly how this can work, view the PBS television series "Yes, Minister!" or its sequel, "Yes, Prime Minister!" which chronicles the interaction between Jim Hacker, a fictional British politician who serves in a ministerial capacity in Her Majesty's cabinet, and the British Civil Service, all of whom know that the government's sole reason for existence is to preserve their bureaucratic positions.

A second, most important issue in this case, involves the nature of the role of the U. S. government in commercial transactions. When a transaction occurs between one private individual and another, to what extent does the U.S. government have a role in maintaining levels of quality? The FAS seems to take the view that complaints must be made officially to be transmitted forward officially, and the complaints made by the Europeans were unofficial in nature. It is true that importers often complain, just as the FAS attaché told the inquiring professor, about quality when, in fact, they're complaining about what they see to have been a bad deal they've made. The USDA is in no position to make a determination about the validity of simple complaints.

It might be mentioned in closing that the Federal Grain Inspection Service was established immediately after these reported incidents to police alleged short weights and inferior quality in agricultural products.

Solutions for Creating a Marketing Plan

Episode Two

a.   The firm's nature is becoming fairly clear in episode two. It is to be a firm specializing in computer servicing. It is to be located in the as yet unnamed home town of the three people who have decided to start it, and they have about $150,000 available to them to do the job. Thus, their geographical scope and their financial resources are limited.

   The company is to be a corporation, appropriately licensed and conforming to the constraints of the various environments impinging on it. It has no sales and profits history as yet, just cash on hand and considerable expertise in computer design and use.

b.   The data provided are designed to lead our heroes to choose to create a firm which will repair PCs, primarily aiming its appeal at the business user. While there are some 118,925 households in the area which own computers, many of those are probably obsolete (or semi-obsolete) 8088 and 80286 units which are used as games machines or for doing homework.

   The 25,895 business firms in the area offer a market with a use level above 90 percent, and it is sure that the larger firms use many, many more than one unit apiece. The estimates indicate that business PCs number about 75,000 units, the vast majority of which can be assumed to be in daily operation. Since the business market uses its computers to make money, a broken unit mustn't stay broken for long if it is to pay its way. In addition, the "office automation" market is the most rapidly growing of all the segments of the computer repair market.

Part 3

Buyer Behavior, Business-to-Business Marketing, and Market Segmentation

A key consideration in the design of marketing mixes is consumer behavior. The acts of consumers as they obtain and use products and services depend on personal and interpersonal influences. The family, reference groups, social classes, and culture are important interpersonal determinants of consumer behavior.

Important personal determinants of consumer behavior are needs, motives, perception, attitudes, and learning. Consumers do not act until a need is demonstrated to them. Motivation depends on which needs have already been satisfied and the consumer's perception of those stimuli which have passed through perceptual filters. The amount of time and effort spent on consumer decision making varies for the three categories of (1) routinized response behavior, (2) limited problem solving, and (3) extended problem solving.

The business market is made up of four components: (1) the commercial market, (2) trade industries (wholesalers and retailers), (3) government organizations, and (4) institutions. Much business-to-business marketing involves managing the supply chain, often by forming strategic alliances. Demand in organizations is different from consumer demand dues to such influences as derived demand, volatile demand, joint demand, and inventory adjustments. Several characteristics differentiate business markets from consumer markets. These include geographic concentration, a relatively small number of buyers, and a unique classification system—the Standard Industry Classification Codes.

Multiple buying influences are common in organizational purchasing because many individuals may be involved in the purchase of a single item. In addition, the question of making, buying, or leasing products may have to be answered. The buying center concept is vital to the understanding of business buying behavior. Government, institutional, and international markets each offer their own set of challenges to the marketer seeking to serve them.

Market segmentation is predicated on the existence of markets, which are people with purchasing power and the authority to use it. Consumer markets, those involving people who purchase products and services for ultimate consumption, are frequently segmented on the bases of geography, demographics, psychographics, and product-related characteristics.

The buying patterns of families depend on their stage in the family life cycle. Engel's laws suggest relationships between level of income and percent of income spent on food, housing, clothing, and other items. The activities, interests, and opinions of consumers usually serve as the basis for psychographic segmentation. Business markets must be analyzed differently than consumer markets because of differences in purpose and characteristics of purchases and purchasing behavior. Industrial markets may be segmented on the bases of geography, nature of the customer, or end use application.

Undifferentiated, differentiated, concentrated, and micromarketing strategies may be chosen to match product offerings to the needs of chosen segments. Once the strategy is chosen, products may be positioned to appeal to a particular segment.

Chapter 7

Consumer Behavior

Chapter Outline

You may want to use the following outline as a guide in taking notes.

I. Chapter Overview — People Are Motivated by Personal and Interpersonal Determinants

II. Interpersonal Determinants of Consumer Behavior

    A. Cultural influences

        1. Core values in U.S. culture

        2. An international perspective on cultural influences

        3. Subcultures

    B. Social influences

        1. The Asch phenomenon

        2. Reference groups

        3. Social classes

        4. Opinion leaders

        5. Household roles

        6. Children and teenagers — the family's new purchasing agents

III. Personal Determinants of Consumer Behavior

    A. Needs and motives

        1. The hierarchy of needs

    B. Perceptions

        1. Perceptual screens

        2. Subliminal perception

    C. Attitudes

        1. Attitude components

        2. Changing consumer attitudes

        3. Modifying the attitudinal components

    D. Learning

        1. Applying learning theory to marketing decisions

    E. Self-concept theory

IV.   The Consumer Decision Process

    A. Problem or opportunity recognition

    B. Search

    C. Alternative evaluation

    D. Purchase decision and purchase act

    E. Postpurchase evaluation

    F. Classifying consumer problem-solving processes

        1. Routinized purchase behavior

        2. Limited problem solving

        3. Extended problem solving

Name _____   Instructor _____

Section _____   Date _____

Key Concepts

The purpose of this section is to allow you to determine if you can match key concepts with the definitions of the concepts. It is essential you know the definitions of the concepts prior to applying the concepts in later exercises in this chapter.

From the list of lettered terms, select the one that best fits each of the numbered statements below. Write the letter of that choice in the space provided.

Key Terms

a. buyer behavior
b. consumer behavior
c. culture
d. subculture
e. status
f. role
g. Asch phenomenon
h. reference group
i. opinion leader
j. need
k. motive
l. perception

m. perceptual screen
n. subliminal perception
o. attitude
p. learning
q. drive
r. cue
s. reinforcement
t. self-concept
u. evoked set
v. evaluative criteria
w. cognitive dissonance

_____ 1. Inner state that directs a person toward the goal of satisfying a felt need.
_____ 2. Features considered in a consumer's choice of alternatives.
_____ 3. Discrepancy between a desired state and the actual state; lack of something useful.
_____ 4. Group with which an individual identifies enough that it dictates a standard of behavior for him or her.
_____ 5. Values, beliefs, preferences, and tastes that are handed down from generation to generation.
_____ 6. Buyer behavior of ultimate consumers.
_____ 7. Behavior that members of a group expect of an individual who holds a specific position within it.
_____ 8. Object existing in the environment that determines the nature of the response to a drive.
_____ 9. One's enduring favorable or unfavorable evaluation, emotional feeling, or pro or con action tendency.
_____ 10. Individual within a group who serves as an information source for other group members.
_____ 11. Changes in behavior, immediate or expected, that occur as the result of an experience.
_____ 12. Occurrence first documented by the psychologist after which it is named that illustrates the effect of a reference group on individual decision making.
_____ 13. Filtering process through which messages must pass.
_____ 14. Number of brands that a consumer actually considers before making a purchase decision.
_____ 15. The real self, self-image, looking-glass self, and ideal self; mental conception of one's self.

_____   16.   Relative position of any individual in a group.
_____   17.   Process by which consumers and industrial buyers make purchase decisions.
_____   18.   Manner in which an individual interprets a stimulus.
_____   19.   Subgroup of a culture with its own distinct mode of behavior.
_____   20.   Strong stimulus that impels action.
_____   21.   Receipt of information at a subconscious level.
_____   22.   Postpurchase anxiety that results when an imbalance exists among an individual's cognitions (knowledge, beliefs, and attitudes).
_____   23.   Reduction in drive that results from an appropriate response.

Name _____   Instructor _____

Section _____   Date _____

Self Quiz

You should use these objective questions to test your understanding of the chapter material. Check your answers with hose provided at the end of the chapter.

While these questions cover most of the chapter topics, they are not intended to be the same as the test questions your instructor may use in an examination. A good understanding of all aspects of course material is essential to good performance on any examination.

True/False

Write "T" for True and "F" for False for each of the following statements.

_____ 1.   The core values of a culture do not change.

_____ 2.   Combining ethnic minorities such as Asians, African-Americans, and Hispanics and treating them as a single, homogeneous market segment is usually a wise strategy.

_____ 3.   Culture is the broadest environmental determinant of consumer behavior.

_____ 4.   The interpersonal determinants of consumer behavior include attitudes, learning, and perception.

_____ 5.   Hispanics are a heterogeneous group because they come from a number of countries and some are more assimilated into the mainstream American culture than others.

_____ 6.   Blacks and Hispanics are of particular importance to marketers of name brand products.

_____ 7.   The formula $B = f(I,P)$ may be interpreted to mean that the behavior of consumers (B) is a function of the interaction of interpersonal determinants (I), such as reference groups and culture, and personal determinants (P), like attitudes, learning, and perception.

_____ 8.   The Asch phenomenon suggests that most consumers are individualists; their decisions are not affected by groups.

_____ 9.   Consumers may be influenced by groups they belong to, groups they desire to associate with, and groups with which they do not want to be identified.

_____ 10.   One explanation of opinion leadership suggests that information flows from mass media such as radio, newspapers and television to opinion leaders, and then from opinion leaders to others.

_____ 11.   One important difference that distinguishes blacks from nonblacks in the United States is shopping activity: blacks shop less than other groups.

_____ 12.   Consumer behavior is the result of the interaction between interpersonal and personal determinants.

_____ 13.   One's role in a group is the relative position that one occupies in that group.

_____ 14.   A person's social class is always determined by the person's income, level of education, family background, and type of dwelling in which he or she resides.

_____ 15.   Opinion leaders can be particularly important in the introduction of new products.

_____ 16.   Puerto Rico is the birthplace of the majority of the United States' Hispanic population, followed by Mexico, Cuba, and the nations of Central America.

_____ 17.   Within the household, syncratic decision making occurs when an equal number of decisions is made by each partner.

_____ 18. In the United States, only whites have a higher per capita percentage of college graduates than do Asians.

_____ 19. Motives are inner states that direct a person toward the goal of satisfying a felt need.

_____ 20. A person who buys a BMW automobile so that he or she will be admired and respected by his or her friends is satisfying a social need.

_____ 21. Attitudes have cognitive, affective, and behavioral components.

_____ 22. Product samples and discount coupons can be effective devices in shaping consumer behavior through reinforcement.

_____ 23. In the average American family, the purchase of insurance is usually a syncratic process.

_____ 24. The statement "My friends see me as an outstanding coach and manager," is an example of the component of self-concept known as the *ideal self.*

_____ 25. The marketing of products such as smoke detectors, insurance, seatbelts, burglar alarms, and safes for valuables appeals to the need for safety as characterized by Maslow's hierarchy.

Multiple Choice

Circle the letter of the word or phrase that best completes the sentence or best answers the question.

26. Consumer behavior includes
    a. purchasing goods and services for personal use.
    b. shopping at stores which carry likely choices to satisfy the individual's felt need.
    c. putting goods and services to use in the home.
    d. awareness of a need for a product by a family member.
    e. all of the items in a through d above.

27. Cultural influences
    a. are the same within the same country.
    b. do not affect consumer behavior.
    c. are inherited; people are born with cultural ideas and values.
    d. can be different for different subcultural groups within the same society.
    e. can be easily modified by marketing activity.

28. Which of the following generalizations about the black, Hispanic, and Asian-American subcultures in the U.S. is correct?
    a. They account for more than 30 percent of the total U.S. population.
    b. The black population is less bargain oriented than the white population.
    c. The Asian subculture in the United States is marked by its diversity.
    d. Neither blacks nor Hispanics are notably brand loyal.
    e. Blacks spend more on tobacco, alcohol, entertainment, and personal care than do whites.

29. For a reference group to significantly influence a person's behavior
    a. the person must belong to the group.
    b. the group must be composed of opinion leaders.
    c. the product purchased must be in common use; it must not be conspicuous or different.
    d. the product purchased must be one that can be seen by others.
    e. the person has to have daily physical or electronic contact with the group.

30. Which of the following correctly describes a consumer behavior characteristic of families?
    a. Most people belong to only one family in their lifetime.
    b. The need for refrigerators and vacuum cleaners depends on the number of families.
    c. Empty nesters are "a small group with few assets."
    d. Traditional families include adult children caring for aged parents.
    e. Personal care items are usually bought syncratically for the home.

31. Self-help cassette tapes which feature relaxing music or the sound of the ocean and, at a level imperceptible to the ear, messages such as "Quit smoking," or "Work smarter, not harder," use
    a. perceptual screening to keep out the lower-level messages.
    b. the concept of subliminal perception to impress the desired message on the listener's subconscious.
    c. our need, according to Maslow, for self-actualization to cause us to take some desired action.
    d. selective perception which allows us to choose to listen to the music or the lower-level message.
    e. the Asch effect as a basis for their operation.

32. Reinforcement can be defined as
    a. any object in the environment that determines the nature of the response to a drive.
    b. the individual's reaction to cues and drive.
    c. changes of behavior which come about as the result of experience.
    d. the reduction in drive that results from an appropriate response to it.
    e. the process by which consumer decisions change over time.

33. Which of the following is a correct description of a specific need?
    a. safety need—purchase of a bulletproof vest for protection from physical harm
    b. social need—joining an exclusive club to achieve recognition and respect
    c. self-actualization need—taking a sea cruise to be with your friends
    d. physiological need—enrolling in an adult education class to develop unrealized potential
    e. esteem need—enrolling in a local health club to increase personal longevity

34. Which of the following is not a good way to ensure that customers will receive an advertising message?
    a. Increase the size of ads in newspapers and magazines.
    b. Use color rather than black and white in newspaper ads.
    c. Create ads that leave it to the imagination of the reader or viewer to fill in missing words or to complete the concept.
    d. Add an additional physical sense, like the sense of smell, to the ad presentation.
    e. Aim advertising at the subconscious level of awareness to avoid viewers' perceptual screens.

35. Which of the following is an example of a comment reflecting the cognitive component of attitude?
    a. "I just love shopping at WalMart."
    b. "I intend to buy a new BMW when I get my next promotion."
    c. "The best food value for the money is available at Schwegmann's."
    d. "It must be a good movie—the stars are my favorites."
    e. "Light blue is my favorite color."

36.   Jahn Hankammer ate dinner at the Bon Ton Cafe because he wanted to use the 20% discount coupon that
       he had clipped from a newspaper ad. He was so impressed with the food and the service that he plans to
       return to the Bon Ton tomorrow night. Which of the following is a correct description of a component of
       the process of learning in this example?
       a.   cue—restaurant service
       b.   response—clip coupon
       c.   reinforcement—cheap price
       d.   cue—newspaper coupon
       e.   drive—desire for money.

37.   "The way you'd like to be" is the
       a.   ideal self.
       b.   real self.
       c.   looking-glass self.
       d.   utopian self.
       e.   none of the above.

38.   Which of the following correctly describes a stage in the consumer decision making process?
       a.   postpurchase evaluation—read newspaper ads to find dealers who sell the desired product.
       b.   problem recognition—discover that any of several brands would be satisfactory for your intended use.
       c.   search—buy the desired product at the nearest store.
       d.   alternative evaluation—create a set of evaluative criteria with which to analyze possible choices
       e.   purchase act—discover that you don't have any toothpaste.

39.   The marketing implications of cognitive dissonance are that
       a.   buyers do not evaluate their purchases after they've paid their money.
       b.   postpurchase evaluation only occurs for low-value products.
       c.   it may be desirable to provide information that supports the chosen alternative.
       d.   dissatisfied customers do not change their behavior in the future.
       e.   consumers will be dissatisfied regardless of the quality or price of the product.

40.   Which of the following would be a likely factor on which a subculture might be based?
       a.   nationality of a group of individuals
       b.   geographical area in which a group of people live
       c.   religious affiliation of a group of people
       d.   whether a group of people live in a rural or an urban area
       e.   all of the above are valid bases for a subculture

41.   The most common cause of problem recognition in the consumer decision process is probably
       a.   possession of an inadequate assortment of products.
       b.   routine depletion of the individual's stock on hand.
       c.   dissatisfaction with the present product or brand.
       d.   a change in the financial status of the consumer.
       e.   information received from advertisements or other people.

42. You are attending a party at the home of a friend and are introduced to "Lieutenant Samuel Jones of the Coast Guard." From this introduction, you know
   a. Mr. Jones' role within a formal aspirational group.
   b. Mr. Jones' status within a formal membership group.
   c. Mr. Jones' social class position in society.
   d. Mr. Jones' role within an informal membership group.
   e. Very little about Mr. Jones; certainly none of the above.

43. Being an opinion leader
   a. goes with the territory. A person who is an opinion leader in one situation will probably be an opinion leader in all situations.
   b. is product and service specific. Knowledge of and interest in the item under consideration motivates leadership.
   c. tends to induce one to delay purchasing new products so as not to make mistakes which will be visible to your followers.
   d. is generally a role that goes with high visibility and upper social class status.
   e. means that your followers expect you to take information from them and to use that information to make decisions for them.

44. When the flow of information about products, retail outlets, and ideas passes from the mass media to opinion leaders and from those opinion leaders to the population,
   a. you have an example of a two-step process of communication.
   b. the flow is what is known as "direct."
   c. the process can be characterized as a "hypodermic needle" communications system.
   d. you have a typical "multistep flow of communications."
   e. none of the above is a good description of what's happening.

45. In the consumer decision process, the gathering of information related to the attainment of any desired state of affairs constitutes
   a. problem recognition.
   b. attitude modification.
   c. evaluation of alternatives.
   d. the search process.
   e. the purchase decision.

46. When an individual opens a savings account for retirement, buys life insurance, or buys a burglar alarm, he/she is probably seeking to satisfy his/her
   a. social needs.
   b. esteem needs.
   c. safety needs.
   d. self-actualization needs.
   e. physiological needs

47. If a marketer were to seek to shape a consumer's response pattern to the marketer's product by reinforcement, a good program to follow might be
   a. first, to distribute cents off coupons of moderate value; then, if a purchase resulted, to include in the
      bought goods a higher value coupon.
   b. first, to distribute free samples of the product accompanied by a substantial cents off coupon; if a
      purchase resulted, to include in the bought goods a coupon of lower value.
   c. first, to advertise the product heavily to the target market; then, if a purchase resulted, offer free
      merchandise by mail to responding buyers.
   d. first, to redesign the product package; then, promote heavily to a new, untapped market segment.
   e. first, to require of all retailers who wished to stock the product that they buy at least ten cases in their
      first order; then, insist that stock levels be maintained at least at that level in all subsequent orders.

48. Which of the following is the most common cause of problem recognition by consumers?
   a. dissatisfaction with the brand or type of good which one is presently using.
   b. routine depletion of one's stock of a product.
   c. realization that one's stock of goods on hand is inadequate to the job one has set oneself; that a broader
      assortment of goods is needed.
   d. changed financial status; one recognizes that one need no longer postpone buying a new car because
      of a raise in pay.
   e. boredom with what one is doing or how one is doing it.

49. In the problem solving process, the "evoked set" includes
   a   all brands and types of product which may be capable of doing the intended job.
   b. only those brands and types of product suitable for the job with which the consumer may have had
      previous experience.
   c. those brands and types of product which the consumer actually considers in making a purchase deci-
      sion.
   d. only one product—the one that's ultimately chosen.
   e. the various problems which the consumer seeks to solve with some scheme to prioritize them.

50. Mel Jacobsen has decided it's time to buy a new car. To help him in his efforts along these lines, he has
bought several issues of *Car and Driver* magazine, has visited several automobile dealerships, and has
carefully read all the sales literature with which they have provided him. He is ready to make his choice
from the four models which he believes meet his needs. Mel's problem solving behavior has been
   a. routinized response.
   b. limited problem solving.
   c. extended problem solving.
   d. extreme problem solving.
   e. excessive problem solving.

Name _____   Instructor _____

Section _____   Date _____

Applying Marketing Concepts

Chang Deng was glad, in a way, to be coming home. After eight years away, first at college in the northeast, then for graduate study at a large southeastern university, it was nice to know she'd soon be seeing her parents, grandparents, and great-grandparents again. To herself she admitted, though, that she was going to have to readjust herself to her family's way of doing things. During her time away from home, she'd gotten used to doing things pretty much her own way, keeping her own hours, and making decisions for herself. She knew that some of that would have to change.

One of the first things that she knew was going to cause difficulty was her desire to have her own apartment near the medical facility where she was to be employed. She knew that, even if Great-grandfather Chang approved, he was going to want to go with her (and probably bring along all the rest of the family) when she went apartment hunting. And she was concerned that he would try and bargain with the landlord over the rent or as to who would pay the utilities. Deng had even seriously considered taking a position far away from home, being quite concerned about the levels of influence she was sure her family was going to bring to bear on her, but she had always felt comfortable in San Jacinto and, after all, there certainly were a lot more young Chinese-Americans there than there had been in Pottstown or Atlanta.

Wondering a little bit about how long it would take for her to brush up on her Chinese and then breathing a sigh, Deng gathered up her possessions and left the plane.

_____ 1. Part of Chang Deng's interest in the numbers of Chinese-Americans in San Jacinto may have had something to do with the fact that ethnic Chinese like to operate in an environment that preserves their ethnic identity.

2. Deng's thoughts about there being "more young Chinese-Americans in San Jacinto than in Pottstown or Atlanta" reflects the fact that
   a. Orientals who live in the east and south have tended to be assimilated into the general population.
   b. the Oriental population of the United States is concentrated primarily on the west coast.
   c. Deng didn't really know where to look to find persons of her own ethnic group. Pottstown and Atlanta have large Oriental populations.
   d. Deng was such an unusual young woman, having a much higher level of education than is typical of Asian-Americans.

3. Deng's worries about apartment shopping stemmed from the Chinese custom(s)
   a. of shopping as a family group.
   b. of allowing buying decisions to be made by a family elder.
   c. of bargaining over almost any purchase.
   d. all of the above were part of her concern.

4.   Deng realized she'd have to brush up on her Chinese because
      a.   her family, like most Chinese-American families, spoke the language at home and when dealing with other ethnic Chinese.
      b.   it's always a good idea to have working knowledge of a second language.
      c.   she knew that her work would require her to use that language a lot.
      d.   Chinese is such a complex language that it must be used constantly or you forget it.

For several years, Adele Cressy has been a successful tennis player. Ranked seventh in her age grouping in her home state, she had long favored the Wilson Graphite Pro/95 racquet in competition. Recently, though, she had been having problems with her old racquet and had decided to invest in a new one. Though she wasn't fabulously wealthy, her medical practice meant that she could afford the best equipment for this special hobby, so she started looking for the best racquet money could buy.

She spoke with friends at the tennis club about their preferences in racquets and became convinced that she would be more credible on the court and would have a psychological advantage if she switched to the PanCourt "Wimbledon Special." Her brother, tennis pro at the club, opposed the change because he thought the PanCourt racquet wasn't as durable as the Wilson. Adele continued to read tennis magazines, talk to friends, and check advertisements of the PanCourt line. Ultimately, she decided to buy the "Wimbledon Special."

Next, she had to decide where to buy her new racquet. The alternatives available to her were two local dealers and a mail-order firm located only 100 miles away, in Capital City. All three of these dealers stocked the racquet she wanted, but the mail-order house's price was substantially less than the other two outlets. Adele finally ordered her racquet from the mail-order house, "Racquets IZ Us."

The following week, her racquet arrived. She immediately drove over to the club to show her brother her new acquisition and convince him she'd made the right decision. Unfortunately, in the middle of their first set she swung at a hard-hit serve and a string broke on her new pride and joy. Adele began to feel doubtful about her purchase. Standing there in front of her brother holding her brand-new racquet with its broken string she would have liked to tell "Racquets IZ Us" what to do with their racquet—keep it!

_____   5.   Adele was mainly concerned with her ideal self.
_____   6.   Need arousal occurred in her because of dissatisfaction with the racquet she already owned.
_____   7.   Adele bought her racquet because of subliminal perception.
_____   8.   Adele is probably a member of the lower class.
_____   9.   Adele's search for alternatives was affected by both personal and interpersonal factors.

10.   Adele's decision to buy the PanCourt because of her friends' influence helped satisfy her _____ needs.
      a.   physiological
      b.   safety
      c.   social
      d.   esteem
      e.   self-actualization

11.   If Maslow's theory of needs is true for Adele, she has at least partially satisfied her _____ needs.
      a.   physiological
      b.   safety
      c.   social
      d.   all of the above
      e.   none of the above

12. For this purchase, the most important influence on Adele was
     a. social class.
     b. reference group.
     c. culture.
     d. attitude.
     e. family.

13. Adele's postpurchase doubt about her purchase is
     a. cognitive dissonance.
     b. subliminal perception.
     c. psychotic imbalance.
     d. psychographic influence.
     e. status loss.

14. Adele may have learned not to buy PanCourt racquets because
     a. reinforcement did not take place.
     b. no drive was present.
     c. her response was inconsistent with her drive.
     d. the cues were correct.

Name _____   Instructor _____

Section _____   Date _____

Experiential Exercises

1. The purpose of this exercise is to help you improve your understanding of consumer behavior by examining the process you used in making a recent purchase. Select a major purchase you made in recent months: a car, clothing, luggage, an appliance or an item of home entertainment electronics. Use this purchase experience to answer the following questions.

    a. How did you become aware of the need to make this purchase?

    b. What sources of information did you use to determine the alternatives that were available to satisfy your needs?

    c. List the brands of product that you considered as alternatives for this purchase.
        My evoked set included:

    d. Circle the brand listed above that you purchased. What factors led you to buy this brand in preference to the others? Was it price, quality, size, performance, color, or some other characteristic or combination of characteristics?

e.   Where did you buy the product? What criteria led you to buy from that place?

f.   Did you experience any cognitive dissonance after this purchase? Do you wish, for example, that you had bought a different brand, or perhaps from a different store, or had postponed your purchase altogether?

g.   Now, make the assumption that you are a marketer of the type of product you purchased. If you wished to market your product to consumers who behaved like you, what would you include in your marketing mix?

Price strategy:

Product strategy:

Promotion strategy:

Distribution strategy:

2. The purpose of this exercise is to analyze the effect which reference groups have on individual consumer behavior. For the purposes of this exercise, your family will be considered a membership group, though your membership in it is involuntary.

You are using this Study Guide presumably because you are taking an introductory course in Marketing at a college or university. Of interest is how you happen to be at this particular school, taking this particular course.

a. How did you make the decision to attend college? List the people who influenced your decision.

b. Who, of the people listed above, are members of your family? (Remember, family includes spouses and children, as well as parents, cousins, aunts, uncles, et cetera.) List the names and relationships below.

c. Were any of the people who influenced you members of the profession or practitioners of the art in which you hope to receive your degree? List the members of this aspirational group.

d. Did you base your decision to attend this school on whether or not any members of your high school class or other group of which you are/were a member were going to attend this school? If so, list the members of this membership group.

Closing note: It is a rare individual who is able truthfully to leave blank any of the categories in the above exercise. If you have, you might consider the following question:

e. List below the names of people who influenced you to attend college so you *wouldn't* turn out like they did. I hope the number of members of this dissociative group is smaller than the number of members of groups b, c, and d.

Name _____ Instructor _____

Section _____ Date _____

Computer Applications

Review the discussion of evoked set and evaluative criteria in Chapter 7 of the text. Then use menu item 6 titled "Evaluation of Alternatives" to solve each of the following problems.

1. Wayne McLemore is faced with the prospect of choosing carpeting for his dining room. Being a less than domestic type, he has decided to approach the problem systematically. He has established that there are four criteria which the new carpet must satisfy. It must be durable, it must be of the right color (a color which will harmonize with McLemore's existing decor), it must be affordable, and it must be easy to maintain. McLemore is considering four brands of carpet: *Everdure*, *Eleganza*, *Majeste*, and *Valuta*. He has assigned to each brand of carpet a score ranging from 1 (poor) to 5 (excellent) on each of the evaluative criteria. These scores are shown below:

Evoked Set Brand	Durability	Evaluative Criteria Color	Price	Maintenance
Everdure	5	3	2	4
Eleganza	4	5	3	3
Majeste	5	2	5	3
Valuta	4	4	1	3

a. Which brand would Wayne select using the overall scoring method?

b. If Wayne thinks that color and price are 50 percent more important than any of the other evaluative criteria, which brand will he select?

c. If Wayne arbitrarily decides that any carpet which scores less than a three on any criterion is unacceptable, which carpet will he select using the overall method?

d.　If Wayne decides to apply the weighted scoring method to the answer to 1c (above), will his decision change?

2.　John and Cynthia Albertson are trying to decide where to buy a new refrigerator. They've already decided that the Kelvinator brand is the one they want, and the problem now is to determine whether they should buy it from Appliance Mart, Smith's Department Store, Discount Appliances, National Furniture Company, or The Warehouse. The Albertsons' evaluative criteria are: convenience of store location, price, credit terms. trustworthiness of sales personnel, and installation. They decide to use a ten point rating scale in making their assessment. Scores range from 1 (unacceptable or not offering the feature) to ten (perfect). The scores assigned jointly by the Albertsons are shown below:

Evoked Set	Evaluative Criteria				
Store	Location	Price	Credit	Trust	Installation
Mart	5	4	5	4	1
Smith's	5	8	9	10	7
Discount	5	9	4	4	3
Furniture	8	8	8	9	7
Warehouse	3	9	4	3	2

a.　Using the overall scoring method, which store would the Albertsons choose?

b.　Suppose the Albertsons decide that trust and installation are twice as important as the other criteria. Which store would they then select?

c.　If, after some discussion, the Albertsons change their minds and decide that price and credit are 50 percent more important than any other criteria, which store will they then select?

d. If the Albertsons decide that they will not buy from a store that receives a rating of less than five on price, credit, trustworthiness, or installation, which store will they select using the overall scoring method?

3. Theophile Boudreaux, a native of Thibodeaux, Louisiana, is considering the purchase of a new fishing boat in which to roam the byways of the Bayou LaFourche. He is considering five models: *Bateau Splendide, Bateau Rapide, Bateau Speciale, Pirogue Grande,* and *Skiff Lafitte.* He has decided to evaluate the boats on the basis of price, engine size, reliability, fuel economy, and how comfortable his old dog, Pheideaux (pronounced Fido), will be riding in the bow. Theophile has rated each model using 4 for excellent, 3 for good, 2 for fair, and 1 for poor. The ratings are shown below:

| Evoked Set | | Evaluative Criteria | | | |
Model	Price	Engine	Reliability	Economy	Comfort
Splendide	2	4	2	1	3
Rapide	3	4	1	2	2
Speciale	4	3	3	2	3
Grande	3	3	3	1	3
Lafitte	2	2	2	1	4

a. Which model will Theophile select using the overall scoring method?

b. Suppose M. Boudreaux considers price twice as important as engine size, reliability, and fuel economy. Comfort is 50 percent more important than engine size, reliability, and fuel economy (Pheideaux is an *old* dog). Which model will M. Boudreaux choose?

c. Monsieur Boudreaux, using the overall scoring method, also has decided that he will not accept a boat that is rated "poor" on reliability or fuel economy. Which model should he select?

d.   If Monsieur Boudreaux had used the weighted scoring method in 3c, would his decision have changed?

Crossword Puzzle for Chapter 7

ACROSS CLUES

1. Behavior members of a group expect of an individual that holds a position within it
2. Object in the environment that determines the nature of response to a drive
4. Discrepancy between a desired state and the actual state
5. Inner state that directs a person toward goal of satisfying a felt need
7. Manner in which a person interprets a stimulus
11. Process by which consumers and organizational buyers make purchase decisions
13. Relative position of any individual in a group
15. Values, beliefs, preferences, and tastes handed down from one generation to the next
16. Enduring favorable or unfavorable evaluation, feeling, or pro or con action tendency

DOWN CLUES

1. Reduction in drive resulting from appropriate response
3. Buyer behavior of ultimate consumers
6. Group with which an individual identifies enough that it dictates a standard of behavior
8. Postpurchase anxiety which results from an imbalance among a person's cognitions
9. Strong stimulus that impels action
10. The real self, the looking glass self, self-image, and ideal self
12. Number of brands a consumer actually considers before making a purchase decision
14. Phenomenon describing effect of a reference group on individual decision making

WORD LIST:

ROLE	CUE	NEED
REINFORCEMENT	MOTIVE	PERCEPTION
ATTITUDE	CONSUMERBEHAVIOR	BUYERBEHAVIOR
EVOKEDSET	DISSONANCE	DRIVE
STATUS	ASCH	CULTURE
REFERENCEGROUP	SELFCONCEPT	

ACROSS

DOWN

WORD LIST

Chapter 7 Solutions

Key Concepts

1.	k	6.	b	11.	p	16.	e	21.	n
2.	v	7.	f	12.	g	17.	a	22.	w
3.	j	8.	r	13.	m	18.	l	23.	s
4.	h	9.	o	14.	u	19.	d		
5.	c	10.	i	15.	t	20.	q		

Self Quiz

1.	T	11.	F	21.	T	31.	b	41.	b
2.	F	12.	T	22.	T	32.	d	42.	b
3.	T	13.	F	23.	F	33.	a	43.	b
4.	F	14.	F	24.	F	34.	e	44.	a
5.	T	15.	T	25.	T	35.	c	45.	d
6.	T	16.	F	26.	e	36.	d	46.	c
7	T	17.	F	27.	d	37.	a	47.	b
8.	F	18.	F	28.	c	38.	d	48.	b
9.	T	19.	T	29.	d	39.	c	49.	c
10.	T	20.	F	30.	b	40.	e	50.	c

Applying Marketing Concepts

1.	T	8.	F
2.	b	9.	T
3.	d	10.	d
4.	a	11.	d
5.	F	12.	b
6.	T	13.	a
7.	F	14.	a

Computer Applications

1. a. Overall Scoring of Brands

   Note: for convenience of notation characteristics have been denoted by the first letter of their name; D = durability, C = color, P = price, and M = Maintenance.

	D		C		P		M		Total
Everdure:	5	+	3	+	2	+	4	=	14
Eleganza:	4	+	5	+	3	+	3	=	15
Majeste:	5	+	2	+	5	+	3	=	15
Valuta:	4	+	4	+	1	+	3	=	12

   Mr. McLemore could choose *Majeste* or *Eleganza* on the basis of total score.

   b. Weighting Color and Price by a factor of 1.5:

	D		C		P		M		Total
Everdure:	5	+	4.5	+	3	+	4	=	16.5
Eleganza:	4	+	7.5	+	4.5	+	3	=	19.0
Majeste:	5	+	3	+	7.5	+	3	=	18.5
Valuta:	4	+	6	+	1.5	+	3	=	14.5

   Eleganza now ranks above *Majeste* as the carpet of choice.

   c. Wayne's newest criterion really simplifies things! Only *Eleganza* scores at or above 3 on every characteristic.

   d. No. See above.

2. a. Overall Scoring of Characteristics

   Note: As above, characteristics are indicated by the first letter of their name; L = Location, P = Price, C = Credit, T = Trust, and I = Installation

	L		P		C		T		I		Total
Mart	8	+	5	+	4	+	5	+	4	=	26
Smith's	5	+	8	+	9	+	10	+	7	=	39
Discount	5	+	9	+	4	+	4	+	3	=	25
Furniture	8	+	8	+	8	+	9	+	7	=	40
Warehouse	3	+	9	+	4	+	3	+	2	=	21

   The Albertsons would buy from National Furniture Company.

b. Weighting trust and installation by a factor of 2:

	L		P		C		T		I		Total
Mart	8	+	5	+	4	+	10	+	8	=	35
Smith's	5	+	8	+	9	+	20	+	14	=	56
Discount	5	+	9	+	4	+	8	+	6	=	32
Furniture	8	+	8	+	8	+	18	+	14	=	56
Warehouse	3	+	9	+	4	+	6	+	4	=	26

The Albertsons would now be forced to choose between National Furniture Company and Smith's.

c. Weighting price and credit by a factor of 1.5, all other criteria receiving a weighting of 1:

	L		P		C		T		I		Total
Mart	8	+	7.5	+	6	+	4	+	5	=	30.5
Smith's	5	+	12	+	13.5	+	10	+	7	=	47.5
Discount	5	+	13.5	+	6	+	4	+	4	=	32.5
Furniture	8	+	12	+	12	+	8	+	9	=	49.0
Warehouse	3	+	13.5	+	6	+	4	+	3	=	29.5

National Furniture becomes the preferred outlet, though Smith's remains a close second.

d. National Furniture Company remains the preferred choice, though Smith's is not eliminated by this criterion.

3. a. Overall Scoring of Characteristics

Note: Characteristics will be labeled by the first two letters of their name: Pr = Price, En = Engine, Re = Reliability, Ec = Economy, and Co = Comfort

	Pr		En		Re		Ec		Co		Total
Splendide	2	+	4	+	2	+	1	+	3	=	12
Rapide	3	+	4	+	1	+	2	+	2	=	12
Speciale	4	+	3	+	3	+	2	+	3	=	15
Grande	3	+	3	+	3	+	1	+	3	=	13
Lafitte	2	+	2	+	2	+	1	+	4	=	11

M. Boudreaux would choose the Bateau Speciale using this system.

b. Rating Price at a factor of 2 and comfort at 1.5 relative to engine size, reliability, and fuel economy

	Pr		En		Re		Ec		Co		Total
Splendide	4	+	4	+	2	+	1	+	4.5	=	5.5
Rapide	6	+	4	+	1	+	2	+	4	=	16
Speciale	8	+	3	+	3	+	2	+	6	=	22
Grande	6	+	3	+	3	+	1	+	6	=	19
Lafitte	4	+	2	+	2	+	1	+	8	=	17

M. Boudreaux would still choose the Speciale, however, the ordering of the second, third, and fourth choices would be changed by the inclusion of these criteria.

c. The only boat that qualifies under this criterion is the Bateau Speciale, which remains the choice of preference.

Crossword Puzzle Solution

Chapter 8

Business-to-Business Marketing

Chapter Outline

You may want to use the following outline as a guide in taking notes.

    I.   Chapter Overview—Participants in the Business Market

    II.   The Nature of the Business market

        A. Differences in foreign business markets

    III.   Managing the Supply Chain

        A. Strategic alliances

    IV.   Characteristics of Business Market Demand

        A. Derived demand

        B. Volatile demand

        C. Joint demand

        D. Inventory adjustments

    V.   Estimating Market Size and Characteristics

        A. Standard industry classification (SIC) codes

        B. Evaluating international industrial markets

    VI.   The Make, Buy, or Lease Decisions

    VII. Characteristics of the Business Market

        A. Geographic market concentration

        B. Size and number of buyers

C. Organizational buyer behavior

    1. Reciprocity

    2. The role of professional buyers

    3. Value analysis

    4. Vendor analysis

VIII. The Buying Center Concept

A. Buying center roles

B. Strategy for marketing to buying centers

C. International buying centers

IX. Classifying Organizational Buying Situations

A. New-task buying

B. The straight rebuy

C. The modified rebuy

X. Developing Effective Business Strategies

A. Challenges of government markets

B. Challenges of institutional markets

C. Challenges of international markets

D. Selling to both consumer and business markets

Name _____   Instructor _____

Section _____   Date _____

Key Concepts

The purpose of this section is to allow you to determine if you can match key concepts with the definitions of the concepts. It is essential that you know the definitions of the concepts prior to applying the concepts in later exercises in this chapter.

From the list of lettered items, select the one that best fits each of the numbered statements below. Write the letter of that choice in the space provided.

Key Terms

a. business-to-business marketing
b. commercial market
c. trade industries
d. supply chain
e. strategic alliance
f. derived demand
g. Joint demand
h. sole sourcing
i. Standard industry classification (SIC) code
j. value added by manufacturing
k. multiple sourcing

l. reciprocity
m. systems integration
n. value analysis
o. vendor analysis
p. buying center
q. new-task buying
r. straight rebuy
s. modified rebuy
t. bid
u. specifications
v. remanufacturing

_____ 1. Written sales proposal from a vendor.
_____ 2. Demand for a business product that depends on demand for a consumer good.
_____ 3. Purchase of goods and services for use in producing other goods and services, to support the daily operations of the organization, or for resale.
_____ 4. Situation in which a purchaser is willing to re-evaluate available options in a repurchase of a good or service.
_____ 5. Written description of a needed good or service.
_____ 6. Practice of extending purchasing preference to suppliers who are also customers.
_____ 7. Demand for a business product that depends on the demand for another business product that is necessary for the use of the first item.
_____ 8. Systematic study of the components of a purchase to determine the most cost-effective way to acquire the item.
_____ 9. Recurring purchase decision in which a customer repurchases a good or service which has performed satisfactorily.
_____ 10. Using just one vendor in a purchasing situation.
_____ 11. Difference between the price charged for a manufactured product and the cost of the its raw materials and other inputs.

_____ 12.   First-time or unique purchase situation that requires considerable effort on the decision maker's part.

_____ 13.   Suppliers involved in the creation and delivery of a good or service.

_____ 14.   Restoring worn-out products to like-new condition.

_____ 15.   Participants in an organizational buying action.

_____ 16.   Individuals and firms that acquire goods and services to be used, directly or indirectly, to produce other goods and services.

_____ 17.   Government classification system that subdivides the business marketplace into detailed market segments.

_____ 18.   Assessment of a supplier's performance in areas such as price, backorders, timely delivery, and attention to special requests.

_____ 19.   Centralization of the procurement function in an internal division or as a service of an external supplier.

_____ 20.   Purchasing from several vendors.

_____ 21.   Partnership formed to create a competitive advantage.

_____ 22.   Retailers or wholesalers that purchase products for resale to others.

Name _____   Instructor _____

Section _____   Date _____

Self Quiz

You should use these objective questions to test your understanding of the chapter material. You can check your answers with those provided at the end of the chapter.

While these questions cover most of the chapter topics, they are not intended to be the same as the test questions your instructor may use in an examination. A good understanding of all aspects of the course material is essential to good performance on any examination.

True/False

Write "T" for True or "F" for False for each of the following statements.

_____ 1. The middle Atlantic is the U.S. region that is ranked highest for value added by manufacturing, as has been the case for many years.

_____ 2. Geographical concentration in the business market greatly influences the marketing strategy used in serving it.

_____ 3. Capital items are short-lived business assets that require a large initial cash outlay.

_____ 4. Buying center participants tend to change as the purchasing process moves through its various stages.

_____ 5. Gatekeepers control the information to be reviewed by other buying center members.

_____ 6. The Census of Manufactures, as well as the Census of Retailing and Wholesaling, is conducted every ten years by the federal government.

_____ 7. Most purchases by government must, by law, be made on the basis of bids (written sales proposals) from potential vendors.

_____ 8. An SIC code will never include more than five digits.

_____ 9. Depreciation is the accounting function of charging a portion of a capital item's cost as a deduction against annual revenues for purposes of determining net income.

_____ 10. Group purchasing is an important factor in institutional markets.

_____ 11. Demand in the business market is often derived from demand in the consumer market.

_____ 12. Organizational buyers are influenced only by rational needs like cost, quality, and reliability of delivery.

_____ 13. Value analysis is an ongoing analysis of a vendor's performance on such features as price, back orders, delivery time, and attention to special requests.

_____ 14. Most organizational goods can be made internally; this is the most common choice of procurement source.

_____ 15. The Standard Industrial Classification system is of little use to sales representatives.

_____ 16. Buying centers are not part of a firm's formal organizational structure, but are informal groups whose composition varies among purchase decisions and firms.

_____ 17. Just-in-time inventory policies involve cutting inventories to an absolute minimum and then requiring vendors to deliver items as they are needed.

____   18.   If the location quotient for a state is greater than 1.0, its manufacturers are producing a larger-than-average share of state output.

____   19.   Systems integration disperses the procurement function throughout the firms so as to be nearer the point of need.

____   20.   Some firms sell only to the business market; a different group sells only to consumers; nobody sells to both organizations and consumers.

____   21.   Marketers who want to maintain straight rebuy situations should concentrate on maintaining a good relationship with the buyer by providing excellent service and delivery.

____   22.   The commercial market includes manufacturing firms, farmers and other resource producing industries, construction contractors, and providers of such services as transportation, public utilities, finance, insurance, and real estate brokerage.

____   23.   Though the number of buyers in any segment of the business market is usually quite large, geographical concentration makes it easy to serve them all.

____   24.   In a buying center situation, people in the influencer's role supply information for the evaluation of alternatives or set buying specifications.

____   25.   The trade industries include retailers and wholesalers that purchase for resale to others.

Multiple Choice

Circle the letter of the word or phrase that best completes the sentence or answers the question.

26.   The business market is also known as
   a.   trade or reseller industries.
   b.   the organizational market.
   c.   the government market.
   d.   the institutional market
   e.   the commercial market

27.   Using value added by manufacturing as an indicator, which of the following groups of states is the biggest business market?
   a.   East North Central
   b.   South Atlantic
   c.   Middle Atlantic
   d.   Desert Southwest
   e.   Northwest Mountain

28.   Bauxite and electricity are both required for the production of aluminum. If the supply of electricity is reduced, there will be an immediate effect on the demand for bauxite. What concept does this represent?
   a.   derived demand
   b.   joint demand
   c.   demand variability
   d.   inventory adjustments
   e.   specific demand

29. Because business buyers are geographically concentrated and relatively few in number,
   a. the marketing channel for industrial goods is typically much longer than for consumer goods.
   b. wholesalers are more frequently used to handle their business than they are in the consumer goods field.
   c. the relationship between business buyers and suppliers is usually direct and often based on face-to-face personal selling.
   d. advertising plays a much larger role in the industrial market than it does in the consumer market.
   e. personal selling is seldom used as the promotional tool of choice by vendors to this market.

30. The largest single source of information to aid marketers in gaining access to the organizational market is
   a. advertising.
   b. trade listings.
   c. a buying center.
   d. the federal government.
   e. distributors' guides.

31. Which of the following properly matches SIC Codes and industry groups?
   a. Book printing: 27; Books: 2732; Printing, publishing, and allied industries: 273
   b. Book printing: 273; Books: 2732; Printing, publishing, and allied industries: 27
   c. Book printing: 2732; Books: 273; Printing, publishing, and allied industries: 27
   d. Book printing: 27; Books: 273; Printing, publishing, and allied industries: 2732
   e. Book printing: 2732; Books: 27; Printing, publishing, and allied industries: 273

32. American Telephone and Telegraph's policy of allowing its divisions to seek out the best deal regardless of the vendor rather than being required to buy from other AT&T units whenever possible, as was the case in the past, reflects a change from
   a. modified rebuy to straight rebuy conditions.
   b. straight rebuy to modified rebuy conditions.
   c. modified rebuy to new-task buying conditions.
   d. straight rebuy to new-task buying conditions.
   e. new-task buying to modified rebuy conditions.

33. Which of the following would you expect to affect an organizational buyer?
   a. the needs of the users of the products being bought
   b. information received from an "influencer" in the buying center
   c. the buyer's own emotional needs
   d. the need for reliability, low cost, and quality from suppliers
   e. All of the above will have some effect on the organizational buyer

34. Value analysis may be defined as
   a. securing needed products at the best possible price.
   b. using a professional buyer to systematize purchasing.
   c. examining each component of a purchase in an attempt either to delete the item or replace it with a more cost-effective substitute.
   d. convening a committee which will be charged with all the buying responsibility for the firm.
   e. evaluating suppliers' performance in categories such as price, back orders, delivery time, and attention to special requests.

35. A competitor seeking to win over another vendor's straight rebuy customers by converting the straight rebuy situation to a modified rebuy should
    a. raise issues that will make the customers reconsider their decisions.
    b. sell other accounts; these accounts are in the other vendor's bag.
    c. hope that the other vendor will maintain adequate delivery and service; this bores customers and makes them more likely to listen to other vendors.
    d. try and convince the customers that the buying situation is entirely new or completely unique.
    e. recognize that a paper clip is a paper clip and try to sell the customers other products.

36. In the buying center, the role filled by the design engineer who develops specifications that only one vendor can meet is the
    a. user.
    b. gatekeeper.
    c. decider.
    d. influencer.
    e. buyer.

37. Most government purchases, by law, must be made on the basis of
    a. written sales proposals.
    b. book value of the item needed.
    c. estimates prepared by government personnel.
    d. cost/benefit studies of the goods required.
    e. the availability of the most graft to the greatest number.

38. Purchase behavior by organizations often tends to be more complex than purchase behavior by consumers because
    a. organizations are more geographically spread out.
    b. organizational buys require the approval of more people.
    c. the item(s) being purchased are always more complex.
    d. there aren't enough sales representatives.
    e. big organizations are very bureaucratic and slow.

39. Which of the following is typically a part of Stage 2 of the new-task buying process?
    a. recognition of a problem, need, or opportunity
    b. search for and identification of potential suppliers
    c. determination of characteristics of and quantity of a needed good or service
    d. selecting an order routine
    e. acquisition and analysis of proposals

40. As a general rule, the buying centers of foreign companies
    a. tend to be easier to identify than those of domestic firms.
    b. will usually be operated by staff, rather than line, personnel.
    c. may well be larger (up to fifty people) than is the case domestically.
    d. are seldom affected by cultural differences in decision making.
    e. are usually unresponsive to political and economic trends.

41. Which of the following organizations would typically be a member of the institutional sector of the market?
    a. Metropolitan Life and Casualty Insurance Company
    b. Merchants Trust and Savings Bank
    c. The American Red Cross
    d. National Stock and Bond Trading Corporation
    e. Rubenstein Men's Clothing Store

42. Which of the following characteristics is typical of the business market?
    a. more money spent on personal selling than advertising
    b. geographical dispersion of members
    c. large number of buyers
    d. purchases are never made for resale, only for use in production
    e. public benefit is primary motivation

43. Which of the following is typical of the practices which have been evident in the federal government market during the last several years?
    a. a requirement that each government agency create its own procurement regulations regardless of the red tape involved
    b. implementation of an executive order which requires that all vehicles owned by the federal government have some military usefulness in the event of war
    c. the influence of social goals such as minority subcontracting programs
    d. development of unit-system costing techniques to reduce the cost of particular government operations
    e. allocation of resources to departments which have shown the greatest ability to spend their budget allotment

44. Which of the following firms would be a member of the commercial segment of the business market?
    a. Bloomingdale's, the well-known department store chain
    b. National Switch and Signal Company, makers of railroad signaling equipment
    c. The Delgado Museum of Art, an endowed public institution
    d. The Training and Development Command of the U. S. Army
    e. The University of Arkansas at Fayetteville

45. When a firm is trying to move a potential customer from a straight rebuy situation to a modified rebuy posture by correctly assessing the factors that would make buyers reconsider their decisions, we have an example of
    a. gatekeeping.
    b. purchase agency behavior.
    c. sales management.
    d. competition.
    e. engineering management.

46. A good definition of the business market should include
    a. recognition that nonprofit organizations are not members.
    b. mention of retailers and wholesalers.
    c. selection of organizational segments prior to production.
    d. a set of guidelines for those who are allowed to join.
    e. a managerial philosophy oriented toward heavy industry.

47.   Occupational Safety and Health Administration inspectors have mandated that Bardyke Paper Company install a system of safety netting in the work area of its warehouse to catch objects that fall from some of the higher storage bins before they reach workers below. Bardyke has no experience with this sort of equipment. The purchasing process would most likely be
      a.   an experimental purchase.
      b.   a relative standard.
      c.   a straight rebuy.
      d.   a new-task purchase.
      e.   a modified rebuy.

48.   Which of the following would be an example of a member of the trade industries?
      a.   The Texas Highway Patrol.
      b.   Lumber Products Company (wood products wholesale and retail)
      c.   National Metal Stamping Co. (produces steel parts)
      d.   Memorial Stadium (a football stadium)
      e.   The Missouri School of Mines (an engineering school)

49.   A small change in the demand for a consumer good that results in a disproportionately large change in demand for a business good
      a.   is an example of the volatile nature of business demand.
      b.   is very unusual. Such conditions don't ordinarily exist.
      c.   occurs because some products are subject to joint demand conditions.
      d.   reflects the demands being made on producers by JIT inventory policies.
      e.   is called reciprocal reaction to market fluctuations.

50.   The practice of extending supply privileges to firms that provide needed supplies is called
      a.   reciprocity.
      b.   reverse reciprocity.
      c.   international trade.
      d.   professional purchasing behavior.
      e.   value analysis.

Name _____   Instructor _____

Section _____   Date _____

Applying Marketing Concepts

George Herrin, director of marketing for Commercial Laundry Equipment Company, was pondering two reports which had just arrived in his office. Both were somewhat disturbing because they told him that his firm had lost sales to competition that he thought was at least a little bit less than fair. In the first instance, Commercial had lost out on a contract to supply transmissions to Longley Washer Company because Longley had decided to buy from Western Gear Corporation. Mr. Herrin felt that the decision had been based, not on the quality of Western's product, but on the fact that Western owned General Sales, Ltd., the big operator of laundromats that bought all their coin-operated washing machines from Longley Washer. In the second case, it appeared as though Commercial had lost out on a U.S. Navy contract for stainless steel spinner tubs to a German firm because the Germans could supply the needed parts at a lower price. The Navy ignored Commercial's arguments that the German product would cost substantially more in the long run because of inferior heat treatment to that of Commercial's product.

_____   1.   In all likelihood, Commercial Laundry Equipment had to supply a written sales proposal for the Navy contract.

_____   2.   The two episodes outlined involved purchases by members of the commercial and government segments of the organizational market.

3.   The case of Longley favoring Western Gear over Commercial was most probably caused by
   a.   bribery.
   b.   reciprocity.
   c.   derived demand.
   d.   threats of force or violence.

4.   The Standard Industry Classification code for Longley Washer Company would lie between
   a.   01-09; agriculture, forestry, and fishing.
   b.   10-14; mining.
   c.   20-39; manufacturing.
   d.   40-49; transportation and other public utilities.
   e.   70-89; services.

5.   The main reason Commercial lost the Navy contract was because
   a.   price was too high.
   b.   their product was of inferior quality.
   c.   the Navy thought they might be an uncertain source of supply.
   d.   they were unable to provide the needed service.
   e.   somebody got bribed.

6. Commercial might well have gotten the Navy contract if
    a. international politics hadn't tainted the decision.
    b. the German product hadn't been vastly superior in design.
    c. it had pressed the issue of foreign ownership of the German firm.
    d. Western Gear hadn't interfered with the sale.

Mercedes-Benz, like most German automobile manufacturers, makes extensive use of components made by other firms: electrical equipment from Robert Bosch; cooling system and air conditioning components from the Behr and Harrison companies; brake parts from Girling, Teves, and even Bendix; and turbosuperchargers from both Garret and Kuhnle Kopp and Kausch (Yes, that's the company's name!). A given Mercedes may contain parts from as many as fifty different manufacturers.

7. If consumer demand for Mercedes-Benz products declined, demand for Garret superchargers would also decline. This is a case of decline. This is a case of
    a. reciprocity.
    b. joint demand.
    c. derived demand.
    d. variable supply.
    e. inventory failure.

8. In deciding to buy components from outside suppliers rather than make them themselves, and in choosing the sources from which those parts would be bought, Mercedes-Benz probably based their decision on
    a. value analysis.
    b. vendor analysis.
    c. a combination of value analysis and vendor analysis.
    d. their desire to be innovative and to be leaders in automotive engineering technology.
    e. their need to keep the price of their cars down.

9. Suppose that Mercedes-Benz management had decided that a two-month inventory of parts was not enough to have on hand to assure that production would continue if the availability of air conditioner compressors was curtailed and increased its stock-on-hand to four months' worth. This would be an example of
    a. demand variability.
    b. conservative thinking.
    c. an inventory adjustment.
    d. derived demand.

10. The Standard Industry Classification for Mercedes-Benz would have been between
    a. 01-09; agriculture, forestry, fisheries.
    b. 10-14; mining.
    c. 20-39; manufacturing.
    d. 40-49; transportation and other public utilities.
    e. 70-89; services.

Name _____ Instructor _____

Section _____ Date _____

Experiential Exercises

1. The purpose of this exercise is to help you understand the complexity of dealing with the global business market. Using a source such as *The Statesman's Yearbook* or the *Area Studies* prepared by the U.S. Department of Defense, or by contacting a nearby office of the Department of Commerce or Department of State, obtain the following information about two nations of your choice and your country (it is suggested the other two be selected from different continents for greater contrast):
(You may choose to expand this table onto extra paper as needed)

	Your Country	Country B	Country C
General: Country Name	_____	_____	_____
Continent	_____	_____	_____
Type of Govt.	_____	_____	_____
GDP per capita	_____	_____	_____
Currency unit/ Exchange rate	_____	_____	_____
Infrastructure: Electrical Std.: Volts/Hertz	_____	_____	_____
Driving Side	_____	_____	_____
Phone System (Units/Pop.)	_____	_____	_____
Commercial: Major Exports	_____	_____	_____
	_____	_____	_____
Major imports	_____	_____	_____
	_____	_____	_____
Prohibited Imports	_____	_____	_____
Restricted Imports	_____	_____	_____
Exchange controls	_____	_____	_____

a. How do you suppose the characteristics listed as "general" affect dealing with that nation's business market?

b. What effect do its international characteristics have on dealing with a particular nation?

c. Discuss how differences in commercial characteristics might affect business relationships among these three countries.

2. The purpose of this exercise is to familiarize you with the marketing of goods and services to government bodies. Visit the office of a government agency located near your campus. You may select from among federal, state, or local organizations. Some agencies whose offices might be convenient for you to visit could include the local school district, your local police or sheriff's department, or city, county, or state administrative offices. Once you have made an appointment to visit, tell your contact person that you'd like to know how that organization buys its equipment and supplies.

a. Ask about the methods the organization uses to purchase equipment and supplies. Is it the job of an individual, a committee, or a higher agency? Record the information below.

b. Ask about the process of requesting bids and getting contracts. Are there any "special" rules that apply to this agency? Record the response below.

c. Ask about the "bid list." Does the agency have one and how is it used, if at all? Record the response below.

Name _____   Instructor _____

Section _____   Date _____

Computer Applications

Review the discussion of the expected net profit (ENP) concept in Chapter 8 of the text. Then use menu item 6 titled "Competitive Bidding" to solve each of the following problems.

1. Harold Handy, president of the Handy Manufacturing Company, makers of the (Yes, you guessed it!) Handy Dandy Industrial Electric Chicken Plucker and Pinfeather Remover, is giving serious thought to the bid he will submit to a large West Coast chicken processor. He would like to make the deal as profitably as possible, and knows that if he misses this sale, there will be other opportunities. The machines normally sell for $38,000, and at that price, Harold believes he has a 40 percent chance of making the sale. He feels that if he reduces his price to $35,000, the probability of purchase will go up to 60 percent. Which price shows the greatest expected net profit?

2. Allison Industrial, Inc., of Tulsa, Oklahoma, has spent $500 million developing a new shale oil extraction pump. The company expects eventually to sell 2,500 of these units, but knows that the market could evaporate if the leading firm in the targeted segment does not buy the pump. One of the company's executives has proposed a price of $650,000 for each unit, while another has suggested that $720,000 would be more appropriate. The marketing research department has assigned a 30 percent probability to the likelihood of the lead customer buying at the higher price and a 70 percent probability to the likelihood of purchase at the lower price. What should Allison Industrial do in this situation?

3. Cemented Armor Corporation has finally perfected its newest product, the ultimate in lightweight military armor plate. The problem now is to convince the right Pentagon officials of the product's superiority. Cemented Armor estimates that, if its product is bought by the military, it will ultimately become part of 1,000 of the new M-89 battle tanks soon to be coming off the production line. The cost to the company of the armor to be installed on the tanks is $120 million. Management is considering two possible bids to submit for this armor: $280,000 and $320,000 per tank. The executive board thinks that the probability of the Army accepting the first price is 65 percent, while the probability of accepting the higher price is 35 percent. Use the ENP formula to determine which of the prices Cemented Armor should bid.

4. Kawakatsu Export Company would like to penetrate the U. S. market with their line of minitractors. Developed primarily for use in truck gardens, the K-10 and K-15 units cost the company $1,000 and $1,500, respectively, delivered in the U. S.. Hideki Takata, Kawakatsu's "man in Los Angeles," has been authorized to negotiate any price above $1,300 for the model K-10 and anything above $1,800 for the K-15. Takata will receive a sales commission of one-third of the difference between the sales price of each tractor and its cost. Takata has assessed the probability of making a sale at each of several alternative prices. He'd very much like to sell at least one unit before month's end and thinks that the best way to go about it would be to make a proposal on a single unit at a reasonable price. His list of prices and probabilities of sale is:

Price	Probability of Sale
$1,650 for a K-10	30 percent
$2,100 for a K-15	35 percent
$1,750 for a K-10	15 percent
$2,250 for a K-15	25 percent
$1,850 for a K-10	5 percent
$2,400 for a K-15	15 percent

What model and price should Takata propose to the contractor?

Crossword Puzzle for Chapter 8

ROSS CLUES

Purchase of goods or services for use in production, operations of the firm, or for resale

Market comprising firms that buy goods and services to be used to produce other goods and services

Systematic study of the components of a purchase to determine most cost-effective way to buy

Restoring worn-out products to like-new condition

Written descriptions of a needed good or service

Nature of demand for a business product that depends on the demand of a consumer product

Centralization of the procurement function within an internal division or external supplier

DOWN CLUES

2. Short for government classification system that subdivides business marketplace into segments

3. Retailers or wholesalers that purchase products for resale to others

4. Suppliers involved in the creation and delivery of a good or service

5. Participants in an organizational buying action

9. Practice of extending purchasing preference to suppliers who are also customers

10. Demand for business product that depends on demand for another business product needed to use it

11. Written sales proposal from a vendor

ORD LIST:

BID
BUSINESSTOBUSINESS
BUYINGCENTER
COMMERCIAL
DERIVED
JOINT
REMANUFACTURING

RECIPROCITY
SIC
SPECIFICATIONS
SUPPLYCHAIN
SYSTEMSINTEGRATION
TRADEINDUSTRIES
VALUEANALYSIS

Chapter 8 Solutions

Key Concepts

1.	t	5.	u	9.	r	13.	d	17.	i	21.	e
2.	f	6.	l	10.	h	14.	v	18.	o	22.	c
3.	a	7.	g	11.	j	15.	p	19.	m		
4.	s	8.	n	12.	q	16.	b	20.	k		

Self Quiz

1.	F	11.	T	21.	T	31.	c	41.	c		
2.	T	12.	F	22.	T	32.	d	42.	a		
3.	F	13.	F	23.	F	33.	e	43.	c		
4.	T	14.	F	24.	T	34.	c	44.	b		
5.	T	15.	F	25.	T	35.	a	45.	d		
6.	F	16.	T	26.	b	36.	c	46.	b		
7.	T	17.	T	27.	a	37.	a	47.	d		
8.	F	18.	T	28.	b	38.	b	48.	b		
9.	T	19.	F	29.	c	39.	c	49.	a		
10.	T	20.	F	30.	d	40.	c	50.	b		

Applying Marketing Concepts

1.	T	6.	c
2.	T	7.	b
3.	b	8.	c
4.	c	9.	c
5.	a	10.	c

Computer Applications

1. Expected Profit from the decision:

    ($35,000 - $30,000) x .60 = $3,000;

    ($38,000 - $30,000) x .40 = $3,200.

    Quote the higher price; the expected payoff is $200 higher.

2. Expected profit from the decision:

At the higher price: 2,500 x $720,000 = $1,800,000,000

Profit: ($1,800,000,000 - $500,000,000) x .30 =

$240,000,000

At the lower price: 2,500 x $650,000 = $1,625,000,000

Profit: ($1,625,000,000 - $500,000,000) x .70 =

$787,500,000

The lower price offers a substantially greater expected net profit than does the higher price. Recall, however, that this is not an either/or situation from the leading firm's point of view. If they refuse to buy *and they can at either price*, Allison is out its $500,000,000. Thus, though the returns IF the leading customer buys look fantastic, should that customer not buy a $500 million loss is going to accrue to Allison.

3. Expected Net Profit from the decision:

At the higher price: $320,000 x 1000 = $320,000,000

Profit: ($320,000,000 - $120,000,000) x .35 =

$70,000,000

At the lower price: $280,000 x 1000 = $280,000,000

Profit: ($280,000,000 - $120,000,000) x .65 =

$104,000,000

The lower price results in a larger expected profit for Cemented Armor Corporation.

4. Expected net profit from the decision:

K-10 at $1,650:	$1,650 - $1,000 = $650 x .30 =	$195
K-15 at $2,100:	$2,100 - $1,500 = $600 x .35 =	$210
K-10 at $1,750:	$1,750 - $1,000 = $750 x .15 =	$112.50
K-15 at $2,250:	$2,250 - $1,500 = $750 x .25 =	$187.50
K-10 at $1,850:	$1,850 - $1,000 = $850 x .05 =	$42.50
K-15 at $2,400:	$2,400 - $1,500 = $900 x .15 =	$135

Mr. Takata should offer his client the K-15 unit at a price of $2,100.

Crossword Puzzle Solution

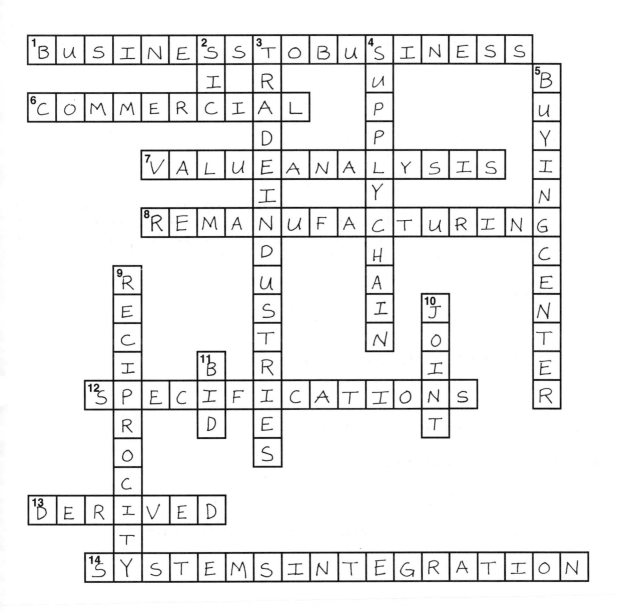

Chapter 9
Market Segmentation, Targeting, and Positioning

Chapter Outline

You may want to use the following outline as a guide in taking notes.

I. Chapter Overview—Understanding the Meaning of the Term "Market"

II. Types of Markets

III. The Role of Market Segmentation

IV. Segmenting Consumer Markets

   A. Geographic segmentation

      1. Geographic Information Systems (GISs)

   B. Demographic segmentation

      1. Segmenting by gender

      2. Segmenting by age

      3. Segmenting by family life cycle stage

      4. Segmenting by household type

      5. Segmenting by income and expenditure patterns

      6. Demographic segmentation abroad

   C. Psychographic segmentation

      1. What is psychographic segmentation?

      2. VALS 2

      3. Psychographics—a global perspective

      4. Using psychographic segmentation

    D. Benefit segmentation

        1. Segmenting by benefits sought

        2. Segmenting by usage rates

        3. Segmenting by brand loyalty

V. Segmenting the Business-to-Business Market

    A. Geographic segmentation

    B. Customer-based segmentation

    C. Segmentation by end-use application

VI. The Market Segmentation Decision Process

    A. Identify market segmentation bases

    B. Develop a relevant profile for each segment

    C. Forecast market potential

    D. Forecast probable market share

    E. Select specific market segments

VII. Target Market Decision Analysis

    A. Applying target market decision analysis

VIII. Strategies for Reaching Target Markets

    A. Undifferentiated marketing

    B. Differentiated marketing

    C. Concentrated marketing

    D. Micromarketing

IX. Positioning

Name _____   Instructor _____

Section _____   Date _____

Key Concepts

The purpose of this section is to allow you to determine if you can match key concepts with the definitions of the concepts. It is essential that you know the definitions of the concepts prior to applying them in later exercises in this chapter.

From the list of lettered terms, select the one that best fits each of the numbered statements below. Write the letter of that choice in the space provided.

Key Terms

a. market
b. consumer goods
c. industrial goods
d. market segmentation
e. geographic segmentation
f. Metropolitan Statistical Area (MSA)
g. Primary Metropolitan Statistical Area (PMSA)
h. Consolidated Metropolitan Statistical Area (CMSA)
i. geographic information system (GIS)
j. demographic segmentation
k. family life cycle
l. Engel's laws
m. psychographic segmentation
n. AIO statements

o. lifestyle
p. VALS 2
q. product-related segmentation
r. 80/20 principle
s. customer-based segmentation
t. end-use application segmentation
u. target market decision analysis
v. undifferentiated marketing
w. differentiated marketing
x. concentrated marketing
y. micromarketing
z. positioning
aa. positioning map
ab. repositioning

_____ 1. Dividing a population into homogeneous groups based on behavioral and life-style profiles developed by analyzing consumer activities, opinions, and interests.
_____ 2. Stages of family formulation and dissolution utilized in demographic segmentation.
_____ 3. Commercially available psychographic segmentation system.
_____ 4. Three general statements on spending behavior: As a family's income increases, the percentage spent (1) on food increases; (2) on housing, household operations, and clothing remains constant; and (3) on other items increases.
_____ 5. Dividing a business-to-business market into homogeneous groups on the basis of product specifications identified by organizational buyers.
_____ 6. Evaluation of potential market segments on the basis of relevant characteristics.
_____ 7. Strategy that directs all of a firm's marketing resources toward serving a small market segment.
_____ 8. A product purchased by the ultimate consumer for personal use.
_____ 9. Major urban area within a CMSA.

_____   10.   Process of dividing the overall market into relatively homogeneous groups with similar product interests.
_____   11.   Computer technology that records several layers of data on the same map.
_____   12.   Dividing a population into homogeneous groups based on characteristics of the consumer's relationship to the product.
_____   13.   Targeting potential customers at basic levels such as by ZIP code.
_____   14.   The way people decide to live their lives, including family, job, social, and consumer activities.
_____   15.   A product purchased for use directly or indirectly in the production of other goods and services.
_____   16.   A group of people who possess purchasing power and the authority and willingness to buy.
_____   17.   Dividing a business-to-business market into homogeneous groups on the basis of how industrial purchasers will use the product.
_____   18.   Major population concentration, including the 25 or so urban giants.
_____   19.   Collection of statements in a psychographic study that reflects the respondent's activities, interests, and opinions.
_____   20.   Dividing a population into homogeneous segments on the basis of characteristics such as age, sex, and income level.
_____   21.   Graphic illustration of how consumers perceive competitive products within an industry.
_____   22.   Strategy used by firms that produce only one product and market it to all consumers using a single marketing mix.
_____   23.   Changing the relative position a product holds in the consumer's mind.
_____   24.   Large, freestanding area for which detailed marketing-related data are collected by the Bureau of the Census.
_____   25.   Dividing a population into homogeneous groups on the basis of population location.
_____   26.   Strategy used by organizations that produce numerous products and use different marketing mixes to satisfy market segments.
_____   27.   Concept that a few heavy users of a product can account for much of its consumption.
_____   28.   Marketing strategy aimed at a particular market segment designed to achieve a certain "position" in the prospective buyer's mind.

Name _____ Instructor _____

Section _____ Date _____

Self Quiz

You should use these objective questions to test your understanding of the chapter material. You can check your answers with those provided at the end of the chapter.

While these questions cover most of the chapter topics, they are not intended to be the same as the test questions your instructor may use in an examination. A good understanding of all aspects of course material is essential to good performance on any examination.

____ 1. "Commercial goods" is a term some marketers use to identify business products not directly used in producing other goods.

____ 2. Henry Ford was one of the pioneers in the segmentation of the U.S. automobile industry.

____ 3. A market requires only people or institutions; there are no additional requirements.

____ 4. Light bulbs sold to lamp manufacturers are business products. Light bulbs sold to consumers to replace light bulbs in their home fixtures are consumer goods.

____ 5. To determine the number of people who are in the automobile market, you would count people who want to buy a car, are not prohibited in some way from owning one, and have purchasing power they can use to buy a car.

____ 6. Single-parent families, single-person households, and nonfamily group households now make up 44 percent of all U.S. households.

____ 7. Automobile tires are classed as consumer goods, not business goods.

____ 8. According to the most recent census, population is growing more rapidly in the Midwest than in any other part of the country.

____ 9. Moorhead, Minnesota is an example of a Primary Metropolitan Statistical Area.

____ 10. Market segmentation is the process of dividing the market into relatively homogeneous groups.

____ 11. Geographic market segmentation of consumers is useful when regional preferences exist.

____ 12. The role of market segmentation is to allow marketers to design one marketing mix that will satisfy all customers of a product.

____ 13. One of the reasons demographic variables are used in market segmentation is because of the vast quantities of such data available.

____ 14. Consumer lifestyles are regarded as components of their individual psychological makeups— their needs, motives, perceptions, and attitudes.

____ 15. The most common approach to market segmentation in the consumer market is benefits segmentation.

____ 16. Though not illegal, it is considered tasteless and unethical to segment a consumer market on the basis of age, sex, income, occupation, or household size.

____ 17. A firm that uses market segmentation assumes that the needs of different targeted segments can best be served with different marketing mixes.

____ 18. Foreign immigration is a major contributor to the growth of population in the western United States.

____ 19. In terms of the family life cycle, mature singles are active investors and heavy mail order buyers.

____ 20. On a global scale, Japan is one of the youngest countries on earth. Short life expectancy and a high birth rate are the major causes of this phenomenon.

____ 21. Product-related segmentation of the toothpaste market by benefits sought might produce segments concerned with price, reducing tooth decay, taste, or brightening the teeth.

____ 22. For census purposes, the term DINKs identifies unmarried people of opposite sexes sharing the same living quarters.

____ 23. Firms which use target market decision analysis ignore the differences in needs and wants among market segments.

____ 24. One of the problems encountered in using demographic segmentation abroad is that some country gather census data only irregularly, while others do not collect demographic data commonly used as bases for segmentation in the United States.

____ 25. Segments which have been identified by psychographic analysis can be expected to behave differently from each other.

Multiple Choice

Circle the letter of the word or phrase that best completes the sentence or best answers the question.

26. Markets require people, a willingness to buy, and
     a. engineering personnel.
     b. purchasing agents.
     c. purchasing power.
     d. authority to buy.
     e. only c and d above.

27. The major difference between consumer and business-to-business markets is
     a. the size of the average purchase.
     b. the reasons for which purchases are made.
     c. the types of goods which are bought.
     d. the educational levels of the buyers.
     e. the length of time spent in negotiation.

28. A basic reason why marketers elect to segment markets is
     a. because it simplifies their decision-making enormously.
     b. that they need some means of simplifying the task of finding buyers for their products.
     c. because the world is too large and is filled with too many diverse people and firms for any one marketing mix to satisfy everyone.
     d. so that when the production line goes into operation, it can turn out the millions of items necessary to secure economies of scale.
     e. so that competition will find it difficult to determine what is going to happen next.

29. Under which of the following conditions may it be impossible to segment the market?
     a. It is possible to measure the market in terms of both purchasing power and size.
     b. It appears feasible to promote to the market segment.
     c. The various segments of the market seem to be large enough to be adequately profitable.
     d. There are no apparent problems in providing the segments of the market with adequate service.
     e. The number of segments in the market are greater than the capacity of the firm to serve them.

30. Which of the following is one of the major population shifts of the last two decades?
    a. to the North from the South and Southwest
    b. to the sunbelt states of the South and Southwest
    c. from the Northeast to the North Central and Midwest areas
    d. to the plains states from the West coast
    e. from the Southern U. S. to Canada

31. At the present time, the proportion of the population which can be expected to move in any given year is about
    a. one-fourth.
    b. one-fifth.
    c. one-sixth.
    d. one-seventh.
    e. one-eighth.

32. A freestanding urban area with an urban center population of 50,000 which exhibits social and economic homogeneity and which has a total population of 100,000 or more would be defined by the U.S. government as a(n)
    a. PMSA
    b. MSA
    c. CMSA
    d. SSMA
    e. OGPU

33. Which of the following is a demographic variable?
    a. an individual's musical preference
    b. the attitude one has toward conservative government
    c. the rate at which one uses a particular product
    d. one's occupation, craft, or trade
    e. an individual's aspirations for the future

34. Which of the following is an example of market segmentation?
    a. An appeal is developed which it is hoped will reach all consumers, regardless of income.
    b. Residents of urban areas and residents of rural areas are approached with exactly the same marketing mix.
    c. An automobile company separates its markets into economy buyers and luxury buyers.
    d. A firm markets its products to all residents of the U.S. with the same single-product marketing mix.
    e. General Foods considers all residents of the United States to be members of its market.

35. The proportion of the population of the United States dwelling on farms
    a. has stabilized at about ten percent of the population.
    b. has ceased to decline and has begun to rise at a rate of about 0.5 percent per year.
    c. has been declining since about 1800 and is now less than three percent of the total population.
    d. is not separately counted by the census, but is estimated to be about 27 percent of the country's population.
    e. varies from census to census with economic conditions; it is now about seven percent of the total population.

36.   A market segment based on the family life cycle concept is
    a.   the high-income segment.
    b.   heavy users of full-sized cars.
    c.   swingers.
    d.   residents of large eastern metropolitan areas.
    e.   middle-aged married persons without children.

37.   According the Engel's laws, an increase in family income should bring
    a.   fewer dollars expended for food.
    b.   fewer dollars expended for housing.
    c.   fewer dollars expended for education and recreation.
    d.   a higher percentage of income spent for housing.
    e.   a lower percentage of income spent for food.

38.   The research into "lifestages" reported in your text notes that, within the family life cycle, older, never-married, separated, or divorced people may be categorized as
    a.   at-home singles.
    b.   single parents.
    c.   starting-out singles.
    d.   mature singles.
    e.   left-alone singles.

39.   Principle-oriented consumers who are mature, home-oriented, well-educated professionals with relatively high incomes are classified by the VALS 2 system as
    a.   fulfillers.
    b.   believers.
    c.   achievers.
    d.   strivers.
    e.   experiencers.

40.   Marketers who want to aim their marketing mix at the segment of the population who are single people living with members of the opposite sex are interested in the government's classification of
    a.   MSAs.
    b.   SSWDs.
    c.   CMSAs.
    d.   DINKs.
    e.   POSLSQs.

41.   A firm that targets as potential customers only neurosurgeons who perform twenty or more of a specific procedure per year is using
    a.   undifferentiated marketing.
    b.   differentiated marketing.
    c.   concentrated marketing.
    d.   micromarketing.
    e.   arbitrary segmentation.

42. Melrose Specialty Company designs and markets to wholesalers of fruits and vegetables a special package of computer software specifically designed to help these firms keep inventory at the peak of condition at all times. Melrose has applied
    a. geographic segmentation.
    b. end-use segmentation.
    c. product segmentation.
    d. marginal segmentation.
    e. demographic segmentation.

43. The stage of the segmentation process which involves describing the life-style patterns, attitudes toward product attributes and brands, brand preferences, product-use habits, and similar characteristics of typical members of each segment is called
    a. developing relevant profiles for each segment.
    b. forecasting market potentials.
    c. selecting specific market segments.
    d. forecasting probable market share.
    e. selecting market segmentation bases.

44. A firm which produces numerous products with different marketing mixes, each of which is designed to satisfy a segment of the market, is said to be practicing
    a. undifferentiated marketing.
    b. mass marketing.
    c. consolidated marketing.
    d. differentiated marketing.
    e. concentrated marketing.

45. Which of the following is an appropriate example of the indicated type of market segment?
    a. geographic—people living within 1.5 miles of a particular shopping center
    b. psychographic—young marrieds with children
    c. demographic—people looking for the lowest cost watch
    d. benefits sought basis—people interested in sports events
    e. demographic—people with a positive attitude toward education

46. The Holt Caterpillar Tractor Company was originally very successful because they developed models of their basic tractor specifically adapted to farming, road-building, earth-moving, and military uses. They applied which of the following types of segmentation?
    a. product
    b. end-use applications
    c. benefits sought
    d. geographic
    e. melodramatic

47. Target market decision analysis
    a. is useful only after market segments have been identified.
    b. is restricted to geographic segmentation.
    c. is a tool used to segment the market on the basis of a single characteristic.
    d. can be used for consumer markets but is too expensive to be used for industrial markets.
    e. is generally done with just one demographic characteristic such as age.

48.   The world's largest city, with a population expected to exceed 28 million residents by the year 2000, is
   a.   Tokyo, Japan..
   b.   New York City.
   c.   Mexico City.
   d.   Rio de Janeiro, Brazil.
   e.   Tianjin, China.

49.   When a manufacturer creates a product such as Chevrolet's "Beau Jacques" pickup truck, which was sold in Louisiana some years ago (the same truck was sold in surrounding states as the "Gentleman Jim" model), it is using
   a.   benefit sought segmentation.
   b.   psychographic segmentation.
   c.   end-use application segmentation
   d.   geographical segmentation.
   e.   arbitrary segmentation.

50.   Which of the following would be more likely to be used as a basis for segmenting the business-to-business, rather than the consumer, market?
   a.   behavioral profiles of people
   b.   age, sex, and other demographic characteristics of people
   c.   benefits sought by people
   d.   location of dense populations of people
   e.   the intended use of the product

Name _____   Instructor _____

Section _____   Date _____

Applying Marketing Concepts

The Wolverine Manufacturing Company has developed a line of disposable work clothing. The clothing can be sold profitably for about half the price of conventional garments. The items are durable enough to withstand several washings if desired, but can be easily disposed of simply by treating them with a special chemical solution. Large manufacturing companies are expected to be a major market for these clothes, with people in the firms' procurement departments expected to be the people with the authority and purchasing power to buy. The company expects the most interest in its products to come from firms in heavy manufacturing where the rigors of the production line destroy clothes at a rapid rate. Executives at Wolverine also foresee a market for their product among individuals who like do-it-yourself projects but don't like to have old, oily, scruffy work clothes lying around the house.

_____   1.   By definition, the real market for disposable clothing is factory production-line workers.
_____   2.   According to Engel's laws, the percent of income spent on clothing stays the same over all levels of consumer income.
_____   3.   Products sold to people who want to use them for their do-it-yourself projects would be classed as commercial goods.

4.   The Wolverine Manufacturing Company is selling disposable clothing as
   a.   business products.
   b.   consumer products.
   c.   both business and consumer products.

5.   The segmentation method most appropriate to Wolverine's attempt to reach the business-to-business market is probably
   a.   geographical.
   b.   end use application.
   c.   product.
   d.   psychographic.

6.   If benefits sought segmentation is used by Wolverine, it should direct its efforts toward people who want
   a.   durability.
   b.   high fashion.
   c.   convenience in use.
   d.   lowest cost clothes.

7.   By selecting heavy production-line manufacturing as a main target market for its disposable work clothing, Wolverine has
   a.   automatically limited itself geographically to those places where that kind of industry exists.
   b.   made it more difficult to segment the market on a geographical basis. Heavy industry is more or less uniformly distributed throughout the country.
   c.   placed no limitations on itself from the point of view of market segmentation.
   d.   restricted itself to only that market for the foreseeable future.

You have recently concluded a month-long visit to your company's main branch in the South American country of Paratina. You were impressed with the differences among the various groups of people you met there. Many of your contemporaries (you're in your early thirties) seemed really wired, working all the time when they weren't partying or rushing off to the beach. Others, about the same age, were much more mellow and laid back. Most of them were established professionals with some measure of success, and you noticed they seemed much more willing to sit back with a glass of good wine, some excellent cheese, and enjoy friendly conversation.

You did notice, though, that many of the women you met, whatever their status in life, seemed strained and on edge. They acted like they had things to do and you were interfering with their getting them done. You felt uneasy in their presence, and often excused yourself to let them get back to what they were doing. Even so, you noticed that many of the older citizens of Paratina seemed to be quite well-off and happy, with a number of them playing golf and tennis at the clubs where you were taken by your hosts and hostesses.

Using the results reported in Backer Spielvogel Bates Worldwide's report, *Global Span*, how would you characterize each of the groups discussed above?

8. Your contemporaries who acted busy, rushed about, and lived at a whirlwind pace would probably be classed by BSBW as
    a. achievers.
    b. adapters.
    c. strivers.
    d. pressured.
    e. traditionals.

9. Your mellow contemporaries are probably
    a. strivers.
    b. traditionals.
    c. adapters.
    d. achievers.
    e. pressured.

10. The women with whom you felt uncomfortable would probably be classed as
    a. strivers.
    b. pressured.
    c. adapters.
    d. traditionals.
    e. achievers.

11. The older people who seemed to be enjoying their lives would be
    a. adapters.
    b. strivers.
    c. achievers.
    d. traditionals.
    e. pressured.

Name _____   Instructor _____

Section _____   Date _____

Experiential Exercises

1. The purpose of this exercise is to help you understand the importance of market segmentation studies in isolating and evaluating markets. You will apply four types of segmentation (geographic, demographic, psychographic, and product-related) to an existing retail store in your home town or in the town where your college or university are located. Make sure you know each of the four types of segmentation before starting this exercise. Select a store with which you are familiar.

    a. Indicate the type of retail outlet you have chosen. (Examples: restaurant, supermarket, clothing store, discount house, home entertainment outlet, et cetera.)

    b. How far from the store do you think most of the patrons live?

    c. What are the demographic characteristics of the people you see shopping in the store?

    Age?

    Sex?

    Family life cycle status?

    Education?

    Income?

d. Do you think that the people who shop regularly at this store have a different psychographic profile from other residents of this city or town? Are there differences in

Activities such as work or entertainment?

Interests such as recreation or food?

Opinions about themselves or culture?

e. How well do you feel the marketing mix of the store fits with the needs and wants of the regular patrons?

Price?

Promotion?

Product and service?

Distribution?

2. The purpose of this exercise is to provide insight into the advantages and disadvantages of following a differentiated, an undifferentiated, a concentrated, or a micromarketing segmentation strategy.

   a. Using a library or first-hand sources (look up firms in the telephone directory and interview them), obtain information on four companies, one with each of the four strategies mentioned above. Compare their histories and current operations.

   Firm name   _____   _____   _____   _____

   Age of firm   _____   _____   _____   _____

   Sales   _____   _____   _____   _____

   Cost of goods _____   _____   _____   _____

   Other costs   _____   _____   _____   _____

   Net worth   _____   _____   _____   _____

   b. Which is the largest firm? the smallest? the newest? the oldest? How do these factors relate to the chosen strategy?

   c. Which firm shows the highest proportion of cost of goods to sales? the lowest? Why do you suppose this is the case?

d. Which firm has the greatest net worth? the least? How do these figures relate to the others you examined?

3. List three items you think most often appear for sale at garage (or yard or carport) sales when people are moving. What service, pricing method, or other marketing strategy can you create to provide these "people on the move" with an alternative to the quick sale/lose money situation they usually seem to face? Suggestion: a two-year sell-back policy on furniture and appliances, or monthly use of a parking lot for group sales.

Yard Sale Item	Service, Pricing Method, Strategy
1.	
2.	
3.	

Name _____   Instructor _____

Section _____   Date _____

Computer Applications

1. The Tyrrell and Richard families have just prepared their household budgets for 1995. Both families expect fairly substantial salary increases at the beginning of the year. The general categories of the items contained in the families' budgets are shown below.

Budget Category	Tyrrell Family Budget 1992	Tyrrell Family Budget 1993	Richard Family Budget 1992	Richard Family Budget 1993
Clothing	$ 3,500	$ 4,200	$ 4,400	$ 7,500
Housing	17,000	20,400	10,000	12,500
Food	12,000	15,600	7,200	8,500
All Other	17,500	19,800	18,400	21,500

2. Ivgeny Yaroslavl is a professional dancer. Since his departure from the National Ballet Company of Turkestan he has established a fine reputation for himself in the United States. His agent has just negotiated contracts for 1995 that should boost his income to $300,000 from the $200,000 he made in 1994. His CPA has also developed a personal budget that reflects his expected income increase in 1995.

Budget Category	1994 Expenses	1995 Expenses
Clothing	$13,200	$ 19,000
Food	22,000	28,000
Entertainment	20,000	30,000
Travel	6,000	9,000
Housing	34,000	40,000
Professional Fees	20,000	30,000
Taxes	60,000	100,000
Savings and Investments	24,800	44,000

After subtracting taxes and the agent's fees from Yaroslavl's gross income to determine net income for 1994 and 1995, determine whether the CPA's proposed budget coincides with Engel's Laws.

3. Dan and Rachelle Valdosta recently consulted their financial advisor to assist them in planning their 1995 spending. The advisor, noting that Rachelle's return to full-time employment would increase the family's income by 20 percent, from $60,000 to $72,000, in the upcoming year, told the couple they could increase their clothing expenditures from $10,000 to $13,000 as long as they held their increases in food spending to $750 (they had been spending $5,000). The advisor also suggested they purchase a new home. Though it would increase their monthly housing costs from $1,200 to $1,440, most of the increase would be tax deductible as interest expense.

    Do the financial advisor's suggestions about clothing, food, and housing conflict with Engel's Laws?

Crossword Puzzle for Chapter 9

ACROSS CLUES

1. Dividing market into homogeneous groups based on nature of the customer/product relationship
3. Marketing strategy that directs all a firm's marketing resources at a small market segment
6. Changing the relative position a product holds in a consumer's mind
9. (Abbr.) Large, freestanding area for which detailed marketing data are collected by Census Bureau
10. People or institutions with the purchasing power, authority, and willingness to buy
12. (Abbr.) Major population concentration, including one of about 25 urban giants
13. Goods or services purchased for use directly or indirectly in production of other products
14. Stages of family formation and dissolution utilized in demographic segmentation

DOWN CLUES

2. Segmentation of a population into homogeneous groups based on age, sex, income, other demographics
3. Goods and services purchased by the ultimate consumer for personal use
4. Segmentation of a population into homogeneous groups based on population location
5. Targeting potential customers at basic levels, such as by ZIP code
7. (Abbr.) Major urban area within a CMSA
8. Process of dividing the total market into homogeneous groups with similar product interests
11. The way people decide to live their lives, incl. family, job, social, and consumer activities

WORD LIST:

BUSINESSPRODUCT	MARKET
CMSA	MICROMARKETING
CONCENTRATED	MSA
CONSUMERPRODUCT	PMSA
DEMOGRAPHIC	PRODUCTRELATED
FAMILYLIFECYCLE	REPOSITIONING
GEOGRAPHIC	SEGMENTATION
LIFESTYLE	

Chapter 9 Solutions

Chapter 8 Solutions

Key Concepts

1.	m	5.	s	9.	g	13.	y	17.	t	21.	aa	25.	e
2.	k	6.	u	10.	d	14.	o	18.	h	22.	v	26.	w
3.	p	7.	x	11.	i	15.	c	19.	n	23.	ab	27.	r
4.	l	8.	b	12.	q	16.	a	20.	j	24.	f	28.	z

Self Quiz

1.	T	11.	T	21.	T	31.	c	41.	d
2.	F	12.	F	22.	F	32.	b	42.	b
3.	F	13.	T	23.	F	33.	d	43.	a
4.	T	14.	T	24.	T	34.	c	44.	d
5.	T	15.	F	25.	T	35.	c	45.	a
6.	T	16.	F	26.	e	36.	e	46.	b
7.	F	17.	T	27.	b	37.	e	47.	c
8.	F	18.	T	28.	c	38.	d	48.	a
9.	F	19.	F	29.	e	39.	a	49.	d
10.	T	20.	F	30.	b	40.	e	50.	e

Applying Marketing Concepts

1.	c	5.	F	9.	d
2.	a	6.	T	10.	b
3.	c	7.	F		
4.	a	8.	c		

Computer Applications

1. The Tyrrell family is in conflict with Engel's laws on their expenditures for food and the items classed as "other." The percentage spent on food should decline and the percentage spent on other items should increase. The Richards are also in conflict with the laws; their expenditures for clothing should decline as a proportion of income, not increase. In addition, their "other" expenditures are budgeted to go up, not down as Engel's laws would postulate.

2. Surprisingly, the only item on the 1995 budget which is in conflict with Engel's laws is housing, which should remain at the same level, 28.3%, in 1995, as in 1994. It has declined to 23.5%.

3. Yes, the advisor's suggested increase in clothing expenditures of 30% in view of a salary increase of only 20% is inconsistent with Engel's laws. The percentage spent on clothing should remain constant. The other suggestions are consistent with Engel's laws.

   NOTE: A number of theoreticians have made note that Engel's laws may no longer be valid. They were formulated in mid-19th century Germany, when and where conditions were vastly different than they are in late 20th century America. Take these exercises with a rather large grain of salt!

Crossword Puzzle Solution

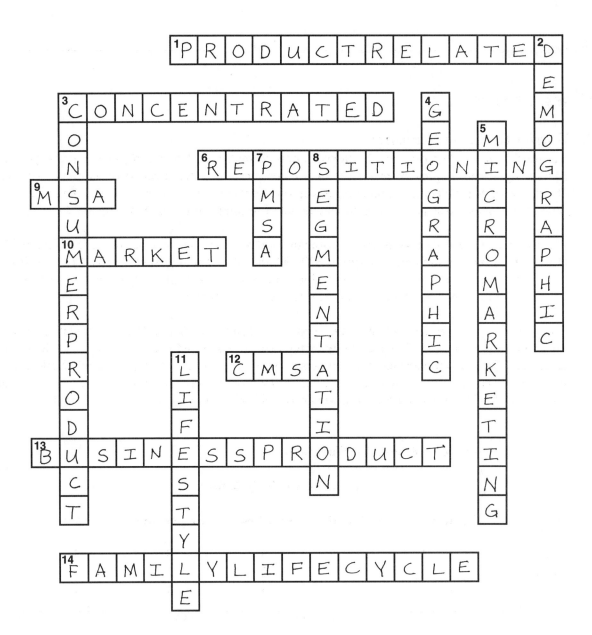

Name _____   Instructor _____

Section _____   Date _____

Cases for Part 3

1. *Warrior Chemical Company*

Warrior Chemical Company has developed a new formulation of household cleaning compound which offers a significant improvement in ease of use and cleaning power over products previously available. Their immediate problem is to decide on an appropriate target market so as to maximize profits. The company has been able to acquire a substantial amount of information to aid in making the decision.

The two variables usually used by firms selling this sort of product are income and stage of family life cycle. The levels of income used are low (up to $29,999 annual income), medium ($30,000 to $60,000 annual income) and high (more than $60,000 annual income). The stages of the family life cycle usually considered are the bachelor, newly married, full nest, empty nest, and solitary survivor.

Four other firms sell products which could be considered similar to Warrior's new formulation. A sample of the members of each of the income-life cycle segments was selected and each member of the sample was asked to try Warrior's product and the four competitive products. These people were then asked to express their preference for the five products by ranking the most preferred as 1 and so on. The average rank assigned to WarChem (the interim name assigned to the Warrior product) is shown in Table P3-1.

Table P3-1: Relative Preference for WarChem

	Family Life Cycle Stage				
Income	**Bachelor**	**Newlywed**	**Full Nest**	**Empty Nest**	**Solitary**
Low	5	5	5	5	5
Medium	3	4	2	3	3
High	1	2	3	4	5

The estimated total unit sales for WarChem's competitors for last year are shown in Table P3-2.

Table P3-2: Last Year's Sales (in Thousands of Units) for Four Competitive Products

	Family Life Cycle Stage				
Income	Bachelor	Newlywed	Full Nest	Empty Nest	Solitary
Low	10,000	8,000	20,000	10,000	2,000
Medium	14,000	12,000	16,000	14,000	10,000
High	6,000	6,000	10,000	12,000	6,000

Finally, the company has estimated the costs of producing one million gallons of WarChem and marketing it to each segment. The selling price has been set at $4.50 per gallon. The cost breakdown is shown in Table P3-3.

Table P3-3:Production and Distribution Costs for Each Segment (in $ millions)

	Family Life Cycle Stage				
Income	Bachelor	Newlywed	Full Nest	Empty Nest	Solitary
Low	$1.2	$1.0	$2.0	$0.8	$1.0
Medium	0.8	1.0	2.2	0.7	1.2
High	0.9	1.0	2.5	0.6	1.5

Questions:

a.   Given this information, which target market should the firm choose?

b. What additional information do you feel is necessary to make his target market decision?

c. It may be difficult to actually get the data in quantitative form as presented in these three tables. Which of the information would be the most difficult to gather? The easiest?

2. *Middlebrook Homes, Incorporated*

Middlebrook Homes, Inc., is in the process of subdividing a tract of land in western Georgia. Although the area is essentially rural in nature, it is located within ten miles of a city of 100,000 and within 60 miles of Atlanta. The company desires to focus in on a target market but is unsure of the consumer characteristics to use in its segmentation.

Middlebrook has hired a newspaper-clipping firm to provide information about recent advertising by other property developers. Typical headlines taken from recent ads for similar single-family, detached dwelling developments read: "Country-style Living with Every Modern Convenience," "The Home-buying Opportunity of the Year FOR ONLY $2,500 DOWN!" and "Total Privacy and a Carefree Lifestyle."

The decisions Middlebrook wants to make include the precise location of the dwellings within the subdivision; whether or not to include or exclude recreational features such as a golf course and swimming pool; whether or not to include a small shopping center in its development plans; the size of home (in square feet) to build; and what sorts of exterior design plans to adopt for the homes which it will build.

Question:

What characteristics do you think Middlebrook Homes should use when determining the target market?

3. *John Huddleston, Househusband*

John Huddleston was beginning to wonder if he had truly become a househusband. Though fully employed, the nature of his work (he was a sales engineer for a manufacturer of milling machines in an area of the country densely covered by factories) was such that, unless an emergency occurred, he could schedule his calls at his own convenience. His wife, who was a commodities broker for a large, Chicago-based commodity trading house, absolutely, positively had to be in the office when the Chicago Board of Trade opened at 8:00 AM, and usually couldn't get away until at least two hours after it closed at 2:00 PM. (The Chicago Board of Trade is the equivalent of the New York Stock Exchange for Commodities—trading in wheat, frozen orange juice, pork bellies, and the like.)

This put most of the household chores squarely back on John. It was he who awakened the kids in the morning, made them breakfast, and drove them to school, his wife having long since left for work. He shopped at the supermarket between calls on customers, and if he had a slack day on his hands, often did laundry and cooked meals. When 3:00 in the afternoon rolled around, John picked up the kids at school, took them to Little League or Soccer practice, and got dinner on the table before Susan, his wife, stumbled in the door.

In the evenings and on weekends, husband, wife, and kids pitched in and kept things on an even keel, Susan often cooking and freezing several days' worth of meals on an assembly line basis. Recently, however, there had been less emphasis on cooking and more on all of them having family fun together whenever possible. John was the first to admit, though somewhat sheepishly, that this had become possible because his cooking had become good enough to rival that of his wife.

John was a happy man; there was no doubt of that in his mind. But he did wonder on occasion if he had become a classic "househusband."

Questions:

a. In what ways does John Huddleston's situation mirror the changes that have taken place in our society in the last 30 years?

b. Of what significance to marketers are scenarios such as the one represented by John as a consumer?

c.   How have the changes evidenced in this case affected the segmentation process for consumer goods?

4. *City Center Cultural Complex*

Janelle Van Dortmund, Executive Director of the City Center Cultural Complex in Springfield, is working on a five-year marketing plan. Part of the planning process involves deciding whether the complex should adopt an undifferentiated marketing strategy, a concentrated strategy, or a differentiated strategy. The Cultural Complex has been in existence for some ten years, and its entire history has been one of financial struggle.

The problem lies, in part, in the fact that within ten miles of the Cultural Complex there are two other, similar facilities with very distinct images. Country Heritage, USA, appeals to people with an interest in music, art, and crafts activities typical of the development of this country as a rural, individually oriented nation of small farmers and dwellers in small towns. The Twenty-first Century, on the other hand, features cultural activities of the most modern sort, from exhibits of the most modern of innovative art to concerts by orchestras and groups so innovative that their names change weekly. Ms. Van Dortmund is well aware that audience studies conducted at cultural centers all across the country have shown that people have very definite likes and dislikes in their cultural pursuits; culture is a very personal thing.

Approximately 20 percent of the residents of Springfield participate in cultural activities of one sort or another on a regular basis. The population has remained stable over the last ten years and will probably not vary much over the next five.

Question:

What marketing strategy would you recommend to Ms. Van Dortmund? Should she adopt a concentrated, differentiated, or undifferentiated strategy? Explain your choice.

Name _____   Instructor _____

Section _____   Date _____

Creating a Marketing Plan: Who's Out There?

The information you will receive in this part will help you to complete Part I.C. of your marketing plan for Latebri Industries, Incorporated.

Episode Three

Having performed the appropriate rituals and filled out the proper forms, Latebri Industries was now duly and properly incorporated under the laws of the state in which it was domiciled. The officers of the corporation were Laura Claire, President; Brian Patrick, Executive Vice President for Systems Analysis; and Terrence Michaels, Executive Vice President for Circuit Design and Repair. Having gotten themselves organized, the three partners decided they needed more information about the nature of the competitive environment if they were to reduce the risk of business failure. They accordingly turned to that standard research volume which the telephone company thoughtfully provides to all of us—but which few of us use to its logical extent—the *Yellow Pages*. Searching through the current *Yellow Page* listings for New Essex, their home city, they discovered 62 firms listed under "Computers—Service and Repair." A telephone survey of these 62 firms revealed that the telephones of four were no longer in service, six were actually located outside the New Essex metropolitan area, and ten repaired only industrial mainframes and did not work on PCs. This left 42 firms remaining active in the market as direct competitors of Latebri.

The partners were aware, however, that a number of computer sales firms serviced computers. Accordingly, they checked their *Yellow Pages* once again, and determined that, of the 164 firms which survived the same sort of culling process as outlined above, 121 (75%) offered repair service, but only 102 (62%) serviced PCs, and only 29 (18%) repaired brands which they did not sell. When asked if they repaired peripherals (printers, modems) 120 (80%) responded in the affirmative. One hundred twenty-one (74%)of the firms offered service contracts to their customers.

Forty-one computer vendors (25%) indicated that they did not repair computers, and 24 of these indicated that they did not make any recommendations to their customers about where they should take their computers should they fail in service. None of the 42 service-only companies received a recommendation from more than two computer dealers.

The partners, who conducted the two surveys themselves, remarked to each other on an aspect of their work which the raw statistics didn't reveal. As Brian put it, "These computer store people don't seem to care about service work at all. In fact, one guy I called said he knew they *sold* computers, but he wasn't sure about repairing them." Laura responded with, "You know, I noticed that even when I was talking to the places that didn't sell computers; you know, the "service and repair" companies. At eight of the firms I talked to, and I did all the service and repair places, they put me on "hold" when I asked if they repaired personal computers."

"You know something else," piped up Terry, "there are over 50 display ads in the "Computers—Dealers" section of the *Yellow Pages*, but only five in the "service and repair section. I wonder why that is?"

Guidelines:

There are both an objective and a subjective component to the analysis of competition. Apply both quantitative and qualitative analysis to the information presented above to complete part I.C. of your marketing plan.

Solutions to Cases for Part 3

1. Warrior Chemical Company

a. To decide on a target market segment, a sequential process must be followed. First, the dollar return for each unit sold into each of the possible segments must be calculated, as in Exhibit P3-1:

EXHIBIT P3-1: Expected Return Per Unit

Income	Bachelor	Newlywed	Full Nest	Empty Nest	Solitary
			Family Life Cycle Stage		
Low	$3.30	$3.50	$2.50	$3.70	$3.50
Medium	3.70	3.50	2.30	3.80	3.30
High	3.60	3.50	2.00	3.90	3.00

Next, these expected returns must be multiplied by the total competitor sales for each segment. The resulting total profit potential for each segment is shown in Exhibit P3-2:

EXHIBIT P3-2: Total Profit Potential ($ Millions)

Income	Bachelor	Newlywed	Full Nest	Empty Nest	Solitary
			Family Life Cycle Stage		
Low	$33.0	$28.0	$50.0	$37.0	$7.0
Medium	51.8	42.0	36.8	53.2	33.0
High	21.6	21.0	20.0	46.8	8.0

The highest profit potentials lie in the medium income empty nest and medium income bachelor segments. These profit potentials, however, do not reflect the preference rankings given the product by these segments. Comparing potentials in rank order, the undesirable segments are those which have lower potential than another segment of similar rank. Since all the low income segments ranked WarChem fifth, the most desirable low income segment would be the full nest; the preferred middle-income segment would be the full nest; and the most desirable high income segment is the bachelor. Using this decision rule, the firm would choose the high income bachelor segment. This segment, however, offers a return of only $21.6 million compared to the $36.8 million offered by the middle income full nest segment. It is quite possible that the potential of an additional $15.2 million in return could overcome the rank difference of 1 and 2 offered by these two segments.

b. It would help to know what ranks were assigned to each of the competitive products in the various segments. In addition, market shares currently held by existing competitors would be of use in evaluating the relative meaning of the ranks assigned to the products.

It was assumed in the analysis that total sales in each segment would behave in the same way based upon aggregate data and consumer rankings. That may not, in fact, be the case. In addition, past history doesn't always predict future performance. It certainly wouldn't hurt to have some information on environmental conditions which might affect the acceptance of WarChem. Legislation may be pending or it could be that another competitor is lurking in the wings.

c.   The most difficult (and expensive) data to gather is probably the consumer preference data shown in Table P3-1. Sampling reliability calls for the use of at least 30 people in each of the fifteen segments, or a minimum of 450 people.

The rest of the data is probably available in secondary sources such as annual reports, newspapers, and financial review publications. Costs of production and distribution are probably the easiest information to generate, since they come from internal sources, but could be in error for a new product.

2. Middlebrook Homes, Inc.

Some characteristics which are probably of importance in segment selection for Middlebrook are geographic location, population demographics, psychographics of potential buyers, and the benefits these people expect to derive from living in a rural setting. Where people presently live will certainly affect their probability of preferring Middlebrook's new development, as will location of the development with respect to the place of employment of the prospective homebuyer. Demographics of importance to this analysis include income distribution data, family life cycle information, and family size characteristics in the area. Newlyweds certainly want a different type of home than do full nesters with a crop of kids in tow.

Behavioral variables affecting the design of the subdivision include attitudes, motivational makeup, benefits desired by potential buyers, and the influence of group pressures. The newspaper clippings lead one to believe that a prime motive for moving to similar subdivisions is the desire for larger living quarters at a price lower than that asked for an urban accommodation of comparable size and similar features.

3. John Huddleston, Househusband

a.   The last thirty years have seen vast, though gradual, changes in American culture and society. Recent data indicate that 70 percent of all adult women are now employed outside the home, and that many of them, like Susan Huddleston, have been successful in jobs that have traditionally been considered male preserves. These changes in the pattern of female employment have had their repercussions in the home. It would not surprise this writer to learn that Mrs. Huddleston's income exceeded that of her husband by some significant amount. Certainly, accommodations of both physical and psychological kinds must be made in acknowledgment of this fact. John is certainly *a* breadwinner for his family, but he is not *the* breadwinner in the family. Many men and women have not been as able to adapt to this realization as John and Susan seem to have been, and this accounts, perhaps, for the fifty percent divorce rate which this country currently faces. Some men, on the other hand, relish the opportunity to spend more time with their wives and children, and with both partners in a marriage gainfully employed, the possibility certainly exists for more family interaction.

b.   Mr. Huddleston is involved in tasks in the marketplace which his father, in all likelihood, would never have performed. He buys groceries, does laundry, cleans house, and cooks meals. The likelihood is that he has developed consumer preferences for products in all the lines related to these activities. It is also not at all unlikely that John shops for other products at the request of his wife and children that his dad never even heard of, let alone bought. Marketers must be aware that laundry detergents, peanut butter, pot roast, and a host of similar products are no longer bought exclusively by women, and modify their marketing mixes accordingly. (It might be mentioned here that firms like Procter and Gamble, Unilever, and Colgate are well aware of these changing patterns, and have not only changed the design of their products to accommodate male preferences, but have even changed the formats of their "daytime dramas" [soap operas] in recognition of increasing male watchership.)

c.   In years past, segmentation of "family" goods could be done on a "mine, yours, ours, and theirs" basis. Some things were men's things, others were women's, and yet others were children's. The dividing line between autonomic, syncratic, and independent decision making was fairly clearcut and distinct. Such is not the case today. The amount of buying behavior which is almost organizational in character with influencers, deciders, buyers, gatekeepers, and users participating in the family purchasing decision is on the increase, as is the buying of atypical goods by both men and women. The segmentation process has been affected by these changing and amplified roles so that constant analysis of who is buying which sorts of goods under what sets of circumstances is necessary if successful segmentation decisions are to be made.

4. City Center Cultural Complex

A concentrated marketing strategy seems to be in order for the City Center Cultural Complex because (1) its resources are limited, (2) the competition are using concentrated strategies, (3) consumers perceive differences among products, and (4) it is likely that this class of product is in the maturity phase of the product life cycle. The complex can't afford to be all things to all people. The competition has staked its claims to specific segments of the market, and the City Center needs to find for itself a similar niche to fill or there is a high likelihood that it will fall by the wayside.

Ms. Van Dortmund should study the marketplace, examining the strategies used by each of her competitors and the tastes of the residents of Springfield before deciding precisely where to target her operation. Obviously, modern and traditional values are well-served. The question now is which segments remain for her to consider as possibilities for her facility.

Solutions to Creating a Marketing Plan

Episode 3

Latebri's analysis of competitive conditions in New Essex involves analysis of three aspects of that environment. First, the firm must consider direct competition from firms specializing in computer service. Of these, there are 42 who are potentially active competitors of Latebri Industries. A second source of possible competition are the firms who engage primarily in the sale of computers, but who also service them (or say they do). Of these there are 102 who *might* be active competitors, but a very interesting statistic in this regard is the fact that only 29 firms indicated that they serviced brands of computers which they did not sell. Latebri will be organized to service *any* brand of computer, so the level of competition with these firms will not be as direct or as intense as with the other firms whose main business is computer service. From a marketing planning point of view, the computer service firms appear to be first-line competitors with the computer sales operations constituting a second line of less serious importance.

The third aspect of the analysis is provided by the subjective comments offered by Laura and Terry. It appears as though the potential competition is not very effective in defining its mission nor in communicating that mission within its own organization or to the using public. A computer service firm whose contact with the community via the telephone doesn't even know whether the firm services PCs—much less eight of them out of 42—indicates that there is a lack of clarity in the firms' statements of their missions and their orientation to the marketplace. One might even say that their consciousness of the process of segmentation is limited, and it is quite likely that one would be right. It is certainly true that firms which deal with high-tech equipment tend to be started and operated by people who are themselves technologists, not marketers, and often suffer from a lack of skills in human interaction as a result. There is obviously weakness among the competition, and they certainly are not very aggressive, as the five display ads from among 42 *Yellow Pages* listings would tend to indicate.

Lacking information on market share, further analysis of the intensity of local competition cannot be undertaken, but it is quite unlikely that such information would be available in a local market situation.

Part 4

Product Strategy

Products are bundles of physical, service, and symbolic attributes designed to satisfy wants. Firms introducing new products must concern themselves with the stages through which the product will pass from the time it is introduced until it is removed from the market. It is important to understand techniques to extend a product's life by extending the product life cycle. The adoption process consumers follow in their acceptance of a new product and factors affecting its speed of acceptance must receive attention by marketers if new products are to be successful.

Products may be classified as either business or consumer products. Consumer products are usually referred to as convenience, shopping, or specialty products. Business products are classified into the six categories of installations, accessory equipment, component parts and materials, raw materials, supplies, and business services.

New product planning is an ongoing activity subject to a number of influences which affect the decision to develop a line of products rather than concentrate on a single product. The stages in the new product development process and four methods of organizing for new product development are reviewed to ensure a thorough knowledge of this subject. Criteria for the deletion of existing products from the product line are also considered.

Very important to product strategy decisions are the availability and use of brand names, symbols, trademarks, and packaging by companies to identify their products. The growth of private brands is a significant topic for today's marketer. Consumer knowledge and acceptance of brands also constitute major considerations in the formulation of strategy. In today's litigious society, product safety has become another important component of strategic decision making.

Defining services requires knowledge of the goods-services continuum. Services are essentially intangible, inseparable from their provider, perishable, difficult to standardize, of highly variable quality, and the buyer nay participate in their development and distribution. There is often a gap between the service received and the consumer's expectation of what that service should have been like. A number of classification systems for services have been proposed. Industries providing services are known as tertiary industries.

The marketing of services is subject to the same environmental influences as is the marketing of goods. Creation of a marketing mix by service providers is somewhat more difficult than is the same task for goods vendors.

Chapter 10

Product Strategy

Chapter Outline

You may want to use this outline as a guide in taking notes.

I.   Chapter Overview—Product Strategy Is a Complex Issue

II.   Defining Product

    A. An International perspective

III.   Classifying Consumer and Business Products

    A. Types of consumer products

        1. Convenience products

        2. Shopping products

        3. Specialty products

    B. Types of business products

        1. Installations

        2. Accessory equipment

        3. Component parts and materials

        4. Raw materials

        5. Supplies

        6. Business services

IV.   The Product Life Cycle

    A. Introductory stage

    B. Growth stage

    C. Maturity stage

    D. Decline stage

    E. Using the product life cycle concepts in marketing strategy

        1. Increasing frequency of use

        2. Increasing the number of users

        3. Finding new uses

        4. Changing package size, labels, or product quality

V.   The Consumer Adoption Process

    A. Adopter categories

    B. Identifying first and early adopters

    C. Rate of adoption determinants

Name _____   Instructor _____

Section _____   Date _____

Key Concepts

The purpose of this section is to allow you to determine if you can match key concepts with the definitions of those concepts. It is essential that you know the definitions of the concepts prior to applying the concepts in later exercises in this chapter.

From the list of lettered terms, select the one that best fits in the blank of the numbered statement below. Write the letter of that choice in the space provided.

Key Terms

a. product
b. convenience product
c. shopping product
d. specialty product
e. installation
f. accessory equipment
g. industrial distributor
h. component parts and materials

i. raw materials
j. supplies
k. MRO item
l. business service
m. product life cycle
n. adoption process
o. consumer innovator
p. diffusion process

____ 1. Finished business products that become part of a final product.
____ 2. Wholesaling marketing intermediary that handles small accessory equipment and operating supplies.
____ 3. Product purchased only after the consumer has made comparisons of competing goods in competing stores on bases such as price, quality, style, and color.
____ 4. Intangible product a firm buys to facilitate its production and operational processes.
____ 5. Product with unique characteristics that cause the buyer to prize it and make a special effort to obtain it.
____ 6. Major capital item, such as a new factory or heavy machinery, that typically is expensive and relatively long-lived.
____ 7. Four stages through which a successful product passes: introduction, growth, maturity, and decline.
____ 8. Industrial product, such as a farm product (wheat, cotton, soy beans) or natural product (coal, lumber, iron ore), used in producing a final product.
____ 9. Series of stages in the consumer decision process regarding a new product, including awareness, interest, evaluation, trial, and rejection or adoption.
____ 10. Capital item, usually less expensive and shorter-lived than an installation, such as a laptop computer.
____ 11. Regular expense items necessary in the firm's daily operation, but not part of the final product.
____ 12. Bundle of physical, service, and symbolic attributes designed to enhance buyer want satisfaction.
____ 13. Product that the consumer wants to purchase frequently, immediately, and with a minimum of effort.

_____ 14.   First purchaser of a new product.
_____ 15.   Acceptance of new products by members of a community or social system.
_____ 16.   Supply for a business categorized as a maintenance item, repair item, or operating supply.

Name _____   Instructor _____

Section _____   Date _____

Self Quiz

You should use these objective questions to test your understanding of the chapter material. You can check your answers with those provided at the end of the chapter.

While these questions cover most of the chapter topics, they are not intended to be the same as the test questions your instructor may use in an examination. A good understanding of all aspects of the course material is essential to good performance on any examination.

True/False

Write "T" for True or "F" for False for each of the following statements.

_____   1.   A broad definition of the word *product* focuses on the physical or functional characteristics of a good or service.

_____   2.   Staple items are consumer products like bread, milk, and gasoline, which must be constantly replenished by the consumer.

_____   3.   Products purchased on the spur of the moment or out of habit are referred to as impulse products.

_____   4.   The burden of promoting convenience products falls largely on the wholesaler and retailer.

_____   5.   Homogeneous shopping products are shopping products that the consumer considers essentially similar to each other.

_____   6.   Price is an important factor in the purchase of heterogeneous shopping products, while styling and quality are more significant in the purchase of homogeneous shopping products.

_____   7.   Specialty products can usually be found in fewer retail outlets than either convenience or shopping products.

_____   8.   Consumer products are classified as convenience, shopping, or specialty products on the basis of the behavior patterns of individual buyers.

_____   9.   The classification system for business products is based on product uses rather than on consumer buying patterns.

_____   10.   Installations can be called the shopping products of the business market.

_____   11.   More decision makers are usually involved in purchasing accessory equipment than are involved in purchasing installations in the business market.

_____   12.   When bought by a firm, leasing and rental of equipment and vehicles, insurance, and legal counsel are examples of business services.

_____   13.   Wholesalers and advertising are more likely to be used by manufacturers of accessory equipment than of either installations or component parts and materials.

_____   14.   Supplies are often called MRO items because they include manufacturing, required, and on-site materials.

_____   15.   The majority of firms in a particular market enter during the maturity phase of the product life cycle.

_____   16.   The product life-cycle concept applies to individual product brands, rather than products or product categories in an industry.

_____ 17.   During the introduction phase of the product life cycle, companies attempting to increase their sales and market share must do so at the expense of competitors.

_____ 18.   An unsought product is one for which the consumer does not yet recognize a need.

_____ 19.   One strategy for extending the product life cycle is to increase the overall market size by attracting new customers who previously have not used the product.

_____ 20.   First adopters of new products are generally older, of lower social status, less well-educated, and less well-off financially than later adopters.

_____ 21.   The degree to which an innovation appears superior to previous ideas is its divisibility.

_____ 22.   The greater the relative advantage of an innovative product over previous ideas, the faster it will be adopted.

_____ 23.   During the evaluation stage of the consumer adoption process, people consider whether or not the product is beneficial.

_____ 24.   The diffusion process is the acceptance of new products and services by the community or social system.

_____ 25.   Price is often a deciding factor in the purchase of raw materials since it is negotiated on a purchase-by-purchase basis between buyer and seller.

Multiple Choice

Circle the letter of the word or phrase that best completes the sentence or best answers the question.

26.   From a marketer's point of view, what people buy when they purchase a product or service is
  a.   a group of physical or functional characteristics.
  b.   attributes that provide satisfaction of a want.
  c.   often nothing more than advice.
  d.   something they cannot do for themselves.
  e.   an absolute necessity for the maintenance of life and limb.

27.   When a consumer sets out to purchase convenience goods he or she
  a.   often visits numerous stores before making a purchase.
  b.   makes comparisons of competing goods on bases such as price, style, or color.
  c.   often lacks complete information about what is sought.
  d.   may be willing to travel a substantial distance and spend a lot of time to get what is wanted.
  e.   rarely visits competing stores or compares price and quality.

28.   Consumer products that are purchased only after making comparisons of competing products in competing stores on the basis of such features as price, quality, style, and color are known as
  a.   shopping products.
  b.   impulse products.
  c.   specialty products.
  d.   staple products.
  e.   demand products.

29.   Shopping products would typically include
  a.   Coca-Cola and Dixie Beer.
  b.   bread, milk, and gasoline.
  c.   clothing, furniture, and appliances such as refrigerators and washing machines.
  d.   Rolex watches and BMW automobiles.
  e.   candy, cigarettes, and newspapers.

30. A consumer product characterized by high price, reliance on personal selling, and image advertising and few retail outlets in its marketing mix would most likely be
    a. a homogeneous shopping product.
    b. an unsought product.
    c. a heterogeneous shopping product.
    d. a specialty product.
    e. a staple product.

31. Which of the following is characteristic of the market for specialty products?
    a. willingness of the buyer to make a special effort to obtain the prized product
    b. buyers have little information about the product they seek
    c. numerous retail outlets serving each geographical area
    d. low-priced goods often lacking a brand name
    e. trial purchases of competing brands made with little financial risk

32. The burden of promoting convenience goods falls largely on
    a. the retailer; it is his desire to stimulate sales.
    b. the wholesaler; retailers don't have the money to promote these goods efficiently.
    c. the manufacturer; retailers often carry competing brands and can't be relied upon to devote effort to one of them.
    d. the government; if more people buy more goods, the economy grows.
    e. a partnership between manufacturer and wholesaler; they can work together efficiently to get the job done.

33. Sales volumes rise rapidly as new customers begin to buy the product and previous users rebuy. Word of mouth and mass advertising induce hesitant buyers to make trial purchases. The stage of the product life cycle is
    a. experimentation.
    b. growth.
    c. introduction.
    d. maturity.
    e. decline.

34. The major problem with the convenience, shopping, and specialty product classification of consumer goods is that
    a. many products are so different that they fall totally outside the scope of the classification.
    b. the system cannot be used in terms of the majority of buyers; it must be applied to a specific individual.
    c. some products fall into the gray areas between categories; they cannot be fitted neatly into one or another of the classifications.
    d. consumers differ in buying patterns; an item that's a shopping good for one person may be a specialty good for someone else.
    e. the system no longer works; human behavior has changed so radically during the last ten years that the system is out of date.

35. The category of industrial goods whose purchase may involve negotiations lasting over a period of several months, the participation of a large number of decision makers, and the provision of technical expertise by the selling company is
    a. raw materials.
    b. accessory equipment.
    c. installations.
    d. component parts and materials.
    e. supplies of various types.

36. People in foreign countries are willing to pay premium prices for American products because
    a. the American products are demonstrably better than local ones.
    b. they have symbolic value as an embodiment of the American dream.
    c. the American products are typically cheaper than local ones.
    d. American products carry a generous warranty.
    e. American products are usually the only ones available for a specific use.

37. Operating supplies are often called "MRO items." The letters MRO stand for the words
    a. manufacturing, research, and organizational.
    b. multiple, random, and obvious.
    c. many, ridiculous, and outrageous.
    d. manual, required, and out-of-stock.
    e. maintenance, repair, and operating supply.

38. The "specialty goods" of the business market are called
    a. MRO items.
    b. raw materials.
    c. accessory equipment.
    d. installations.
    e. supplies.

39. In the industrial market, finished goods that become part of the final product are called
    a. accessory equipment.
    b. component parts and materials.
    c. maintenance items.
    d. repair items.
    e. mechanical attachments.

40. The firm's objective in the introductory stage of the product life cycle is to
    a. extend the cycle as long as possible.
    b. improve warranty terms and service availability.
    c. emphasize market segmentation.
    d. stimulate demand for the product.
    e. price competitively.

41. Efforts to extend the product life cycle should begin
    a. toward the end of the introductory stage.
    b. early in the maturity stage.
    c. toward the middle of the growth stage.
    d. in the latter part of the maturity stage.
    e. as the product enters the decline stage.

42. Kraft General Foods' promotion of Crystal Light as a diet drink during January, traditionally a low sales volume month for the product, is an example of extending the product life cycle by
    a. increasing frequency of use of the product.
    b. finding new uses for an existing product.
    c. increasing the number of users of Crystal Light.
    d. changing package size, label, or product quality.
    e. physically modifying the product for a new market.

43. The determinant of the rate of adoption of an innovative product that describes the degree to which the innovation is consistent with the values and experiences of potential adopters is its
    a. relative advantage.
    b. compatibility.
    c. possibility of trial.
    d. observability.
    e. complexity

44. The stage of the adoption process which has been reached when an individual becomes sufficiently involved with a new product to begin to seek information about it is
    a. awareness.
    b. evaluation.
    c. interest.
    d. trial.
    e. rejection.

45. Promoting oatmeal as a cholesterol reducer, wax paper as a food covering for microwave cooking, and mouthwash as an aid in preventing gum disease are examples of extending a product's life cycle by
    a. increasing the product's frequency of use.
    b. increasing the number of people who use the product.
    c. changing the package size, label, or product quality.
    d. creating a new product service component for the firm.
    e. finding new uses for the product.

46. People who purchase a new product almost as soon as it's available in the market are known as
    a. traditional shoppers.
    b. barefoot pilgrims.
    c. members of the late majority.
    d. laggards.
    e. consumer innovators.

47. First adopters of innovative new products tend to be
    a. older than those who adopt later.
    b. less mobile than those who adopt later.
    c. better educated than those who adopt later.
    d. more likely to rely on word-of-mouth than later adopters.
    e. people who change jobs very seldom.

48.   The stage of the adoption process during which consumers consider whether or not the product is benefi-
       cial is
       a.   adoption/rejection.
       b.   interest.
       c.   trial.
       d.   evaluation.
       e.   awareness.

49.   Johnson and Johnson's offer to consumers of a free trial pair of its innovative disposable contact lenses
       enhanced which of the stages of the adoption process?
       a.   awareness and interest
       b.   interest and evaluation
       c.   evaluation and trial
       d.   trial and adoption
       e.   evaluation and rejection

50.   The degree to which the superiority of a new product is demonstrable in terms of lower price, physical
       improvement, or ease of use is a measure of the product's
       a.   communicability.
       b.   relative advantage.
       c.   complexity.
       d.   divisibility.
       e.   compatibility.

Name _____   Instructor _____

Section _____   Date _____

Applying Marketing Concepts

Mosca Tancredi was very busy. It was a nasty day outside, and the bad weather had stimulated him to analyze his company's sales records. He was both pleased and confused by what he saw there. Mosca's firm, Tancredi Enterprises, manufactured products which were used by both consumers and industry. From their new plant in Richland, Washington, they shipped "Tancredi Trous," a line of high fashion men's pants, all over the United States. The pants were in such demand, Mosca knew, that people would literally drive a hundred miles to a store that sold them in order to buy a pair. The firm's other soft goods line, a coverall widely used by service firms, had long been a satisfactory performer in the industrial marketplace. One of the firm's hard lines, the TanJar Therapeutic Chair, seemed to have fallen on hard times. Developed five years before, sales had grown slowly for three years, then rapidly for another two years. Now, however, things were not so rosy. Competitors had begun to appear and Mosca felt that prices and profits from the chair were being squeezed by their activities. The other hard line in the Tancredi stable, the Tantic Precipitator, a device used to remove dust from "clean rooms" in electronics factories and laboratories in hospitals and pharmaceuticals plants, continued to do well. Mosca was glad he'd had the good luck to realize that hospitals and pharmaceutical companies could use the precipitator just when the electronics market for the thing seemed to be peaking out. He wondered if perhaps he could do the same thing with the therapeutic chair. So far, most sales had been made to chiropractors and physical therapists for use in treating their patients, but Mosca knew that the chair could also be used as a very convenient workstation for people doing clerical work because of all the adjustments that could be made to it. He began to think about the possibilities.

1. Into which category of consumer goods could "Tancredi Trous" best be placed?
   a. convenience
   b. homogeneous shopping
   c. heterogeneous shopping
   d. specialty
   e. impulse

2. Tancredi's line of workman's coveralls are probably treated by industry as
   a. installations.
   b. shopping goods.
   c. accessory equipment.
   d. supplies.
   e. raw materials.

3. The TanJar chair is in which stage of the product life cycle?
   a. introduction
   b. growth
   c. maturity
   d. decline
   e. death

4. Mosca's deliberations about development of the TanJar chair into a workstation for clerical employees
    a. reveal his desperation; the idea is obviously ludicrous.
    b. have definite possibilities; it would extend the product life cycle by finding a new use for the product.
    c. would offer the possibility of extending the product life cycle by adding new users to the product's market.
    d. could conceivably extend the product life cycle by increasing the frequency with which the chair is used.

5. From Tancredi Enterprises' point of view, their new plant is
    a. a specialty product.
    b. an installation.
    c. accessory equipment.
    d. a convenience product.
    e. none of the above.

6. Mosca's development of the hospital and pharmaceutical industry market for the Tantic precipitator was
    a. a good example of extending the product life cycle by finding new users for the product.
    b. pure luck; he couldn't do that again in a thousand years.
    c. an example of product life cycle extension through a change in product packaging or quality.
    d. a very astute example of how a product can be changed from a shopping good to a specialty good by advertising.

Milos Millstone, general sales manager for Langston Hose and Tube Company, was checking sales figures for two of his products. The first, type TAA31, was a new variety of industrial tubing that Langston had introduced three years ago. Sales had increased the two years following introduction, but had begun to decline in the last quarter of the current year. Several competitors had introduced similar tubing a year after Langston's new product introduction. When Milos lowered prices on TAA31, sales had recovered, and total industry sales continued to increase but at a slower rate than during the previous year.

The second type of tubing Milos was examining was type CKY022A. This was a semirigid tube that had been available for twenty years. Once widely used as a component in the domestic aircraft industry, sales had been declining for a number of years, and Langston remained one of the few makers of this type of tubing. Milos had recently learned, however, that a number of East Asian aircraft firms still used this type of tubing and might be willing to talk about buying it from Langston.

7. The type TAA31 tubing is in which stage of the product life cycle?
    a. introduction
    b. growth
    c. maturity
    d. decline
    e. death

8. If Milos were to discover that this tubing could be used to make novel and decorative lighting fixtures, there might be a good chance that
    a. he could extend the product life cycle by finding new users for the product.
    b. he could extend the product life cycle by developing this new use for the product.
    c. he could forget about making industrial tubing and go strictly into the lighting fixture business.
    d. he could repackage the tubing and sell it to hobbyists for use in their aquariums and fish tanks.

9. The Type CKY022A tubing is in which stage of its product life cycle?
   a. introduction
   b. growth
   c. maturity
   d. decline
   e. death

10. If Milos succeeds in convincing the East Asian aircraft companies to buy CKY022A tubing from his firm, he will have extended the product life cycle by
    a. finding a new use of for the product.
    b. changing the product's package and label.
    c. getting firms to use the product more often.
    d. increasing the number of users of the product.
    e. improving the customer service available from his firm.

Name _____ Instructor _____

Section _____ Date _____

Experiential Exercises

1. The product life cycle consists of four stages: introduction, growth, maturity, and decline.
   a. Name a consumer product that you believe to be in the introduction stage of its product life cycle. What characteristics of the market for the product led you to place it in that stage?

   b. Name a consumer product that you believe to be in the growth stage of its product life cycle. What characteristics of the market for the product led you to place it in this stage?

   c. Name a consumer product that you believe to be in the maturity stage of its product life cycle. What characteristics of the market for the product led you to place it in this stage?

    d. Name a consumer product that you believe to be in the decline stage of its product life cycle. What characteristics of the market for that product led you to place it in that stage?

2. For each of the products listed in Exercise 1 of this section indicate whether the product is a convenience, shopping, or specialty good. Give your reasons for your choice of product classification.

    a. Product:

       Classification:

       Reasons:

    b. Product:

       Classification:

       Reasons:

c. Product:

Classification:

Reasons:

d. Product:

Classification:

Reasons:

3. How would these products be classified if they were sold in the business market?

a. Product:

Classification:

Reasons:

b. Product:

Classification:

Reasons:

c.   Product:

Classification:

Reasons:

d.   Product:

Classification:

Reasons:

4.   The pace of technology is such that products are often introduced, develop through a portion of what might
be their natural growth, and go into early decline as new products take their place. Sometimes, though, a
product which was seemingly obsolete will suddenly experience a renewal as some previously unperceived
advantage gives it "a new lease on life." For each of the products or concepts mentioned below, examine the
product's initial introduction to the marketplace, subsequent events, and the current status of this particular
technology. Use the product life cycle and the concept behind its extension as the basis for your analysis.

a.   Laserdiscs

b.   Tube-type electronic equipment (especially sound amplifiers)

c. Electric automobiles

d. Cooking out-of-doors

e. Miniaturization

Name _____   Instructor _____

Section _____   Date _____

Computer Applications

Review the discussion of return on investment (ROI) in Chapter 10 of the text. Then use menu item 10 titled "Return on Investment" to solve each of the following problems.

1. Brian's Company (Pty.), Ltd., of Alice Springs, Northern Territory, Australia, is engaged in the development of a new feeding system for sheep. It is estimated that it will cost $6 million to develop the new system. The firm expects to sell $30 million worth of the systems, producing a profit of $3 million. What is the ROI for this product? (All figures in U. S. dollars)

2. "Laissez le Bon Temps Roulez!, Inc.," franchises its new pub concept internationally. The company projects that a franchisee will earn $150,000 in the first year of operation based upon $750,000 in sales. The total investment for a franchise owner is $1,200,000 which includes franchise fees, building, equipment, and operating capital. What is the typical first year's ROI for a new Laissez le Bon Temps Roulez! outlet? (Laissez le Bon Temps Roulez!, by the way, means "Let the Good Times Roll!")

3.   Embols and Symblems, Ltd., of Pudney-on-Slope (the entire town leans slightly to the left), Yorkshire, England, was recently awarded a patent on a new screen printing process such as is used on T-shirts and similar apparel. The new system causes the ink to bond with the fibres of the garment so that the colors never fade, regardless of how many times it is washed. The owners estimate it would cost about $3,600,000 to successfully commercialize the process. Royalties would bring in about $24 million, but costs of research and development, legal fees, taxes, and other expenses are expected to reduce net income to about $9,000,000. What is the expected ROI on this invention?

4.   The Merlman Company produces replacement parts for obsolete automobiles. They have been approached by the DeSoto Collectors' Club of America to discuss the feasibility of Merlman producing parts for the Club's particular make of car. Merlman executives estimate that they could sell $45 million worth of DeSoto parts over the life of their investment. However, tooling would cost $6 million, and the flow of profits would be about $900,000 per year from sales. Calculate the ROI for the proposed DeSoto parts.

Crossword Puzzle for Chapter 10

CROSS CLUES

. Equipment of a capital nature usually less expensive and shorter lived than installations

. Bundle of physical, service, and symbolic attributes designed to enhance consumer satisfaction

. Acceptance of new goods and services by members of the community or social system

. Products purchased only after the consumer has compared competing products in competing stores

. Process involving learning about new products, trying them, and finally deciding to use/reject

. Finished parts from one producer that become part of the final product of another producer

DOWN CLUES

1. Includes the basic stages of introduction, growth, maturity, and decline

4. Goods and services the consumer wants to purchase frequently, immediately, and with small effort

5. Capital goods for business use with long lifetimes, such as factories and mainframe computers

7. Among the first 2.5 percent of the people who adopt a new product

8. Products possessing some unique characteristic that causes buyers to prize those brands

10. In industry, maintenance items, repair items, or operating supplies

WORD LIST:

ACCESSORY	INNOVATOR
ADOPTION	MROITEM
COMPONENTPARTS	PRODUCT
CONVENIENCE	PRODUCTLIFECYCLE
DIFFUSIONPROCESS	SHOPPING
INSTALLATION	SPECIALTY

Chapter 10 Solutions

Key Concepts

1.	h	6.	e	11.	j	16.	k
2.	g	7.	m	12.	a		
3.	c	8.	i	13.	b		
4.	l	9.	n	14.	o		
5.	d	10.	f	15.	p		

Self Quiz

1.	F	11.	F	21.	F	31.	a	41.	b
2.	T	12.	T	22.	T	32.	c	42.	a
3.	T	13.	T	23.	T	33.	b	43.	b
4.	F	14.	F	24.	T	34.	c	44.	c
5.	T	15.	F	25.	F	35.	c	45.	e
6.	F	16.	F	26.	b	36.	b	46.	e
7.	T	17.	F	27.	e	37.	e	47.	c
8.	F	18.	T	28.	a	38.	d	48.	d
9.	T	19.	T	29.	c	39.	b	49.	c
10.	F	20.	F	30.	d	40.	d	50.	b

Applying Marketing Concepts

1.	d	5.	b	9.	d
2.	d	6.	a	10.	d
3.	c	7.	c		
4.	b	8.	b		

Computer Applications

1. The investment is $6,000,000, yielding a return of $3,000,000 for an ROI of 50 percent.

2. The required investment is $1,200,000, which yields a yearly return of $150,000. The ROI is $150,000/$1,200,000 or 12.5 percent.

3. The investment in the process is $3,600,000. Return of $9,000,000 on the invested amount would result in an ROI of $9,000,000/$3,600,000, or 250 percent.

4. Tooling of $6,000,000 would yield a return of $900,000 per year, a return of 15 percent ($900,000/$6,000,000).

Crossword Puzzle Solution

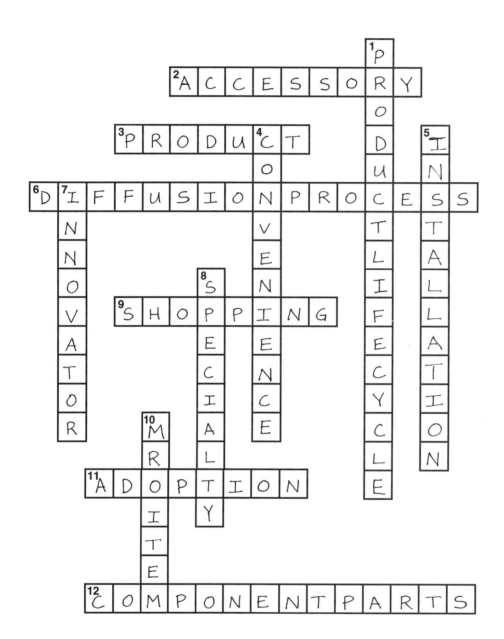

Chapter 11

Product Mix Decisions and New Product Planning

Chapter Outline

You may want to use the following outline as a guide in taking notes.

I. Chapter Overview—Product Mix, Product Development, Product Decisions

II. The Existing Product Mix

    A. Line extension

    B. Cannibalization

III. The Importance of Product Lines

    A. Desire to grow

    B. Optimal use of company resources

    C. Increasing company importance in the market

    D. Exploiting the product life cycle

IV. New Product Planning

    A. Product development strategies

        1. Market penetration

        2. Market development

        3. Product development

        4. Product diversification

V. Organizing for New Product Development

    A. New product committees

    B. New product departments

    C. Product managers

    D. Venture teams

VI.   The New Product Development Process

   A. Idea generation

   B. Screening

   C. Business analysis

   D. Development

   E. Test marketing

   F. Commercialization

VII.   Product Deletion Decisions

VIII. Product Identification

   A. Brands, brand names, trademarks, and brand equity

   B. Characteristics of effective brand names

   C. Protecting trademarks abroad

   D. Measuring brand loyalty

   E. Brand extensions and brand licensing

   F. Family brands and individual brands

   G. Manufacturers' brands and private brands

      1. Generic products

      2. The growth of private brands

IX.   Packaging

   A. Protection against damage, pilferage, and spoilage

   B. Assistance in marketing the product

   C. Cost-effective packaging

   D. The metric system

   E. Labeling

      1. Green labeling

      2. Universal product code

X   Product Safety

   A. Consumer Product Safety Commission

   B. The concept of product liability

Name _____   Instructor _____

Section _____   Date _____

Key Concepts

The purpose of this section is to allow you to determine if you can match key concepts with their definitions. It is essential that you know the definitions of the concepts prior to applying the concepts in later exercises in this chapter.

From the list of lettered terms, select the one that best fits each of the numbered statements below. Write the letter of that choice in the space provided.

Key Terms

a.	product mix	q.	brand equity
b.	product line	r.	generic name
c.	line extension	s.	brand recognition
d.	cannibalizing	t.	brand preference
e.	product positioning	u.	brand insistence
f.	product manager	v.	brand extension
g.	venture team	w.	brand licensing
h.	task force	x.	family brand
i.	phased development	y.	individual brand
j.	parallel approach	z.	manufacturer's (national) brand
k.	concept testing	aa.	private brand
l.	test marketing	ab.	generic product
m.	brand	ac.	label
n.	brand name	ad.	Universal Product Code
o.	brand mark	ae.	product liability
p.	trademark		

_____   1.   Stage of brand acceptance at which consumer is aware of the existence of a brand but does not prefer it to competing brands.

_____   2.   Brand name that has become a generally descriptive term for a product.

_____   3.   Allowing another firm to use a brand name for a fee.

_____   4.   Brand that has been given legally protected status for exclusive use by its owner.

_____   5.   Brand name owned by a wholesaler or retailer.

_____   6.   Series of related goods offered by a firm.

_____   7.   Assortment of product lines and individual offerings.

_____   8.   Item characterized by a plain label, little or no advertising, and no brand name.

_____   9.   Interdisciplinary group on temporary assignment that works through functional departments to examine new product issues.

_____   10. New product development organization consisting of specialists from different functional areas.

_____   11. Stage of brand acceptance at which the customer will accept no alternatives and will search extensively for the good or service.

_____ 12.   Strategy of giving an item in a product line its own brand name rather than identifying it by a family brand name.

_____ 13.   Special code on packages that is read by optical scanners.

_____ 14.   Measuring consumer attitudes and perceptions of a product idea prior to its actual development.

_____ 15.   Stage of brand acceptance at which the customer will select one brand over competitive offerings based on previous experience with it.

_____ 16.   Use of a popular brand name for a new product entry in an unrelated product category.

_____ 17.   Symbol or pictorial design used to identify a product.

_____ 18.   Buyer's perception of a product's attributes, uses, quality, and advantages and disadvantages.

_____ 19.   New product that is closely related to other products in the firm's existing line.

_____ 20.   Selecting a city or television coverage area typical of a new market and introducing a new product with a marketing campaign in this area.

_____ 21.   Sequential pattern whereby a product is developed in an orderly series of steps.

_____ 22.   Brand name used for several related products.

_____ 23.   Concept that manufacturers and marketers are responsible for injuries and damages caused by their products.

_____ 24.   Brand name owned by a manufacturer or other producer.

_____ 25.   Individual given complete responsibility for determining objectives and marketing strategies for an individual product or product line.

_____ 26.   Name, term, sign, symbol, design, or some combination of these used to identify the products of a firm.

_____ 27.   Descriptive part of a product's package, listing brand name or symbol, name and address of manufacturer or distributor, composition and size of product, and recommended uses.

_____ 28.   Part of a brand consisting of words or letters that comprise a name used to identify and distinguish a firm's offerings from those of competitors.

_____ 29.   A product taking sales from another offering in the same product line.

_____ 30.   Teams of design, manufacturing, marketing, sales, and service people who are involved with development from idea generation to commercialization.

_____ 31.   Added value that a certain brand name gives to a product in the marketplace.

Name _____   Instructor _____

Section _____   Date _____

Self Quiz

You should use these objective questions to test your understanding of the chapter material. You can check your answers with those provided at the end of the chapter.

While these questions cover most of the chapter topics, they are not intended to be the same as the test questions your instructor may use in an examination. A good understanding of all aspects of the course material is essential to good performance on any examination.

True/False

Write "T" for True or "F" for False for each of the following statements.

_____ 1. Width of assortment refers to the number of products in a firm's marketing mix.

_____ 2. An established firm initiates product planning by first assessing its current product mix.

_____ 3. If a new product takes sales away from an existing product in the same line, it is said to be cannibalizing the line.

_____ 4. A company marketing only a single product is often more important to both consumers and intermediaries than is the firm with a line of products.

_____ 5. "Line extension" refers to the development of individual offerings that appeal to different market segments and are different from the existing product line.

_____ 6. New products introduced into markets where the firm already has an established position are called flanker brands.

_____ 7. A market penetration strategy concentrates on developing new products for new markets.

_____ 8. Nearly one-third of the resources American firms invest in product innovation is spent on products that are commercial failures.

_____ 9. Test marketing often suffers from the distortion that occurs when competitors reduce the selling price of their products in the test market area during the period of the test.

_____ 10. Test marketing of consumer durables such as home computers is often a long, drawn-out process because of the possible losses a company may suffer if the testing is not thorough enough.

_____ 11. Phased development of new products works well for firms that dominate mature markets and develop variations on existing products. It works less well for firms affected by rapidly-changing technology.

_____ 12. The decision to prune old, marginal products from the product line usually should be made during the late maturity or early decline stage of the product life cycle.

_____ 13. Trademark protection can be secured only for the pictorial or design portion of a product's brand.

_____ 14. A brand mark is a symbol or pictorial design; it is the part of the brand that cannot be vocalized.

_____ 15. Effective brand names are easy to pronounce, recognize, and remember.

_____ 16. Brand equity acts as a competitive disadvantage to a firm because it is almost impossible to realize the value of the equity in increased sales.

_____ 17. If the brand name of a trademarked product becomes the name by which that class or type of product in general is known, the original owner may lose the exclusive right to use it.

_____ 18.   During the stage of brand acceptance called brand recognition, consumers will choose a product over its competitors if, it is available.

_____ 19.   Trade names and trademarks should not be confused. a trade name identifies a company while a trademark identifies a company's products.

_____ 20.   Family brands are more expensive to market than individual brands because a new promotional campaign must be developed to introduce each new product to its target market.

_____ 21.   Individual brand names should be used for products which are dissimilar and family brand names for those which are similar in quality and use.

_____ 22.   Products characterized by plain labels, little or no advertising, and no brand names are called private brands.

_____ 23.   Brand licensing gives a firm added exposure in the marketplace and an extra source of income from the royalties it receives, which can be as much as eight percent of wholesale sales.

_____ 24.   Packaging plays a very small role in product safety; after all, most products aren't used until after they have been removed from the package.

_____ 25.   Product liability refers to the concept that, beyond making sure that their products will do the job they have been advertised to do, manufacturers and marketers have no responsibility for injuries and damages caused by those products.

Multiple Choice

Circle the letter of the word or phrase which best completes the sentence or answers the question.

26.   The number of product lines a firm offers defines
   a.   the width of assortment within its product mix.
   b.   the length of assortment within its product mix.
   c.   the depth of assortment within its product mix.
   d.   the length of assortment within its product line.
   e.   the width of assortment within its product line.

27.   Kimberly-Clark's doubling of its investment in plants in Europe reflects that it views the area appropriate for
   a.   a market penetration strategy.
   b.   a product development strategy.
   c.   a product positioning strategy.
   d.   a product diversification strategy.
   e.   a market development strategy.

28.   When a firm's product development orientation is toward increasing sales of existing products in existing markets, it is practicing a strategy of
   a.   product positioning.
   b.   market development.
   c.   product development.
   d.   market penetration.
   e.   product diversification.

29. When a single individual sets product prices, develops advertising and sales promotion programs, and works directly with the sales force of a product, you have a
    a. new product committee in action.
    b. product manager structure.
    c. venture team.
    d. new product department.
    e. product diversification strategy.

30. The most common organizational arrangement for new-product development is the
    a. new-product department.
    b. product manager system.
    c. new-product committee.
    d. the venture team arrangement.
    e. the idea-generation concept.

31. That part of the product development process which is designed to determine consumer reactions to a product under normal conditions is called
    a. idea generation.
    b. concept testing.
    c. screening.
    d. business analysis.
    e. test marketing.

32. Which of the following is a drawback to test marketing?
    a. If the test is carefully controlled, consumers will not be aware that it is taking place.
    b. After the test has been going on for a few months, the firm can estimate the product's likely performance in a full scale introduction.
    c. Test marketing can cost up to $1,000,000 depending on the size of the test market city and the cost of buying media to advertise the product.
    d. The residents of the test market should represent the overall population in such characteristics as age, sex, and income.
    e. Test market locations are typically chosen so that they are of a manageable size.

33. The primary reason why long-lived durable goods are seldom test marketed is because
    a. of the major financial investment required for their development, the need to establish a distribution network for them, and the parts and servicing required.
    b. the act of test marketing communicates company plans to competitors prior to introduction of the product.
    c. competitors who learn about the test market often cut prices in the test area, distribute cents-off coupons, or take other actions to disrupt the experiment.
    d. firms are afraid their competitors will "pirate" their ideas and rush into production with copycat products.
    e. test market locations are so difficult to find.

34. The approach to development of a new product which uses teams of design, marketing, manufacturing, sales, and service people who are involved with the product from idea generation to commercialization is called
     a. phased development.
     b. parallel development.
     c. the Program Evaluation and Review Technique.
     d. the Critical Path Method.
     e. sequential scheduling.

35. Monsanto sold All detergent to Lever Brothers because
     a. of shortages of raw materials which made the product no longer profitable to manufacture and sell.
     b. the product had gone into the decline stage of its product life cycle and the company's executives felt it should be "pruned" from the product mix.
     c. the only reason they had added it to their product mix in the first place was to provide a complete line of goods for their customers. They no longer felt this obligation.
     d. the product did not really fit into a product mix which was largely composed of business goods.
     e. the company had only been acting as agent for Lever Brothers in the first place.

36. The right of exclusivity granted the owner of a brand by trademark registration
     a. includes any pictorial designs used in the brand.
     b. covers the brand name of the product.
     c. includes brand name abbreviations such as "Coke" for "Coca-Cola."
     d. preserves the brand owner's right to slogans such as "It's Miller Time."
     e. extends to all of the conditions mentioned in a through d.

37. When a company uses a single brand name for several related products, it is practicing
     a. family branding.
     b. individual branding.
     c. national branding.
     d. private branding.
     e. institutional branding.

38. Which of the following is more true of individual branding than of family branding?
     a. A promotional outlay benefits all of the products in the product line.
     b. It is easier to introduce a new product to retailers and to the consumer.
     c. It can be used when products are of dissimilar quality without harming the firm's product image.
     d. Consumers who have a good experience with one of the firm's products will be more likely to purchase another.
     e. It should be used for products which are generally similar in use and in market characteristics.

39. Marketers typically face the decision to delete products from the product mix during
     a. the late introduction and early growth stages of the product life cycle.
     b. the late maturity and early decline stages of the product life cycle.
     c. the late growth and early maturity stages of the product life cycle.
     d. the late introduction or early decline stages of the product life cycle.
     e. late in the decline stage of the product life cycle.

40. The market share held by generic products
    a. has remained stable at about seven percent for those types of products where generics are available.
    b. has been increasing steadily since their introduction in 1977.
    c. decreases during periods of recession and increases as the economy improves.
    d. represents as much as 40 percent of sales for some classes of products.
    e. increases during recessions but subsides when the economy improves.

41. The main purpose of oversized packaging, such as the plastic or paperboard boxes in which prerecorded audio tapes are sold, is to
    a. provide extra physical protection to the contents.
    b. prevent spoilage of the product by tampering.
    c. assist in the marketing of the product by providing convenience of access to it.
    d. reduce pilferage by shoplifters by making the product too bulky to fit conveniently into a pocket or purse.
    e. be a cost-effective way of facilitating goods handling.

42. Which of the following is a good example of using a package to assist in marketing a product?
    a. packaging beer in brown or green bottles
    b. providing tamper-resistant seals on food and medicine containers
    c. designing the package so that it can be put to some other use after the product it contains has been expended
    d. designing the package so that the product will not be deformed or crushed in shipment
    e. choosing from among alternative package designs the one which will adequately protect the contents at least cost

43. The stage of the development of brand loyalty during which consumers, relying on previous experience with the product, will choose it over its competitors if it is available, is called brand
    a. preference.
    b. insistence.
    c. aggravation.
    d. realization.
    e. recognition.

44. The Universal Product Code
    a. is a device which allows consumers to determine how long it has been since a product they are buying was produced.
    b. is a circular emblem displayed on many packages certifying that the product is manufactured to "universal standards."
    c. is a numerical code read by optical scanners that print the item and its price on the cash register receipt.
    d. is a law that specifies that the labels on packages all over the world contain the same type and quantity of information.
    e. is a standard of ethics for the manufacturers of consumer goods that sets forth their customer relations policy.

45. Brands offered by wholesaler and retailers are usually called
    a. family brands.
    b. private brands.
    c. individual brands.
    d. generic brands.
    e. extended brands.

46.   The original, historical objective of packaging was
       a.   as a tool to assist in marketing the product.
       b.   to offer physical protection for the product.
       c.   to be cost-effective.
       d.   to establish and "identity" for the product.
       e.   to provide convenience in storage, use and disposal.

47.   The federal law which has had the greatest impact on product safety has been
       a.   the Toxic Substances Act of 1968.
       b.   the Fair Packaging and Labeling Act of 1966.
       c.   the Product Safety Standards Act of 1987.
       d.   the Consumer Product Safety Act of 1972.
       e.   the Magnusson-Moss Consumer Products Warranty Act of 1973.

48.   The concept that manufacturers and marketers may be responsible for injuries and damage caused by their
       products is called
       a.   corporate social responsibility.
       b.   the premise of extended warranty.
       c.   customer relations.
       d.   the rule of individual responsibility.
       e.   product liability.

49.   Which of the following was a brand name but has become generic through common usage over the years?
       a.   Nylon
       b.   Jell-O
       c.   Xerox
       d.   Hoover
       e.   Frigidaire

50.   Creating a package design which features a gold crest with a heavy maroon accent is a way of assisting in
       marketing the product by
       a.   making the product more convenient to use.
       b.   producing a package that can be easily reused.
       c.   establishing the product's identity through package design.
       d.   producing a package which is cost-effective.
       e.   protecting the product against damage, pilferage, or spoilage.

Name _____   Instructor _____

Section _____   Date _____

Applying Marketing Concepts

Riverside Candy Company has been in business for over fifty years. The company was founded in 1934 to manufacture and distribute *Riverside Ramps*, a hard caramel confection in bar form that the company still carries in its product mix. Over the years, the company has added to its line of candies, and now sells *Riverside Rollers*, round, hard candies, *Riverside Ripples*, a bar candy with alternating vanilla/chocolate stripes, and *Riverside Rapids*, a fast-dissolving candy specially designed for use by joggers and runners "for quick energy on the go." Each Riverside candy item is packaged in a distinctive brown and cream wrapper featuring the Riverside trade-mark.

1. The type of branding which Riverside has traditionally used is
    a. individual branding.
    b. family branding.
    c. dealer branding.
    d. generic branding.
    e. indeterminate branding.

2. Just recently, Riverside was approached by a large supermarket chain that wants to buy *Riverside Rapids* to be packaged in their own wrappers and sold under their name. The supermarket brand is a
    a. generic brand.
    b. national brand.
    c. individual brand.
    d. family brand.
    e. private brand.

3. Riverside has received an offer from the Fuchida Leisure Foods Company of Tokyo. They want to produce candy products using Riverside's recipes and bearing Riverside's brand in Japan, where a craze for American food (sort of like the Sushi craze here) is under way. If Riverside agrees, they will have
    a. implemented a market penetration strategy.
    b. begun a product positioning sequence.
    c. given Fuchida a brand license.
    d. decided to actively pursue market development.
    e. diversified their product mix.

4. Though it is unlikely that such a thing would ever happen, suppose that some of Riverside's Rollers suddenly began exploding while on store shelves and in consumers' homes. Which federal agency do you suppose would show the greatest interest?
    a. Federal Energy Regulatory Commission.
    b. Bureau of Alcohol, Tobacco, and Firearms.
    c. Consumer Products Safety Commission.
    d. Directorship of the Federal Reserve System.
    e. National Electrical Products Purchasing Commission.

5. If Riverside decided to branch out into the production of flavored syrups for use by sellers of snow cones and decided to create a new brand, such as "Best Taste," for that line, it would be
    a. developing a new family brand for the syrup line.
    b. individually branding the syrups.
    c. making a serious mistake; users of Riverside candies aren't going to be interested in snow cone syrups.
    d. in violation of law; each food product must bear the brand name most closely associated with its maker.

"OK, people, settle down," Sam Delaney called the group to order. "We've got a lot to do today. This is our third meeting this year, and we've got four items on the agenda. First, as some of you know, Mel Oustalet will be replacing Leslie Hussman as our engineering member until Leslie gets back from the hospital. If you haven't heard, it was a boy! Next, I've got three new concepts I want you to take with you and look over." He handed out large brown envelopes to six of the other seven people in the room. "You'll find the preliminary appraisal forms for each attached to their descriptions."

Gesturing toward the person who didn't get and envelope, he continued. "I'd like to introduce Mia Cascabel to all of you. She'll be handling the New Era line when we introduce it next month. I've given her all the information we generated during our deliberations, but she may need to talk to some of you about details as we get closer to the intro date."

Everyone shook hands with Mia across the table and she excused herself to go back to her office. Sam started handing out slim volumes of paper bound in green to each person remaining. "Here are the preliminary results from Hahnville. As you can see, models K-30 and K-31 are doing well, but K-32 isn't really selling."

"Well, Sam, that's sort of what we expected from our earlier research, isn't it?," said a tall man halfway down the table.

"Yes, Jack," replied Sam.

"I'd be inclined to recommend we drop the K-32," said Jack, who was from manufacturing. "It's got too many bells and whistles, anyway."

"How do the rest of you feel?" asked Sam, scanning the table.. Everyone was in agreement, as nodding heads indicated. "Good, then it's done. Our next meeting will be next week, same time, same place. Thank you all." And they filed from the room.

6. The above is most probably a transcript of a meeting of Wendover Industries'
    a. flight products venture team.
    b. new product department.
    c. new product committee.
    d. separately funded delivery department.

7. The members of the group were given the documents in the brown envelopes so they could
    a. begin the process of idea generation.
    b. examine them and give their input to the screening process.
    c. do a business analysis on the information in the envelopes.
    d. test market the information in the envelopes.
    e. commercialize the information given them.

8. Mia Cascabel is probably
    a.   the product manager for the New Era line.
    b.   a visitor to company headquarters.
    c.   a research analyst whose work the firm has used.
    d.   nobody important.

9. The "results from Hahnville" probably had to do with
    a.   some preliminary concept testing Wendover was doing.
    b.   a jury of executive opinion done at company headquarters.
    c.   a survey of several thousand consumers.
    d.   the results of test marketing a new product line.
    e.   deciding whether or not to drop an old line.

Name _____   Instructor _____

Section _____   Date _____

Experiential Exercises

1. The purpose of this exercise is to help you understand the requirements of package design. You are being asked to design a package for a new product. This package must bear the information required by law, must have visual appeal, must protect the product and be cost-effective. Dimensions will be limited, for reasons of distribution, to a rectangular configuration six inches long by two inches wide by 3/4 inch deep. You may use any material you choose so long as it satisfies the requirements above. The package need not be rigid so long as those specifications are met.

    Choose *one* of the following products:

    a. A family cereal called *Mountain Nuggets*, an all-natural product containing nuts and dried pears and lightly sweetened with dark molasses.
    b. A snack food called *Tri-Pro*, whose basic ingredients are dried beef, sunflower seeds, and cheese solids, and which contains three times the protein of any other snack food on the market.
    c. An instant dessert called *Fudge A Little*, a creamy, low calorie dish with a bottom layer of brownies and a top layer of pudding.

    Your package will contain 3-3/4 ounces of the product. The first two products can be eaten as-is, but the *Fudge A Little* must be mixed with eight fluid ounces of skim milk for preparation.

    Don't be afraid to let your creative juices flow, but realize that practical considerations must also govern your design.

2. Using library sources such as *The Wall Street Journal*, *Advertising Age*, and *Marketing News*, investigate sources for the last year or so, seeking news of new-product introductions into the market. Continue until you have found at least one example of each of the following strategies.

a.) *Market penetration*

Nature of new product:

Name of Company:

Why is this an example of market penetration?

b.) *Market development*

Nature of Product:

Name of Company:

Why is this market development?

c.) *Product development*

Nature of Product:

Name of Company:

Why is this product development?

d.) *Product diversification*

Nature of Product:

Name of Company:

Why is this an example of product diversification?

Name _____   Instructor _____

Section _____   Date _____

Computer Applications

Review the discussion of alternative approaches to evaluating alternatives in the text. Then use menu item 6 titled "Evaluation of Alternatives" to solve each of the following problems.

1. Standard Coffee Company is considering one of three package designs for its ground coffee. The firm has identified three major factors to consider in making this decision: product protection, promotional appeal, and ease of storage. Standard's management has scored each of the package designs on a scale of 1 (poor) to 5 (excellent) for each of the three decision factors. These scores are shown below:

| Package | Decision Factors | | |
Design	Protection	Appeal	Storage
A	4	3	2
B	2	5	3
C	4	3	4

a. Which package design would the company select using the overall scoring method?

b. Suppose that management considers package appeal to be 100% more important than any other decision factor. Which package design would be selected?

c. Suppose that management, using the overall scoring method, also decides that it will not accept any package design that scored less than 3 for ease of storage. Which package design would be selected?

d. Would your response to question c change if management used the weighted scoring method?

2. Darmstadt Quelle, one of Germany's premier bottlers and distributors of spring water, is planning to introduce a new line of flavored spring waters into the French market. They have created five possible brand names which might be used for these products and have tested their impact on a sample of 5,000 French citizens. The citizens were categorized on the basis of whether they were previous users, current users, or had never been users of bottled water. A five-point scale ranging from 1 (poor) to 5 (excellent) was used. The rankings are as follows:

Brand Names	Previous Users	Marketing Impact with Current Users	Never Users
Artiste	4	3	4
Benefice	3	4	5
Charmant	4	2	3
Delicieux	5	4	4
Espresif	3	4	3

a. Which brand name would be chosen using the overall scoring method?

b. Suppose that management considers the brand name's impact with current users and never users to be 100 percent more important than its impact with previous users. Which brand name would be selected?

c. Suppose that management decides it will not accept a brand name rated less than 4 by any group. Using the overall scoring method with this additional stipulation, which brand name would be chosen?

d. Would your answer to question c changed if the weighted scoring method were used?

3. Alabama Book Company, a distributor of paperback books in Huntsville, is considering five new retail display racks. There are three major factors to be considered in making the decision on the new rack: promotional appeal; maximum display inventory; and cost. Management has scored each of the display designs on a scale of 1 (poor) to 5 (excellent) for each of the decision factors. These scores are shown below:

Display	Promotional Appeal	Maximum Inventory	Cost
A	5	3	5
B	4	4	3
C	3	5	2
D	3	4	3
E	5	4	4

a.   Which display would the firm select using the overall scoring method?

b.   Suppose that management considers cost the least important decision factor. Promotional appeal and maximum inventory are considered 100% more important than cost. Which display would be selected?

c.   Suppose that management, using the overall scoring method, also decides that it will not purchase any display scoring less than 4 on any decision factor. Which display would be selected?

d.   Would your response to c change if management used the weighted scoring method?

Crossword Puzzle for Chapter 11

ACROSS CLUES

4. Assortment of product lines and individual offerings
7. What manufacturers and marketers may bear if their products cause damage or injury
11. Brand acceptance level where consumer is familiar with brand and will choose it on this basis
13. Name, term, sign, symbol, design, or some combination used to identify the products of a firm
14. The descriptive part of a product's package, often containing a great deal of information
17. Item characterized by a plain label with no advertising or brand name

DOWN CLUES

1. Abbreviation for the special code on packages read by optical scanners
2. Brand name owned by a wholesaler or retailer
3. Series of related products offered by a firm
5. Stage of brand acceptance when the consumer is aware of brand's existence but does not prefer it
6. Group on temporary assignment that works through departments examining new product issues
8. Brand that is legally protected and is exclusive to its owner
9. Added value that a certain product name gives that product in the marketplace
10. Brand acceptance is such that the consumer will accept no alternatives and will search for choice
12. Brand name used for several related products
15. Words or letters used as a name to identify and distinguish a firm's products
16. Sequential pattern in which a product is developed in an orderly series of steps

WORD LIST:

BRAND	LABEL	PRIVATE
BRANDEQUITY	LIABILITY	RECOGNITION
BRANDNAME	LINE	TASKFORCE
FAMILYBRAND	PHASED	TRADEMARK
GENERICPRODUCT	PRODUCTMIX	UPC
INSISTENCE	PREFERENCE	

Chapter 11 Solutions

Key Concepts

1.	s	7.	a	13.	ad	19.	c	25.	f	31.	q
2.	r	8.	ab	14.	k	20.	l	26.	n		
3.	w	9.	h	15.	t	21.	i	27.	ac		
4.	p	10.	g	16.	v	22.	x	28.	n		
5.	aa	11.	u	17.	o	23.	ae	29.	d		
6.	b	12.	y	18.	e	24.	z	30.	j		

Self Quiz

1.	F	11.	T	21.	T	31.	e	41.	d
2.	T	12.	T	22.	F	32.	c	42.	c
3.	T	13.	F	23.	T	33.	a	43.	a
4.	F	14.	T	24.	F	34.	b	44.	c
5.	F	15.	T	25.	F	35.	d	45.	b
6.	T	16.	F	26.	a	36.	e	46.	b
7.	F	17.	T	27.	e	37.	a	47.	d
8.	F	18.	F	28.	d	38.	c	48.	e
9.	T	19.	T	29.	b	39.	b	49.	a
10.	F	20.	F	30.	c	40.	e	50.	c

Applying Marketing Concepts

1.	b	6.	c
2.	e	7.	b
3.	c	8.	a
4.	c	9.	d
5.	a		

Computer Applications

1. a. Using the Overall Scoring Method:

$$
\begin{array}{llccccccl}
 & & \text{Criteria} & & & & & & \\
 & & P & A & S & & P & = & \text{Protection} \\
\text{Design} & A = & 4 + & 3 + & 2 & = 9 & A & = & \text{Appeal} \\
 & B = & 2 + & 5 + & 3 & = 10 & S & = & \text{Ease of Storage} \\
 & C = & 4 + & 3 + & 4 & = 11 & & &
\end{array}
$$

The design chosen would be C.

b. Weighting appeal 100% more important than either of the other factors:

    Criteria

		P		A		S		
Design	A =	4	+	6	+	2	=	12
	B =	2	+	10	+	3	=	15
	C =	4	+	6	+	4	=	14

The chosen design would change to design B.

c. The chosen design would have to be C. It has the highest score and no disqualifier.

d. The answer would be B. The weighting of appeal redeems this design from rejection.

2. a. Using the Overall Scoring Method:

    Impact with

		P		C		N						
Brand	Artiste	4	+	3	+	4	=	11		P	=	Previous users
	Benefice	3	+	4	+	5	=	12		C	=	Current users
	Charmant	4	+	2	+	3	=	9		N	=	Never users
	Delicieux	5	+	4	+	4	=	13				
	Espresif	3	+	4	+	3	=	10				

Delicieux Brand would be chosen under overall scoring.

b. If impact with current users and never users were 100% more important than impact with previous users:

    Impact with

		P		C		N		
Brand	Artiste	4	+	6	+	8	=	18
	Benefice	3	+	8	+	10	=	21
	Charmant	4	+	4	+	6	=	14
	Delicieux	5	+	8	+	8	=	21
	Espresif	3	+	8	+	6	=	17

Delicieux Brand is now tied with Benefice Brand as the choice with 21 points.

c. All the brands except Delicieux would be excluded from consideration by this criterion. Delicieux would become the brand chosen.

d. The combination of criteria would restore Benefice to a tie with Delicieux.

3. a. Using the Overall Scoring Method:

Criteria

		A		I		C					
Display	A	5	+	3	+	5	=	13	A	=	Appeal
	B	4	+	4	+	3	=	11	I	=	Inventory
	C	3	+	5	+	2	=	10	C	=	Cost
	D	3	+	4	+	3	=	10			
	E	5	+	4	+	4	=	13			

Displays A and E would be tied for chosen display.

b. Using a weighting of 100% for Appeal and Inventory considerations:

Criteria

		A		I		C		
Display	A	10	+	6	+	5	=	21
	B	8	+	8	+	3	=	19
	C	6	+	10	+	2	=	18
	D	6	+	8	+	3	=	17
	E	10	+	8	+	4	=	22

Display E becomes the display of choice.

c. This decision rule would exclude all of the displays except E from consideration.

d. The decision would not change. Although Display A now meets the criteria, E wins out on points.

Crossword Puzzle Solution

Chapter 12

Marketing of Services

Chapter Outline

You may wish to use this outline as a guide in taking notes.

I.   Chapter Overview—Are Goods and Services Totally Different?

II.   What Are Services?

III.   The Importance of the Service Sector

IV.   Characteristics of Services

     A. Intangibility

     B. Inseparability

     C. Perishability

     D. Difficulty of standardization

     E. Buyer involvement

     F. Variable quality

V.   Service Quality

     A. Determinants of service quality

     B. Gap analysis

     C. The service encounter

VI.   Types of Consumer and Business Services

VII.   Environments for Service Firms

    A. Economic environment

    B. Social-cultural environment

    C. Political-legal environment

    D. Technological environment

    E. Competitive environment

        1. Competition from goods

        2. Competition from government

        3. Outsourcing in the service sector

VIII. The Marketing Mix for Service Firms

    A. Service strategy

    B. Pricing strategy

    C. Distribution strategy

    D. Promotional strategy

Name _____   Instructor _____

Section _____   Date _____

Key Concepts

The purpose of this section is to allow you to determine if you can match key concepts with their definitions. It is essential that you know the definitions of the concepts prior to applying the concepts in later exercises in this chapter.

From the list of lettered terms, select the one that best fits in the blank of the numbered statement below. Write the letter of that choice in the space provided.

Key Terms

a.   goods-service continuum
b.   service
c.   service quality
d.   gap

e.   service encounter
f.   tertiary industry
g.   productivity
h.   relationship quality

_____   1.   Output as measured by the production of each worker.
_____   2.   Expected and perceived quality of a service offering.
_____   3.   Difference between expected and perceived service quality.
_____   4.   Industry involved in the production of services.
_____   5.   Intangible task that satisfies consumer and business user needs.
_____   6.   Method of visualizing the differences and similarities between goods and services.
_____   7.   Actual interaction point between the buyer and the service provider.
_____   8.   Buyer's trust in and satisfaction with a seller.

Name _____   Instructor _____

Section _____   Date _____

Self Quiz

You should use these questions to test your understanding of the chapter material. You can check your answers with those provided at the end of the chapter.

While these questions cover most of the chapter topics, they are not designed to be the same as the test questions your instructor may use in an examination. A good understanding of all aspects of the course material is essential to good performance on any examination.

True/False

Write "T" for True and "F" for False for each of the following statements.

_____ 1. Marketing programs for services are typically developed very differently than are those for products.

_____ 2. Use of the "goods-service continuum" is necessary because so many products have both a good and a service component.

_____ 3. Service products are often difficult to identify because they come into existence at the same time they are bought and sold.

_____ 4. One thing that definitively separates goods from services is tangibility; a pure service is never tangible.

_____ 5. Service imports account for a substantial part of the U.S. trade deficit.

_____ 6. The idea that consumer perceptions of the service provider become their perceptions of the service is called variability.

_____ 7. Since personal selling and advertising cannot show the service itself, they must communicate the benefits of using the service.

_____ 8. Because buyers are often incapable of judging service quality prior to purchase, reputations of service vendors frequently become key factors in buying decisions.

_____ 9. Services are perishable because, when stored in inventory, they tend to deteriorate rapidly.

_____ 10. It is often possible to standardize offerings among sellers of the same service.

_____ 11. There is often substantial interaction between the service provider and the customer in the production and marketing of services.

_____ 12. Among the determinants of service quality, empathy refers to the willingness and readiness of employees to render service.

_____ 13. The intangibility of services tends to make buyers rely on objective analyses of services and their sellers when making buying decisions.

_____ 14. If a firm provides a higher standard of service than the buyer expects, then a favorable gap between expected service quality and perceived service quality exists.

_____ 15. The buyer's perception of service quality is likely to be determined during the service encounter.

_____ 16. A motion picture theater provides people-based services, while a law firm's services are equipment-based.

_____ 17.   According to Colin Clark, the most advanced stage of the growth of service industries occurs when the majority of the labor force is engaged in tertiary industries.

_____ 18.   One reason for the rapid growth of business service firms is that they are frequently able to serve the customer's needs more cheaply than the customer can.

_____ 19.   Few service businesses are regulated and when they are they are more loosely regulated than other forms of private enterprise.

_____ 20.   Application of new technology is one way productivity in the service sector has been improved in recent years.

_____ 21.   Direct competition between goods and services seldom occurs because it is impossible to satisfy service needs through the substitution of goods.

_____ 22.   Entrepreneurial service providers may find themselves in direct competition with government or its agencies in the provision of certain services.

_____ 23.   Price negotiation is an important part of many professional service transactions.

_____ 24.   Sales promotion is widely used in services marketing, with sampling, demonstrations, premiums, and contests being the favored vehicles.

_____ 25.   An innovative service company may gain a competitive edge by finding new ways to distribute its services.

Multiple Choice

Circle the letter of the phrase or sentence that best completes the thought or answers the question.

26.   The development of a marketing program for a service typically begins with
a.   the development of a marketing mix to satisfy a market segment.
b.   investigation, analysis, and selection of a market segment.
c.   the realization that marketing a service is radically different than is marketing a physical product.
d.   creation of the service in recognition of universal need for it.
e.   definition of the specific limits of the capacity of the developer to perform the service.

27.   Which of the following most closely approximates a pure service?
a.   having your car washed and waxed by a "detailing" company
b.   repairs made to your television set when a major component fails
c.   purchasing a security package for your home from Westec; the package includes an alarm system as well as periodic visits during the day and night by Westec patrols
d.   buying a set of tires and having them mounted and balanced at a local Firestone store
e.   enjoying a meal at Galatoire's or any other fine restaurant

28.   The immediate handling of an emergency at a medical center, prompt record of frequent flyer mileage, and an attorney who returns phone calls before the end of the business day are examples of service providers'
a.   reliability.
b.   assurance.
c.   empathy.
d.   responsiveness.
e.   variability.

29. Services are difficult to demonstrate at trade shows, to display in retail stores, to illustrate in advertisements, and to sample because
    a.   they are perishable.
    b.   they are inseparable from their provider.
    c.   they are usually not standardized.
    d.   of interaction between buyer and seller.
    e.   they are intangible.

30. Which of the following best illustrates the perishability of services?
    a.   They do not have features that can be seen, heard, smelled, tasted, or touched.
    b.   In consumers' minds, those who provide the service are the service.
    c.   They cannot be produced ahead of time and stored in inventory in anticipation of periods of peak demand.
    d.   Consistency of quality is difficult to achieve even in the services provided by a single seller.
    e.   The consumer often plays a major role in the determination of when and how the service is going to be performed.

31. Which of the following is the best example of an equipment-based service?
    a.   an accounting practice
    b.   a firm of lawyers
    c.   a public relations company
    d.   a dental practice
    e.   an advertising agency

32. Gap analysis involves
    a.   measuring the distance between a person's teeth with a view toward eliminating the spaces between them.
    b.   examining the difference between consumers' expectations of a quality of service and their perceptions of the service they have received.
    c.   determining how much of what a politician promised during his/her campaign is delivered once elected.
    d.   ascertaining how reliable, responsive, and empathetic service providers can be.
    e.   careful consideration of the difference between consumer expenditures for services and purchases of business service during a stated period of time.

33. Word-of-mouth, service switching, and service loyalty are
    a.   the classifications into which the outcomes of a service encounter may be categorized.
    b.   three of the determinants of service quality.
    c.   techniques traditionally used to define whether a product is a service or a good.
    d.   characteristics of services that can be measured accurately.
    e.   devices used by the federal government to determine the reliability of a supplier.

34. Most explanations of the sharp increases in spending for services and the rapid development of service industries in the United States since World War II are predicated on
    a.   a return to a more subsistence-oriented lifestyle calling for less dependence on manufactured goods and more on individual skills.
    b.   a shifting from primary industries to secondary industries in the American economy.
    c.   the changes associated with a maturing economy and the byproducts of rapid economic growth.
    d.   liberation of women from the home and into the work force, distributing expertise more uniformly across the manufacturing sector of the economy.
    e.   a decline in American productivity which has called for additional people to be employed in "cleaning up" the mess we have made of this continent.

35. Direct competition between goods and services is inevitable because
    a. of the tangible nature of each.
    b. of the type of labor which is used in each.
    c. internal competition between goods is almost nonexistent.
    d. goods and services are both intangibles.
    e. competing goods and services often provide the same basic satisfactions.

36. Which of the following is true of the market for business services?
    a. The growth in spending for business services has been less significant than that for consumer services.
    b. Many firms purchase business services because they do not have the equipment or the expertise to perform a particular, specialized task which an outside source can provide.
    c. The profitability of business-service providers is questionable; intense competition makes the field marginal.
    d. Many business services provided by outside operations cost more than if the purchasing firm did them themselves.
    e. Most business services are purchased as a mark of prestige rather than for any economic or practical reason.

37. Which of the following is an example of a service not available a few years ago but now in demand in the U.S.?
    a. janitorial services provided by separate companies to business users
    b. personal services such as haircutting and styling in a salon environment
    c. automotive repairs done by dealers at their service facilities
    d. leisure consultants to advise consumers how to spend their spare time
    e. travel agencies which will book single airfares or package tours on request

38. The most primitive stage of the growth of service industries, according to economist Colin Clark, is characterized by
    a. the vast majority of an economy's population being engaged in farming, hunting, fishing, and forestry.
    b. an economy based on manufacturing activities.
    c. the majority of labor being engaged in tertiary industries.
    d. a shift from capitalist to socialist economic theory.
    e. implementation of widespread land reforms with landowners being stripped and the land being deeded to the serfs.

39. The increasingly common practice among service firms of having data entry done in countries such as Hungary is an example of
    a. competition between a service and a good for the same market.
    b. competition between private enterprise and a government service.
    c. competition between a for-profit and not-for-profit organization.
    d. restriction by government of the type of service a firm can provide.
    e. outsourcing in the service sector

40. The use of virtual reality software for purposes such as avoiding errors in hospital design is an example of
    a. how the shortage of human help has forced the use of such stopgap measures to minimize the use of people and maximize use of machines.
    b. how people's expectations have changed; a few years ago, no one would have accepted such an idea.
    c. an effort to improve productivity in the service sector of the economy; using such measures, output per person employed can be increased.
    d. experimentation with technology which may or may not prove to be successful or acceptable.
    e. yet another effort to weaken the bargaining power of unions at the negotiating table.

41. The paradoxical nature of the competitive environment in the market for services is best exemplified by the fact that
    a. people want services but very often do not wish to pay what they are worth to get them.
    b. internal competition is fierce for all except the most marginal kinds of services.
    c. competition often comes not from other services but from goods manufacturers or from government-provided services.
    d. despite uniform ease of entry, some segments of the service market remain almost totally unserved.
    e. high levels of profitability have not drawn service providers into the service sector in anything like the volume one would ordinarily expect.

42. Which of the following is the best example of a service normally provided only by government?
    a. communications
    b. security in one's old age
    c. medical care
    d. security of one's person and property
    e. none of these are services which are exclusive to government

43. Express Mail is an example of a government service
    a. which has direct competition from the private sector.
    b. which was created to serve a market segment too small to profitably be served by commercial interests.
    c. which has as its main market the government itself.
    d. provided only to a limited number of users of a preferential basis.
    e. offered on an experimental basis to develop better communication networks within the nation's communications system.

44. The most commonly used segmentation method applied by service marketers is
    a. geographic.
    b. psychographic.
    c. demographic.
    d. product-based.
    e. economic.

45. Dry cleaning, shoe repair, and similar personal services are usually classed as
    a. shopping services.
    b. specialty services.
    c. impulse services.
    d. emergency services.
    e. convenience services.

46. Price competition for many services is limited because
    a. of rapid price increases across the board; over the last 20 years, service prices have risen over 100% more than goods prices.
    b. production, marketing, and administrative costs must be covered regardless of competitive conditions.
    c. of the involvement of employees in the pricing process.
    d. of close regulation by federal, state, or local government agencies, as in the case of utilities.
    e. of the relative fewness of suppliers compared to the size of the market.

47.   The financial planning firm that uses as a promotional theme a retired schoolteacher relaxing in Arizona thanks to a retirement account he established years ago is
   a.   attempting to create a favorable image of the company.
   b.   attempting to make a service look like a good.
   c.   using the promotion as a prospecting tool for sales representatives.
   d.   showing the tangible benefits of purchasing an intangible service.
   e.   increasing the importance of personal selling in the marketing mix.

48.   With which of the following is the service marketer typically more concerned than the goods marketer?
   a.   storage of the product.
   b.   continuing personal relationships between producers and users of the product.
   c.   relationships among intermediaries in the channel of distribution.
   d.   inventory cost and control problems.
   e.   transportation of product from source to point of delivery.

49.   Distribution channels for services are typically
   a.   simpler and shorter than those for goods.
   b.   longer and more complex than those for goods.
   c.   less personal and more institutional than those for goods.
   d.   agents or brokers.
   e.   characterized by extensive use of sophisticated materials handling equipment.

50.   Linking a service to a concrete image or symbol such as the insurance industry has done with its umbrellas, rocks, and blankets is an example of
   a.   creative presentation of a tangible product.
   b.   attempting to make services tangible.
   c.   how firms attempt to personalize their services.
   d.   the dehumanizing effect of promotion.
   e.   some really weird thinking; who really thinks of insurance companies in these terms?

Name _____   Instructor _____

Section _____   Date _____

Applying Marketing Concepts

John Alberts is a landscape architect who has been in practice some fifteen years. His clients are primarily large business firms, among them Integrity Outdoor Advertising Company, one of the nation's largest owners of billboards and other outdoor advertising displays. John is somewhat concerned because his contract with Integrity will expire soon, and he knows that he will be facing competition to continue the beautification of the land surrounding the company's billboards all over the Southeast. He knows that the executives of the company are very happy with his work, and he feels that they think of him as "their" architect. The other firms competing for the contract have sent in "sales teams" to try and convince Integrity to do business with them, and each executive has mentioned to John what a turnoff the presentations have been, dealing primarily with costs and only marginally with aesthetics. This has made him feel better, because he knows his prices are competitive, and the plantings he has provided to Integrity to carry out his designs have been only the best stock. Despite this, he knows he's going to have to be prepared to offer his very best as the renewal date approaches.

1. Clients who rent Integrity's billboards are purchasing
   a. a pure service or something very close to it.
   b. something which is predominantly a service with some goods included.
   c. something which mixes products and services in roughly equal proportions.
   d. something which is predominantly a product with a somewhat smaller service component.
   e. a pure good.

2. Given that Mr. Alberts provides the plantings which are used in his work of beautifying Integrity's billboard locations, his position on the goods-services continuum is
   a. at the service end; what he does is a pure service.
   b. certainly not a pure service; he is dealing in goods as well.
   c. well toward the goods end of the continuum; his services are a minor part of the total offering he's providing.
   d. at the goods end; his product is purely goods.
   e. at both ends; the services he provides are totally separate from whatever goods may be involved.

3. John is hoping to retain the contract because he feels that he is in a position to provide the one thing that the other competitors don't seem to have,
   a. size and scale of operations.
   b. effective sales personnel who can really hammer home a concept.
   c. the ability to do the job the company wants done.
   d. the ability to cut costs at every opportunity, doing an acceptable job at the lowest expenditure.
   e. a personal relationship with company executives and their trust in his relationship with him.

4. Judging by what you know of John's clients, how would you categorize the nature of his services?
   a. They are directed toward the industrial market and are people based.
   b. They are directed to the consumer market and are equipment based.
   c. They are industrially oriented and are equipment based.
   d. They are consumer oriented and are people based.
   e. They are consumer based and are performed by unskilled workers.

5. John's recognition that he's going to have to be prepared to offer his "very best" as the end of his current contract draws near implies
   a. that he feels he's going to have to bribe Integrity officials to secure renewal of his relationship with them.
   b. that he hopes to hit them with his very best designs just before his contract runs out.
   c. that John knows that he's going to have to negotiate with the Integrity people to secure a renewal of his contract.
   d. that John feels there's little hope his contract will be renewed.
   e. that he hasn't done a very good job for Integrity in the past.

Sally Smith, owner of Sally Forth, Inc., is assessing the progress of her new business venture, shopping for people who don't have time to shop for themselves. A phone call to Sally Forth with a request that a birthday present be bought for a six year old boy nephew and sent to the child's address can be fulfilled the same day the request is made. Sally Smith is quite pleased; she has had to hire five additional shoppers to handle the avalanche of requests for things that people need to buy but can't find time to go out and get. The twenty percent surcharge over the cost of any merchandise purchased doesn't seem to bother many of the people who call to request the service.

6. Sally Forth provides
   a. a consumer service that's equipment based.
   b. a business service that's people based.
   c. a consumer service that's people based.
   d. a business service that's equipment based.
   e. a business service with a product component.

7. The need for a service like Sally Forth grows out of changes in the
   a. economic environment.
   b. social/cultural environment.
   c. political/legal environment.
   d. technological environment.
   e. competitive environment.

8. If intended use were the basis, Sally Forth would be classed as a
   a. consumer convenience service.
   b. consumer specialty service.
   c. diversified consumer service.
   d. general business service.
   e. specialty business service.

Name _____ Instructor _____

Section _____ Date _____

Experiential Exercises

1. Get a small notebook and, for the space of two days, describe each service that you use. You may ride the bus, get a haircut, cash a check at the bank, or pick up your drycleaning. You may elect to create a table of uses for very frequently used services such as speaking on the telephone. At the end of the second day, fill in the information below.

    a. Total number of different services used:

    b. Most frequently used service:

        How many times was this service used?

    c. Pure services used: (List them)

    d. Mixed goods/services used: (List them)

2. Acquire a copy of a *Yellow Pages* Telephone Directory. Open the directory to a randomly-chosen page and, starting with the classification which opens or continues on the left-hand page, decide whether that and the next ninety-nine classifications list companies who provide predominantly goods or predominantly services. Report the results of your efforts below.

    a. Proportion of service providers:

    b. Proportion of goods providers:

3. Acquire a copy of a general-circulation magazine like *Time, U.S. News and World Report*, or *People*. Also get a copy of a business publication like *Business Week, Forbes*, or *Barrons*. Examine the display advertisements in both publications (display ads, for our purposes, are ads of a quarter-page or more in size). In each case,

    a. What is the total number of ads?

        General Circulation   _____

        Business   _____

    b. How many in each case are for services? for goods?

        General Circulation   Goods   _____   Services   _____

        Business   Goods   _____   Services   _____

    c. Are there differences in proportions between the two? If so, how would you account for them?

Name _____ Instructor _____

Section _____ Date _____

Computer Applications

1. Rinaldo Moto, Sp.A., of Livorno, Italy, a firm that specializes in the repair of small motorcycles, is considering the acquisition of a similar firm, Riparatura Mecanica, in Verona. the asking price for the Verona firm is £It. 1,000,000,000 (about $500,000). Mecanica currently earns a return of £It. 300,000,000 ($150,000) on annual revenues of about £It. 1,500,000,000 ($750,000). If the purchase were to be made, what would be the return on investment?

2. Leroy Terwilliger, owner and operator of Service Solicitations, a firm specializing in soliciting funds for charitable institutions, has received the assignment of soliciting St. Louis, Missouri, for the American Safe Homes Association. Mr. Terwilliger has determined that St. Louis contains a total of 575,000 households, of which some 55,000 he has classified as type A (high value contributor). Another 120,000 households have been determined to be in class B (medium value contributor), and the remaining 400,000 are in class C (low value contributor). Mr. Terwilliger estimates that contact with a high value contributor should take 20 minutes if a contribution is to be successfully solicited. It should be possible to realize a contribution from a class B contributor in 15 minutes, and from a class C household in ten. Mr. Terwilliger has 12 weeks to complete the solicitation. If Mr. Terwilliger's solicitors, each of whom works a 36 hour week, spends 50 percent of his or her time calling on designated accounts, 35 percent traveling, and the remaining 15 percent filling out reports, how many solicitors should Mr. Terwilliger assign to St. Louis?

3. The Milazzo Group, Inc., is a financial planning firm headquartered in Dallas. Jose Antonio Milazzo, the owner, realizes that he needs to develop a closer relationship with some of Dallas' 2,700 pension and profit sharing plan administrators than with others. He has broken the administrators down into three groups. The "A" group, administrators of plans with more than $10,000,000 invested, requires 30 minutes a week to serve each of its 300 members. The "B" group, of whom there are 800, are the administrators whose plans range in size between $5 and $10 million. They require 15 minutes a week. The "C" administrators, comprising the remaining 1,600 in the area, can be dealt with in five minutes each a week. Mr. Milazzo's financial counselors work 40 hour weeks and can devote 80 percent of their time to dealing with plan administrators, leaving 20 percent to handle paperwork. How many financial counselors are needed to handle the workload?

Crossword Puzzle for Chapter 12

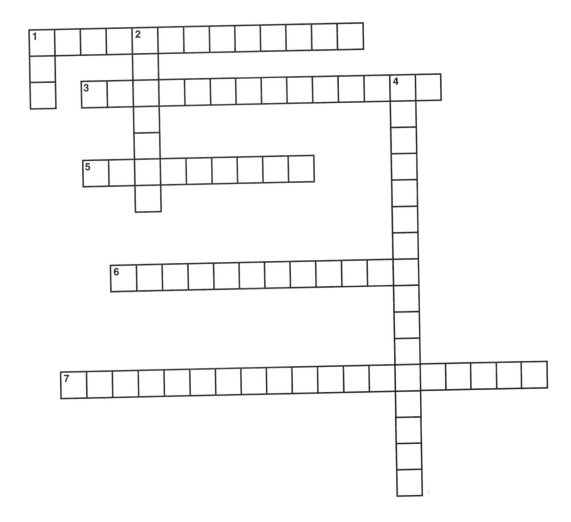

ACROSS CLUES

1. First name of continuum used to visualize similarities and differences between goods, services
3. Expected and perceived quality of a service offering
5. In terms of service, the actual interaction point between buyer and service provider
6. Ratio of output to input of goods and services in a region, an industry, or by individual workers
7. Buyer's trust in and satisfaction with a seller

DOWN CLUES

1. Difference between expected service quality and perceived service quality
2. An intangible task that satisfies consumer or business user needs
4. An industry involved in the production of services

WORD LIST:

ENCOUNTER
GAP
GOODSSERVICES
PRODUCTIVITY

RELATIONSHIPQUALITY
SERVICEQUALITY
SERVICE
TERTIARYINDUSTRY

Chapter 12 Solutions

Key Concepts

1.	g	5.	b
2.	c	6.	a
3.	d	7.	e
4.	f	8.	h

Self Quiz

1.	F	11.	T	21.	F	31.	d	41.	c
2.	T	12.	F	22.	T	32.	b	42.	e
3.	T	13.	F	23.	T	33.	a	43.	a
4.	T	14.	T	24.	F	34.	c	44.	c
5.	F	15.	T	25.	T	35.	e	45.	e
6.	F	16.	F	26.	b	36.	b	46.	d
7.	T	17.	T	27.	a	37.	d	47.	b
8.	T	18.	T	28.	d	38.	a	48.	d
9.	F	19.	F	29.	e	39.	e	49.	a
10.	F	20.	T	30.	c	40.	c	50.	b

Applying Marketing Concepts

1.	a	5.	c
2.	b	6.	c
3.	e	7.	b.
4.	a	8.	a

Computer Applications

1. ROI = Net profit/Amount Invested = $150,000/$500,000 = 30%

    Alternatively, ROI = Net profit/sales x sales/investment =

    $150,000/$750,000 x $750,000/$500,000 =

    30%

2. Class A =   55,000 households
    Class B =   120,000 households
    Class C =   400,000 households

    Time required: 55,000   x 20 minutes = 1,100,000 min.
                     120,000   x 15 minutes = 1,800,000 min.
                     400,000   x 10 minutes = 4,000,000 min.
    The total time required = 6,900,000 min. or 115,000 hours

    Time available from each solicitor:

    36 hours x .50 x 12 = 216 hours

    Number of solicitors required = 115,000/216 = 532.4 = 533

3. Class A =   300 administrators
    Class B =   800 administrators
    Class C =   1,600 administrators

    Total time: 300 x   30 min. =   9,000 min. or 150 hrs./week
                   800 x   15 min. = 12,000 min. or 200 hrs./week
                  1600 x   5 min. = 8,000 min. or 133.33 hrs./week
    for a grand total of 483.33 hrs./week

    Time available from each financial counselor:

    40 hours x .80 = 32 hours per week.

    Number of personnel needed: 483.33/32 = 15.10 = 16

Crossword Puzzle Solution

Name   _____   Instructor   _____

Section   _____   Date   _____

Cases for Part 4

1. *Ontario Chemicals and Coatings, Ltd.*

Louis Sherbrooke, product manager for Ontario Chemicals and Coatings, was wondering what to do with one of the firm's new products, Tempadhere. Tempadhere, an adhesive designed for use as a temporary "tacking agent" to hold large sheets of steel in alignment for final assembly by welding, had recently been developed by OCC as a by-product of one of its major chemical processes. The product had tremendous holding power, which was its major advantage over other tacking agents used in the metal fabrication industry.

The product had been on the market only a couple of weeks when complaints began to pour in from dissatisfied users. The apparent problem was that the product worked too well! Users found that it was exceedingly difficult to remove from their weldments once fabrication had been completed, interfering with further processing and assembly. "Well, it looks like we're going to have to pull Tempadhere off the market," said Richard Hartmann, vice-president of production for OCC. "Surely we can find other uses for such a product."

Question:

What was this company's definition of a product? How does this differ from the definition with which you have become familiar in this course?

2. *Little People Toys*

Little People Toys are high quality products marketed throughout the United States and Canada. They are usually sold in specialty toy stores and in a few of the best department stores.

Since prices in toy shops are normally higher than prices in the usual toy outlets, big people who shop in toy shops are usually more interested in quality and service than in price. Research evidence gathered by Little People suggests that most people who have made a purchase of a Little People toy continue to buy the Little People brand when they purchase toys in the future.

Question:

What kind of consumer goods are represented by the Little People line of toys? Why do you suppose this is so?

3. *Maldinado Manufacturing Company*

Recent years have seen a number of financial crises at Maldinado Manufacturing because the company seems to be unable to introduce new products in timely fashion. Competitors always seem to introduce the innovations and Maldinado ends up copying these products. By the time Maldinado has a product ready to go into the marketplace, competitors are already well established with their innovations and Maldinado is forced to compete mainly on a price basis.

In the past, Vito Maldinado, the company's president, had depended on the sales and production staffs to come up with new product ideas. Those who had ideas got temporary relief from some of their other duties to see their ideas through actual development and marketing.

This procedure had caused problems. Not only did it move workloads around, it also resulted in no one having the ultimate responsibility for developing new products. Vito knows something must be done soon, so he is trying to create a better way to assign the responsibility for new product development within his organization.

Question:

How can Mr. Maldinado assure that someone is responsible for developing new products?

4. CBS, Incorporated[1]

In October, 1987, CBS, Incorporated, in cooperation with the U.S. Product Safety Commission, announced a voluntary recall and replacement of the plastic bodies of its "Clippety Clop," "Comanche," and "Colt" ride-on toy "Wonder" horses because the plastic body might break during use.

CBS had received 105 complaints that the body of the toy had broken without warning while being ridden, causing the rider to fall suddenly. Forty of these incidents resulted in injuries such as cuts, scrapes, and bruises.

Over 114,000 of these ride-on toys, produced and distributed to retailers between March 1984 and May 1986, had been sold nationally for approximately $60 each. The defective toys had been produced prior to June 1986 by the Wonder Unit of CBS Toys. Only toys with control numbers (stamped on the belly) of 86206 or less were affected.

Consumers were warned to *immediately* stop using the toy and retailers were warned to remove affected toys from sale. A toll-free number was provided for questions concerning replacement of the product and identification of potentially defective items.

A statement from the Consumer Products Safety Commission, attached to the recall document, read in part "an estimated 325 million potentially hazardous products have been called back from the marketplace and consumers since 1973 (when CPSC was created). Most of these were voluntarily recalled by manufacturers, who established programs to repair or replace the products, or to refund the purchase price."

Questions:

a. What is the significance of the voluntary recall of these products by CBS, Inc.? Relate product liability to the recall.

---

[1]Abstracted from "CBS 'Wonder' Spring Ride-on Horses Recalled," A *Consumer Product SAFETY ALERT*, Washington: U.S. Consumer Product Safety Commission), October 1987.

b.   How significant do you suppose pressure brought to bear by the CPSC was in causing CBS to issue the recall?

5. *Industrial Health Services*

Al Newman is thinking of leaving Industrial Health services and setting up his own industrial medical clinic. For the last seven years, Dr. Newman has been the medical director and examining physician for IHS, which specializes in examining managerial personnel of local businesses.

These examinations are usually carried out in the manager's office. Some firms have their executives examined every two years as a matter of course, others when they are applying for an increase in life or medical insurance benefits for their employees.

Over the last seven years, Dr. Newman has gotten to know a number of the high-level executives of numerous local firms and feels that they would come with him rather than remain with IHS if he should leave. He knows, though, that IHS is a large firm with a good local and regional reputation in this somewhat specialized field. He is wondering whether the move which he is contemplating would be a wise one.

Questions

a.   What are some of the characteristics of the market for services which make Dr. Newman's idea potentially viable?

b.   What are some of the characteristics of the market for services that make Dr. Newman's idea potentially risky?

6.   *Seagull Computer Corporation*

Seagull Computer Corporation was started in 1987 in Sam Seagull's garage in West Charlotte, North Carolina. In the beginning, the majority of Sam's customers were people who had read his ads in publications like *Computer Shopper* and *PC Source* magazines and ordered by mail. The first year's sales totaled $100,000, which represented 41 units. There are literally thousands of direct selling microcomputer assemblers in the United States, most of which produce "IBM clones." These are machines which emulate the behavior of an IBM micro but are typically sold at a lower price.

Sam's computers were and are no exception. In fact, they are about as indistinguishable from other clones as peas in a pod in terms of design, features, and price. Sam decided, however, that he was going to be like Marshall Field and not just give lip service to the idea that "the customer is always right," but make sure that his customers were. Sam installed a 24-hour a day WATTS line staffed with trained computer *users*, not technicians (though those were available as backup if the users couldn't help.) This line, called the HELP! number, would answer *any* question from *any* Seagull purchaser about *any* problem they might be having with their machine. The HELP! operators would bend over backward to be of assistance, even repeating procedures step-by-step over and over if necessary. If the problem proved to be a bad part, a new one was sent out immediately by Federal Express or the customer was advised where to take their unit for repair, depending on their desire and the terms of their warranty. Though it wasn't publicized, Seagull often made good on components on which the warranty had expired or helped customers by assembling special cables for them—free of charge. In the meantime, Seagull Computers continued to be built with good components and at a level of technology compatible with that of the industry as a whole. Though Sam continued to advertise as before, many new customers said they had been sold by people who already owned Seagull computers.

1993's sales were $1,220,000,000 (555,000 units) and the firm hired its 2000th employee on May 14th. Sam Seagull expressed pleasure at his company's success by throwing a major party for employees, customers, and the community.

Questions

a. Where would you position Seagull Computer Corporation on the goods/services continuum? Justify your answer.

b. Outline the segmentation strategy you believe this firm to be using.

Name _____ Instructor _____

Section _____ Date _____

Creating a Marketing Plan: Where Do We Go From Here?

The information you will receive in this part will help you to complete all of Part II of your marketing plan for Latebri Industries, Incorporated.

Episode Four

As episode four begins, we find our young entrepreneurs discussing their long-term plans for the company. They are examining their resources, and attempting to match the potential in the marketplace to their abilities and potentials. They quickly recognized that the potential for the kind of service they planned to offer was quite substantial. If the information they had was correct, then the potential in the local market could be as much as $18,200,000 per year, growing at a rate of somewhere between 14 and 33% per annum. Their resources, on the other hand, were limited to the $150,000 they had on hand, plus their own educations and talents.

Meanwhile, there were already 42 potentially active competitors in the market, with some 102 others who might someday pose a threat. On the other hand, many of these potential competitors had displayed little marketing "savvy" to the partners when they had conducted their market survey.

Laura was the first to speak. "Listen, guys," said she, "we have to set some kind of goals for ourselves or we won't have anything to work toward. What do you say we start with the long run and work our way back to the present? I figure that, if we play our cards right, we can hold onto at least one percent of the market in five years. What do you think? That would be at least $300,000 in volume by then. Do you think we can get that big a market share? We'd have to do at least $100,000 this year and grow by at least 32 percent a year to get there in five years."

"Do you think that's aiming high enough?" asked Terry. "We've got to get this operation going, which we know is going to cost at least $110,000 if we do it right. We're sure to lose money unless we get a pretty big chunk of the market pretty quick."

"On the other hand," said Brian, "if we aim too high and don't achieve our goals, we may think we've failed when we're really doing well. I figure that we'd be better off looking at bottom line profits rather than share of the market. I think we ought to look to make at least ten percent profit on sales."

"Look," said Laura, "I'll agree with both of you. I sure hope we can latch on to one percent of this market. I hope we can make ten percent on sales. But remember, we have to do this the customer's way. I think we should be open 24 hours a day, seven days a week. That should give us a real advantage over the other companies in the market. Sure, it'll cost a little more at first, but we'll build customer loyalty and probably generate more up-front money from maintenance contracts that way. Besides, I think we're all being too conservative. Remember, we're going *after* this market, not just giving it lip service. We really should expect to lose money for the next couple of years. But we'll be offering people what they need, and it's sure to pay off in the long run."

Guidelines:

a.   Where are Laura, Terry, and Brian getting the figures they are using in these discussions?

b.   Remember that a lot of what happens depends on how actively our heroes pursue their business. Enthusiasm and dedication do count, if the market offers sufficient potential in the first place. Summarize their objectives and complete Parts II. A., II. B., and II. C. in your marketing plan.

Solutions to Cases for Part 4

1. Ontario Chemicals and Coatings, Ltd.

This company is obviously a "product-oriented" firm. Stuck with a by-product which happened to be uniquely sticky, the firm tried to dispose of it by adapting it to a use for which it was not suited. This firm would probably define a product as "something we can sell to customers."

A firm should, in fact, be marketing oriented. Instead of merely trying to get rid of a by-product, they should examine it from a marketing point of view—a view toward satisfying needs. Such a view would have led to the pretesting of this product before its introduction and apparent failure, and the failure could have been avoided.

2. Little People Toys

The Little People line are specialty consumer goods. Since customers who have once purchased these toys continue to buy them, they fall into the specialty goods category.

3. Maldinado Manufacturing Company

There are four alternative strategies which can be used to approach the problem of new product development: (1) a new-product committee, (2) a new product department, (3) product management, and (4) venture teams.

The problems experienced by Maldinado are typical of those experienced by firms which haven't recognized the need for establishing specific methods for locating the responsibility for new product development. New product development plays such a vital role in keeping an organization alive that it is hard to overemphasize the need to establish a formal set of procedures for evaluating new products and for locating the responsibility for this function in an enterprise.

4. CBS, Incorporated

a. A failure rate of 105 items out of a production run of 14,000 is rather high by today's standards. Though representing less than 1/10 of one percent of output, such a rate of failure is unacceptable, especially where children are involved. Children are defenseless, and a product which offers the possibility of harming a child is an unacceptable product on its face. "Wonder" horses, in one guise or another, have been in production for at least 25 years and enjoy a well-deserved reputation as a sturdy, simple toy which will last for a very long time. This is a classic case of a totally no-win situation, regardless of whether the manufacturer is concerned for ethical reasons or not. A lawsuit brought by the parent of an injured child is just exactly the kind of thing which can destroy a firm's reputation, not to mention generating costs far in excess of the cost of a product recall of this type. It is obvious that this action *had* to be taken. One might question whether CBS acted quickly enough, and in fact it seems that they might have, because they modified the mold in which these bodies were cast in April of 1986, but we don't know *all* the facts in the case and can't really draw that conclusion.

b. It does not appear that CPSC pressure had very much to do with the recall. The phrasing of the notices infers that manufacturers have been rather cooperative with the CPSC in recalling potentially dangerous products. Moreover, it was mentioned that CBS Toys had received the 105 complaints, not the CPSC, which might well lead one to believe that CBS was the instigator of the action, not CPSC. CPSC does, in fact, provide an excellent avenue for manufacturers who discover a potentially dangerous defect in a product to get the word to consumers and dealers quickly, efficiently, and cheaply. The CPSC's *SAFETY ALERTS* receive wide distribution to pediatricians, toy stores, and others concerned with child safety.

5. Industrial Health Services

The characteristic of service most likely to work in Dr. Newman's favor is also one which may make the move risky: the inseparability of the service and the service-provider. If, indeed, the people whom he has examined over the last seven years think of him as the service-provider and speak for their companies, he may do quite well. If, on the other hand, they think of IHS as the service-provider, he may find himself with no business at all. This characteristic of services is related to their intangibility. It is possible that Dr. Newman may benefit or suffer, as well, from the difficulties with service standardization. If he can approach the companies with something they see as better for their purposes, or give them the same thing at a lower price, he may do well. But he's going to have to work very hard to demonstrate that he is, in fact, capable of doing exactly what he has been doing these last seven years. Then, he was IHS; now, he's Dr. Al Newman. There could be a perceived difference between the two.

6. Seagull Computer Corporation

a. Seagull Computer Corporation is certainly selling a combination of goods and services, so it is not at one extreme or other of the continuum. On the other hand, it looks like Sam Seagull's devotion to customer satisfaction positions the company more significantly toward the service end of the continuum than its competitors. A clone is, after all, a clone, but a clone with a high level of customer commitment is another thing entirely. One would suspect from the mention of word-of-mouth and from the rapid growth of company sales that the service provided by Seagull is of a much higher order than is typical in the mail-order microcomputer industry. In short, what we have here is a company which has used a commitment to service to change an otherwise undistinguished product into one with quite a good reputation.

b. Microcomputers sold by mail are still usually sold to commercial/industrial users. Seagull's use of publications like *Computer Shopper* and *PC Source* is consistent with the idea that it is seeking a market that sees the microcomputer as a tool, rather than as an entertainment product or a toy. Not all industrial or commercial users of computers are large corporations with large numbers of micros in service. Many are small, maybe even one-person operations that need computer support of their operations, but even more importantly need support for their computers. The evidence suggests that Seagull's segment of the market is professional individuals and small businesses with one or perhaps a few micros that are used as tools by people whose interest is in having them available when needed, as needed, with a minimum of hassle.

Solutions for Creating a Marketing Plan

Episode Four

a.   The partners are getting their figures from the data given in this episode as well as information from previous episodes. Their estimate of a repair market for PCs of $18,200,000 in the local area was based on the $3.5 billion estimate for the national market multiplied by New Essex' proportion of that population, some 0.52%. The $300,000 projection for one percent of the market five years hence was arrived at by compounding $182,000 (currently one percent of the market) at 14 percent for five years, the current year being uncompounded, and is actually $307,390. This is a very lowball or conservative estimate of market potential, as using the projected rate of growth for "office automation" repair would generate a volume prediction of some $569,500 for the fifth year hence. Laura's comment about doing $100,000 this year and growing at a rate of 32% to achieve the $300,000 volume derives from the same source: her assumption of $100,000 in volume this year and $300,000 in five years.

b.   It appears that our heroes have decided that their objectives are to be one percent of the market in five years and a rate of profitability of ten percent on sales at the end of that time. They recognize that, in the meantime, they are likely to lose money for a few years to come, but they are prepared to do so in order for their firm ultimately to succeed. Their business philosophy seems very marketing oriented, with a 24 hour a day operation envisioned. They want their customers to be happy with their service and hope to build customer loyalty which will ultimately result in the writing of a lot of service contracts. Later information may call for revision of the objectives and policies set at this point in the plan.

Part 5

Distribution Strategy

Distribution strategy, the method used to put the product in the possession of the consumer at the right time and place, is an integral part of marketing strategy. Product, price, and promotion, are all related to distribution strategy as part of the marketing mix.

A distribution channel may be a single transaction between producer and ultimate user or an extremely complex set of interrelationships including several successive independent firms taking title to goods or assisting in the transfer of title to those goods. Dual channels are often used to match product availability to the needs of users. "Reverse" channels have had to be developed to handle product recalls, warranty service, and returnable containers.

The institutions which are involved in marketing channels include producers, wholesaling intermediaries, retailers, and facilitating agencies. The marketing channel begins with the producer, who often must actively seek wholesaling intermediaries and retailers to distribute the product. The producer must be prepared to compensate and otherwise to motivate the others to perform their functions in an effective manner. Producers often have a choice of several alternative channels to use and must devise strategies to gain acceptance of their product.

Wholesaling intermediaries include manufacturer-owned facilities, independent individuals and firms that take title to goods or assist in the passage of title from producers to retailers or business users, and retailer-owned cooperatives and buying offices. Manufacturer-owned facilities include sales branches, sales offices, trade fairs, and merchandise marts.

Among the independents, merchant wholesalers actually take title to the goods they intend to sell. They thus engage in speculative buying in the hope that purchasers will be found. Merchant wholesalers develop long-term relationships with manufacturers and retailers or industrial users.

Agents and brokers are independent wholesaling middlemen who perform primarily a selling function. There are five types: commission merchants, auction houses, brokers, selling agents, and manufacturers' agents.

Products may be made available in the marketplace through channels providing intensive, selective, or exclusive distribution. Regardless of the desired level of intensity of distribution, the type of channel used will play a significant role in channel strategy. The battle for channel captaincy—a dominant position in the channel—has resulted in development and resolution of a number of types of channel conflicts. Now, in addition to the traditional, loosely organized channel, there are three classes of vertical marketing systems (VMS) which can be used. These three types include the corporate, administered, and contractual VMSs.

Retailers buy for resale to the ultimate consumer. Numerous types of retailers exist. Retailing changes in an evolutionary process as products, institutional structures, and consumer buying habits change. Because of this, at any given point in time there may be a number of different forms of retail institutions in existence competing

382 Part 5 Distribution Strategy

for the same consumer market. Many recent trends in retailing, such as scrambled merchandising, hypermarkets, planned shopping centers, and teleshopping, are evidence that retailers are attempting to provide consumers with increased shopping convenience.

Physical distribution is the mechanism which facilitates the operation of marketing channels. It is certainly not enough that title is transferred from manufacturer to wholesaler to retailer, it is also necessary that product move from source to ultimate user. Physical distribution functions, usually through facilitating agencies, to move, store, and keep track of the product as it transits from producer through the channel of distribution to the ultimate user. These functions must be performed in a timely, efficient, and effective manner. The objective is to achieve a stated level of customer service at least total overall cost. The physical distribution manager chooses from among alternative transportation, warehousing, inventory control, order processing, and materials handling methods to achieve this objective.

© 1995 by The Dryden Press. All rights reserved.

Chapter 13

Channel Strategy and Wholesaling

Chapter Outline

You may want to use the following outline as a guide in taking notes.

I. Chapter Overview—How Do Products Get From Manufacturer to Ultimate User?

II. Distribution Channels

    A. The role of distribution channels in marketing strategy

    B. Wholesaling intermediaries

    C. Types of distribution channels

    D. Dual distribution

    E. Reverse channels

III. Types of Wholesaling Intermediaries

    A. Manufacturer-owned facilities

    B. Independent wholesaling intermediaries

IV. Retailer-owned Cooperatives and Buying Offices

V. Channel Leadership

    A. The battle for shelf space

    B. Channel conflict

    C. The gray market

VI. Channel Strategy Decisions

    A. Selection of a distribution channel

VII.   Determining Distribution Intensity

    A. Intensive distribution

    B. Selective distribution

    C. Exclusive distribution

VIII.   Vertical Marketing Systems

    A. Corporate system

    B. Administered system

    C. Contractual system

Name _____ Instructor _____

Section _____ Date _____

Key Concepts

The purpose of this section is to allow you to determine if you can match key concepts with their definitions. It is essential that you know the definitions of the concepts prior to applying the concepts in later exercises in this chapter.

From the list of lettered terms, select the one that best fits each of the numbered statements below. Write the letter of that choice in the space provided.

Key Terms

a. distribution channel
b. marketing intermediary
c. wholesaler
d. wholesaling intermediary
e. direct selling
f. direct marketing
g. business distributor
h. dual distribution
i. reverse channel
j. sales branch
k. sales office
l. trade fair
m. merchandise mart
n. merchant wholesaler
o. rack jobber
p. cash-and-carry wholesaler
q. truck wholesaler
r. drop shipper
s. mail-order wholesaler
t. agents and broker

u. commission merchant
v. auction house
w. broker
x. selling agent
y. manufacturer's agent
z channel captain
aa. slotting allowances
ab. gray goods
ac. intensive distribution
ad. selective distribution
ae. exclusive distribution
af. exclusive-dealing agreement
ag. closed sales territory
ah. tying agreement
ai. vertical marketing system
aj. corporate marketing system
ak. administered marketing system
al. contractual marketing system
am. franchise

_____ 1. Agent wholesaling intermediary that takes possession of goods when they are shipped to a central market for sale, acts as the producer's agent, and collects an agreed-upon fee at the time of sale.

_____ 2. Limited-function merchant wholesaler that performs most wholesaling functions except financing and delivery.

_____ 3. Establishment maintained by a manufacturer that serves as a warehouse for a particular sales region, thereby duplicating the services of independent wholesalers; carries inventory and processes orders to customers from available stock.

_____ 4. Agent wholesaling intermediary that does not take title to or possession of goods and whose primary function is to bring buyers and sellers together.

_____ 5. Marketing intermediary in a business channel.

_____ 6. Agent wholesaling intermediary responsible for the marketing program of a firm's product line.

_____ 7. Arrangement between a marketing intermediary and a manufacturer that requires the intermediary to carry the manufacturer's full product line in exchange for an exclusive dealership.

_____   8.   Direct communication, other than personal sales contacts, between buyer and seller.

_____   9.   VMS in which channel coordination is achieved through the exercise of power by a dominant channel member.

_____   10.   Full-function merchant wholesaler that markets specialized lines of merchandise to retail stores and provides the services of merchandising and arrangement of goods, pricing, maintenance, and stocking of display racks.

_____   11.   Dominant and controlling member of a marketing channel.

_____   12.   Fees paid by manufacturers to retailers for shelf space.

_____   13.   Arrangement between a manufacturer and a marketing intermediary that prohibits the intermediary from handling competing product lines.

_____   14.   Comprehensive term describing both wholesalers and agents and brokers.

_____   15.   Path that goods follow from consumers back to the manufacturer.

_____   16.   Establishment that brings buyers and sellers together in one location for the purpose of permitting buyers to examine merchandise before purchase.

_____   17.   Policy in which a firm chooses only a limited number of retailers to handle its product line.

_____   18.   Policy in which a firm grants exclusive rights to a wholesaler or retailer to sell in a particular geographic area.

_____   19.   VMS characterized by formal arrangements among channel members.

_____   20.   Restricted geographic selling region specified by a manufacturer for its distributors.

_____   21.   Business firm, either wholesale or retail, that operates between the producer and the consumer or business user, sometimes called a middleman.

_____   22.   Independent wholesaling intermediaries that may or may not take possession of goods but never take title to them.

_____   23.   Policy in which the manufacturer of a convenience item attempts to saturate the market.

_____   24.   VMS in which there is single ownership of each stage in the distribution channel.

_____   25.   Limited-function merchant wholesaler that receives orders from customers and forwards them to producers who ship directly to the customers.

_____   26.   Network in which a firm uses more than one distribution channel to reach its target market.

_____   27.   Direct sale contact between buyer and seller.

_____   28.   Wholesaling intermediary also called a jobber or distributor.

_____   29.   Contractual arrangement in which a wholesaler or retailer (the franchisee) agrees to meet the operating requirements of a manufacturer or other franchiser.

_____   30.   Goods manufactured under licenses abroad and then sold in the U.S. market in competition with their U.S.-produced counterparts.

_____   31.   Preplanned distribution channel organized to be cost-effective and achieve improved distribution efficiency.

_____   32.   Periodic show at which manufacturers in a particular industry display wares for visiting retail and wholesale buyers.

_____   33.   Agent wholesaling intermediary who represents a number of manufacturers of related but noncompeting products and receives a commission.

_____   34.   Limited-function merchant wholesaler that utilizes catalogs instead of a salesforce to contact customers in an attempt to reduce transportation costs.

_____   35.   Wholesaling intermediary that takes title to the goods it handles.

_____   36.   Manufacturer's establishment that serves as a regional office for salespeople but does not carry inventory.

_____   37.   Entity consisting of marketing institutions and their interrelationships responsible for the physical and title flow of goods and services from producer to consumer or industrial user.

_____   38.   Limited-function merchant wholesaler that markets perishable food items.

_____   39.   Permanent exhibition facility in which manufacturers rent showrooms to display products for visiting retail and wholesale buyers, designers, and architects.

Name _____   Instructor _____

Section _____   Date _____

Self Quiz

You should use these questions to test your understanding of the chapter material. You can check your answers with those provided at the end of the chapter.

While these questions cover most of the chapter topics, they are not intended to be the same as the test questions your instructor may use in an examination. A good understanding of all aspects of the course material is essential to good performance on any examination.

True/False

Write "T" for True and "F" for False for each of the following statements.

_____ 1. One of the functions of a distribution channel is to adjust discrepancies in assortment by the process of sorting.

_____ 2. Distribution channels play a key role in the creation of form, time, and possession utility.

_____ 3. Possession utility is created only when title to the goods passes from the producer or the intermediary to the purchaser.

_____ 4. Marketing intermediaries facilitate the exchange process by reducing the number of marketplace contacts.

_____ 5. Direct channels of distribution are much more important in the consumer market than in the business market.

_____ 6. Small retailers rely on wholesalers as buying specialists that ensure a balanced inventory of goods produced in various parts of the world.

_____ 7. Agent wholesalers are typically used in industries where there are a large number of small producers; their primary function is to bring buyers and sellers together.

_____ 8. The producer to agent to business user channel is typically used when the unit of sale of a product is small and the cost of product transportation is relatively high.

_____ 9. Distribution channels for not-for-profit organizations tend to be long, complex, and indirect.

_____ 10. Dual distribution occurs when a manufacturer uses more than one wholesaler or retailer in any given market to reach the selected target market segment.

_____ 11. If a state or the federal government should pass a law requiring the use of returnable bottles for beer and soft drinks, it would be forcing the creation of a reverse channel of distribution.

_____ 12. Retailers are becoming more likely to become channel captains these days as large retail chains assume traditional wholesaling functions and may even dictate design specifications to manufacturers.

_____ 13. When marketing intermediaries are used by service firms, they are usually agents or brokers.

_____ 14. Horizontal conflict within a distribution channel occurs when members of the channel at different levels, such as wholesalers and retailers, disagree.

_____ 15. Retailers' practice of demanding fees for stocking new products is called "reverse charge-off."

_____ 16. Exclusive-dealing agreements, closed sales territories, and tying agreements are per se illegal — that is, illegal in and of themselves.

_____ 17. A tying agreement is a contract between a manufacturer and a wholesaler or retailer which prohibits the retailer or wholesaler from carrying competing products.

_____ 18. Retailers are prohibited from buying gray market goods because foreign licensees have no right to sell outside the countries for which the license was granted.

_____ 19. A wholesaler is a wholesaling intermediary, but not all wholesaling intermediaries are wholesalers.

_____ 20. Wholesaling intermediaries successfully transfer the risk-taking function to other members of the channel of distribution, bearing little of it themselves.

_____ 21. Some, but not all, wholesaling intermediaries assume the inventory function and its associated costs.

_____ 22. Large retailers that bypass wholesalers and deal directly with manufacturers make the functions previously performed by wholesaling intermediaries unnecessary.

_____ 23. It is not unusual for a wholesaler to earn as little as 1.5 percent net profit as a percent of net sales.

_____ 24. "Value-added services" is another factor that has contributed to the reduction in wholesale profit margins because it represents a cost to wholesaling intermediaries not offset by revenue.

_____ 25. The basic distinction between a manufacturer's sales office and a sales branch is that the sales office carries inventory and the sales branch does not.

_____ 26. When they serve the business market, full-function merchant wholesalers usually market machinery, inexpensive accessory equipment, and supplies.

_____ 27. Rack jobbers are limited-function merchant wholesalers because they have restricted their activities to certain specialized types of merchandise.

_____ 28. Auction houses bring buyers and sellers together, operating in businesses such as frozen foods, real estate, and used machinery, where there are a large number of small suppliers and purchasers.

_____ 29. Drop shippers typically operate in industries where goods are bulky and customers typically make purchases in carload lots.

_____ 30. Brokers can serve as a reliable channel for manufacturers seeking regular, continuing service because their ability to "make a market" places them in a unique position in the wholesale marketplace.

_____ 31. If a manufacturer decides to use a selling agent to handle its merchandise, it should realize that the selling agent will typically assume full control of its marketing program.

_____ 32. Manufacturers' agents differ from selling agents in that a manufacturer's agent takes the entire output of its principal, while the selling agent usually is only one of a number of such intermediaries being used by that manufacturer.

_____ 33. In recent years, brokers and agents have improved their performance to such an extent that they are expected to have captured about 65 percent of the wholesale market by the year 1998.

Multiple Choice

Circle the letter of the word or phrase that best completes the sentence or answers the question.

34. In the industrial market, you would expect most installations and accessory equipment to be sold
   a. directly from producer to ultimate user.
   b. to the ultimate user through wholesalers.
   c. through agents who sell to wholesalers who then sell to the ultimate user.
   d. directly through agents to the ultimate user.
   e. by retailers direct to the ultimate user.

35. The so-called "traditional" channel of distribution for consumer goods involves
    a. distribution by a producer through wholesalers and retailers to the consumer.
    b. distribution by a producer through retailers to the consumer.
    c. only a producer and the ultimate user of the product.
    d. manufacturers, agents, wholesalers, and retailers.
    e. distribution by producers to the user through wholesalers and agents.

36. Which of the following would be a reverse channel of distribution?
    a. A manufacturer ships high style clothing direct to a retailer.
    b. A supermarket receives returnable bottles from consumers and ships them back to the bottling plant to be sterilized and refilled.
    c. A manufacturer of industrial installations custom-designs a metal stamping plant for Kaiser Industries.
    d. The Electromatic Corporation supplies the State of Delaware with a complete traffic control system for the City of Wilmington.
    e. Your little brother sets up a stand in front of the house and, using lemons and sugar he's filched from the pantry, becomes a small businessman selling lemonade to passersby.

37. A dual distribution system is best exemplified by
    a. the use of insurance companies to absorb some of the risks of doing business.
    b. creation of a channel of distribution to handle the return of recyclable materials to factories for reprocessing.
    c. the practice by some social welfare agencies of opening neighborhood offices to be more convenient to their clients.
    d. the use of its own sales force and a system of outside jobbers by a manufacturer of mechanics' tools.
    e. the action of an agent who brings together orange growers and wholesale grocers to create a market for fresh fruit.

38. In addition to their use as a device to facilitate recycling, reverse channels of distribution are often used
    a. for the distribution of services; intangible goods call for unique relationship between producer and ultimate user.
    b. in the industrial market for the distribution of high-tech products where a substantial degree of customization is required.
    c. for the handling of products which have been recalled by their maker or which must be returned to the factory for repairs.
    d. when a very short channel of distribution is called for by some characteristic of the product or the market.
    e by facilitating agencies to facilitate the performance of the services they render.

39. Of the following statements about channel captaincy, which is most true?
    a. Historically, the role of captain in the channel has tended to be filled by the retailer, though in recent years wholesalers and manufacturers have increased their influence.
    b. Although the influence of wholesalers in the channel of distribution has been on the increase in recent years, they are still largely in the shadow of producers and retailers.
    c. Retailers are increasingly assuming the role of channel captain; their control of the limited space in their stores contributes to their power, as does the size and volume of retail chains.
    d. Manufacturers seldom fill the role of channel captain; the intense competition among them precludes any single one becoming particularly powerful.
    e. Wholesalers exercise perhaps the greatest amount of power of all possible participants in the distribution channel because only they have the ability to bring producer and user together.

40.   Slotting allowances are most often paid
    a.   by manufacturers if they want retailers to carry their new, relatively unknown and unresearched products.
    b.   by retailers to prevent maunfacturers from selling high-demand products to competitors.
    c.   by retailers who are so dependent on sales of a particular product that they'll pay a substantial premium to get it.
    d.   by manufacturers who are concerned that their permission to use a customer's warehouse space to store excess inventory will be revoked.
    e.   when shelf space is shifted from one brand to another even though they both sell at the same price.

41.   Which of the following is an example of vertical channel conflict?
    a.   conflict between two or more wholesalers
    b.   conflict among a group of retail florists
    c.   conflict among drug, variety, and discount stores all of which sell the same branded products
    d.   conflict between company-owned and independently-owned retail outlets in the same chain
    e.   conflict between manufacturers and retailers which develops when the retailers develop private brands

42.   The basic antidote to channel conflict is
    a.   strict enforcement of all legal and contractual provisions of the relationship among the members of the channel.
    b.   effective leadership of the channel by the channel captain to create the spirit of being members of the same organization among members of the channel.
    c.   for those members of the channel who don't agree with the way things are going to abandon that channel and start their own.
    d.   creation of an integrated, single-company controlled channel from production to retail sale to prevent any conflict.
    e.   dissolution of the channel by the channel captain; conflict can never be overcome, only contained.

43.   A firm with a broad product line is usually able to sell directly to retailers or industrial users because
    a.   it has enough items in its line to publish a catalog.
    b.   larger total sales permit selling costs to be spread over a variety of products.
    c.   it can afford more sales representatives than can a limited line producer.
    d.   buyers like to do business with big companies that can easily satisfy their needs.
    e.   it does not need a large number of customers to survive.

44.   Among the market factors which determine the structure of a distribution channel is
    a.   the perishability of the product.
    b.   the product's requirement for regular service.
    c.   whether the product is designed for the consumer or the industrial market.
    d.   the fact that a producer who is financially strong can hire its own sales force.
    e.   that the single-product firm often discovers that direct selling is an unaffordable luxury.

45.   Some firms are forced to develop unique distribution channels because
    a.   independent marketing intermediaries do not adequately promote their offerings.
    b.   there is such a small market for their offerings that intermediaries refuse to handle them.
    c.   they wish to hold onto the lion's share of the profits from their products.
    d.   their products are so unique that no one exists to deal in them.
    e.   they have such a bad reputation as suppliers that intermediaries will not handle their products.

46. Which of the following is most true of exclusive distribution?
    a. Some market coverage may be sacrificed by choosing this policy, but the loss is offset by the image of quality and prestige which is created.
    b. Mass coverage and low unit prices make the use of wholesalers almost mandatory with this policy.
    c. The firm reduces total marketing costs and establishes better working relationships within the channel by choosing this policy.
    d. Adoption of this policy allows the consumer to buy the product with a minimum of effort.
    e. Cooperative advertising can be used for mutual benefit and marginal retailers can be avoided.

47. An exclusive-dealing agreement
    a. restricts the geographical territory of each of a producer's distributors.
    b. requires that a dealer who wishes to become the exclusive dealer for a producer's products to also carry other products of that producer.
    c. is legal if the producer's or dealer's sales volume represents a substantial percentage of total sales in the market area.
    d. prohibits the distributors from opening new facilities or marketing the manufacturer's products outside their assigned territories.
    e. prohibits a marketing intermediary from handling competing products.

48. Tying agreements are illegal when
    a. they lessen competition.
    b. they are horizontal in nature.
    c. they limit the geographical territory in which the product may be sold.
    d. they tie the marketing intermediary to the producer or service provider by not allowing that intermediary to carry competing products.
    e. they are required by producers as assurance that the marketing intermediary will devote total concentration to the producer's product line.

49. If a group of retailers were to start their own wholesaling operation, purchasing ownership shares in it and agreeing to buy a minimum percentage of their inventory from it, they would have created
    a. a corporate marketing system.
    b. a retail cooperative.
    c. a wholesaler-sponsored voluntary chain.
    d. an administered marketing system.
    e. a franchise system.

50. Wholesaling involves the activities of persons or firms that
    a. sell in significant amounts to ultimate consumers.
    b. deal largely with retailers.
    c. sell primarily to business users.
    d. do the majority of their business with other wholesale intermediaries.

51. In the most technical sense, the term "wholesaler"
    a. should be applied only to merchant wholesale intermediaries.
    b. applies across the board to all those institutions that are intermediaries in the channel of distribution.
    c. can be applied only to full-service marketing intermediaries.
    d. should be used only to describe a firm that deals in business goods.
    e. cannot be used to describe a firm that does not offer credit to its customers.

52. In a channel of distribution which includes eight manufacturers and 20 retailers, the presence of a single wholesaler would reduce the number of transactions needed to satisfy demand from
    a. 112 to 32.
    b. 160 to 28.
    c. 80 to 32.
    d. 240 to 96.
    e. 120 to 24.

53. The marketing function being performed by wholesalers when they provide their customers with new product specifications and communicate to manufacturers about the market acceptance of their offerings is
    a. buying.
    b. financing.
    c. risk taking.
    d. providing market information.
    e. reducing market contacts between manufacturers and end users.

54. Which of the following states the fundamental principle of marketing which applies to channel decisions?
    a. You can eliminate some of the members of a marketing channel, but you can't eliminate the marketing functions that must be performed.
    b. When a particular member of a marketing channel is eliminated, the cost of channel operation is always reduced.
    c. Channels of distribution operate in such a way that it is virtually impossible to change the structure of an existing channel.
    d. Eliminating independent wholesalers from a marketing channel should increase profit margins of other channel members by at least ten percent.
    e. The structure of a marketing channel is such that changes in the structure often result in changes in the functions that must be performed.

55. The profit margins earned by independent wholesaling intermediaries are
    a. low, ranging between one percent for food wholesalers to five percent for durable goods wholesalers.
    b. roughly equal to the profit margins earned by other American businesses; between four and 11 percent.
    c. among the highest of all American businesses, averaging nine percent.
    d. increasing as the number of wholesaling intermediaries declines.
    e. being eroded even further by their provision of "value-added services" to their customers.

56. Sales offices and branches, as identified in your text, are examples of
    a. independent merchant wholesaling intermediaries.
    b. independent agent wholesaling intermediaries.
    c. retailer-owned cooperatives or buying offices.
    d. manufacturer-owned facilities.
    e. brokers used only in certain industries.

57. A manufacturer-owned facility that serves as a regional office for salespeople but does not carry an inventory is a
    a. merchandise mart.
    b. brokerage house.
    c. manufacturer's representative.
    d. sales branch.
    e. sales office.

58. An independently owned, permanent facility that provides space in which manufacturers display their wares for visiting retail and wholesale buyers is an example of a
    a. sales branch.
    b. trade fair.
    c. public warehouse.
    d. merchandise mart.
    e. brokerage house.

59. The yearly gathering at High Point, North Carolina, during which furniture manufacturers display their wares for visiting retail and wholesale buyers is an example of a
    a. manufacturer's agency.
    b. retail buying office.
    c. public market.
    d. merchandise mart.
    e. trade fair.

60. Which of the following is a full-function merchant wholesaler.
    a. a commission merchant.
    b. a rack jobber.
    c. an auction company.
    d. a truck wholesaler.
    e. a drop shipper.

61. Which of the following product assortments would you expect to find being handled by an auction company?
    a. bread, tobacco products, potato chips, candy
    b. hardware, cosmetics, jewelry, sporting goods
    c. tobacco, used cars, art works, livestock, furs
    d. health and beauty aids, housewares, paperback books, compact discs
    e. industrial chemicals, building materials

62. Commission merchants
    a. are prevalent in the marketing of agricultural products, commonly handling grain, produce, and livestock.
    b. operate largely in industries characterized by large numbers of small buyers and sellers, like real estate.
    c. are often referred to as "independent marketing departments" because they can be responsible for a firm's marketing program.
    d. are conventionally called "manufacturer's reps" in the trade and represent a number of related but noncompeting product lines.
    e. are responsible for over 30 percent of the sales of all agent wholesaling intermediaries.

63. A wholesaler's pricing strategy is in large part determined by
    a. the nature of competition in that segment of the market.
    b. the extent of the services it renders.
    c. the demands of its customers; those who can't compete on price will not survive.
    d. its promotional budget; those who promote a lot must charge more.
    e. the seasonality of the merchandise it sells.

64.   In general, the primary ingredient of a wholesaling intermediary's promotional program is
a.   advertising.
b.   sales promotion.
c.   personal selling.
d.   specialties, like calendars and imprinted pencils.
e.   free merchandise given to sweeten the sales pot.

65.   From the point of view of pricing strategy, which of the following wholesaling intermediaries could you expect to charge the most to its customers.
a.   selling agents.
b.   manufacturer's agents.
c.   drop shippers.
d.   rack jobbers.

Name   _____   Instructor   _____

Section   _____   Date   _____

Applying Marketing Concepts

The Merriman Company, a retailer located in Little Rock, Arkansas, is in the process of analyzing its relationships with its various suppliers and customers. Company management has discovered, as it expected, that most purchasing of soft goods (clothing, piece goods, furs) by the company is directly from the manufacturer of the item. Some of Merriman's other lines, however, are bought in a very different manner. Household electrics, if the quantity to be bought is large enough, can often be bought directly from the producer. If the order is small or if repair parts are needed, however, a local industrial distributor is often the source of products from the same manufacturers. Merriman people also seem to be spending an inordinate amount of time handling goods which have been returned to the store for shipment back to manufacturers for repair under warranty or because a recall order was issued. The company also found that, in recent years, the furniture department, which has its own separate building and has always been somewhat autonomous in its operations, has gone heavily into office furniture and supplies, and sells more furniture, fixtures, and supplies to local businesses than it does household furnishings to the company's traditional customers.

Executives realize that times have changed, but are somewhat puzzled by all these relationships, and to top it all off, they have been approached by several other medium-sized retailers with the proposal that they all get together and set up their own captive wholesaling operation to sell to themselves so they can buy in larger overall quantities and save some money.

1. Merriman typically purchases soft goods
   a. through a "traditional" consumer goods channel.
   b. through a channel direct from producer to retailer.
   c. wherever they can be gotten at the best price.
   d. only during peak seasons.
   e. from wholesalers specializing in soft goods.

2. Merriman' purchases of household electrics indicate the presence of
   a. collusion which probably violates the Sherman Act.
   b. much confusion in Merriman's buying department.
   c. a dual distribution system for this class of product.
   d. the inadequacy of Merriman's inventory control system.
   e. a high level of demand for this merchandise in Little Rock.

3. The time which Merriman personnel are spending handling merchandise which is to be sent off for repair or other manufacturer adjustment should tell you that
    a. Merriman must handle very inferior goods; quality merchandise simply shouldn't be giving that much trouble.
    b. the channel of distribution from those manufacturers to Merriman must be somehow in disarray.
    c. times have changed a lot; in years past it would have been the retailer's responsibility to make good on these items.
    d. Merriman has become involved in reverse channels of distribution; these typically appear under these conditions.
    e. Merriman's New York buying group needs to be made aware of the deficiencies in the goods they are shipping.

4. Merriman's furniture department
    a. appears to have become a wholesale operation in office furnishings and supplies and probably should be set up that way and the retail furniture and home furnishings department separated from it.
    b. seems to be one of the most efficient parts of the Merriman operation.
    c. is acting as a producer rather than as a marketing intermediary.
    d. is engaging in direct distribution, acting as agent for a broad range of manufacturers.
    e. serves primarily as the base for a reverse channel of business equipment and supplies.

5. If Merriman joins with the other retailers to create the wholesale operation they will have created a
    a. wholesaler-sponsored voluntary chain.
    b. franchise.
    c. corporate marketing system.
    d. administered marketing system.
    e. retail cooperative.

Indiana Hardware and Supply Company of Kokomo sells hand and electric tools and supplies in several different ways. The company publishes a quarterly catalog that it mails to any retailer with which it has done more than $500 worth of business during the three months before the mailing. It also operates a fleet of trucks that it dispatches on weekly routes to regular customers (over $1,500 in business during the last three months) in its operating area. These trucks carry a selection of the most popular items in the company's line for immediate delivery, and the drivers can take orders for any other items a customer needs for delivery on the next trip.

If an account is sufficiently large ($10,000 in volume during the last three months), Indiana Hardware will even dispatch a truck to make immediate delivery of any order and will carry the balance owed on an open account for thirty days. Certain items in the Indiana Hardware line are now handled by a special division of the company that visits all customers at least once a month and replenishes their stock of "expendable items"—packaged screws, nuts, and washers; wiring devices, and very small tools like screwdrivers. They even put the merchandise on display for the customers and keep track of inventory as well. The company calls this division the "small stuff" department.

_____   6.   Even though it operates in several ways, Indiana Hardware remains a merchant wholesaler.

7. In serving its smaller customers (more that $500 but less than $1,500 in sales), the company acts like a
    a. drop shipper.
    b. cash-and-carry wholesaler.
    c. mail-order wholesaler.
    d. broker.
    e. rack jobber.

8. Indiana Hardware handles its middle-sized accounts ($1,500—$10,000) like a
   a. truck wholesaler.
   b. manufacturers' agent.
   c. drop shipper.
   d. commission merchant.
   e. selling agent.

9. Indiana Hardware's large accounts are handled as if the company was a
   a. manufacturers' sales branch.
   b. drop shipper.
   c. limited-function wholesaler.
   d. full-function wholesaler.
   e. commission merchant.

10. In terms of the way it operates, the "small stuff" division of Indiana Hardware is a
    a. trade fair.
    b. merchandise mart.
    c. drop shipper.
    d. rack jobber.
    e. public warehouse company.

Name _____ Instructor _____

Section _____ Date _____

Experiential Exercises

1. The purpose of this exercise is to investigate the extent to which dual (or an even more extended case, multiple) distribution exists in the market for a single, extremely common, product. Consider the simple wall-mounted light switch. For those with a technical background, the most common of these are the single-pole, single-throw type sometimes known as the one-way switch.

    a. Discuss the channel of distribution which might bring such a switch to a consumer for do-it-yourself installation.

    b. What channel of distribution do you suppose an institution like your college or university uses to buy the same switch? How does this differ from the consumer channel?

    c. When a home is being newly constructed, the electrical contractor purchases switches to install in the job. How and where does this individual buy them and how did they get there?

d.   The unhandy consumer may have to bring in an electrician to replace a switch in the event that one burns out in his or her home. Examine the channel of distribution that his switch is likely to follow.

Compare your analysis of each of the above channels with those of your classmates. Don't be surprised if there are significant differences in the channels which you have isolated for each of the product-users we've mentioned.

2.   The purpose of this exercise is to familiarize you with the wholesalers located in your area.

Using the *Yellow Pages* of the telephone directory and a map of a city in your area, plot the locations of wholesalers in the various categories listed below. Use the space provided to explain any patterns you find. If the *Yellow Pages* prove inadequate for the task, consult the city directory or contact the city's Chamber of Commerce and inquire where a directory of local wholesalers might be obtained.

a.   Plumbing fixtures and supplies

b.   Fresh and frozen meats

c.   Major appliances

d.   Fresh fruits and vegetables

Name _____   Instructor _____

Section _____   Date _____

Computer Applications

Review the discussion of decision tree analysis and inventory turnover in Chapters 3 and 13 of your text. Then use menu item 2 titled "Decision Tree Analysis" to solve problems 1 and 2 and item 10 titled "Inventory Turnover" to solve problems 3, 4, and 5.

1. Belinda's Feline Fashions is a ten store chain of pet stores specializing in products for cat owners (or, some would say, products for people who are owned by cats). Belinda Gilliam operates her mini-chain from a headquarters in Dayton, Ohio. Over the last ten years, the firm has grown so that sales are now averaging $2 million per year. Ms. Gilliam has been approached by CatFancy, a leading producer of cat care products. They have proposed that BFF become an exclusive intermediary for their products. The arrangement would be that BFF would have geographical exclusivity in their market area but would have to carry only the CatFancy line. The offer looks good to Ms. Gilliam because the CatFancy line is of excellent quality and is well advertised and has a strong consumer preference. She is of the opinion that her sales would increase by ten percent if she took the offer. Ms. Gilliam, when carefully questioned, indicated that she was "quite sure" (70 percent) that her opinion would be vindicated if she took the CatFancy offer. She did indicate that there was a "remote chance" (30 percent) that sales would decline ten percent with only the CatFancy line to sell.

   a. Should Belinda accept the CatFancy offer?

   b. Mel Moffett, Belinda's accountant, disagrees with her. He thinks that there is a 90 percent chance that BFF sales would decline by ten percent because of the loss of customers who are loyal to brands that would have to be dropped from BFF's line if the offer is accepted. If he is right, should Belinda accept the offer?

2. Steve Geraci, who owns an auto parts store in Pullman, Washington, has been approached by a salesman from the Spokane Auto Supply Company, a large wholesaler-sponsored voluntary chain. On the face of it, the deal the chain is offering looks pretty good, and Steve is considering dropping the independent wholesaler from whom he's been buying. The brands carried by Spokane Auto Supply are all well-known with reputations for good quality. The salesman concluded his presentation with the comment that Steve "should be able to increase sales by 45 percent" over his current $2 million.

Steve, however, is no dummy. He has talked to several other firms which have gone with Spokane Auto Supply and feels that there's only a 50 percent chance that he will achieve the 45 percent increase the salesman promised. The other side of the coin is that there is a 50 percent chance that his volume will drop by 50 percent if he goes with the voluntary chain. It seems that deliveries by Spokane Auto Supply are often slow and unreliable, and customers don't like waiting for delivery.

a.   Should Steve continue to buy from the independent wholesaler or should he switch to Spokane Auto Supply?

b.   Judy Collara, Steve's partner, disagrees with his assessment of the Spokane Auto Supply deal. She believes that the only risk of not achieving the 45 percent increase in sales depends on whether National Auto Supply decides to open a store in Pullman. She knows they have been studying the feasibility of such an action for a long time and that there is an 80 percent probability that they'll move into town in the next year. If that happens, sales will drop by fifty percent if she and Steve stay with the independent wholesaler. If, on the other hand, they switch to Spokane Auto Supply, sales will drop only 20 percent. If Judy is right, what should they do?

3.   Joseph Meringer is a rack jobber in Pocatello, Idaho who services drug stores and pharmacies throughout the state. At the beginning of the year a physical inventory determined that he had 1,800,000 items with a total value at retail of $2,646,000. At year's end he had 2,364,000 items worth $3,121,272. His sales were $24,000,000. What was Joseph's turnover rate for the year?

4. In a discussion at a cocktail party the other evening, Joe Smith mentioned that his wholesale firm maintained an average inventory at retail of some $2,600,000. A nosy friend recalled that he had read recently where Joe's company had annual sales of $29,250,000. Curious but not very expert, the friend has come to you asking you to compute the turnover rate for Joe Smith's company. What is that rate?

5. Lindqvist Machine Company of Minneapolis handles an extensive assortment of machine tools and related equipment. A physical inventory taken in January revealed that the company had on hand $16,754,000 worth of equipment (not including equipment at the Lake Woebegon branch, which seems somehow to have disappeared in its entirety). Sales during the year were $76,355,000, and at year's end a new inventory indicated on-hand goods to the tune of $15,550,000 (Lake Woebegon remains missing). Disregarding Lake Woebegon—which seems the safer case, somehow—what was the turnover rate for Lindqvist Machine? All figures are at cost.

Crossword Puzzle for Chapter 13

ACROSS CLUES

1. Goods made under license abroad and sold in the U.S. in direct competition with U.S. versions
5. Wholesaling intermediary that takes title to goods it handles: also called jobber, distributor
8. Interrelated marketing institutions responsible for flow of goods and services to users
9. Type of vertical marketing system with formal agreements among channel members
11. Direct communication on a nonpersonal basis between buyer and seller
13. Manufacturer-owned facility that carries inventories and processes orders from available stock
15. Full-function wholesaler that merchandises goods for retailers; maintains and stocks racks
16. Permanent facility in which mfrs. rent showrooms to display goods to buyers, designers, and architects
17. Periodic show at which mfrs. in a particular industry display goods to visiting buyers

DOWN CLUES

2. Distribution network in which a firm has more than one channel to reach its target market
3. Marketing intermediary in a business channel
4. Abbreviation for preplanned channel designed to be cost effective and achieve improved efficiency
6. VMS in which channel coordination is achieved through use of power by dominant channel member
7. Contractual arrangement in which a wholesaler or retailer agrees to meet standards set by another
10. First name of a wholesaling intermediary that takes title to the goods it handles
12. Agent wholesaling intermediary whose main function is to bring buyers and sellers together
14. First name of limited function merchant wholesaler usually found marketing perishable foods

WORD LIST:

ADMINISTERED
BROKER
BUSINESSDISTRIBUTOR
CONTRACTUAL
DISTRIBUTIONCHANNEL
DIRECTMARKETING

DUAL
FRANCHISE
GRAYGOODS
MERCHANDISEMART
MERCHANT
RACKJOBBER

SALESBRANCH
TRADEFAIR
TRUCK
VMS
WHOLESALER

Chapter 13 Solutions

Key Concepts

1.	u	9.	ak	17.	ad	25.	r	33.	y
2.	p	10.	o	18.	ae	26.	h	34.	s
3.	j	11.	z	19.	al	27.	e	35.	n
4.	w	12.	aa	20.	ag	28.	c	36.	k
5.	g	13.	af	21.	b	29.	am	37.	a
6.	x	14.	d	22.	t	30.	ab	38.	q
7.	ah	15.	i	23.	ac	31.	ai	39.	m
8.	f	16.	v	24.	aj	32.	l		

Self Quiz

1.	T	16.	F	31.	T	46.	a	61.	c
2.	T	17.	F	32.	F	47.	e	62.	a
3.	F	18.	F	33.	F	48.	a	63.	b
4.	T	19.	T	34.	a	49.	b	64.	c
5.	F	20.	F	35.	a	50.	e	65.	d
6.	T	21.	T	36.	b	51.	a		
7.	T	22.	F	37.	d	52.	b.		
8.	F	23.	T	38.	c	53.	d		
9.	F	24.	T	39.	c	54.	a		
10.	F	25.	F	40.	a	55.	a		
11.	T	26.	T	41.	e	56.	d		
12.	T	27.	F	42.	b	57.	e		
13.	T	28.	F	43.	b	58.	d		
14.	F	29.	T	44.	c	59.	e		
15.	F	30.	F	45.	a	60.	b		

Applying Marketing Concepts

1.	b	6.	T
2.	c	7.	c
3.	d	8.	a
4.	a	9.	c
5.	e	10.	d

Computer Applications

1. a.   ($2,200,000)(.70) + ($1,800,000)(.30) = $2,080,000.

    The CatFancy offer seems to offer an $80,000 advantage over current conditions, Belinda's assessment being a reasonable one.

    b.   ($2,200,000)(.10) + ($1,800,000)(.90) = $1,840,000

    If Mr. Moffett is correct, the offer should be declined.

2. a.   ($2,900,000)(.50) + ($1,000,000)(.50) = $1,950,000

    Mr. Geraci should hold fast with his current supplier.
    The $2,000,000 level of sales should not change.

    b.   ($2,000,000)(.20) + ($1,000,000)(.80) = $1,200,000
    if the old supplier is used.

    ($2,900,000)(.20) + ($1,800,000)(.80) = $2,020,000
    if the switch is made to the new supplier.

    The switch should be made to the new supplier.

3. Turnover rate = Sales/Average Inventory

    Sales = $24,000,000

    Average Inventory = ($2,646,000 + $3,121,272/2 = $2,883,636

    Turnover rate = $24,000,000/$2,883,636 = 8.32

4. Turnover rate = Sales/Average Inventory = $29,250,000/$2,600,000 = 11.25

5. Turnover rate = Sales/Average Inventory

    Sales = $76,335,000

    Average Inventory = ($16,754,000 + $15,550,000)/2 = $16,152,000

    Turnover rate = $76,335,000/$165,152,000 = 4.73

Crossword Puzzle Solution

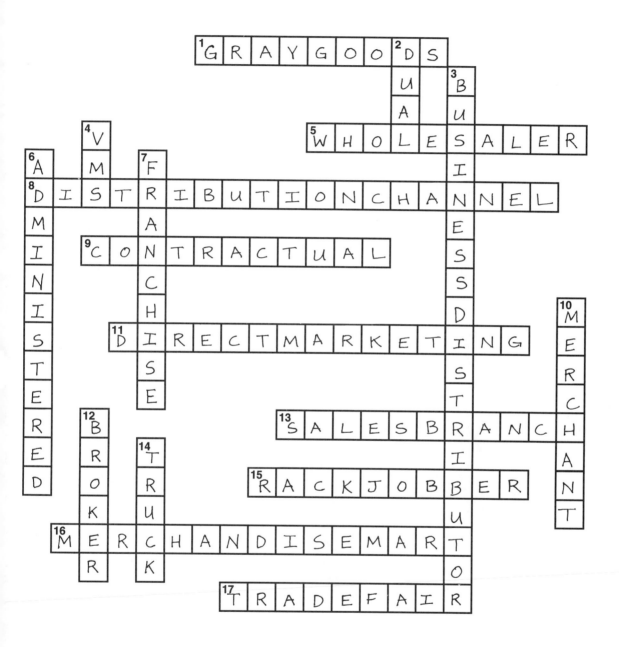

Chapter 14

Retailing

Chapter Outline

You may wish to use the following outline as a guide for taking notes.

    I.   Chapter Overview—Retailing: Selling products to the ultimate consumer

    II.   Evolution of Retailing and the Wheel of Retailing Hypothesis

    III.   Retailing Strategy

        A. Target market

        B. Merchandise strategy

        C. Customer service strategy

        D. Pricing strategy

            1. Markups

            2. Markdowns

        E. Location/Distribution strategy

            1. Planned shopping centers

            2. Other distribution decisions

        F. Promotional strategy

        G. Store atmospherics

    IV.   Types of Retailers

     V.   Classification by Shopping Effort

    VI.   Classification by Services Provided

VII.   Classification by Product Lines

    A. Specialty stores

    B. General merchandise retailers

        1. Variety stores

        2. Department stores

        3. Mass merchandisers

        4. Discount houses

        5. Off-price retailers

        6. Hypermarkets

VIII.   Classification by Location of Retail Transactions

    A. Direct selling

    B. Direct-response retailing

    C. Automatic merchandising

IX.   Classification by Form of Ownership

    A. Chain stores

    B. Independent retailers

X.   Scrambled merchandising

Name _____   Instructor _____

Section _____   Date _____

Key Concepts

The purpose of this section is to allow you to determine if you can match key concepts with their definitions. It is essential that you know the definitions of the concepts prior to applying the concepts in later exercises in this chapter.

From the list of lettered terms, select the one that best fits in the blank of the numbered statement below. Write the letter of that choice in the space provided.

Key Terms

a. retailing
b. wheel of retailing
c. retail image
d. markup
e. markdown
f. planned shopping center
g. electronic data interchange (EDI)
h. selling up
i. suggestion selling
j. atmospherics
k. specialty store
l. limited-line store
m. category killer

n. general merchandise retailer
o. variety store
p. department store
q. mass merchandiser
r. discount house
s. off-price retailer
t. outlet mall
u. hypermarket
v. home shopping
w. chain store
x. scrambled merchandising

_____ 1. Retail sales technique of convincing the customer to buy a higher priced item than he or she had originally intended.
_____ 2. Large store that handles a variety of merchandise including clothing, household goods, appliances, and furniture.
_____ 3. Store that charges lower-than-normal prices but may not offer services such as credit.
_____ 4. Store that carries a wide variety of product lines, all of which are stocked in some depth.
_____ 5. Group of retail stores planned, coordinated, and marketed as a unit.
_____ 6. Retail sales technique that attempts to broaden the consumer's original purchase to add related items, special promotions, or holiday or seasonal merchandise.
_____ 7. Store that stocks a wider line of goods than a department store but usually does not offer the same depth of assortment.
_____ 8. Amount by which the retailer reduces the original selling price of a product.
_____ 9. Shopping center that consists entirely of off-price retailers.
_____ 10. Exchange of orders and other business documents in machine-readable format.
_____ 11. Retailer that sells well-known brand name clothing at less than typical prices.

_____ 12.   Retailing practice of carrying dissimilar product lines in an attempt to generate additional sales volume.

_____ 13.   Amount added to the cost of an item to determine its selling price.

_____ 14.   Use of cable television to sell products via telephone order.

_____ 15.   Combination of physical characteristics and amenities that contribute to a store's image.

_____ 16.   Retailer that offers a large assortment within a single product line or a few related product lines.

_____ 17.   All activities involved in the sale of products and services to the ultimate consumer.

_____ 18.   Retailer that offers an extensive range and assortment of low-price merchandise.

_____ 19.   One of a group of retail stores that are centrally owned and managed and handle essentially the same product lines.

_____ 20.   Consumers' perception of the store and the shopping experience it provides.

_____ 21.   Hypothesis stating that retailers generally gain a competitive foothold by offering lower prices through reduction or elimination of services. Once established, they add services, raise prices, and become vulnerable to new low-price outlets.

_____ 22.   Giant mass merchandiser of soft goods and groceries that operates on a low-price self-service basis.

_____ 23.   Retailer that combines huge selection and low prices with a single product line.

_____ 24.   Retailer that typically handles only part of a single product line.

Name _____ Instructor _____

Section _____ Date _____

Self Quiz

You should use these questions to test your understanding of the material in this chapter. You can check your answers with those provided at the end of the chapter.

While these questions cover most of the chapter topics, they are not intended to be the same as the test questions your instructor may use in an examination. A good understanding of all aspects of the course material is essential to good performance on any examination.

True/False

Write "T" for True or "F" for False for each of the following statements.

_____ 1. Retailers often perform an important feedback role by obtaining information from customers and transmitting it to manufacturers and other channel members.

_____ 2. Innovations in retail institutions typically illustrate the marketing concept in action because they have emerged to satisfy consumer wants.

_____ 3. General stores were doomed by the fact that their habit of carrying a large assortment of items from a small number of product lines made them vulnerable to competition from limited-line and specialty outlets.

_____ 4. Suburban shopping center development, convenience food stores, and vending machines are excellent examples of the "wheel of retailing" in action.

_____ 5. One of the most pronounced trends in retailing today is decreased market segmentation.

_____ 6. The 1950s' innovation of discount department stores in suburban locations offered consumers convenient parking and lower prices in return for reduced services.

_____ 7. In an attempt to counter competition from specialty and discount stores, many department stores have eliminated high-overhead, low-profit lines such as toys, appliances, sporting goods, and furniture.

_____ 8. Retailers' marketing decisions center on the fundamental steps of selecting a target market and developing a retailing mix to satisfy the chosen market.

_____ 9. The basic objective of providing services such as gift wrapping, alterations, bridal registries, and interior designers is to attract and retain target customers.

_____ 10. Marketing research is not an important factor in the development of retail product strategies because retailing is so segmented that the decision to appeal to a particular segment determines product strategy.

_____ 11. The retailer is the member of the marketing channel who is directly responsible for the prices consumers pay.

_____ 12. The amount of markup used by a retailer is typically determined by the number and types of services it provides and the rate of inventory turnover.

_____ 13. The higher the rate at which a retailer turns over inventory, the greater the markup required for covering costs and generating a profit.

_____ 14.   The markup on selling price for a product which a retailer purchases for $.60 and sells for $1.20 is 100%.

_____ 15.   If you know the selling price and cost of a good, you can compute the markup based both on selling price and cost.

_____ 16.   Airport retailing, which caters to travelers stranded between flights, is beginning to catch on in the United States.

_____ 17.   Location may be the determining factor in the success or failure of a retail business.

_____ 18.   If a good is to be marked down, the markdown percentage may be determined by dividing the dollar amount of the markdown by the new or "sale" price.

_____ 19.   The smallest of the types of planned shopping center is the community shopping center which usually contains only 10 - 30 stores.

_____ 20.   Atmospherics includes physical characteristics and amenities both internal and external to the store that are designed to attract customers and satisfy their shopping needs.

_____ 21.   It isn't a regional shopping center unless it has at least 500,000 square feet of shopping space.

_____ 22.   If "selling up" is used without due regard for customers' real needs, they become dissatisfied with that retailer and the potential for repeat sales will be substantially diminished.

_____ 23.   Convenience retailers typically include furniture stores, appliance retailers, gasoline stations, and some barber shops.

_____ 24.   Many people are quite surprised to learn that supermarket profit margins are usually in the range of eight to nine percent of sales.

_____ 25.   Category killers, which include stores like Toys "R" Us and Home Depot, combine huge selections and low prices in a single product line.

_____ 26.   A department store is actually a series of limited-line and specialty stores under one roof.

_____ 27.   Off-price retailers take advantage of special price offers from manufacturers and offer fewer services than traditional retailers, which helps keep their prices low.

_____ 28.   Scrambled merchandising refers to the practice of locating goods randomly in the store to force consumers to search for what they need.

Multiple Choice

Circle the letter of the word or phrase that best completes the sentence or best answers the question.

29.   The "wheel of retailing" concept
   a.   postulates that new types of retailers gain a foothold in the marketplace by entering at a fairly high price level and offering a complete service package.
   b.   seems to fit the development of such outlets as department stores, chain stores, and supermarkets.
   c.   applies most appropriately to the development of suburban shopping centers, convenience stores, and vending machines.
   d.   theorizes that, after a new type of marketing institution has established itself in the market, it changes its ways of operating by reducing prices and services until an opportunity is created for a new kind of institution to enter the marketplace.
   e.   relates best to the demise of the general store in the U.S.

30.   A store or other retail outlet's "retail image" is
   a.   the owner's perception of the store and the shopping experience it provides.
   b.   its suppliers' perceptions of the store's operating philosophy, place in the market, and profitability.
   c.   consumers' perceptions of the store and the shopping experience it provides.
   d.   competitors' perceptions of the store and the market niche it occupies.
   e.   always consistent with the expectations of the owner, competitors, and the shopping consumer.

31.   One of the most dominant trends in modern retailing is
a.   the tendency for retailers to concentrate their efforts in one or another part of the country and to avoid the national market.
b.   a strong pull toward combining market segments into larger, less homogeneous targets for marketing effort.
c.   for firms to abandon the markets in which they have been most strongly entrenched for the longest periods of time and to strike out into new fields of endeavor.
d.   for firms that used to seek to serve the mass market to shift their strategy to target more narrowly defined segments.
e.   the thrust toward segmentation on highly ethnic grounds.

32.   The use of cable television networks to sell merchandise through telephone orders is an example of
a.   the subset of direct-response retailing known as home shopping.
b.   proving to be much less successful than was formerly hoped.
c.   a type of direct selling known as party selling.
d.   selling through an electronic catalog.
e.   catalog retailing.

33.   If a retailer purchases a refrigerator from its supplier for $350 and offers it for sale for $650, the markup on selling price for this item, rounded to the nearest whole percent, is
a.   24 percent.
b.   30 percent.
c.   35 percent.
d.   46 percent.
e.   54 percent.

34.   Jones Brothers Floor Tile Company just bought an odd lot of some really nice Italian ceramic tile. The tile cost 65 cents per square foot and the brothers usually mark up their merchandise 35 percent on selling price. What should be the asking price on this tile? (Rounded to the nearest cent.)
a. $0.88 per square foot
b. $1.00 per square foot
c. $1.22 per square foot
d. $1.64 per square foot
e. $2.00 per square foot

35.   The Market has overbought fresh cauliflower and is going to take a markdown on it to get it out the door before it goes bad. If the original price was $1.29 per head and a markdown to $0.89 per head is taken, what is the percent markdown? (Round to the nearest percent)
a.   31 percent
b.   37 percent
c.   45 percent
d.   69 percent
e.   73 percent

36.   A neighborhood shopping center is usually characterized by
a.   a market size of from 20,000 to 100,000 persons; the facility is usually anchored by a branch of a local department store.
b.   a size of from five to 15 stores serving 5,000 to perhaps as many as 50,000 persons.
c.   the presence of some professional offices such as those of physicians, dentists, and attorneys.
d.   a theme park on site somewhat like a mini Disney World.
e.   at least 400,000 square feet of shopping area.

37. When a salesperson in a store suggests that a new tie certainly would go well with that new shirt you just bought, he or she is practicing
     a. suggestion selling.
     b. selling up.
     c. use of atmospherics.
     d. franchising.
     e. simple selling.

38. When a store focuses its merchandising efforts on accessible locations, long store hours, rapid checkout service, and adequate parking facilities, it would be reasonable to assume, considering classification by shopping effort, that it is
     a. a shopping store.
     b. a variety store or specialty store.
     c. a mass merchandiser like an off-price retailer.
     d. a department store.
     e. some kind of convenience store.

39. Using classification by level of service provided as a base, a store that provides little or no product service or advice and specializes in staple convenience goods purchased frequently would be classed as
     a. an hypermarket.
     b. a self-realization store.
     c. a specialty store.
     d. a limited-service store.
     e. a convenience store.

40. Specialty stores
     a. typically carry only convenience and shopping goods.
     b. practice scrambled merchandising to a substantial extent.
     c. typically handle only part of a single product line.
     d. are run primarily by large chains; independents are rare.
     e. tend to be very large-scale operations in both physical size and sales volume.

41. Using product lines carried as the basis for classification, supermarkets are
     a. specialty stores.
     b. single-line stores.
     c. mixed merchandise marketers.
     d. convenience stores.
     e. limited-line stores.

42. When one considers that profit margins in supermarketing are as low as they are, one recognizes
     a. why the supermarket industry seems to be dying out; there's certainly no money to be made in it.
     b. why supermarkets are constantly pleading with government for tax breaks and special concessions to help them stay in business.
     c. why the number of supermarkets is decreasing year by year.
     d. why supermarkets are becoming even more selective about the merchandise they carry and are reducing the number of items made available to the public month by month.
     e. how important rapid inventory turnover is to a supermarket if it is to produce sufficient return-on-investment to justify its continued operation.

43. A general merchandise retailer which specializes in well-known brand name clothing bought on special and offered to the public at prices reflecting the savings realized is a(n)
    a. off-price retailer.
    b. department store.
    c. discount house.
    d. hypermarket.
    e. catalog retailer.

44. The newest wave of true discount houses is these stores which require customers to purchase memberships and operate on a no-frills, cash-and-carry basis. They are called
    a. factory-direct retail stores.
    b. variety stores.
    c. micromarkets.
    d. mass merchandisers.
    e. warehouse clubs.

45. Party selling, as used by firms like Stanley Home Products Company, is a variation of
    a. direct-response retailing.
    b. suggestion selling.
    c. direct selling
    d. selling up.
    e. overselling.

46. Discount houses, off-price retailers, and hypermarkets are all examples of
    a. mass merchandisers.
    b. department stores.
    c. catalog retailers.
    d. specialty stores.
    e. small-scale independent retail merchants.

47. Mass merchandisers have made a place for themselves in the retail marketplace by emphasizing
    a. low prices for not-so-well-known products, high turnover of goods, and reduced services.
    b. low prices for well-known brand name products, high turnover of goods, and reduced services.
    c. high prices for well-known brand name products, low turnover of goods, and a high level of quality service.
    d. low prices for well-known brand name goods, high turnover of goods, and a high level of quality service.
    e. low prices for well-known brand name goods, low inventory turnover, and a high level of quality service.

48. Department stores have been vulnerable to competition from mass merchandisers, among others, because
    a. they have relatively high operating costs, averaging from 45 to 60 percent of sales.
    b. they have been slow to adapt to conditions in the marketplace, often refusing to take competitive action from motives of tradition.
    c. their suburban locations isolated them from the real bases of their markets.
    d. their bare-bones approach to merchandising has turned a lot of people off to the way they do business.
    e. of their refusal to modernize their central city locations to provide the convenience factors people are looking for.

49.   The hypermarket
    a.   originated in Germany and has spread throughout Europe and the Middle East.
    b.   differs from a supermarket primarily in the merchandise carried and not so much in size and operating philosophy.
    c.   usually features over 200,000 square feet of selling space stocked with a wide selection of grocery items and general merchandise at discount prices.
    d.   has not as yet had marked success in any market in which it has thus far been introduced. It may be a blind alley in retail evolution.
    e.   is another name for the warehouse club type of retail store.

50.   The nation's largest retail chain is now
    a.   K-Mart Corporation of Benton Harbor, Michigan.
    b.   The Kroger Grocery and Baking Company of Cincinnati.
    c.   Sears, Roebuck and Company of Chicago.
    d.   Wal-Mart Stores of Bentonville, Arkansas.
    e.   Delchamps, Incorporated of Mobile, Alabama.

51.   Vending machines
    a.   have now become as common world-wide as they are in the United States.
    b.   are among the most profitable of all retailing institutions, averaging eight percent profit on sales.
    c.   are limited in growth potential by their inability to accept credit or debit cards.
    d.   have now become a $30 billion a year industry in the United States.
    e.   really got their start right after the First World War, selling books and magazine on the streets of Detroit.

52.   Scrambled merchandising refers to
    a.   the fact that most retailers are so disorganized that they do not know what their merchandise inventory includes, much less how much of each item is on hand.
    b.   the practice of allowing merchandise normally housed in one department to be shifted to another department for a special sales event, thus "scrambling" the inventory.
    c.   the practice of buying up stock from failed stores and mixing it in with fresh stock purchased for normal inventory, a questionable practice at best.
    d.   the habit which many consumers have gotten into of failing to replace merchandise which they have decided not to buy back on the proper shelves, dumping it instead any old place in the store, thus scrambling the merchandise.
    e.   the practice of carrying dissimilar lines in an attempt to generate additional sales volume.

Name _____   Instructor _____

Section _____   Date _____

Applying Marketing Concepts

Back Court, Inc., is an independently owned retail store that sells tennis racquets, balls and accessories, and tennis clothes for men, women, and children. In addition, it offers a complete repair department and its specialists can restring a racquet to any customer's desires. Through an arrangement with a group of local professional tennis players, lessons are available for interested players.

_____   1.   Because of its combination of merchandise and services, Back Court, Inc. practices scrambled merchandising.

_____   2.   Back Court, Inc., is a good candidate to engage in direct selling.

_____   3.   Back Court, Inc.'s product lines would be easy to market via teleshopping.

_____   4.   If the store added a line of snow skis, it would be engaging in scrambled merchandising.

_____   5.   In order to compete with the large chain stores Back Court, Inc., should carry exclusive lines, provide superior service, and stress their knowledge of local market conditions.

6. This store would be classed as a
    a.   specialty store.
    b.   general merchandise store.
    c.   department store.
    d.   limited-line store.
    e.   discount house.

7. If a store like Back Court, Inc., requires convenient access by at least 150,000 people to survive, which of the following locations would be most advantageous for it?
    a.   neighborhood shopping center
    b.   community shopping center
    c.   suburban shopping center
    d.   regional shopping center
    e.   central business district

8. If this store sold only racquets, it would be an example of a
    a.   specialty store.
    b.   general merchandise store.
    c.   department store.
    d.   limited-line store.
    e.   mass merchandiser.

9. If Back Court, Inc., hired an interior designer to make the interior of the store resemble a tennis club, it would be attempting to use
    a. distribution to attract a target market.
    b. product/service strategy to attract buyers.
    c. retail image to attract a target market.
    d. location to attract customers.
    e. product/service strategy to attract new customers.

10. Back Court, Inc., is thinking about publishing a catalog and taking orders by phone and mail. They would send the ordered merchandise to the customer by mail or private carrier. What type of nonstore retailing would this be?
    a. catalog retailing
    b. direct-response retailing
    c. automatic merchandising
    d. off-price retailing
    e. direct selling

Joy and Larry Fein have operated Fein's corner market for over thirty years. During all that time, they have operated their store the way they thought their customers would want them to. They open the doors at seven in the morning and close at ten at night seven days a week. Their parking lot is large and well lighted, and they make sure there are never more than three people in line at the cash register. They have always been very proud of the fact that their store kept away from what they referred to as faddish merchandise and stuck to the basics. Good quality meats, breads, dairy products, and standard fruits and vegetables. And everything in the store, without exception, was Kosher for all Jews—Orthodox, Conservative, and Reformed. Of course, not all their clientele was Jewish, hence they remained open on the Sabbath with the help of their non-Jewish employees.

11. In terms of the shopping effort required to shop at Fein's, the store is a
    a. shopping store.
    b. convenience store.
    c. specialty store.
    d. self-selection store.
    e. full-service retailer.

12. Looking at the product lines carried by Fein's we would have to come to the conclusion that the store was
    a. a specialty store.
    b. a limited-line store.
    c. a general merchandise store.
    d. a general store.
    e. a variety store.

13. Considering their pride in their resistance to carrying dissimilar lines of merchandise from the basics of grocerydom, it should be concluded that the Feins
    a. have resisted the temptation to go into scrambled merchandising.
    b. should move with the times and broaden their merchandise assortment.
    c. have accommodated themselves to the inevitable pressures of the need to make a profit by adding lines which scrambled their merchandise assortment.
    d. have successfully practiced selling up on their customers.
    e. know how to apply suggestion selling.

14. Fein's corner market, as far as we know, is
    a. a member of a corporate retail chain.
    b. a member of a wholesaler-sponsored voluntary chain.
    c. a member of a retail cooperative.
    d. an independent retail institution.
    e. a subsidiary of a holding company.

15. The fact that all the merchandise at Fein's is completely Kosher indicates that the Feins
    a. have applied geographic segmentation to choose a market segment.
    b. have used psychographic segmentation to choose a market segment.
    c. have segmented the market demographically.
    d. have applied segmentation by end-use to their marketplace.
    e. have done little, if any, segmentation of the market.

Name _____   Instructor _____

Section _____   Date _____

Experiential Exercises

1. Planned shopping centers have become so common in the United States that we often take them for granted. In this exercise you will examine planned shopping centers from a professional point of view.
    a. Using a map of a city near your campus or home, carefully plot the location of every planned shopping center. Next, scale the distance by road between each center. Now answer the following questions.

    1) What are the logical reasons for the location of each planned shopping center?

    2) If you were to build a neighborhood shopping center in or near the city, where would you build it? Why?

b. Visit a planned shopping center and draw a plan showing the location of each retail store in the center. (If the center being visited has more than 100 stores, draw a plan of only one section or level of it.) Show all parking areas and walkways. Select a group of four stores immediately adjacent to each other and classify them according to the bases that follow.

Store Name	Customer Effort	Services Provided	Product Lines	Ownership
1.				
2.				
3.				
4.				

c. If you were able to rent space in the shopping center you visited, what kind of store would you open? Why? In what part of the center would you prefer to rent? Why?

2. The purpose of this exercise is to familiarize you with the use of scrambled merchandising by various retail outlets. You will examine several stores with different basic product mixes and attempt to determine the degree to which they are involved in scrambled merchandising.

Visit three retail stores which are convenient for you to reach. Each store should have a different basic product mix than the others. Some suggested stores might be a supermarket, a hardware store, a pharmacy, a camera store, a furniture store, or even a toy store. For each store, acquire the following information. Be prepared to ask store personnel enough questions to complete each of the questions which follow.

Store 1:   Store Name _____

             Basic Product Line _____

             Dissimilar Lines Carried_____

             Approximate percentage of selling space devoted to unrelated lines_____

             Logic behind carrying the unrelated lines _____

             _____

Store 2:   Store Name _____

             Basic Product Line _____

             Dissimilar Lines Carried _____

             Approximate percentage of selling space devoted to unrelated lines_____

             Logic behind carrying the unrelated lines _____

             _____

Store 3:   Store Name _____

             Basic Product Line _____

             Dissimilar Lines Carried _____

             Approximate percentage of selling space devoted to unrelated lines_____

             Logic behind carrying the unrelated lines _____

             _____

a.   Are there any similarities, store to store, in the information you have gathered? Are they a function of

     customer effort considerations?

     services offered?

     store ownership?

product lines carried?

b. How would you say these stores are dissimilar in their approaches to scrambled merchandising? Are the dissimilarities a function of

customer effort considerations?

services offered?

product lines carried?

store ownership?

Name _____   Instructor _____

Section _____   Date _____

Computer Applications

Review the discussion of markups and markdowns in Chapter 14 of the text. Then use menu item 11 titled "markups" to solve problem 1. Use menu item 12 titled "markdowns" to solve problem 2. Use both on problem 3.

1. Melanie Scott imports native art from Paraguay and markets it to young, upwardly mobile people. Twice a year, Melanie flies down to Paraguay to meet with local artists and purchase items she thinks her customers will like. As soon as she returns from each of these trips, she publishes a catalog in which each item she has bought is pictured and described along with its price. Most of the products she sells are marked up 70% of the selling price. On her last trip, she discovered a new studio in Villarrica whose artists were producing truly exceptional work. She immediately contracted to take their entire yearly output of sculptures (only 150 units) at a price of $200 each. Because of their exceptional quality, Melanie feels she can get twice her normal markup on cost for these sculptures.

    a. What is Melanie's normal markup on cost?

    b. What will be the catalog price for these sculptures?

2. Aimee Thomas, whose dress shop has accumulated an inventory of unsold formal dresses, has decided to have a sale to reduce the on-hand stock. She paid an average of $75 each for the dresses, and normally marks them up 70 percent on cost. She intends to offer the dresses in a newspaper ad for $85 apiece.

    a. What would be her normal average retail price for these dresses?

b.   What is the average markdown percent she's applying for the sale?

3.   Dryden Harcourt, who purchased his home on lovely McGraw Hill (just south of Prentice Hall) in southern England some years ago, decided to place it on the market. His estate agent (real estate broker), P.W.S. Kent of Random Houses, suggested he list it at £750,000. He had paid £500,000 for it, so he was pleased that Kent thought he could get more. His neighbor, Dow Jones, suggested that he also decide on the least he'd accept for his home in a negotiated deal. Dryden thought £650,000 would be acceptable. Dryden was in luck! Allyn Bacon, an American retiring from business in the U.S., made an offer of £700,000, which he accepted.

a.   What was the percent markup on selling price of the original offering price for Mr. Harcourt's home?

b.   What percent markdown was he willing to take to make the sale?

c.   What percent markup on cost did he realize on the actual sale?

d.   What percent markdown did he actually take on the sale?

Crossword Puzzle for Chapter 14

CROSS CLUES

5. Use of cable television to sell products via telephone orders
8. Process involving exchange of orders and other business documents in machine-readable form (Abbr.)
9. All activities involved in the sale of goods and services to the ultimate consumer
11. Shopping center that consists entirely of off-price retailers
12. Amount added to the cost of an item to determine its selling price
13. Store offering a large assortment within a single product line or a few related product lines

DOWN CLUES

1. Giant soft goods and grocery mass merchandiser that operates on a low-price, self-service basis
2. Sales technique that attempts to broaden customer's original purchase to add related items
3. Group of centrally owned and managed stores that handle essentially the same product line
4. Retailer that combines huge selection and low prices within a single product line
6. Sales technique of convincing the consumer to buy a more expensive item than originally intended
7. Retailer that offers an extensive range and assortment of low-price merchandise
9. Customers' perception of the store and the shopping experience it provides
10. Amount by which the retailer reduces the original selling price of an item
11. A retailer selling well-known name brand clothing at less than usual prices

WORD LIST:

CATEGORYKILLER
CHAINSTORE
EDI
HOMESHOPPING
HYPERMARKET
LIMITEDLINE
MARKUP
MARKDOWN

OFFPRICE
OUTLETMALL
RETAILING
RETAILIMAGE
SELLINGUP
SUGGESTIONSELLING
VARIETYSTORE

Chapter 14 Solutions

Key Concepts

1.	h	6.	i	11.	s	16.	l	21.	b
2.	p	7.	q	12.	x	17.	a	22.	u
3.	r	8.	e	13.	d	18.	o	23.	m
4.	n	9.	t	14.	v	19.	w	24.	j
5.	f	10.	g	15.	j	20.	c		

Self Quiz

1.	T	11.	T	21.	F	31.	d	41.	e	51.	d
2.	T	12.	T	22.	T	32.	a	42.	e	52.	e
3.	F	13.	F	23.	F	33.	d	43.	a		
4.	F	14.	F	24.	F	34.	b	44.	e		
5.	F	15.	T	25.	T	35.	c	45.	c		
6.	F	16.	T	26.	T	36.	b	46.	a		
7.	T	17.	T	27.	T	37.	a	47.	b		
8.	T	18.	T	28.	F	38.	e	48.	a		
9.	T	19.	F	29.	b	39.	d	49.	c		
10.	F	20.	T	30.	c	40.	c	50.	d		

Applying Marketing Concepts

1.	F	6.	d	11.	b
2.	F	7.	d	12.	b
3.	F	8.	a	13.	a
4.	T	9.	c	14.	d
5.	T	10.	b	15.	c

Computer Applications

(All calculations of Markups are in percentages)

1. a   Markup on Cost = Markup on S. P./(100%-Markup on S.P.) =
$$70\%/30\% = \underline{233.33\%}$$

   b.   If Melanie adheres rigorously to her markup calculations, she will list these items in her catalog for $1,133.34. I would suggest, however, a price of $1,150.

   Selling Price = $200 + $200(466.67%) = $1,133.34
   This may also be done by computing markup on selling price
   Markup on S. P. = Markup on Cost/(100% + Markup on Cost)
$$466.67/566.67 = \underline{82.35\%}$$

   Selling Price = Cost/(100%-Markup on S. P.) =
$$\$200/17.65\% =$$
$$\underline{\$1,133.34}$$

2. a.   Normal selling price = Cost + Cost(Markup on Cost) =
$$\$75 + \$75(.70) = \underline{\$127.50}$$

   b.   The markdown percentage =
   Dollar Amount of Markdown/New "Sale" Price =
$$\$42.50/\$85 = \underline{50\%}$$

3. a.   Markup on Selling Price = Selling Price - Cost/Selling Price x 100

   [£750,000 - £500,000)/£750,000] x 100 = 33.33%

   b.   Percent markdown = Money amount of markdown/ New "Sale" price x 100

   (£100,000/£650,000) x 100 = 15.38%

   c.   Markup on cost = Money markup/Cost x 100 =

   (£200,000/£500,000) x 100 = 40%

   d.   Percent markdown = (Money amount of markdown/ New "Sale" Price) x 100

   (£50,000/£700,000) x 100 = 7.14%

Crossword Puzzle Solution

Across:
5. HOME SHOPPING
8. EDI
9. RETAILING
11. OUTLET MALL
12. MARKUP
13. LIMITED LINE

Down:
1. HYPERMARKET
2. SUGGESTION SELLING
3. CHAINS
4. CATEGORY KILLER
6. SELLING UP
7. VARIETY
9. RETAIL LIMIT
10. MARKDOWN
11. OFF PRICE
11. LOTORE (LOT STORE)

Chapter 15

Physical Distribution

Chapter Outline

You may wish to use the following outline as a guide in taking notes.

I. Physical Distribution—From Production Line to Consumer

II. Importance of Physical Distribution

III. Physical Distribution System

    A. The problem of suboptimization

    B. Customer service standards

IV. Elements of the Physical Distribution System

    A. Transportation

        1. Rate Determination

        2. Transportation deregulation

        3. Classes of carriers

        4. Major transportation modes

        5. Freight forwarders—transportation intermediaries

        6. Supplemental carriers

        7. Intermodal coordination

    B. Warehousing

        1. Automated warehouses

        2. Location factors

    C. Inventory control systems

    D. The just-in-time system

    E. Electronic data interchange (EDI)

    F. Order processing

    G. Protective packaging and materials handling

Name _____ Instructor _____

Section _____ Date _____

Key Concepts

The purpose of this section is to allow you to determine if you can match key concepts from this chapter with their definitions. It is essential that you know the definitions of the concepts before applying the concepts in later exercises in this chapter.

From the list of lettered terms, select the one that best fits each of the numbered statements below. Write the letter of that choice in the space provided.

Key Terms

a. physical distribution
b. value-added service
c. system
d. suboptimization
e. *maquiladoras*
f. customer service standards
g. class rates
h. commodity rate
i. Storage warehouse

j. Distribution warehouse
k. economic order quantity (EOQ) model
l. Just-in-time system
m. stockout
n. materials handling
o. unitizing
p. containerization

_____ 1. An organized group of components linked according to a plan for achieving specific objectives.
_____ 2. Inventory control system designed to minimize costs by providing goods and services in a timely manner.
_____ 3. Activities concerned with the efficient movement of finished goods from the end of the production line to the consumer.
_____ 4. Standard transportation rate established for shipping various commodities.
_____ 5. Facility designed to assemble and then redistribute products to facilitate rapid movement to purchasers.
_____ 6. Method of determining optimal order quantity by trading off inventory holding costs and order processing costs.
_____ 7. Process of combining as many packages as possible into one load in order to expedite product movement and reduce damage and pilferage.
_____ 8. Special transportation rate granted by carriers to shippers as a reward for either regular use or large-quantity shipments.
_____ 9. Inventory item that is unavailable for shipment or sale.
_____ 10. Process of combining several unitized loads of products into a single load to facilitate intertransport changes in transportation modes.
_____ 11. Condition in which individual objectives are achieved at the expense of broader organizational objectives.
_____ 12. All activities involved in moving products within plants, warehouses, and transportation terminals.

____ 13.   Quality of service that a company wants its customers to receive.
____ 14.   Traditional warehouse in which products are stored prior to shipment.
____ 15.   An improved or additional service offering not normally available to customers.
____ 16.   Mexican assembly plants located near the U. S. Border.

Name _____   Instructor _____

Section _____   Date _____

Self Quiz

You should use these questions to test your understanding of the material in this chapter. You can check your answers with those provided at the end of the chapter.

While these questions cover most of the topics in the chapter, they are not intended to be the same as the test questions your instructor may use in an examination. A good understanding of all aspects of the course material is essential to good performance on any examination.

True/False

Write "T" for True and "F" for False for each of the following statements.

_____ 1. Total distribution costs in the United States amount to approximately 15 percent of the nation's gross domestic product.

_____ 2. The terms transportation and physical distribution can be used interchangebly.

_____ 3. The cost of physical distribution represents almost half of total marketing costs.

_____ 4. Historically, managers have attempted to cut costs by improving the efficiency of goods production.

_____ 5. By providing consumers with place and possession utilities, physical distribution contributes to implementing the marketing concept.

_____ 6. A growing part of the logistics service industry is made up of full-service companies that help firms plan and execute distribution plans in other countries.

_____ 7. Each component of a system operates independently of every other component in the system.

_____ 8. Suboptimization occurs when a specified level of customer service is achieved while the total cost of physically moving and storing products as they go from point of production to the point of ultimate purchase is minimized.

_____ 9. Firms may segment markets based on different levels of customer service.

_____ 10. The reduction of any physical distribution cost should be made with the goal of maintaining the required level of customer service.

_____ 11. Because of deregulation it is not now possible to simultaneously increase service levels while decreasing transportation costs.

_____ 12. The single largest expense item in physical distribution is the cost of inventory control systems.

_____ 13. In transportation, negotiated rates are sometimes called special rates and are the standard rate for every commodity moving between any two places.

_____ 14. Common carriers are for-hire carriers that serve the general public with regulated rates and services.

_____ 15. Deregulation of the transportation industry has brought with it real cost savings that benefit U.S. producers, distributors, and consumers.

_____ 16. Motor carriage represents the most efficient mode of transportation for bulky commodities over long distances.

____ 17.   Though many people are barely aware of its existence, the network of 214,000 miles of pipelines that crisscrosses the United States ranks second only to the railroads in number of ton-miles of cargo transported per year.

____ 18.   One of the factors that limits the use of the pipeline medium is its speed; the average pipeline shipment moves along at a rate of only three to four miles an hour.

____ 19.   United Parcel Service, Federal Express, and the U. S. Postal Service are examples of freight forwarders.

____ 20.   A make-bulk center is a type of distribution warehouse that consolidates several small shipments into one big one and delivers it to its destination.

____ 21.   The Economic Order Quantity (EOQ) model is based on a trade-off between the cost of goods bought by a company and the cost of processing orders for those goods.

____ 22.   Shrink packaging involves binding a unitized load in a plastic that shrinks when it cools after heating, thus securing the elements of the load together.

____ 23.   Wal-Mart's automatic electronic ordering of another pair of jeans of the same style and size from their supplier when a pair is sold is an example of utilizing electronic data interchange.

____ 24.   America's "just-in-time" inventory system is an adaptation of the Soviet "Krasny Krim" system that involves moving inventory to production facilities only as it is needed.

____ 25.   With the unification of the European Economic Community, prices will be driven up to the highest level prevailing in any EEC country.

Multiple Choice

Circle the letter of the phrase or statement that best completes the sentence or best answers the question.

26.   According to your text, physical distribution costs in the United States now amount to
   a.   over half of total marketing costs and about 15 percent of GNP.
   b.   about a third of all marketing costs and about ten percent of GNP.
   c.   almost half of all marketing costs and more than 15 percent of GNP.
   d.   almost a quarter of all marketing costs and 20 percent of GNP.
   e.   40 percent of all marketing costs and 12 percent of GNP.

27.   A term which can be used interchangeably with physical distribution is
   a.   logistics.
   b.   transportation.
   c.   inventory adjustment.
   d.   customer satisfaction standardization.
   e.   suboptimization.

28.   One of the major reasons for the increased attention to physical distribution activities by management is
   a.   recognition of their effect on production efficiency in factories.
   b.   the realization that transportation is the primary source of competitive advantage in today's markets.
   c.   the importance of reducing the cost of every aspect of the physical distribution process.
   d.   recognition of their role in providing customer service.
   e.   that these activities have been neglected for many years and as a result the system is on the brink of collapse.

29. The study of physical distribution is one of the classic examples of
     a. high comedy in the field of business management.
     b. the systems approach to business problems.
     c. errors magnified by the efforts made to correct them.
     d. a complex analysis reduced to simplistic terms.
     e. examination of a process going nowhere at a faster and faster rate.

30. The objective of an organization's physical distribution system is
     a. to deliver the goods faster and better than the competition.
     b. to satisfy all the firm's customers all the time with the best quality products delivered in the most rapid
         fashion from a storage facility operated at the highest level of efficiency.
     c. to develop the most modern, high-tech transportation network in the firm's marketplace so as to
         reduce competition and improve customer service.
     d. to serve each manager with the minimum cost-profile of the distribution function under his supervi-
         sion.
     e. to establish a specified level of customer service while minimizing the costs involved in physically
         moving and storing product as it moves from point of production to the point of ultimate sale.

31. Suboptimization frequently occurs in physical distribution because
     a. each logistics activity is judged by its ability to achieve certain management objectives some of which
         are at cross-purposes with each other.
     b. there is too much emphasis on customer service and not enough emphasis on reducing the cost of each
         physical distribution function.
     c. too ambitious a level of customer service is chosen as a standard, thereby driving up operations costs.
     d. inventory management fails, causing the system to run out of stocks of important goods just when
         they're needed most.
     e. firms find themselves operating out-dated, old-fashioned warehouses and can't afford to develop
         better, more efficient facilities.

32. Which of the following would be a valid customer-service standard?
     a. All shipments will be sent motor freight unless another mode is specified by the customer.
     b. Shipment will be made open-account to firms rated BAA or better by Dun and Bradstreet; all others
         must pay cash with their order.
     c. Ninety percent of all orders are filled within twenty-four hours after receipt; all orders will be filled
         within forty-eight hours after receipt.
     d. Returns will be accepted only with prior approval by our management and then only if it can be
         proven that the goods were bought from us within the last fifteen days.
     e. We dry-store merchandise ordered from us for seventy-two hours after we receive the order; after
         that, it is returned to stock and the customer is charged 15 percent for restocking.

33. The largest single expense item in physical distribution is
     a. the cost of warehousing; storage is more expensive every year.
     b. materials handling; moving goods inside the storage facility is always a costly process.
     c. order processing; the volume of orders pouring into the distribution system has driven the cost of this
         function up more than any other.
     d. transportation; despite new media and new forms of organization in the field, costs have rapidly
         escalated.
     e. inventory control; increased hijacking, pilferage, and other forms of "shrinkage" have driven up the
         cost of this function

34.   In transportation, this type of rate allows the shipper and the carrier to negotiate a rate to be charged for a particular service. Such a rate is called
   a.   a class rate
   b.   a contract rate.
   c.   a special rate.
   d.   a commodity rate.
   e.   an insider rate.

35.   The current trend toward deregulation of the nation's transportation media began with the
   a.   Motor Carrier Act of 1976.
   b.   Airline Deregulation Act of 1977.
   c.   Staggers Rail Act of 1978.
   d.   Celler-Kefauver Act of 1952.
   e.   Stanford-McCauley Amendment to the Sherman Act, passed in 1966.

36.   If a freight carrier offers its services to the public, operates under a regulated system of rates and services, and must seek approval from a regulatory body to operate, it is
   a.   a contract carrier.
   b.   a designated carrier.
   c.   a private carrier.
   d.   a common carrier.
   e.   a bulk carrier.

37.   The common unit of traffic volume for transportation media is the
   a.   hundredweight (cwt.).
   b.   "short box" (an 8 foot by 10 foot container).
   c.   palletload (a 48" x 60" x 42" cubic measure).
   d.   Britonne (2,240 pounds weight or 160 stone.)
   e.   the ton-mile (one ton moved through a distance of one mile).

38.   Despite the shrinkage which their portion of U. S. freight volume has suffered over the last forty years, railroads still dominate other carriers by
   a.   carrying about 47 percent of all shipments sent.
   b.   forcing other media to follow their rate schedules.
   c.   moving freight faster and better than any other medium.
   d.   handling 37 percent of total ton-mile volume.
   e.   commanding over 90 percent of the long-haul volume.

39.   One of the results of deregulation of the U.S. transportation industry has been
   a.   reduction of the number of railway cars in service by 27 percent.
   b.   an increase in the cost of the national logistics system; since 1986, it has risen by $60 million.
   c.   a decrease in the number of trucking companies serving the contiguous 48 states from 4,000 to 132.
   d.   a lessening of intermodal cooperation as rail and motor freight have become more direct competitors.
   e.   the necessity to lay many thousands of miles of railroad track to handle the loadshift to that medium.

40.   Motor carriage's primary advantage over the other transportation media is
   a.   its ability to move bulky commodities efficiently over long distances.
   b.   its capacity to safely carry natural gas and oil products at a very low cost.
   c.   relatively fast, consistent service for both large and small shipments.
   d.   speed; motor carriage is nearly twice as fast as the next fastest medium.
   e.   its ability to handle the paperwork involved in effectively shipping goods.

41.   For which of the following cargo lists would water carriage be the most likely choice?
    a.   finished lumber, coal, automobiles, industrial chemicals
    b.   clothing, food products, furniture and fixtures, machinery
    c.   minerals and ores, bulk chemicals, petrochemicals
    d.   natural gas, coal slurries, crude oil, jet fuel
    e.   cut flowers, microchips, medical instruments, precision tools

42.   If you sought to ship a product by the least-cost method, the obvious choice would be
    a.   railroad.
    b.   motor freight.
    c.   pipeline.
    d.   air freight.
    e.   water carrier.

43.   The warehouse most often used by firms facing seasonal fluctuations in the supply of or demand for their products is
    a.   a make-bulk center.
    b.   a storage warehouse.
    c.   an automated warehouse.
    d.   a distribution warehouse.
    e.   a break-bulk facility.

44.   The just-in-time system
    a.   has an inherent expectation that deliveries will be made at the time they are needed.
    b.   involves maximizing inventory at the place of production, rather than in warehousing facilities.
    c.   works best when the products involved have a number of variations.
    d.   is unaffected by the great physical distances that often lie between supplier and customer in this country.
    e.   usually depends on direct relationships between supplier and customer with no intervening intermediaries, especially in the United States.

45.   If a product which a customer has ordered is not available for shipment or sale, one has
    a.   a credit check condition.
    b.   to make a credit to a sales account.
    c.   to record the Universal Product Code of the item.
    d.   to compensate by using a different transportation method.
    e.   a stockout.

46.   Automated warehouses are capable of
    a.   providing major savings for high-volume distributors such as grocery chains.
    b.   reducing labor costs and worker injuries.
    c.   lowering the amount of pilferage, fires, and breakage.
    d.   all of the effects mentioned above.
    e.   none of the things mentioned above.

47.   Freight forwarders are considered to be transportation intermediaries because they
   a.   buy shipping services at the LTL or LCL rate and charge their clients the TL or CL rate for them.
   b.   buy shipping services at the TL or CL rate and charge their clients the LTL or LCL rate for them.
   c.   buy shipping services at the TL or CL rate and charge their clients a price between that rate and the LTL or LCL rate for them.
   d.   serve carriers by booking shipments for them; they do the paperwork and the carriers just move the goods.
   e.   serve as arbitrators in the event of a conflict between a shipper and a common carrier.

48.   Which of the following is a legitimate example of a supplemental carrier?
   a.   Norfolk Southern Railroad Company
   b.   Federal Express Company
   c.   Northwest Airlines
   d.   United Gas Pipeline Company
   e.   Canal Barge Company, Inc.

49.   Containerization involves
   a.   combining as many packages as possible into one load, preferably on a pallet.
   b.   properly packing each item of a shipment into its own carton or container.
   c.   recording the exact contents of each package which becomes part of a shipment.
   d.   combining several unitized loads; a standardized shipping container is typically used.
   e.   moving products within a manufacturer's plant and warehouses; special "tote boxes" are used.

50.   Aalsmeer Greenhouses' adaptation of nature to the needs of its customers through controlling the blooming date of roses is an example of
   a.   a value-added service.
   b.   a logistical problem.
   c.   liaison between a U.S. company and a European one.
   d.   an inventory control process in action.
   e.   foreign accommodation of U.S. Customs regulations.

Name _____   Instructor _____

Section _____   Date _____

Applying Marketing Concepts

Saltaformaggio Specialties is a chain of retail stores catering to gourmet cooks. The company stocks everything the avid kitchen craftsman or craftswoman might need. Pots, pans, spoons, measuring devices, all the bells and whistles—you name it, they've got it.

Saltaformaggio's history has been short but exciting. Founded only eight years ago as a small store in Pontchatoula, Louisiana, the company now has over 250 stores nationwide. This rapid growth has brought not only profits but also problems. The main problem facing Saltaformaggio's founder and chief executive, Helmut Oberraeder, is the challenge of physical distribution.

The company has over 300 suppliers scattered all over the country. At present, each supplier receives orders from and ships directly to each Saltaformaggio store. Store managers are responsible for all shipping and materials-handling related to their stores. Mr. Oberraeder realizes that the system is causing problems. Suppliers charge more for small shipments to the stores than they would for large shipments to a company warehouse. Moreover, if Saltaformaggio buys in larger quantities, it can get the benefit of quantity discounts it is not now receiving.

There is also a problem with delivery; shipments are often late or simply don't arrive at the company's stores. Recently, store managers have begun to complain about having to inspect incoming shipments for defective merchandise, do paperwork on returns to suppliers, and handle special orders, all of which are very time-consuming. Personnel at company headquarters, meanwhile, are up in arms over their lack of control of buying activities at the local stores and their lack of information about inventory. To top it all off, sales are being lost because of too many stockouts in the retail stores.

Something must be done! Mr. Oberraeder has received several suggestions from other members of management, from lower-level employees who work in the affected areas of the company, and even from a certain number of irate customers. He has disregarded those suggestions that would have been too personally painful or physically impossible (leaping from high windows <u>does</u> hurt; let's not get into the physical impossibilities). Others he has given substantial thought. One of the more interesting suggestions involves setting up a central, automated warehouse to receive all supplier shipments. From that location, goods could be shipped to the stores by common carrier. A second suggestion is to set up several automated warehouses rather than one to cut down on delivery time.

Before a meaningful decision can be made, a number of questions must be answered. Two of these are: Should the company buy a fleet of trucks or use common carriers? Should all buying, goods returns, and so forth be coordinated by the main office?

_____   1.   To have an integrated physical distribution system, Saltaformaggio's should consider using the EOQ model of inventory control.
_____   2.   Because avoiding stockouts is so important to a firm like Saltaformaggio's, the just-in-time system of inventory control would probably not be a very good choice for them.

_____   3.   Automated warehouses are probably quite feasible for the needs of a firm like Saltaformaggio's.
_____   4.   Freight forwarders should be used by Saltaformaggio's, especially if the company does buy a fleet of trucks.
_____   5.   The Motor Carrier Act of 1980 could be of benefit to the company if they decide to use common carriers.

6. What type of warehouse is the company thinking of installing?
    a. a storage warehouse
    b. a distribution warehouse
    c. a make-bulk facility
    d. a manufacturing warehouse
    e. a bonded warehouse

7. A key function of the warehouse the company is thinking of building is
    a. unitizing.
    b. containerizing.
    c. breaking bulk.
    d. long term storage.
    e. making bulk.

8. If the company uses a common carrier to deliver orders to the individual stores, what type of rate would it be charged?
    a. a class rate
    b. a commodity rate
    c. a special rate
    d. a negotiated rate
    e. a flat rate

9. If Saltaformaggio's were to install a physical distribution system, a basic systems orientation would require the inclusion of certain features. Others would remain optional. Which of the following would constitute an optional feature in such a system?
    a. order processing
    b. inventory control
    c. intermodal coordination
    d. customer service
    e. materials handling

10. If the company is losing sales due to stockouts in stores, then
    a. customer service standards are not being met.
    b. the stores are too far from the suppliers.
    c. the company needs to hire better store managers.
    d. customers are demanding too much; the company should take an "if we don't have it, you probably don't need it" posture.
    e. a careful analysis of the salesmen's activity sheets is in order; they're probably overselling some lines.

Melrose Manufacturing Company, a maker of farm machinery located in the community of Bugtussle, Texas, is facing something of a crisis in its operations. It has been approached by a representative of a foreign country which wants to buy 5,000 of the firm's mule-drawn earth augers. Melrose knows nothing whatsoever about international trade. In addition, the company is in no position to lay in the supplies and materials to build 5,000 of the machines. In a good year, they might sell 500 of them in the domestic market. Of course, the foreign country said they'd send an inspector to approve the machines as they came off the production line and pay for them on the spot. Melrose would be expected to prepare the machines for shipment, for which the foreign nation would compensate them. Each machine has overall dimensions of seven feet in width, six feet, eight inches in height, and nine feet, six inches in length. They would all be going to the same destination, the capital of the foreign nation, Blagoveshchensk. This city is several hundred miles from the ocean and the highway system between it and the port of Chimutsk is appalling. It does, however, have good road connections with the interior of the country and an excellent airport. The nation's rail system is uniformly good.

____ 11. If Melrose undertakes this job themselves, they should be prepared to allocate 36 hours of employee time to preparing the paperwork to go along with each shipment of augers.

____ 12. If the earth augers are shipped in containers, there is increased danger of damage to them because they cannot be seen through the solid walls of the container.

____ 13. All of the activities of preparing the augers for shipment up to the time they're turned over to a transportation company constitute warehousing from Melrose's point of view.

14. In recognition of Melrose's total ignorance of international distribution,
   a. they should probably turn this deal down; there is no practical way to satisfy their customer.
   b. they should get in touch with a good foreign freight forwarder; such people specialize in just this sort of thing.
   c. they probably need to get in touch with the U. S. Department of State.
   d. they should send one of their people off to the State University to take one of those courses in foreign trade.
   e. there is little to be said; such ignorance inevitably leads to business failure.

15. Faced with an apparent shortage of funds to undertake this foreign contract, Melrose looks like
   a. an excellent candidate for just-in-time inventory management; the customer's willingness to pay as machines come off the production line means Melrose can minimize inventory investment at no penalty to itself.
   b. it may have to undertake only a part of the contract or subcontract it out to someone who is better funded.
   c. a company which cannot seize upon opportunity when it presents itself.
   d. it may be in financial trouble and a likely candidate for a takeover bid by a larger, better funded firm.
   e. just another small-time country manufacturer that doesn't know what it's doing.

16. The best way to prepare the augers for shipment would probably be
   a. to crate each of them individually; their dimensions are so large no other method makes sense.
   b. to unitize each machine on its own pallet; that way each machine would be complete on arrival.
   c. to containerize the machines in the largest standard container (40 feet in length); since all the machines are going to the same destination, this is the sensible way to solve the problem, shipping four machines per container.
   d. in whatever fashion is most convenient; after all, they now belong to the foreign government and damages are their problem.
   e. to turn them over to the foreign government at the end of the production line and let them worry about it.

17.   A recommended shipping route for these products would be
   a.   from Bugtussle to Dallas by truck; thence to Blagoveshchensk by air freight.
   b.   from Bugtussle to Houston by truck; thence to Chimutsk by container ship, and from Chimutsk to Blagoveshchensk by truck.
   c.   from Bugtussle to Houston by truck; thence to Chimutsk by container ship, and from Chimutsk to Blagoveshchensk by rail.
   d.   from Bugtussle to Houston by truck; thence to Jacksonville, Florida, by train; from Jacksonville to Chimutsk by container ship, and thence to Blagoveshchensk by truck.
   e.   from Bugtussle to Los Angeles by train; thence to Yokohama by unscheduled steamer (not container ship); to Port Moresby, Papua-New Guinea, by sailing schooner; from Port Moresby via Bombay to Chimutsk by outrigger canoe; thence to Blagoveschchensk by yak caravan.

Name _____   Instructor _____

Section _____   Date _____

Experiential Exercises

1. The purpose of this exercise is to familiarize you with the workings of the transportation system and its interrelationship with the other features of the physical distribution system.

    Visit the nearest office of a firm in as many of the transportation media as you can conveniently reach: a railroad company, a motor freight carrier, an airline company, a barge or steamship line, and a pipeline company. (If you are in an isolated location, this may be a major task. Persist at it and do the best you can.)
    a. Ask a representative of each company what kind of service it renders from your location. Are there regularly scheduled arrivals and departures? How frequently? To and from what locations? Note below the information you receive.

    Medium:

    Services offered:

    Schedule:

    Locations:

    (Repeat format for each medium. Use additional paper as needed.)

b.   Ask to see the company's "tariff schedule." What does this document reveal?

c.   Ask a representative of each company if there are any "special" services they render at your location. Note these below.

d.   Comment on the similarities and the differences you have observed in the methods of operation, quoting of tariffs, and other features of the firms you have visited.

2. Visit a storage warehouse and a distribution warehouse located near your home or school. (Many public warehouses, particularly those operated by "transfer and storage" companies, are storage warehouses. Warehouses operated by wholesale grocery companies, hardgoods wholesalers, and other vendors to local retailers are often distribution warehouses. Check your *Yellow Pages* and make some phone calls before embarking on your visits.)

a. Discuss the differences in physical characteristics between the two types of warehouse.

b. How does the level of activity compare between the storage warehouse and the distribution warehouse?

c. Discuss the similarities and the differences you have observed between the materials handling equipment and activities at the two types of facility.

d. Discuss the niche which each of these warehouses occupies in the physical distribution process.

Name _____   Instructor _____

Section _____   Date _____

Computer Applications

Review the discussion of economic order quantity (EOQ) in Chapter 15 of the text. Then use menu item 13 titled "Economic Order Quantity" to solve the following problems.

1. Luis Ramirez-Bientempo must determine the EOQ for the ink used in the printing plant where he works. He has talked with the head press operator and the maintenance department and has learned that last year's consumption of ink was 82,600 pounds. The ink averaged $.50 per pound in price. It costs the company 25 percent of cost to carry ink in inventory for a year, and placing an order costs $103. It is estimated that current year consumption of ink will be 97,500 pounds.

    a. Calculate the EOQ for ink for this year.

    b. Calculate the EOQ for ink for last year, assuming all costs and prices were the same then as they are now.

c. Determine the correct order size for this year if the supplier of the ink decides that all orders must be in even increments of 1,200 pounds (a palletload).

2. Southern Microchip is a medium-sized wholesaler of computer memory chips located in Buckatunna, Mississippi. Lee Willard, the inventory manager, is getting ready to lay in a new stock of 30686 CPU chips. Each chip costs $594.26 from the manufacturer. Lee knows he will need 25,000 chips in the course of the year. It costs him $55 to place an order, and due to special conditions, each chip's holding cost is 30 percent of its price. If the 30786 chip is made available during the year, Lee knows he'll need 10,000 of those. They are expected to cost $700 each, but require no special storage conditions, so holding only runs ten percent of the price per year. Ordering cost is the same.

a. How many 30686 chips should Lee order at a time?

b. How many of the 30786 constitute an optimal order?

Crossword Puzzle for Chapter 15

ACROSS CLUES

5. Activities concerned with efficient movement of finished goods from factory to the consumer
6. Type of transportation rate given by carriers to shippers as reward for regular use or large volume
8. Organized group of components linked according to a plan for achieving specific objectives
10. Process of combining as many packages as possible into one load
12. Type of warehouse in which goods are kept prior to shipment
13. Control system designed to minimize costs by providing inventory in timely manner

DOWN CLUES

1. Improved or additional service offering not usually available to customers
2. Inventory item that is unavailable for delivery or sale
3. Condition in which individual objectives are achieved at the expense of broader objectives
4. Process of combining several unitized loads of products into a single load
7. Standard transportation rate established for shipping various commodities
9. Warehouse designed to assemble and redistribute goods to facilitate rapid movement to consumers
11. Method of determining optimal order quantity by trading off holding costs against ordering costs

WORD LIST:

CLASS
COMMODITY
CONTAINERIZATION
DISTRIBUTION
EOQMODEL
JITSYSTEM
PHYSICALDISTRIBUTION

STORAGE
STOCKOUT
SUBOPTIMIZATION
SYSTEM
UNITIZING
VALUEADDEDSERVICE

Chapter 15 Solutions

Key Concepts

1.	c	6.	k	11.	d	16.	e
2.	l	7.	o	12.	n		
3.	a	8.	h	13.	f		
4.	g	9.	m	14.	i		
5.	j	10.	p	15.	b		

Self Quiz

1.	T	11.	F	21.	F	31.	a	41.	c
2.	F	12.	F	22.	T	32.	c	42.	e
3.	T	13.	F	23.	T	33.	d	43.	b
4.	T	14.	T	24.	F	34.	b	44.	a
5.	F	15.	T	25.	F	35.	b	45.	e
6.	T	16.	F	26.	c	36.	d	46.	d
7.	F	17.	F	27.	a	37.	e	47.	c
8.	F	18.	T	28.	d	38.	d	48.	b
9.	T	19.	F	29.	b	39.	a	49.	d
10.	T	20.	T	30.	e	40.	c	50.	a

Applying Marketing Concepts

1.	T	6.	b	11.	T	16.	c
2.	T	7.	c	12.	F	17.	c
3.	T	8.	a	13.	F		
4.	F	9.	c	14.	b		
5.	T	10.	a	15.	a		

Computer Applications

1. a. $EOQ = \sqrt{[(2 \times 97{,}500 \times 103)/(.25)(.50)]} = $
             $\underline{12{,}676 \text{ Pounds per order}}$

     Eight orders would be placed. This would result in the purchase of some 101,408 pounds of ink, but the overage could be corrected for next year.

     b. $EOQ = \sqrt{[(2 \times 82{,}600 \times 103)/(.25)(.50)]} = $
             $\underline{11{,}668 \text{ Pounds per order}}$

     If seven orders are placed, the company will come up short by 924 pounds; better to place eight orders and correct on next year's projections.

     c.   The calculated EOQ remains the same as in (a); the manufacturer is, in effect, forcing purchases in 1,200 pound increments, so Luis would order eleven pallets (13,200 pounds) per order. He could then order either eight such batches (105,600 pounds) and correct in next year's estimate, or place seven standard orders (92,400 pounds) and one order for five pallets (6,000 pounds) if he wished to minimize carryover inventory.

2. a. $EOQ = \sqrt{(2)(25{,}000)(55)/594.26(.30)}$ $= 124 \text{ units}$

     b. $EOQ = \sqrt{(2)(10{,}000)(55)/700(.10)}$ $= 125 \text{ units}$

     The similarity of the EOQs in this case is accounted for by the lower demand and lower carrying cost of the 30786 chip as opposed to the 30686, despite the higher price of the 786.

Crossword Puzzle Solution

The crossword solution contains the following answers:

Across:
- 5. PHYSICAL DISTRIBUTION
- 6. COMMODITY
- 8. SYSTEM
- 10. UNITIZING
- 12. STORAGE
- 13. JIT SYSTEM

Down:
- 1. VALUE ADDED
- 2. STOCKOUT
- 3. SUBPTIMIZATION
- 4. CONTAINERIZATION
- 7. CLASS
- 8. SERVICE
- 9. DISTRIBUTION
- 11. EOQ MODEL

Name _____   Instructor _____

Section _____   Date _____

Cases for Part 5

1. Leonhardt Farms, Inc.

Roy Leonhardt, owner and chief executive of Leonhardt Farms, a large head vegetable operation near Fresno, California, is considering a suggestion made to him by his son, Roy, Jr., a recent graduate of Cal State. Junior has suggested that the family corporation, now one of the largest independent growers of lettuce and cabbage on the West Coast, abandon its long-standing relationship with the Greengrocer Wholesale Food Brokerage Company and handle its own distribution. Junior contends that Leonhardt's own railroad sidings and truck fleet are adequate to handle outbound shipments and that the special services available from the railroads, like diversion in transit, will make it possible for Leonhardt to process orders that come in during the picking season even after the lettuce and cabbage have been shipped.

Dad is not so eager to abandon the relationship between the farm and Greengrocer. Greengrocer has always been very efficient in preselling Leonhardt's output before it was harvested, and paid promptly. Roy never had to bother with worrying about the mechanics of getting the goods where they were needed. He simply shipped in carload lots where Greengrocer told him to. Now he was concerned. Junior seemed so confident in their ability to handle this new state of affairs.

Question:

Before making a decision, what are some additional factors that Mr. Leonhardt had better consider before implementing Roy, Junior's, plan?

2. *Aquaplane Industries, Incorporated*

Aquaplane Industries, a well-established boat builder with yards in Jacksonville and Pensacola, Florida, and Brownsville, Texas, builds and sells twenty to thirty-four foot pleasure boats designed specifically for salt-water uses. Since the company's beginning in 1956, sales have grown steadily during periods of economic growth and have been stable during downturns of the economy. Recently, however, John Massa, sales manager for Aquaplane, has been under pressure from Harbie Mellner, the company president, to increase sales and profits. John believes this can best be done through the company's existing marketing channels. After analyzing his firm's distribution pattern, Massa has come to the conclusion that increased sales through marinas, the company's only distributors, are unlikely.

An additional marketing channel for Aquaplane has been suggested by Rick Mingus, a volume used-car dealer in a major Gulf Coast city. Mingus wants to sell Aquaplane boats on his used-car lots, because "for many middle-class customers the choice is between a second car and a boat." Mingus has pledged to promote Aquaplane boats aggressively and, in return or an exclusive dealership, to carry no competing line of boats.

John realizes that marketing channels do change over time, and he is interested in experimenting with new channel arrangements. Perhaps this new channel would increase sales and profits for Aquaplane.

Questions:

a.   What factors constitute important considerations for Aquaplane's decision?

b. What steps should be included in the selection of a new marketing channel?

c. Should Massa accept Mingus' offer?

3. *Mimi's Mart*

Mimi Delachaise, owner of Mimi's Mart, a medium-sized supermarket located in Plaisance, a growing southern city of 15,000, has enjoyed ten years of successful operation. Recently, however, her dreams of an uncomplicated existence were rudely disrupted when Market Giant Stores, a national discount supermarket chain, announced plans to build a store in a new shopping center located at the southern edge of Plaisance.

Market Giant is an efficient chain that sells on a high-volume, low-price basis. Not only does Market Giant sell national brand merchandise at low prices, it also has an excellent house brand, Market Gold. Market Gold is a fast-selling line of food products that is always priced a few cents less than national brands. Market Giant also stocks an economy brand called Mighty Good that attracts some buyers.

Ms. Delachaise realizes that Mimi's Mart can't compete on a price basis. She is hoping, however, that the fine, friendly service and excellent reputation of her store will keep her customers from leaving to shop at Market Giant.

Garrison Alidont, general manager of Alidont Grocery Supply Company, has proposed that Ms. Delachaise join his organization. Alidont pointed out that this organization, a voluntary chain of thirty-five independent supermarkets, buys in quantity and obtains discounts similar to those enjoyed by Market Giant. In addition, his organization has its own line of branded merchandise, Gourmet Delight, which is comparable in quality and price to Market Gold. Alidont alleged to Ms. Delachaise that if she joined his chain she could "compete with Market Giant in every way."

Questions:

a.   What benefits can a voluntary chain provide a retailer?

b.   Should Ms. Delachaise accept Mr. Alidont's invitation to join his voluntary chain?

4. Printemps du Nord

Printemps du Nord, a Montreal-based medium-priced department store, is considering opening an outlet in Duquesne City, a town of some 300,000 located in a northern state of the U.S. Two locations are under serious consideration by Printemps. The first would be in a new, medium-sized shopping center located at the opposite end of town from a five-year-old, existing center which contains the flagship location of Duquesne City's only home-owned department store chain.

The new shopping center will contain a department store which could be Printemps), a grocery store, a hardware store, a variety store, a drug store, a discount department store, a bank, and about thirty specialty shops. The developer of the new shopping center has asked Printemps to be the department store. It is understood that if Printemps does not accept, the home-owned chain will probably take that location.

Some of Printemps' people are in favor of the new shopping center location. Their enthusiasm is tempered, however, by the belief that if the branch is not profitable in four years, there could be financial problems. The other location which is being examined by Printemps is in the central business district of Duquesne City. Even though the home-owned department store closed its downtown location five years ago to move to the shopping center, there is another department store in the CBD which is doing well. In addition, the federal government is planning a major office complex downtown, and there are strong rumors that a major New York corporation shifting its corporate headquarters to a location in downtown Duquesne City.

Printemps officials are somewhat turned off to the new shopping center because there will be a discount department store located there. They feel the discounter will provide serious competition. Printemps, because it offers higher levels of service and a repair facility for appliances, can't match the prices of the discount operation. The shopping-center developer can't be talked out of that feature of the center.

Question:

What action do you think Printemps du Nord should take?

5. *Milkmaid Manufacturing Company*

Milkmaid Manufacturing Company makes mechanical milking machines sold through dealers. They are thinking of changing their distribution system. Currently, each dealer maintains a small inventory of one or possibly two of the bulky milkers and storage units. Final assembly of milker/storage units takes place at one of four Milkmaid strategically-located warehouses before shipment to dealers takes place. Common carriers are used to ship the units from the main plant to the regional warehouses and from the regional warehouses to the dealers.

There have been problems with this system of late. Carrier service has at times been poor. Some deliveries have been late and others have arrived in damaged condition. Melrose Mescaline, marketing manager for Milkmaid, has been searching for alternatives that will reduce dealer complaints and, if at all possible, reduce physical distribution expense. You have been called in to render your expert opinion.

Questions:

a.   What alternative transportation arrangement would you suggest Milkmaid consider? Should it buy or lease its own trucks, use a contract carrier, or possibly resort to some sort of intermodal transportation?

b.   What do you think of Milkmaid's assembly and storage ware-houses? Is there a better way to provide for storage and assembly?

6. Wilson Publishing Company

Wilson Textbook Company published college textbooks which are used throughout the United States and Canada. Textbooks are ordered by college bookstores as soon as professors place orders for their courses. All orders are filled from the company plant located at Ridiculous Falls, Ohio.

Every term a number of professors are late ordering books. This creates a flurry of activity at the beginning of every semester. Recently, the number of late orders has been growing, and delivery of some texts has been as late as two weeks after the beginning of classes. Needless to say, complaints from professors and students have increased in number and virulence. The management of Wilson, however, sees no way to solve the problem as long as professors continue to place late orders.

Questions:

a. What changes would you suggest be made in Wilson's distribution system?

b. Should Wilson attempt to advise professors to order early? Can company salespeople obtain accurate order estimates? In other words, can the order-processing system be improved?

Name _____   Instructor _____

Section _____   Date _____

Creating a Marketing Plan: Let's Find a Place to Hang Our Hats

The information which you will receive in this episode should allow you to complete Part III. C. of your marketing plan.

Episode Five

"If I ever have to look at another dump like that last one, I'll quit!" was Laura's vehement comment after she and Brian drove away from the address the commercial real estate agent had given them. She and the guys knew what they needed: a place of about 2,000 square feet, part warehouse/service area, part office, located near the center of concentration of the businesses in New Essex. The problem seemed to be that the places they felt they could afford suffered from one or more fatal flaws, like inadequate wiring or lack of securability—after all, the place was going to be full of computers, test equipment, and components.

"Let's try one more place, 'L,'" said Brian, the ever-optimistic. Now that we've established our credit with MicroDevices and KLB, we can get going as soon as we get a place. It was rare luck that we were able to buy those two service vans the telephone company ordered but never had delivered. I doubt that we could have found such nice machines anywhere else for the price. It's a good thing your uncle is in the automobile business and knew about them."

"That's true. I guess I can't expect everything to go smoothly all the time. Didn't you say you had seen an ad in today's paper for a place that it sounded like we could use?" asked Laura.

"Yes," replied Brian, "it's right around the next corner. Let's take a look." And so saying, they turned the corner and parked next to a nicely-maintained concrete block building. "I see there's someone here," said Laura, pointing to a small van parked next to the open side door of the structure.

"Maybe we can get in and take a look," was Brian's reply, "or maybe whoever's there can tell us something about the place." They approached the open door.

Thirty minutes later they emerged in the company of an older man. "The place is just perfect, Mr. Cressy. We'll have our attorney call yours tomorrow to iron out the details, but I think we've got a deal," said Laura, shaking hands with the older man. "Very good, Ms. Claire," was his response, "I think you'll find the building and the location are perfect for your plans." Later, back at Laura's house, where Terry was waiting, the threesome sat down to organize their thoughts. Terry passed out sheets of paper to the other two and said, "Here are the suppliers we've arranged to buy from and the lead times from each one. Obviously, we're going to have to stock more deeply on parts from some of these people than from others."

Table P6-1: Suppliers, Items Supplied, and Lead Times

Supplier	Items Supplied	Lead Time
Action Electronics	Mechanical Parts	7 days
KLB Corporation	Electronic Parts	7 days
New Haven Electronics	Electronic Parts	7 days
LL Melwer	Electronic Devices	7 days
NPN Electronics	Mechanical Parts	7 days
Data Exchange	Printer Parts	14 days
Micro Devices	Electrical Devices	30 days
Okidata	Printer Parts	30-90 days
Epsom	Printer Parts	30-90 days
NEC	Printer Parts	30-60 days
Star Micronics	Printer Parts	30-60 days
Panasonic	Printer Parts	30-45 days
Data Products	Printer Parts	30 days

"Why do these printer people take so long to fill orders?" asked Brian. "I guess because all those parts are imported, and maybe they make less money from selling them than they do from selling finished goods," replied Terry. "Anyway, those lead times are what they told me, so I guess we'd better proceed accordingly."

"Right, let's order the stuff we're going to need to have on hand when we open the doors. I suppose we'd better plan for the full length of time for replenishment on those printer parts, so get what you think we'll need for the longest lead time when you order," Laura told Terry. "You guys get on home now, and we'll meet again tomorrow morning to get the lease finalized with the lawyer."

Guidelines:

Review the requirements of Part III.C. of your Marketing Plan, and, using the information in this episode, complete that Part of the plan.

Solutions to Cases for Part Five

1. Leonhardt Farms, Inc.

Wholesale middlemen exist because they perform services for their producer and their retailer customers. Mr. Leonhardt should give a great deal of consideration to the services Greengrocer Wholesale Brokerage has performed for him before implementing his son's suggestion. At this moment, it is doubtful the Mr. Leonhardt knows who the firms are that have traditionally bought his lettuce and cabbage. It is doubtful that they are aware of him, even if he does package his product in Leonhardt Farms boxes for shipment to market. The implication is that the wholesale intermediary has been functioning in the capacity of a marketing department for Leonhardt Farms. As a result, the Farms have no sales personnel, no immediate contact with their ultimate customers, and no means of assuring, at least for the immediate future, a market for their output. I would therefore advise Mr. Leonhardt to table—not discard, but table—young Roy's suggestion. Meanwhile, young Roy should be assigned to gather information about the nature of the overall channel structure in fresh head vegetables and to learn how these vegetables are sold into that market by producers that do not use wholesale intermediaries. He should be sent to learn more about the availability of those special transportation services he was talking about. They may or may not be appropriate for products like this. (In fact, they are, but there are many details which would have to be ironed out before they could be effectively used.)

In short, it may, at some time in the foreseeable future, be possible to implement young Roy's suggestion, but for the moment Leonhardt Farms is certainly not in a position to dismiss Greengrocer Wholesale and go out on their own.

2. Aquaplane Industries, Inc.

a. The idea of selling boats through a used car dealership should be considered in the context of the following variables, among others, before a response is made to Mr. Mingus' offer:

In terms of consumer perceptions:
Is a used car lot an appropriate place, from the viewpoint of consumers, to shop for a boat? Is the image of used car lots and salespeople consistent with the image of new boats?

In terms of product characteristics:
Can a used car dealership provide the necessary level of service and maintenance required for this class of boat? Will Mingus' personnel be able to properly describe the features of the Aquaplane line? Again, is the image of the used car lot consistent with the image of the Aquaplane line?

In terms of distribution:
How would the marinas that currently carry the Aquaplane line feel about the addition of the new distribution channel? What should the functional (trade) discount for a used car dealer be?

From the producer's point of view:
Does Aquaplane really need a new channel? How much money is there to finance such a channel?

These questions begin the discussion of the desirability of Aquaplane selecting marketing intermediaries, particularly the one which has surfaced. Aquaplane needs to develop a set of specific criteria to apply in the selection of new channels and their members.

b. The steps used in selecting a new channel of distribution are described in this section. The first step is to analyze the market, product, producer, and competitive factors. The second step is to determine the level of intensity of distribution desired.

c. No, I don't think the Mingus offer should be accepted. A used car lot is not a very appropriate place to look for a large, offshore boat. Used car dealers haven't the necessary image, nor do they possess the right kind of repair facilities for a product like this. Their personnel aren't knowledgeable about boats and would have to be trained to do the job correctly. To top it all off, I imagine it would be rather difficult to find a used car lot located conveniently close to a body of water big enough to demonstrate a boat in this class.

3. Mimi's Mart

a. Voluntary chains provide retailers with several benefits. First, the chain's buying power allows the independent to get product cheaper than would be the case if the independent had to make every purchase from a marketing intermediary. In addition, the voluntary chain can usually provide a private label that the independent can call its own, giving customers the same priceline choices as at the major chains. The private label provides some name recognition among customers who have shopped other members of the voluntary chain. Most voluntary chains also provide management information that the independent would have to buy elsewhere for more money. And finally, the wholesaler can provide to Mimi information on product movement and prices that she does not now get.

b. The voluntary chain looks like a good competitive move on Mimi's part. Before going with Mr. Alidont, however, she should shop around to see if there might be an alternative voluntary or perhaps a retailer's cooperative she could join that will offer better benefits or prices on goods and services of similar quality. Mimi must respond to the challenge posed by Market Giant or she will become uncompetitive, and in the compete-or-die world of modern business, surely perish.

4. Printemps du Nord

Printemps du Nord should move into the new shopping center. If they do not, they will be leaving the suburbs solely to the local department store. The discount department store is not the problem Printemps seems to think it is. Many shopping centers feature a discounter and a full-service store as their anchor outlets. Generally, people do not shop for the same goods at the two sorts of stores (and some people do not shop one or the other sort, period!). They do *not* want to go downtown and slug it out with the other store presently located there. Central business districts are risky locations in which to locate a department store nowadays. In general, they have experienced economic decline, but some have begun to resurge and offer real opportunity. There is insufficient information in the case to suggest that the time is ripe for Duquesne City to move back downtown. The only real risk is that the new shopping center will bomb and Printemps will not succeed in this market.

5. Milkmaid Manufacturing Company

a. Milkmaid can choose from a number of transportation alternatives, including:

Contract carriers
Company owned carriers
Leased carriers
A new common carrier.

The intermittent nature of Milkmaid's shipping schedule—it is obvious they don't ship milking machines on anything like a regular schedule—tends to rule out the purchase of their own truck or the lease of one for an entire year. The best bet for this company is probably a change of common carrier of the use of a contract carrier on an as-needed basis. The contract carrier, because of the closer relationship between this form of carrier and its user, offers the better choice in this case.

b. A change to contract carriers solves the obvious problem of being forced to maintain four regional warehouses for assembly purposes. Better service, able to make longer hauls with less risk of damage, may make it possible to assemble complete milker units at the factory and ship them direct to dealers. There isn't enough information in the case to make a final decision, but it is reasonable to expect that the idea of reducing the number of assembly facilities will occur to the serious student who reads this case.

6. Wilson Publishing Company

a. One can but wonder how centrally located Ridiculous Falls, Ohio, is to Wilson's market. Even if it is reasonably central, a single facility hardly seems enough to serve the needs of all the country's colleges and universities. Subsidiary distribution centers in, say, northern California, Texas, South Carolina, and Connecticut would spread the load across the entire population of students and make delivery time to any given school shorter.

b. Late orders are not always the professor's fault. Sure, some of us put off book ordering till the last minute, but some schools engage in the "last minute shuffle," changing the courses professors teach up until the last week or so before classes are to meet. Wilson has absolutely no control over this sort of behavior, but might experiment with some of the following ideas:

Increase sales practitioners' bonuses for accurate estimates of demand.

Reward sales practitioners who get bookstore orders early.

Reward bookstores for early ordering.

Place a surcharge on late orders.

Increase book prices for late orders.

Use telemarketing to call bookstores and request early orders.

Set up a 1-800 number for late orders.

Ship late orders Federal Express—at the purchaser's expense.

Wilson should assign someone the task of establishing a better procedure for receiving and shipping orders. A combination of the answers to question (a) and one or more of the other suggestions mentioned in this answer would help the company minimize late orders. There will always, however, be emergency orders.

Solutions for Creating a Marketing Plan

Episode Five

Latebri Industries, as a service organization, occupies a somewhat unusual position in the distribution channel. Technically, they are merchant wholesalers in that the goods they purchase are purchased for resale to industrial or trade users. Their position in the local market is such, however, that they will be treated as retailers by local wholesalers and sold merchandise at what is usually referred to as "the wholesale price." Recognition of this fact is probably beyond most of your students, but it makes an interesting point because it is directly related to the "intention of the buyer" difficulty in identifying whether a specific transaction is a retail or a wholesale sale—it all depends on the intention of the buyer. At any rate, Latebri will be participating in a marketing channel in which they will be acting as a middleman for parts and components and a direct provider of repair and related services. The table (Table P6-1) outlines the specific lines of goods which they will keep in stock, though we do not know as yet their relative quantities. Needless to say, the rather radical differences in lead times among the various suppliers is going to have a pronounced effect on the absolute quantities of certain of the goods which will have to kept on hand.

The youngsters have already acquired most of the physical distribution facilities they are going to need: two delivery (or field service) vans and a combination shop/warehouse/office. They are probably also going to need some materials handling equipment, like a carrycart and perhaps a handtruck for some of the heavier and bulkier equipment which they will be moving.

Their location was chosen to make them physically convenient to the greatest number of businesses. Obviously, they took some care in the choice. They are certainly aware of the need for a secure location, a particular consideration for firms which handle high-value merchandise or merchandise which has a high appeal in the resale market (or to be fenced).

Their major physical distribution characteristics, in my estimation, should be accessibility, speed, and a low rate of damage to merchandise while it is in their hands. They should also, in the context of the textbook, offer frequent departures and flexibility of scheduling, though these features are perhaps redundant to mention in this context. It is important to remember that their operating philosophy is "minimum downtime" for their customers. Moreover, I think it is significant that one of the things they were looking for was a building that wasn't a "dump." While physical beauty is not a necessary attribute of a facility devoted to this sort of activity, it sure doesn't hurt to produce an attractive appearance when customers come to drop off or pick up equipment. More will be said on this under promotion.

Part 6

Promotional Strategy

Promotion is one of the most dynamic and severely criticized aspects of marketing. Closely related to the process of communication, it is the marketing activity charged with providing information, increasing demand, differentiating products, accentuating their value, and stabilizing sales. Promotional mix elements include personal selling and nonpersonal selling (subdivided into advertising, sales promotion, and public relations). Effective promotional strategy requires that these elements be properly mixed.

Nonpersonal selling includes advertising, sales promotion, and public relations. *Advertising*, any nonpersonal sales presentation carried by a medium and usually directed to a large number of potential customers, is an important part of modern business.

Sales promotion is the name applied to assorted nonrecurrent and somewhat extraordinary nonpersonal selling efforts. The basic types of sales promotion include: point-of-purchase displays; specialty advertising; trade shows; samples, coupons, and premiums; contests; and trading stamps.

Public relations activities are often used to supplement other promotional efforts in the marketing mix. Publicity, part of public relations, obtains favorable media coverage for a firm without payment to the media.

Integrated marketing communications coordinates all promotional efforts with a customer focus. Teamwork is essential to IMC's success. An optimal promotional mix depends on the nature of the market, the nature of the product, stage in the product life cycle, price of the product, and funds available for promotion.

The objectives of promotion form the basis for the promotional budget. Traditional methods of allocating a promotional budget are percentage of sales, a fixed sum per unit, meeting the competition, and task-objective.

Personal selling, a vital part of the promotional mix, has evolved from the old-time peddler to today's professional sales practitioner. The sales process usually follows seven steps beginning with prospecting and qualifying and ending with follow-up after the sale has been made. The content and emphasis of the sales presentation depends on whether the sales practitioner is responsible for order processing, creative selling, or missionary sales. A personal sales force means sales management. Someone must recruit, train, organize, supervise, pay, and evaluate sales practitioners and act in a boundary-spanning role between them and upper-level management.

Chapter 16

Introduction to Promotion

Chapter Outline

You may want to use the following outline as a guide in taking notes.

    I.   Chapter Overview—the Elements of the Promotional Process

    II.   The Communications Process

    III.   Objectives of Promotion

         A. Provide information

         B. Increase demand

         C. Differentiate the product

         D. Accentuate the product's value

         E. Stabilize sales

    IV.   The Promotional Mix

         A. Personal selling

         B. Nonpersonal selling

    V.   Integrated Marketing Communications

         A. The importance of teamwork

    VI.   Developing an Optimal Promotional Mix

         A. Nature of the product

         B. Role of databases in effective IMC efforts

         C. Nature of the product

D. Stage in the product life cycle

E. Price

F. Funds available for promotion

VII.   Pulling and Pushing Promotional Strategies

VIII. Budgeting for Promotional Strategy

IX.   Measuring the Effectiveness of Promotion

X.   The Value of Promotion

A. Social importance

B. Business importance

C. Economic importance

Name _____   Instructor _____

Section _____   Date _____

Key Concepts

The purpose of this section is to allow you to determine if you can match key concepts with their definitions. It is essential that you know the definitions of the concepts prior to applying the concepts in later exercises in this chapter.

From the list of lettered terms, select the one that best fits in the blank of the numbered statement below. Write the letter of that choice in the space provided.

Key Terms

a. promotion
b. marketing communications
c. AIDA concept
d. promotional mix
e. personal selling
f. advertising
g. sales promotion
h. trade promotion
i. public relations
j. publicity
k. integrated marketing communications (I.M.C.)
l. Pulling strategy
m. Pushing strategy
n. Percentage-of-sales method
o. fixed-sum-per-unit method
p. task-objective method
q. fixed-sum-per-unit method

_____ 1. Promotional budget allocation method in which a firm defines its goals and then determines the amount of promotional spending needed to achieve them.

_____ 2. Marketing activities other than personal selling, advertising, and publicity that stimulate consumer purchasing and dealer effectiveness.

_____ 3. Transmission from a sender to a receiver of messages dealing with the buyer-seller relationships.

_____ 4. Stimulation of demand by disseminating commercially significant news or obtaining favorable media presentation not paid for by an identifiable sponsor.

_____ 5. Traditional expansion of the steps that lead to a purchase decision.

_____ 6. Informing, influencing, and persuading the consumer's purchase decision

_____ 7. Interpersonal influence process involving a seller's promotional presentation conducted on a person-to-person basis with the prospective buyer.

_____ 8. Firm's communications and relationships with its various publics.

_____ 9. Effort by a seller to stimulate demand by final users, who will exert pressure on the distribution channel to provide the good or service.

_____ 10. Budget allocation method in which promotional expenditures are a predetermined dollar amount for each sales or production unit.

_____ 11. Promotional budget allocation method that matches competitors' promotional outlays on either an absolute or relative basis.

_____ 12. Coordination of all promotional activities to produce a unified promotional message that is customer-focused.

_____ 13.   Blend of personal selling and nonpersonal selling created by marketers in an attempt to achieve promotional objectives.

_____ 14.   Paid, nonpersonal communication through various media by a sponsor that is identified in the message and hopes to inform or persuade members of a particular audience.

_____ 15.   Budget allocation method in which the funds allocated for promotion during a given time are based on a specified percentage of either past or forecast sales.

_____ 16.   Effort by a seller to members of the marketing channel to stimulate personal selling of the good or service.

_____ 17.   Sales promotion techniques aimed at marketing intermediaries rather than ultimate consumers.

Name _____   Instructor _____

Section _____   Date _____

Self Quiz

You should use these questions to test your understanding of the material in this chapter. You can check your answers with those provided at the end of the chapter.

While these questions cover most of the chapter topics, they are not intended to be the same as the test questions your instructor may use in an examination. A good understanding of all aspects of the course material is necessary to good performance on any examination.

True/False

Write "T" for True and "F" for False for each of the following statements.

_____ 1. For communication to be effective, it is only necessary that the message be understood by the sender.

_____ 2. In E. K. Strongs's acronym, AIDA stands for attention, interest, desire, and action.

_____ 3. Feedback to a communication may take the form of attitude change, purchase, or even nonpurchase of a good or service.

_____ 4. A promotional program seeking to increase primary demand is aimed at increasing the desire for a specific brand of product.

_____ 5. Noise in the communications process always results from some sort of mechanical or electronic failure in the communications equipment.

_____ 6. The primary objective of most promotion is to increase the demand for a specific product or service.

_____ 7. Hotels and motels, which ordinarily have high occupancy during the weekends from tourist guests, often promote special midweek packages at reduced rates to boost business occupancy.

_____ 8. The sign in the Bucharest hotel lobby read: "The lift is being fixed for the next day. During this time we regret you will be unbearable." This is an example of how noise from the process of translation can creep into a communication.

_____ 9. A differentiated demand schedule for a product, in contrast to one which is homogeneous with respect to competition, permits more flexibility in marketing strategy, such as price changes.

_____ 10. If a nonpersonal promotion is designed to stimulate demand for a product or service by obtaining favorable presentation of it on radio, TV, or on the stage without having to pay for it, it is publicity.

_____ 11. Personal selling is generally the most effective form of promotion when there is mass consumption of a product and a geographically dispersed market.

_____ 12. In the introductory stage of the product life cycle, personal selling is heavily emphasized to inform the marketplace of the merits of the new product or service.

_____ 13. Low-unit-value products are typically promoted using a heavy proportion of advertising in the promotional mix.

_____ 14. A pulling promotional strategy relies on personal selling to convince members of the channel of distribution to spend extra time and effort promoting the vendor's product.

_____   15.   Industrial firms generally spend more of their promotional budget for advertising than personal selling, while the reverse is true for consumer goods companies.

_____   16.   Promotion is subject to diminishing returns; that is, at some point in time an increase in promotional spending will fail to produce a corresponding increase in sales.

_____   17.   The ideal method of allocating a promotional budget is to increase the budget until no further money is available to be spent for promotion; in other words, to use every penny you can lay your hands on for promotion.

_____   18.   The use of the single-source research system has revolutionized the evaluation of consumer advertising and sales promotion.

_____   19.   Criticisms of advertising which focus on words such as "tasteless" and "obnoxious" ignore the fact that no commonly accepted set of values exists within our social framework. In other words, there's no such thing as "bad taste," only your taste and my taste.

_____   20.   Probably the most common way to set promotional budgets, the "fixed-sum per unit method" applies a predetermined money allocation to each unit of sale or production.

_____   21.   A traditional method of allocating promotional outlays involves simply meeting competition dollar for dollar or on a percentage basis; it is thought that this method merely preserves the status quo—everybody keeps their market share but nobody moves ahead.

_____   22.   Quantitative measures of the effectiveness of each promotional mix component for a specified market segment are now available.

_____   23.   Among the indirect methods of evaluating the effectiveness of advertising are recall and readership measurements.

_____   24.   Integrated marketing communications frequently result in a competitive advantage for marketers' efforts to reach and serve their target market.

_____   25.   When a new prescription drug receives FDA approval, the drug firm selling it must switch its promotional strategy from consumer advertising to personal selling.

Multiple Choice

Circle the letter of the phrase or sentence that best completes the sentence or best answers the question.

26.   An effective message must
   a.   be understood by the receiver.
   b.   stimulate the receiver's needs and suggest an appropriate method of satisfying them.
   c.   be understood by the sender.
   d.   gain the receiver's attention.
   e.   achieve all of the above objectives.

27.   The AIDA concept proposed by E. K. Strong over sixty years ago explains
   a.   why Giuseppe Verdi named his opera in this peculiar fashion.
   b.   the steps that lead to a purchase decision.
   c.   the relationship among ability, intelligence, dedication, and activity in the marketing process.
   d.   the structural relationships among variables in the development of the promotional mix.
   e.   the various components of the promotional process: advertising, indoctrination, description, and acceptance.

28.   In the communications process, the receiver's interpretation of the message is known as
   a.   feedback.
   b.   transmission.
   c.   encoding.
   d.   decoding.
   e.   noise.

29. The major advantage of this form of promotion are that it can be more accurately monitored than some of the alternatives, produces an immediate consumer response, attracts attention and creates product awareness, and provides short-term sales increases. This promotional tool is
    a. advertising.
    b. personal selling.
    c. sales promotion.
    d. public relations.
    e. publicity.

30. Of the following, which is most correctly an example of noise in the marketing communications process?
    a. An advertisement is incorrectly assumed to be a news program by a viewer who tunes in a little late.
    b. A viewer of the President's State of the Union message refuses to believe a word of it because he/she is a member of a different political party.
    c. An individual isn't there when a promotional message appears on television.
    d. Viewers laugh off a tornado alert because they've never been through a twister and don't believe in the danger.
    e. A commercial is presented at the right time, to the right audience, using the correct advertising medium.

31. A newspaper advertisement which emphasizes such items as descriptions of merchandise, prices, and store hours is most likely designed to
    a. differentiate the merchandise from competitive merchandise in the same marketplace.
    b. lay emphasis on the product's value.
    c   provide market information.
    d. stabilize sales of the products over a period of time.
    e. promote the business rather than the products themselves.

32. If promotion is successful in increasing the demand for a product or class of products, the result should be
    a. retaining the same level of sales by lowering the price.
    b. an increase in sales without a corresponding decrease in price.
    c. a decline in sales volume despite a lowering of the price.
    d. stabilization of sales volumes and prices across the industry.
    e. erratic changes in sales volumes which seem to have no relationship to price levels.

33. In the communications process, feedback refers to
    a. the receiver's response to the message.
    b. the receiver's interpretation of the message.
    c. interference at some stage in the communications process.
    d. the transfer mechanism by which the message is delivered.
    e. the translation of the message into understandable terms.

34. The original form of promotion, the one with the longest history, is
    a. advertising; advertising messages have even been found on the walls of the ruins of Pompeii.
    b. public relations; the Phoenicians were always very careful to keep on good terms with their customers and competitors.
    c. sales promotion; it is recorded that the ancient Greeks often offered premiums and prizes to employees who sold more than their quota.
    d. personal selling; presumably, the very first exchanges in trade were made by two individuals acting face-to-face.
    e. publicity; no one knows for sure when publicity began, but Pepsi bottles at least three thousand years old have been found at stage level in the ruins of the Greek theatre at Catharsis.

35. Advertising, sales promotion, and public relations are all
    a. paid communications through various media that include identification of the sponsor and which hope to inform or persuade members of a particular audience.
    b. examples of promotion through mass media such as newspapers, television, radio, magazines, and billboards.
    c. particularly appropriate methods of promoting products that rely on sending the same promotional message to large audiences.
    d. nonrecurrent promotional methods used on an irregular basis.
    e. examples of forms of nonpersonal selling.

36. A firm's communications and relationships with its various publics defines
    a. public relations.
    b. publicity.
    c. advertising.
    d. sales promotion.
    e. personal selling.

37. Royal Caribbean Cruise Lines' advertising emphasizing the quality, service, and amenities of its cruises most exemplifies promotion's ability to
    a. provide information to potential customers.
    b. accentuate a product's value by pointing out its greater ownership value.
    c. differentiate one product from another even when those products are virtually identical.
    d. stabilize sales of a product with a seasonal market.
    e. create demand among nonusers of the product class.

38. The fact that highly standardized products with minimal servicing requirements are less likely to depend on personal selling than are custom products that are technically complex is an example of the way
    a. the nature of the market influences the promotional mix.
    b. the stage in the product life cycle affects the promotional mix.
    c. the nature of the product affects the promotional mix.
    d. the product's price affects the promotional mix.
    e. the funds available for promotion affect the promotional mix.

39. The stage of the product life cycle that most often shows the heaviest emphasis on personal selling as a promotional tool is
    a. later maturity.
    b. mid-growth.
    c. decline.
    d. early maturity.
    e. introduction.

40.   If a manufacturer begins advertising a new good to consumers before that good has even become available to wholesale and retail intermediaries in the channel of distribution, it is probably using a
a.   pushing strategy to secure distribution at the wholesale level of the channel.
b.   thrust-off promotion to get the product adopted by the members of the channel before the public becomes aware of it.
c.   mixed-bag strategy designed to create the proper atmosphere for product introduction to the consumer market.
d.   pulling strategy to develop end-user demand so that final consumers will force retailers and wholesalers to stock the product.
e.   forced-choice program to make channel members decide which of two competing products they're going to stock.

41.   Which of the following combinations of sales promotional techniques is increasing in popularity with food marketers as a means of gaining consumer support?
a.   extensive use of newspaper inserts and cents-off coupons
b.   consumer advertising using interactive home computing equipment and production of self-sponsored TV programs
c.   increasingly elaborate point-of-purchase displays and manufacturer salesmen "pitching" the product in the stores
d.   sponsorship of special events and unusual sampling settings such as out-of-store locations.
e.   mechanized promotions such as robots serving the product and use of comparison tests loaded in favor of the sponsor's product.

42.   Evidence suggests that sales initially lag behind promotion
a.   for structural reasons—stocking retail shelves, low initial production, and lack of buyer knowledge.
b.   because promotional efforts are often misdirected in the beginning, aiming at markets that don't develop.
c.   because the promotional budget is too small to support a sufficiently high level of sales in the beginning.
d.   because diminishing returns are typical during this period of product availability—spending more on promotion doesn't yield greater sales.
e.   for no apparent reason; there is insufficient data on which to base any conclusions.

43.   The method of allocating a promotional budget most consistent with the marketing concept is
a.   to try and get every nickel you can lay your hands on and spend it largely on advertising.
b.   to spend equally on advertising, sales promotion, and personal selling.
c.   to increase the promotional budget until the cost of each additional increment equals the additional revenue received.
d.   to match what the competition spends either dollar for dollar or percent for percent.
e.   to allocate a fixed sum for advertising and when it's gone, it's gone.

44.   The most common way of establishing promotional budgets is most likely the
a.   marginal analysis method.
b.   percentage-of-sales method.
c.   fixed amount available method.
d.   fixed-sum-per-unit method.
e.   method described by Svoboda in *Alligators and Advertising*.

45. Effective use of the task-objective method of budget allocation depends on
    a. defining realistically the communication goals the promotional mix is expected to achieve.
    b. having available a very large sum of uncommitted funds to support the promotional program.
    c. understanding the necessity for a concentration of funds on advertising and the lesser importance of personal selling.
    d. retarding the promotional expenditure flow until results are apparent.
    e. carefully hoarding monies from one year to the next until they can be most effectively spent.

46. Personal selling is considered to be more important than advertising during which phase(s) of the purchasing process?
    a. prepurchase and postpurchase
    b. time of purchase and postpurchase
    c. time of purchase
    d. prepurchase
    e. postpurchase

47. Given the capacity to control for other variables operating in the marketplace, most marketers would prefer to measure promotional effectiveness using
    a. standard statistical tools such as mean difference testing.
    b. direct-sales-results tests which would reveal the impact on sales of every dollar spent on advertising.
    c. indirect evaluation of effectiveness using such devices as recall and readership analysis.
    d. sales inquiries and studies of attitude change caused by promotion.
    e. traditional methods based on the expertise of company executives.

48. Promotion has assumed a degree of social importance if for no other reason than that
    a. government administrative decisions eventually determine what is acceptable practice in the marketplace.
    b. most modern business institutions cannot survive in the long run without promotion.
    c. business enterprises recognize the importance of promotional efforts.
    d. many television commercials contribute to cultural pollution.
    e. it has become an important factor in campaigns to achieve socially oriented objectives.

49. Comments such as "Most advertisements assume I'm an idiot" and "Advertising is almost always in bad taste" relate to
    a. the importance of advertising to the economy.
    b. advertising's role in perpetuating undesirable stereotypes.
    c. advertising's importance in the business sphere.
    d. relationships we've all noticed between advertising and mental capacity.
    e. perceptions of the social importance of advertising.

50. Promotion can be said to be economically important because
    a. it provides employment for thousands of people.
    b. it increases sales volumes, thus lowering per-unit cost.
    c. it subsidizes the communications and entertainment media.
    d. it performs all of the functions outlined above.
    e. None of the above constitutes a valid reason to call promotion "important" in any fashion.

Name _____   Instructor _____

Section _____   Date _____

Applying Marketing Concepts

It's always a little rough to report for work at a new place for the first time, and John Weiler admitted to himself that he felt a little uneasy about his new job at Commonwealth Industries, one of Australia's best known makers of industrial control systems. Replacing a promotions manager who had been there for twenty-five years was not an enviable task. It didn't take John long to get into the swing of things and settle down to a long, close look at the company's promotional program.

Some things were pretty much as he expected them to be. As an industrial supplier, Commonwealth followed fairly conventional advertising and personal selling practices. John was disturbed, however, when he discovered that there was no mechanism by which the comments and actions of customers were reported back to his department. He also observed that many of the company's promotional pieces—advertisements, catalogs, and mailers—were badly written and hard to understand.

He also felt he had cause to worry about the company's relationship with the local community. Fences surrounding the plant bore signs saying "No Trespassing—Keep Out" and the main gate, which was guarded by armed security personnel, was even more intimidating with its "Stop—Show Identification—Authorized Personnel Only" sign. Such isolation seemed a bit much to John, as did the fact that Commonwealth had no athletic teams playing in the local junior or adult leagues.

1. Commonwealth's promotional program probably
   a. puts more emphasis on personal selling than on advertising.
   b. puts more emphasis on advertising than on personal selling.
   c. emphasizes personal selling and advertising about equally.
   d. uses neither personal selling nor advertising.
   e. relies on publicity to carry the burden of promotion.

2. John's concern about the lack of a way for him to get to know customers' comments and actions indicates he was concerned
   a. about the effectiveness of his sales promotion program.
   b. about the degree to which his advertising money was being wasted on fancy artwork by the layout department.
   c. that feedback from the marketplace was not being used to make adjustments to the company's programs and practices.
   d. that his position in the company was isolated from the decision makers at headquarters.
   e. that salesmen weren't doing their jobs in the field properly.

3. Difficulty in understanding an advertising message, catalog entry, or the terms of a mailer means
    a. that Commonwealth Industries must be on the verge of failure.
    b. very little; these sorts of things are used merely to get the customer's attention.
    c. that someone in the production department probably wrote the catalogs.
    d. that there is a very real danger that enough noise will be created in the communications channel to defeat the intent of the communication.
    e. that someone has probably been trying to do two jobs at once: write advertising and learn to read.

4. Commonwealth Industries' seeming isolation from the local community is probably evidence
    a. of a weakness in their public relations program.
    b. of the fact that they've got something to hide at their plant location.
    c. that the president of the company really did say "Bah, humbug!" last Christmas when approached by the local Church Fund.
    d. of the low level of competitiveness in the industrial controls market these days.
    e. of good legal thinking; the company certainly doesn't want to have to worry about paying for injuries to unauthorized persons on its grounds. It's better to shoot them for trespassing before they can hurt themselves.

Darkstar Development Company, a manufacturer of specialty photographic film used by astronomers, has retained you as its promotion manager. At present, Darkstar film is sold to wholesalers in units of six cassettes to a case, which is the standard unit for sales and cost analysis purposes. Promotional expenditures are allocated on a per case basis at the rate of $18 per case shipped.

5. Which of the following promotional budgeting techniques is Darkstar Development using?
    a. percentage of sales
    b. fixed sum per unit
    c. meeting competition
    d. task-objective method
    e. spend what you have

6. If ten percent of total sales had been the promotional allocating rule, the method would have then been
    a. percentage of sales.
    b. fixed sum per unit.
    c. meeting competition.
    d. task-objective method.
    e. marginal analysis method.

Name _____   Instructor _____

Section _____   Date _____

Experiential Exercises

1. The importance of the various promotional tools differs depending on which phase of the purchasing process the product's buyer has reached. Review your text concerning the roles which advertising and personal selling play during the prepurchase, time of purchase, and postpurchase phases of this process and then

   a. List three products and develop a promotional device to reach people during the posttransactional period.

      1. (Example) Automobile. Send the proud new purchaser of the BMW 750iL a letter congratulating him/her on his/her good taste in buying such a fine machine. Specifically mention the name of the "representative" who will be handling warranty service of the car (should any be required!) with a telephone number and address.

      2.

      3.

b.   Using the three products from part a, show how your use of promotion would differ in the pretransactional stage.

   1.   Automobile

   2.

   3.

c.   How do the objectives of promotion differ among the three stages of the purchasing process?

2. Social Customs, Holidays, and special occasions provide many opportunities for unique promotional approaches. We are all familiar with the custom of giving gifts on birthdays, of erecting decorated evergreen trees for Christmas, and of shooting fireworks on the Fourth of July. In this exercise, you will examine a bit more closely these social institutions.

a. List three customs, holidays, or special occasions observed in a foreign country of your choice and relate them to some special good or service that is called for. Then create some promotions that could be used in connection with the event. Make sure you do enough background investigation of the local culture to avoid any disastrous missteps.

Custom	Good or Service	Promotion

1.

2.

3.

b. Create your own three special occasions, holidays, or customs that would call for parties, gift-giving, or human sensitivity. Show products or services that would be required and suggest promotions that could be applied to each.

Custom	Good or Service	Promotion

1.

2.

3.

Name _____ Instructor _____

Section _____ Date _____

Computer Applications

Review the discussion of the alternative methods of allocating promotional budgets in Chapter 16 of the text. Then use menu item 13 titled "Promotional Budget Allocations" to solve each of the following problems.

1. Early Bird, a chain of coffee shops in Denver, has allocated $300,000 for its 1996 promotional budget. The allocation was based upon using the same percentage of sales as had been used during 1995. During 1995, the chain generated sales of $4,000,000 and spent a total of $240,000 on promotion. How much revenue does Early Bird expect to produce in 1996?

2. Giovanni Bianco, director of marketing for Vinos Finos, Inc., is working up his 1996 promotional budget. His historical sales and promotional figures are as follows:

Year	Sales for Year	Spent on Promotion
1991	$1,240,000	$ 87,600
1992	1,360,000	97,720
1993	1,440,000	104,400
1994	1,480,000	105,520
1995	1,504,000	112,800
1996	1,550,000 (est.)	?

Bianco has also discovered sales and promotional outlay figures on his three biggest competitors for 1995. During that year, Vins Superieurs sold about $1,640,000 worth of wine on a promotional budget of $95,120; Vinhos Portugesas sold about $2,800,000 with a promotional budget of $170,800, and Winos Northamericanos did about $3,000,000 on a promotional expenditure of $180,000.

a.   What percentage of 1995 sales should Bianco include in his 1996 promotional budget if he bases it on the percentage of sales used in 1995? How many dollars would go for promotion?

b.   Suppose Mr. Bianco decides to use the average percentage over the last five years as the basis for his 1996 promotional budget. What percentage would be included? And how many dollars would that be?

c. Suppose he based his budget for promotion on the average of the percentage expenditures of his three closest competitors. What percentage would he use? How many dollars would be appropriated for promotion?

3. Jomo Kallakaw, manager of the Finest Kind Seafood Market and Florist Shop, has decided to budget a fixed sum per unit to determine the correct promotional budget for 1996. He is going to base the exact amount on the average for other seafood markets/florist shops in his area. Available data revealed the following:

Shop	Per Unit Promotional Expenditure*
A	$17
B	28
C	35
D	45
E	50

*A unit is twelve dozen of anything—cod or roses, it doesn't matter.

Jomo expects 1996 sales to be 2500 units. How much should he allocate per unit to promotion in 1996? What will his total promotional budget be?

4. The Okaloosa Tribal Company of Belzoni, Mississippi, was founded by the Indian tribe of the same name to develop the tribe's native ability to build prefabricated wooden structures. The firm's growth has been substantial, and the high quality of the finished product and its genuine "American" design has won it high praise from architects and buyers alike. Jack Whitelaw, tribal chief and business manager of the company, is working on the promotional budget for 1996. Sales and promotional expenditure records since 1990 are summarized below:

Year	Sales	Promotion as a Percent of Sales
1990	$ 5,000,000	4.0
1991	6,200,000	4.6
1992	7,600,000	5.0
1993	8,400,000	5.2
1994	10,800,000	5.4
1995	11,900,000	5.5

The sales forecast for 1996 is $12,800,000. The firm's four major competitors have sales and promotional budgets as follow:

Competitor (Tribe)	Annual Sales (Est.)	Promotional Budget (Est.)
Calcasieu	$ 7,600,000	$319,200
Choctaw	8,400,000	596,400
Chickasaw	13,400,000	670,000
Catahoula	18,400,000	993,600

a. What percentage of 1996 sales should the Okaloosa Tribal Company include in its 1996 promotional budget if the budget is based on the percentage allocated for 1995 sales? How many dollars would be earmarked for promotion?

b. Suppose the average percentage spent over the last six years is to be the percentage allocated in 1992. What percentage would be allocated? How many dollars?

c. Jack Whitelaw is concerned that perhaps meeting competition is a better idea than simply spending to one's own average. He wonders if perhaps he should base spending for promotion on the average percentage outlays of his four major competitors. What percentage would be used if this were done? How many dollars would this be?

Crossword Puzzle for Chapter 16

CROSS CLUES

1. Firm's communications and relationships with its various publics
2. Strategy of promoting to members of the marketing channel so they will promote to their customers
3. Informing, persuading, and influencing the consumer's purchase decision
4. Blend of personal and nonpersonal selling by marketers in attempt to achieve objectives
5. Paid, nonpersonal communication through media by an identified sponsor to inform or persuade
6. Sales promotion techniques aimed at marketing intermediaries rather than ultimate consumers
7. Promotional budget allocation method where current funds are a portion of past/forecast sales

DOWN CLUES

2. Promotional budget allocation method where goals are defined and money budgeted to achieve them
3. Displays, trade shows, coupons, premiums, contests, demonstrations, for example
5. Traditional explanation of the steps leading to purchase: attention, interest, desire, action
6. Person-to-person promotional presentation by seller's representative with prospective buyer
8. Strategy which depends on stimulating demand by final users who pressure suppliers to deliver

WORD LIST:

ADVERTISING
AIDACONCEPT
PERCENTAGEOFSALES
PERSONALSELLING
PROMOTION
PROMOTIONALMIX

PUBLICRELATIONS
PUSHING
PULLING
SALESPROMOTION
TASKOBJECTIVE
TRADEPROMOTION

Chapter 16 Solutions

Key Concepts

1.	q	6.	a	11.	p	16.	m
2.	g	7.	e	12.	k	17.	h
3.	b	8.	i	13.	d		
4.	j	9.	l	14.	f		
5.	c	10.	o	15.	n		

Self Quiz

1.	F	11.	F	21.	T	31.	c	41.	d
2.	T	12.	T	22.	F	32.	b	42.	a
3.	T	13.	T	23.	T	33.	a	43.	c
4.	F	14.	F	24.	T	34.	d	44.	b
5.	F	15.	F	25.	F	35.	e	45.	a
6.	T	16.	T	26.	e	36.	a	46.	c
7.	F	17.	F	27.	b	37.	b	47.	b
8.	T	18.	T	28.	d	38.	c	48.	e
9.	T	19.	T	29.	c	39.	e	49.	e
10.	T	20.	F	30.	a	40.	d	50.	d

Applying Marketing Concepts

1.	a
2.	c
3.	d
4.	a
5.	b
6.	a

Computer Applications

1. Promotional Budget: 1995 Sales = $4,000,000;
    Promotional Budget = $240,000

    Basis for allocation = Budget/Sales = $240,000/$4,000,000 = 6 percent

    1996 budget = $300,000 = 6 percent of sales;
    $300,000/.06 = $5,000,000

2. a. The 1996 budget to be the same percentage of sales as the 1995 expenditure:

    1995 Budget = $112,800; 1995 Sales $1,504,000
    Budget percent = $112,800/$1,504,000 = 7.5 percent

    1996 budget = $1,550,000(.075) = $116,250

    b. The 1996 budget based on the average of the last five years:

Spent on promotion over the last five years:	$508,040
Sales for the last five years:	$7,024,000
Proportion spent:	7.23 percent

    1996 budget = $1,550,000(.0723) = $112,065

    c. The 1996 budget based on the average expenditures of the three competitors:

Spent by them on promotion:	$445,920
Wine sold by them:	$7,440,000
Average of their expenditures:	6 percent

    1996 budget = $1,550,000(.06) = $93,000

3. Seafood/Florist shop promotional budget:

    Average per unit expenditure of five competing shops = $35

    Finest Kind expenditures = 2500 units($35) = $87,500

4. a. Same percentage as allocated in 1995:

    The percentage was 5.5 percent.

    $12,800,000(.055) = $704,000

    b. The average percentage expenditure over the last six years:

    4.0 + 4.6 + 5.0 + 5.2 + 5.4 + 5.5 = 29.7/6 = 4.95 %

    $12,800,000(.0495) = $633,600

c. Average percentage expenditures of four competitors:

Calcasieu:	$319,200/$7,600,000	=	4.2%
Choctaw:	$596,400/$8,400,000	=	7.1%
Chickasaw:	$670,000/$13,400,000	=	5.0%
Catahoula:	$993,600/$18,400,000	=	5.4%

Average percentage expended = 5.425 percent

$12,800,000(.05425) = $694,400

Crossword Puzzle Solution

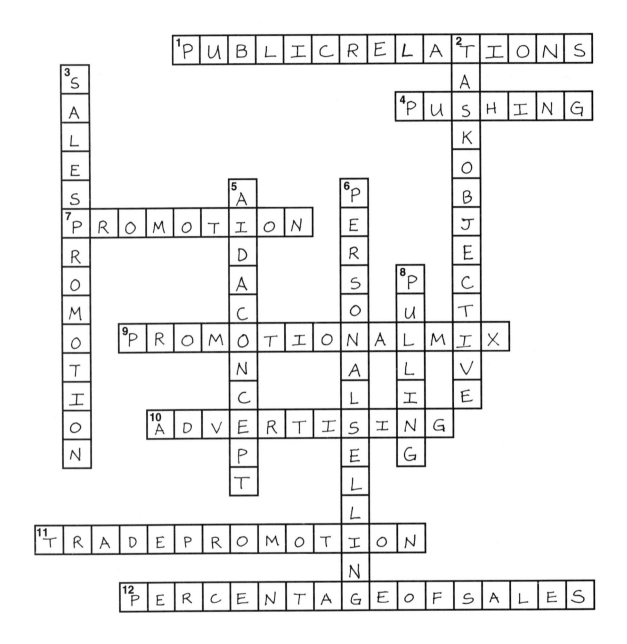

Chapter 17

Advertising, Sales Promotion, and Public Relations

Chapter Outline

You may wish to use the outline that follows as a guide in taking notes.

I.   Chapter Overview—The Nonpersonal Elements of Promotion

II. Advertising

    A. Evolution of advertising

    B. Advertising objectives

    C. Translating advertising objectives into advertising plans

III. Types of Advertising

IV. Media Selection

    A. Television

    B. Radio

    C. Newspapers

    D. Magazines

    E. Direct mail

    F. Outdoor advertising

    G. Other advertising media

    H. Growth of interactive media

V.   Media Scheduling

VI. Organization of the Advertising Function

VII.   Creating an Advertisement

    A. Comparative advertising

    B. Celebrity testimonials

    C. Retail advertising

    D. Cooperative advertising

VIII.   Assessing the Effectiveness of an Advertisement

    A. Pretesting

    B. Post-testing

IX.   Sales Promotion

    A. Point-of-purchase advertising

    B. Specialty advertising

    C. Trade shows

    D. Samples, coupons, and premiums

    E. Contests

    F. Trading stamps

    G. Trade promotion

X   Sponsorship

    A. Growth of sponsorships

    B. How sponsorship differs from advertising

    C. Assessing sponsorship results

    D. Using sponsorship in a promotional strategy

XI.   Public Relations

Name _____   Instructor _____

Section _____   Date _____

Key Concepts

The purpose of this section is to allow you to determine if you can match key concepts with their definitions. It is essential that you know the definitions of the concepts before applying the concepts in later exercises in this chapter.

From the list of lettered terms, select the one that best fits in the blank of the numbered statement below. Write the letter of that choice in the space provided.

Key Terms

a. advertising
b. product advertising
c. institutional advertising
d. informative advertising
e. persuasive advertising
f. reminder advertising
g. advocacy advertising
h. interactive media
i. media scheduling
j. advertising agency
k. comparative advertising

l. retail advertising
m. cooperative advertising
n. pretesting
o. posttesting
p. sales promotion
q. point-of-purchase advertising
r. specialty advertising
s. trade promotion
t. public relations
u. sponsorship
v. publicity

_____ 1. Promotion that seeks to announce the availability of and develop initial demand for a good, service, organization, person, place, idea, or cause.

_____ 2. Sharing of advertising costs between the manufacturer and the retailer of a good or service.

_____ 3. Nonpersonal selling of a good or service.

_____ 4. Assessment of an advertisement's effectiveness after it has been used.

_____ 5. Promotion seeking to reinforce previous promotional activity by keeping the name of the good, service, organization, person, place, idea, or cause in front of the public.

_____ 6. Timing and sequencing of advertisements.

_____ 7. Promoting a concept, an idea, a philosophy, or the goodwill of an industry, company, organization, place, person, or government agency.

_____ 8. Stimulation of demand for a good, service, place, idea, person, or organization by disseminating significant news or obtaining favorable media presentation not paid for by the sponsor.

_____ 9. Display or other promotion located near the site of the actual buying decision.

_____ 10. Marketing specialist firm that assists advertisers in planning and implementing advertising programs.

_____ 11. Communication channels in which message recipients actively participate in promotional efforts.

_____ 12. Firm's communications and relationships with its various publics.

_____ 13. Competitive promotion that seeks to develop demand for a good, service, organization, person, place, idea, or cause.

_____ 14. Paid public communication or message that presents information or a point of view bearing on a publicly recognized, controversial issue.

_____ 15. Sales promotion technique that involves the distribution of articles such as key rings and ball point pens that bear the advertiser's name, address, and advertising message.

_____ 16. Nonpersonal selling by stores that offer goods or services directly to the consuming public.

_____ 17. Assessment of an advertisement's effectiveness before it is actually used.

_____ 18. Nonpersonal selling effort that makes direct or indirect promotional comparisons with competing brands.

_____ 19. Paid, nonpersonal communication through various media by business firms, nonprofit organizations, and individuals who are identified in their messages and who hope to inform or persuade members of particular audiences.

_____ 20. Marketing activities other than personal selling, advertising, and publicity that stimulate consumer purchasing and dealer effectiveness.

_____ 21. Sales promotion geared to intermediaries rather than consumers.

_____ 22. Provision of funds for a sporting event or cultural activity in exchange for a direct association with the event or activity.

Name _____   Instructor _____

Section _____   Date _____

Self Quiz

You should use these questions to test your understanding of the chapter material. You can check your answers with those provided at the end of the chapter.

While these questions cover most of the chapter topics, they are not intended to be the same as the test questions your instructor may use in an examination. A good understanding of all aspects of the course material is essential to good performance on any examination.

True/False

Write "T" for True and "F" for False for each of the following statements.

_____   1.   Since the end of World War II, advertising and related expenditures have risen at roughly the same rate as the gross national product.

_____   2.   The nation's two leading advertisers—Philip Morris Companies and Procter and Gamble—spend more that $2 billion per year on advertising.

_____   3.   One of the major reasons for the growth of advertising worldwide is innovations in transportation and communication.

_____   4.   The first advertising agency in the United States was organized by George P. Rowell in 1844.

_____   5.   In ancient Rome, a sign outside a building showing a bucket signified that the business at that location was a dairy.

_____   6.   Advertising attempts to condition the consumer to adopt a favorable viewpoint toward the promotional message.

_____   7.   Novice advertisers are often less concerned with the technical aspects of advertisement construction than they should be, concentrating instead on the more basic steps, such as market analysis.

_____   8.   Product advertising is the type that comes to the average person's mind when someone mentions advertising.

_____   9.   Institutional advertising is concerned with reinforcing previous promotional activity by keeping the name of the subject of the previous effort before the public.

_____ 10.   Advocacy advertising is sometimes known as institutional advertising.

_____ 11.   The objective of media selection is to achieve adequate media coverage without going beyond the identifiable limits of the potential market.

_____ 12.   Most newspaper advertising revenues come from national advertisers, while television derives the bulk of its revenues from local sources.

_____ 13.   It has been estimated that, by 1998, four out of five American homes will subscribe to a cable system.

_____ 14.   Among the disadvantages of television advertising is its lack of impact, flexibility, and prestige.

_____ 15.   Radio is a low cost advertising medium with a high immediacy factor.

_____ 16.   Magazines are divided into three basic categories—consumer, farm, and business publications.

_____ 17.   A growing, but controversial form of advertising in the United States is cinema advertising, which has been popular in Europe for many years.

_____ 18. Interactive media are based on electronic technology and are limited to use in the United States.

_____ 19. Effective use of an advertising agency requires that the agency have thorough knowledge of the advertiser's product, competitors' strategy, and available media that can be used to reach consumer and trade markets.

_____ 20. Post-testing is generally more desirable that pretesting of advertising because of the potential cost savings.

_____ 21. Sales promotional techniques may be used by all members of a marketing channel: manufacturers, wholesalers, and retailers.

_____ 22. Specialty advertising began when early automobile vendors began giving their customers free keychains as a souvenir of their visit to the showroom.

_____ 23. Premiums are items given free or at reduced cost when another product is purchased.

_____ 24. Public relations is an efficient indirect communications channel for promoting products, although its objectives typically are broader than those of other components of promotional strategy.

_____ 25. Two thirds of the $2.6 billion spent annually by commercial sponsors goes to musical and cultural events.

Multiple Choice

Circle the letter of the word or phrase that best completes the sentence or best answers the question.

26. In ancient Rome, a sign hanging on a building showing a boy being whipped indicated
   a. that the construction was a jail.
   b. that the building contained a school.
   c. that the structure housed a slave market.
   d. that the owner of the building had been imprisoned for beating his employees.
   e. that the edifice contained a temple to Apollo, who, in his human form, had often suffered the pain of the whip.

27. Marketers use a positioning strategy
   a. to distinguish their goods or services from those of the competition.
   b. to prevent the intrusion into the market of new products or services.
   c. to avoid making direct comparisons between one product and another.
   d. to enhance a dominant share of the market.
   e. as a desperate move when a product market is dying.

28. In television, a national advertising spot is
   a. a locally developed and sponsored commercial.
   b. a scheduled program sponsored by a national advertiser.
   c. sponsorship of a major cultural or sports event.
   d. non-network broadcasting used by a general advertiser.
   e. network advertising by a local advertiser.

29. Advertising that seeks to develop initial demand for a good, service, organization, person, place, idea, or cause is called
   a. product advertising.
   b. persuasive advertising.
   c. informative advertising.
   d. reminder advertising.
   e. comparative advertising.

30. Advertising that strives to reinforce previous promotional activity by keeping the name of the product, organization, person, place, idea, or cause before the public is called
   a. selective advertising.
   b. reminder advertising.
   c. informative advertising.
   d. selective advertising.
   e. persuasive information.

31. Advocacy advertising is really a special form of
   a. corporate product advertising.
   b. informative institutional advertising.
   c. reminder life-cycle advertising.
   d. informative political advertising.
   e. persuasive institutional advertising.

32. Radio advertising now accounts for about
   a. five percent of all national advertising and 13 percent of local sales.
   b. 26 percent of total advertising revenues.
   c. seven percent of total advertising revenues and ten percent of local expenditures.
   d. 18 percent of national advertising revenues but only four percent on a local basis.
   e. 31 percent of all advertising revenues locally and nationally.

33. Which advertising medium offers the advantages of immediacy, low cost, flexibility, practical and low-cost audience selection, and mobility?
   a. radio
   b. television
   c. newspapers
   d. magazines
   e. direct mail

34. Some of the disadvantages of using the newspaper medium as an advertising vehicle are
   a. lack of flexibility found in other media, long lead time between ad placement and appearance.
   b. short life span, relatively poor reproduction quality, and haste in reading.
   c. high cost, loss of control of the promotional message, and public distrust of the medium.
   d. consumer resistance to the medium and high per-person acquisition cost.
   e. the necessity for an extremely brief message and lack of aesthetics in the eyes of the public.

35. The term that describes the number of different persons or households exposed to an advertisement during a certain period of time is
   a. frequency.
   b. density.
   c. gross rating.
   d. reach.
   e. volume penetration.

36. Outdoor advertising is particularly effective
    a. in rural locations where the message can be seen at a great distance.
    b. when placed along lightly traveled arteries so that people can pay more attention to the advertising and less to driving.
    c. when fairly large blocks of print are used to communicate the desired information.
    d. in metropolitan districts and other high-traffic areas.
    e. when placed so that foot traffic is forced to detour around the billboards to get where it's going.

37. Within most businesses, the advertising function is usually set up as
    a. a line department reporting directly to the chief executive officer of the company.
    b. a staff department reporting to the vice-president or director of marketing.
    c. a home-office department housed in the engineering division.
    d. a staff department with responsibility directly to the president of the firm.
    e. a functional division of the company with its own vice-president and an equal voice in company policymaking with all other divisions.

38. The top three advertising agencies in the world, ranked by worldwide billings, are
    a. all located in Tokyo, within three blocks of each other on the Ginza.
    b. American and are headquartered in New York.
    c. WPP Group of London, the Interpublic Group of Companies, and Saatchi and Saatchi, both of New York.
    d. Chan Lee of Hong Kong, Komatsu of Tokyo, and Wetherill and Sons of Sydney.
    e. Appleseed of London, L'Avertence of Paris, and Noticias Commercial and Publicidad General of Madrid.

39. The final step in the advertising process is
    a. choice of a medium to carry the message.
    b. definition of a target market to which to appeal.
    c. retention of an advertising agency to develop the program.
    d. deciding on the positioning of the product with respect to the competition.
    e. development and preparation of an actual advertisement.

40. In an advertisement, the part of the ad that actually names the sponsor and may include the company's address and phone number is called the
    a. headline.
    b. subhead.
    c. upper body.
    d. lower body.
    e. signature.

41. According to the authors of your text, too many advertisers fail to
    a. suggest how readers can buy the product if they want it.
    b. tell the reader what the product actually is.
    c. identify themselves and establish their credibility.
    d. gain our intention with their message.
    e. include a headline; all ads must have a headline.

42. One of the things that users of comparative advertising must be certain about is that they
    a. are the industry leader; followers don't do well with comparative advertising.
    b. make comparisons that can't be checked; you can say anything as long as no one can disprove it.
    c. are able to prove their claims; comparative advertising that can't be backed up has been known to produce lawsuits.
    d. not mention specifically what they are comparing with their product; that way, nobody can squawk even if the point of the comparison is obvious.
    e. make no comparisons that have any meaning; the public won't know the difference, anyway.

43. The primary advantage of using big-name personalities as product spokespeople is that they may
    a. improve product recognition in an environment filled with competing advertising.
    b. allow a company to pay less attention to trends; their credibility is inherent and doesn't vary with fashion.
    c. create a new and amplified level of interest in the company.
    d. can create interest in the company, especially when the personality has no apparent relationship with the product.
    e. allow the company to be less creative; using personalities lets them carry the load so the rest of the program can slide a little.

44. The basic problem with retail advertising is that
    a. it varies widely in its effectiveness.
    b. consumers are often suspicious of retail price ads.
    c. source, message, and shopping experience affect consumer attitudes toward these ads.
    d. retail stores often treat advertising as a secondary activity, rarely using advertising agencies.
    e. it accounts for such a sizable portion of annual advertising expenditures.

45. When a manufacturer pays a part of a retailer's cost of advertising the manufacturer's products, it is practicing
    a. demonstrative advertising.
    b. comparative advertising.
    c. retailer-sponsored advertising.
    d. testimonial advertising.
    e. cooperative advertising.

46. When interviewers from McCann-Erickson ask heavy users of a product which of two alternative advertisements would convince them to purchase it, they are conducting a
    a. sales conviction pretest.
    b. blind product pretest.
    c. dummy ad test.
    d. recognition pretest.
    e. aided recall test.

47. The post-test of advertising effectiveness in which interviewers ask people who have read selected magazines whether they have read various ads in them is
    a. the Gallup and Robinson *Unaided Recall Test.*
    b. the *Starch Readership Report.*
    c. Burke's *Day-After Interview System.*
    d. *AdWatch*, a joint venture of the Gallup Organization and *Advertising Age.*
    e. Inquiry Corporation's *Split Runs.*

48.   Looked at from the point of view of dollars spent on the activity,
   a.   advertising and sales promotion are virtually tied on a year to year basis on the amount spent on each.
   b.   advertising accounts for roughly twice as much promotional spending each year as does sales promotion.
   c.   sales promotion actually leads advertising in terms of the dollars spent on each.
   d.   public relations and sales promotion together still don't approach the dollar value of advertising each year.
   e.   Sales promotion lags both advertising and public relations in yearly expenditures.

49.   The practice during the Middle Ages of giving wooden pegs inscribed with artisan's names to prospective customers so they could use them to hang up their armor has developed into the modern practice called
   a.   couponing.
   b.   sampling.
   c.   trade show promotion.
   d.   public relations.
   e.   specialty advertising.

50.   Every year, packaged goods marketers spend more than $900 million distributing 277 billion
   a.   point-of-purchase displays to retailers all over the United States.
   b.   specialty advertising pieces to potential customers in the industrial and consumer markets.
   c.   samples of product to consumers in stores, by mail, and by hand.
   d.   trading stamps through more than 1.5 million supermarkets, service stations, and small businesses.
   e.   coupons through print media throughout the country.

Name _____   Instructor _____

Section _____   Date _____

Applying Marketing Concepts

Your job as national advertising manager for Kumquat Soap has become a source of great frustration to you. You know that your product is superior to any other cleansing and beauty soap on the market and that the addition of genuine kumquat oil (kumquats, for those unfamiliar with them, are small, very tart citrus fruits with a light, delightfully scented, highly concentrated oloeoresin in their peel) makes your product an excellent deodorant and antiperspirant. It is also a totally natural product, containing only organically produced ingredients. But your firm is so small (less than one percent of the market) that you can't afford to buy advertising like Procter and Gamble, Lever Brothers, Colgate, or any of the other "big boys" of the industry. Faced with this problem, you are considering how best to use your rather modest advertising budget.

1. Convinced that your very modest share of the market is due to the fact that the majority of the population doesn't know of your product, you feel that you must use your advertising to tell them who and what you are. The type of advertising to use in this instance would be
   a. product advertising.
   b. persuasive advertising.
   c. advocacy advertising.
   d. reminder advertising
   e. informative advertising.

2. Very aware that your unique selling proposition requires the use of an advertising medium which will be highly selective, speedy in effect, highly personalized, and capable of delivering a complete message, you choose as your major medium
   a. local newspapers.
   b. direct mail.
   c. specialty magazines.
   d. outdoor advertising.
   e. radio.

3. Convinced that part of the reason your market share is so small is because very few people have ever tried your product, you authorize your local sales representatives to stand near the display of your product in local stores and give away miniature bars of Kumquat Soap you've had made up. This promotional technique is
   a. the form of sales promotion known as sampling.
   b. point-of-purchase advertising.
   c. pretesting: recipients of the free bars get to pretest them before buying your soap.
   d. sales promotion by means of specialty advertising.
   e. sales promotion through the use of a premium.

4. Upon reflection, you decide that one way to improve your competitive position would be by advertising your product in such a way as to point out its obvious superiority to Zest, Dial, Irish Spring, and other well-known bath soaps, each of which would be mentioned by name. This type of advertising is called
   a. competitive advertising.
   b. compulsive advertising.
   c. comparative advertising.
   d. "cause" advertising.
   e. corporate advertising.

5. Further thought convinces you that making a frontal attack on all the major soap companies might not be the best way to develop Kumquat's market. You consider, however, creating for Kumquat an advertising program which will stress its all-natural formulation. Such a program would position your product against the competition by its
   a. applications.
   b. product class.
   c. attributes.
   d. user characteristics.
   e. competitive position.

Amanda Hazlenut has the task of assembling her firm's advertising plan for the next fiscal year. She has reviewed the information she was able to gather very carefully. Her Firm, Fungus Importers, a major international trader in mushrooms, truffles, and related products from Europe and the Far East, spent over $1 million on advertising last year, but Amanda isn't sure what happened to the money. Top management at FI set no specific promotional objectives, though they did spend a lot on audience analysis reports and research aimed at identifying the characteristics of the readers of the ads for the company's products. Invoices from research suppliers also note that a substantial sum was paid to McCann-Erickson for some pretesting of ads, and a firm called, Pens, Calendars, and Mugs, Inc., was paid several thousand dollars from the promotional budget.

6. Ms. Hazlenut will probably be unable to come to any conclusions concerning the success of last year's advertising program because
   a. no audience analysis was undertaken.
   b. no objectives were set.
   c. pretesting was done incorrectly.
   d. media choices were improperly made.
   e. the budget was too small for analysis.

7. The research which was done to identify the characteristics of the firm's audience was
   a. a pretest of the company's advertising.
   b. a wise use of a portion of the advertising budget.
   c. budgeted as a test of the achievement of advertising objectives.
   d. a posttest of advertising effectiveness.
   e. the perfect test of the validity of promotional objectives.

8. The money paid to McCann-Erickson probably went for
   a. galvanic skin response measurements.
   b. the use of a hidden camera to photograph eye movement of ad readers.
   c. studio screening of ads for selected consumers.
   d. blind product tests.
   e. sales conviction tests.

9. The money paid to Pens, Calendars, and Mugs, Inc., was probably for
    a. specialty advertising items like mushroom desk sets and "Fungus-of-the-Month" calendars.
    b. participation in industrial and consumer trade shows.
    c. production of materials to be used in company sales contests.
    d. manufacture of miniature samples of company products to be given as inducements to buyers.
    e. bribes paid to obscure European officials to sign permits allowing the exportation of truffles and other trifles.

Name _____   Instructor _____

Section _____   Date _____

Experiential Exercises

1. Some products lend themselves better to advertising in one medium than in another.
    a. For each of the media mentioned below, list a product or products frequently advertised in that medium. Then explain why you think that medium is commonly chosen for the product you listed.

    1. Medium: Newspapers

        Product: Foods

        Why: Consumers who cook can compare prices from the ads and can take the newspaper with them when shopping.

    2. Medium: Magazines

        Product:

        Why:

    3. Medium: Television

        Product:

        Why:

4. Medium: Radio

Product:

Why:

5. Medium: Direct Mail

Product:

Why:

6. Medium: Outdoor

Product:

Why:

b. For each of the products you listed in part a, indicate what type of sales promotion might be used and how it would best be used.

	Product	Sales Promotion	How Used
1.	Food	Coupon	Place in Newspapers to encourage product sale.
2.			
3.			
4.			
5.			
6.			

2. Your text lists six major types of advertising. Each of these types of advertising lends itself to a different application. Find three advertisements that you think are particularly good examples of different types of ads. List below why you think these examples are particularly good.

a. Type of Advertisement:

Sponsor:

Why particularly appropriate:

b. Type of Advertisement:

Sponsor:

Why particularly appropriate:

c. Type of Advertisement:

Sponsor:

Why particularly appropriate:

3. Every student of marketing should have the opportunity to determine whether or not he or she is creative. In this exercise you will create a one-page advertisement for a particular product or service.

    a. Choose a product or service about which you have some knowledge either from work experience or as a consumer.

        Product Chosen:

    b. Choose whether you will produce a one-page magazine ad or a thirty-second radio spot.

        Medium chosen:

        Why this medium?

    c. If you chose the print medium (magazine), you may produce your ad manually, using a computer publishing program such as Ventura Publisher, or by cut-and-paste from existing magazines. When you have finished, be prepared to identify the headline, subheads (if any), illustrations, body copy, and signature.

    d.) Write and record your thirty-second spot, if you chose the radio medium. Does your ad have the same parts as a print ad? Identify as many similar parts as you can.

Name _____   Instructor _____

Section _____   Date _____

Computer Applications

Review the discussion of the cost-per-thousand criterion in Chapter 17 of the text. Then use menu item 15 titled "Advertising Evaluations" to solve each of the following problems.

1. Eldon Womble manages the aircraft accessories division of Firebrand Industries, the world's largest manufacturer of hot-air balloon burners, fuel tanks, and related supplies. He knows he must narrow the number of magazines being considered for the 1996 "Firebrand Flyer" advertising campaign from eight to three before meeting with the executive committee to make recommendations on the handling of 1996's print advertising. The information below summarizes cost and readership figures for the eight magazines he's been looking at. He also has enumerated the percent of each magazine's readership he believes matches the "Firebrand persona."

Magazine	Four Color Page Rate	Total Readers (in millions)	Percentage Firebranders
Flameout	$11,500	3.2	17
Airman	17,500	4.0	21
Liftoff	13,000	3.6	21
Aeronaut	36,000	19.6	11
Balloonist	28,000	10.6	13
Franklin's	7,500	2.4	27
Spacetime	34,500	15.2	16
Outthere	26,000	8.4	19

a. Which of the eight magazines has the lowest CPM if total readers are considered? Which has the highest CPM?

b. Which of the eight magazines has the lowest CPM if only target market readers are considered? Which has the highest?

2. Louise Anglaterra is in charge of magazine advertising for The Boulders, a resort on Monte Sano, just outside Huntsville, Alabama. She is examining the figures on six major national magazines as candidates for this year's advertising.

a. Given the information below, which magazine has the lowest CPM? The lowest CPM for male readers? For female readers?

Magazine	Four-color Page Rate	Total Readers (in 000s)	Men (in 000s)	Women (in 000s)
Travel News	$36,375	11,375	3,473	7,902
Leisure Time	45,187	9,335	5,575	3,760
Outdoors	32,675	7,300	4,220	3,080
Movin' On	46,200	18,940	8,790	10,150
MountainTops	27,750	5,365	4,045	1,320
Vacationspot	40,367	7,180	3,645	3,535

3. After reviewing the readership profiles for the six magazines included in problem 2, Louise has developed the following estimates of the percentages of male and female readers of each magazine who exactly match the profile of The Boulders' target customers:

Percentage of Readers in Target Market

Magazine	Male Readers	Female Readers
Travel News	49	21
Leisure Time	32	34
Outdoors	24	22
Movin' On	26	38
MountainTops	34	16
Vacationspot	22	29

a. Which of the six magazines has the lowest CPM for male readers who match the target profile? The highest?

b. Which magazine has the lowest CPM for female readers who match the target profile? The highest?

4. Aksel Nordhoff is an advertising buyer specializing in radio for Bingham, Bongham, Bopham, and Bashem, an advertising agency specializing in heavy-duty saturation advertising. Aksel wants his message to reach people between the ages of 18 and 49 in the Mobile, Alabama, area during drive time, while they're going to and from work. He has narrowed the choices to four stations, each of which offers the format he thinks will attract his target listeners.

Radio Station	Cost for 30 Second Spot	All Ages	Total Listeners Ages 18-34	Ages 35-49
KRGA	$190	25,000	6,500	6,000
KABB	200	28,000	5,600	7,000
KMOB	250	42,000	16,800	12,600
KKIK	290	70,000	21,000	17,500

a.   Which of the four stations has the lowest overall CPM? Which is the most expensive on a CPM basis?

b.   Which of the four stations has the lowest CPM for listeners aged 18-34? Which is most expensive for this group?

c.   Which of the four stations will reach Mr. Nordhoff's target customers at the lowest CPM?

Crossword Puzzle for Chapter 17

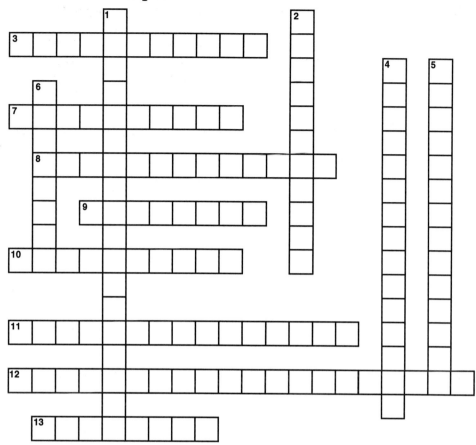

ACROSS CLUES

3. Paid, nonpersonal communication in media by identified sponsors who seek to inform or persuade
7. Type of advertising that seeks to develop demand for a good, service, person, place, etc.
8. Advertising promoting the goodwill of an industry, company, or government agency, for example
9. Advertising type that promotes a point of view on a publicly recognized, controversial issue
10. Assessment of an advertisement's effectiveness before it's actually used
11. A firm's communications and relationships with its various publics
12. Sales promotion technique that involves use of key rings, etc., that bear the advertiser's name
13. Short form of name of marketing specialist firm used to assist with a firm's advertising task

DOWN CLUES

1. Advertising designed to sell a good or service
2. Advertising that announces availability of and develops initial demand for a good, service, etc.
4. Advertising displays or other promotion located near the site of actual buying decision
5. Sales promotion geared to intermediaries rather than consumers
6. Advertising that seeks to reinforce previous promotional activity

WORD LIST:

ADVERTISING
ADVOCACY
ADAGENCY
INSTITUTIONAL
INFORMATIVE
PERSUASIVE
POINTOFPURCHASE

PRETESTING
PRODUCTADVERTISING
PUBLICRELATIONS
REMINDER
SPECIALTYADVERTISING
TRADEPROMOTION

Chapter 17 Solutions

Key Concepts

1.	d	6.	i	11.	h	16.	l	21.	s
2.	m	7.	c	12.	t	17.	n	22.	u
3.	b	8.	v	13.	e	18.	k		
4.	o	9.	q	14.	g	19.	a		
5.	f	10.	j	15.	r	20.	p		

Self Quiz

1.	F	11.	T	21.	T	31.	e	41.	a
2.	T	12.	F	22.	F	32.	c	42.	c
3.	T	13.	F	23.	T	33.	a	43.	a
4.	F	14.	F	24.	T	34.	b	44.	d
5.	F	15.	T	25.	F	35.	d	45.	e
6.	T	16.	T	26.	b	36.	d	46.	a
7.	F	17.	T	27.	a	37.	b	47.	b
8.	T	18.	F	28.	d	38.	c	48.	c
9.	F	19.	T	29.	c	39.	e	49.	e
10.	F	20.	F	30.	b	40.	e	50.	e

Applying Marketing Concepts

1.	e	5.	c	9.	a
2.	b	6.	b		
3.	a	7.	d		
4.	c	8.	e		

Computer Applications

1. a. Cost per thousand readers of available magazines:

    CPM = Cost of ad/Circulation (in thousands)

Flameout	=	$11,500/3,200	=	$3.594 per thousand
Airman	=	$17,500/4,000	=	$4.375
Liftoff	=	$13,000/3,600	=	$3.611
Aeronaut	=	$36,000/19,600	=	$1.837
Balloonist	=	$28,000/10,600	=	$2.641
Franklin's	=	$7,500/ 2,400	=	$3.125
Spacetime	=	$34,500/15,200	=	$2.270
Outthere	=	$26,000/8,400	=	$3.095

    Aeronaut, at $1.837 per thousand, seems the least costly of the magazines on this basis, and Airman, at $4.375 per thousand, the highest.

    b. Adjusting for the target market:

    Cost per thousand in Firebrand's market =
    (Cost per thousand)/(percent of readers in target mkt.)

Flameout	=	$3.594/.17	=	$20.594 per thousand
Airman	=	$4.375/.21	=	$20.833
Liftoff	=	$3.611/.21	=	$17.195
Aeronaut	=	$1.837/.11	=	$16.700
Balloonist	=	$2.641/.13	=	$20.315
Franklin's	=	$3.125/.27	=	$11.574
Spacetime	=	$2.270/.16	=	$14.187
Outthere	=	$3.095/.19	=	$16.289

    The most cost-effective way to reach Firebrand's potential customers is apparently through Franklin's Magazine, with a per thousand target customer cost of $11.574.

2. Cost per thousand readers of available magazines:

Travel News	=	$36,375/11,375	=	$3.198
Leisure Time	=	$45,187/9,335	=	$4.840
Outdoors	=	$32,675/7,300	=	$4.476
Movin' On	=	$46,200/18,940	=	$2.439
MountainTops	=	$27,750/5,365	=	$5.172
Vacationspot	=	$40,367/7,180	=	$5.622

    The lowest aggregate CPM is Movin' On, at $2.439 per thousand readers.

If only male readers are to be considered, then corrections should be made as follows:

Travel News	=	$36,375/3,473	=	$10.474 per thousand
Leisure Time	=	$45,187/5,575	=	$8.105
Outdoors	=	$32,675/4,220	=	$5.861
Movin' On	=	$46,200/8,790	=	$5.329
MountainTops	=	$27,750/4,045	=	$6.860
Vacationspot	=	$40,367/3,645	=	$11.075

Movin' On becomes the least cost medium to reach males, at $5.329 per thousand, while Vacationspot is now the most expensive, at $11.075 per thousand.

If only female readers are important, the following corrections are necessary:

Travel News	=	$36,375/7,902	=	$4.603 per thousand
Leisure Time	=	$45,187/3,760	=	$12.018
Outdoors	=	$32,675/3,080	=	$10.609
Movin' On	=	$46,200/10,150	=	$4.552
MountainTops	=	$27,750/1,320	=	$21.023
Vacationspot	=	$40,367/3,535	=	$11.419

Movin' On is also the least cost medium to reach females, at only $4.552 per thousand, while MountainTops, at $21.023 per thousand, is most expensive.

3. Adjusting the cost per thousand of magazine advertising to the desired market segment:

a. Males matching the Spa's market:

Travel News	=	$10.474/.49	=	$21.375 per thousand
Leisure Time	=	$ 8.105/.32	=	$25.328
Outdoors	=	$ 5.861/.24	=	$24.421
Movin' On	=	$ 5.329/.26	=	$20.496
MountainTops	=	$ 6.860/.34	=	$20.176
Vacationspot	=	$11.075/.22	=	$50.341

MountainTops becomes the most effective vehicle for reaching the Spa's male customers, and Vacationspot the least effective, with costs per thousand of $20.176 and $50.341, respectively.

b. Females matching the Spa's market:

Travel News	=	$ 4.603/.21	=	$21.919 per thousand
Leisure Time	=	$12.018/.34	=	$35.347
Outdoors	=	$10.609/.22	=	$48.223
Movin' On	=	$ 4.552/.38	=	$12.303
MountainTops	=	$21.023/.16	=	$131.394
Vacationspot	=	$11.419/.29	=	$39.376

Movin' On remains the vehicle of choice to reach women who match the Spa's user profile, with a cost of $12.303 per thousand, while MountainTops is least efficient, at $131.194 per thousand.

4. a. Lowest overall CPM for four radio stations:

KRGA	=	$190/25	=	$7.600 per thousand.
KABB	=	$200/28	=	$7.143
KMOB	=	$250/42	=	$5.952
KKIK	=	$290/70	=	$4.143

KKIK, at <u>$4.143</u> per thousand, is least expensive.
KRGA is most expensive at <u>$7.60</u> per thousand.

b. Lowest CPM, ages 18-34:

KRGA	=	$190/6.5	=	$29.231 per thousand
KABB	=	$200/5.6	=	$35.714
KMOB	=	$250/16.8	=	$14.881
KKIK	=	$290/21	=	$13.809

KKIK, at <u>$13.809</u> per thousand, is least expensive.
KABB, which charges <u>$35.714</u> per thousand, is the highest.

c. Lowest CPM, ages 18-49:

KRGA	=	$190/12.5	=	$15.20 per thousand
KABB	=	$200/12.6	=	$15.873
KMOB	=	$250/29.4	=	$8.503
KKIK	=	$290/38.5	=	$7.532

For Mr. Nordhoff's purposes, KKIK is the best choice.

Crossword Puzzle Solution

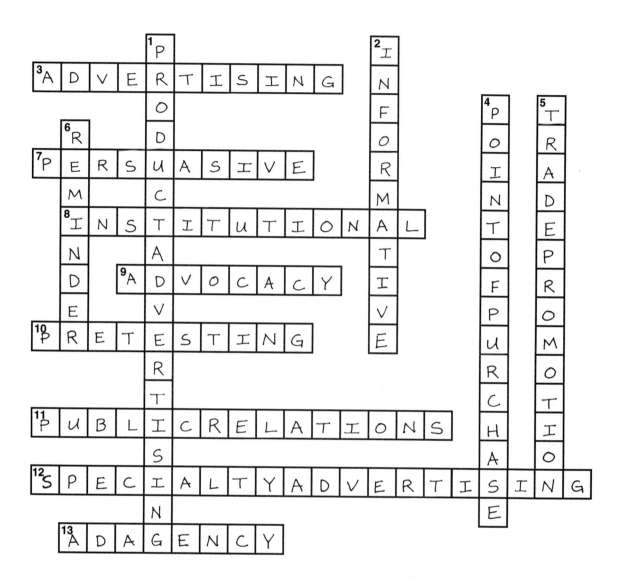

Chapter 18

Personal Selling and Sales Management

Chapter Outline

You may want to use the following outline as a guide in taking notes.

I.   Chapter Overview—Interpersonal Influence in Marketing

II.   The Evolution of Personal Selling

III. The Three Selling Environments

IV. Sales Tasks

    A.   Order processing

    B.   Creative selling

    C.   Missionary sales

V.   The Sales Process

    A. Prospecting and qualifying

    B. Approach

    C. Presentation

    D. Demonstration

    E. Handling objections

    F. Closing

    G. Follow-up

VI.   Managing the Sales Effort

    A. Recruitment and Selection

    B. Training

    C. Organization

    D. Supervision

    E. Motivation

    F. Compensation

    G. Evaluation and control

VII.   Sales Force Automation

Name _____   Instructor _____

Section _____   Date _____

Key Concepts

The purpose of this section is to allow you to determine if you can match key concepts in the chapter with their definitions. It is essential that you know the definitions of the concepts before using the concepts in later exercises in this chapter.

From the list of lettered terms, select the one that best fits the numbered statement below. Write the letter of that choice in the space provided.

Key Terms

a. personal selling
b. relationship selling
c. field selling
d. team selling
e. over-the-counter selling
f. telemarketing
g. order processing
h. creative selling
i. missionary sales
j. prospecting
k. qualifying
l. approach

m. precall planning
n. presentation
o. canned approach
p. closing
q. follow-up
r. sales management
s. boundary-spanning role
t. major accounts organization
u. expectation theory
v. commission
w. salary
x. sales quota
y. sales force automation (SFA)

_____ 1. Describing a product's major features and relating them to a customer's problems or needs.
_____ 2. Postsale activities designed to assure that a person who has made a recent purchase will become a repeat customer.
_____ 3. Personal selling function of identifying potential customers.
_____ 4. Sales manager's role of linking the sales force with the other elements of an organization's internal and external environments.
_____ 5. Planning, organizing, staffing, motivating, compensating, evaluating, and controlling a sales force to ensure its effectiveness.
_____ 9. Identifying customer needs, pointing them out to customers, and completing orders; typical of selling at the wholesale and retail levels.
_____ 11. Sales practitioner's initial contact with a prospective customer.
_____ 12. Personal selling which involves a considerable degree of analytical decision making on the buyer's part, requiring skillful presentation of proposals for solutions that meet the customer's needs.
_____ 13. Establishment of a sustained buyer-seller relationship.
_____ 14. Stage of the personal selling process at which the salesperson asks the customer to make a purchase decision.
_____ 15. Face-to-face sales presentations made at prospective customers' homes or places of business.

_____ 16.   Level of expected sales or profits for a territory, product, customer, or salesperson against which actual results are compared.

_____ 17.   Use of information collected during prospecting and qualifying and during previous contacts with the prospect to tailor the approach and presentation to match the customer's needs.

_____ 18.   Use of specialists from other functional areas to help sell a product.

_____ 19.   Interpersonal influence process involving a seller's promotional presentation conducted on a person-to-person basis with the buyer.

_____ 20.   Memorized sales talk used to ensure uniform coverage of the selling points that management has deemed important.

_____ 21.   Promotional presentation involving use of the telephone on an outbound basis by salespeople or an inbound basis by customers who initiate calls to obtain information and place orders.

_____ 22.   Incentive compensation directly related to the sales or profits generated by the salesperson.

_____ 23.   Determining that a prospect has the need, income, and purchase authority necessary to become a potential customer.

_____ 24.   Theory that motivation depends on the expectations an individual has of his or her ability to perform a job and how that performance relates to attaining rewards that the individual values.

_____ 25.   Use of various technologies to make the sales function more efficient and competitive.

Name   _____   Instructor   _____

Section   _____   Date   _____

Self Quiz

You should use these questions to test your understanding of the material in this chapter. You can check your answers with those provided at the end of the chapter.

While these questions cover most of the chapter topics, they are not intended to be the same as the test questions your instructor may use in an examination. A good understanding of all aspects of the course material is essential to good performance on any examination.

True/False

Write "T" for True and "F" for False for each of the following statements.

_____ 1. Expenditures for advertising almost always exceed expenditures for personal selling in the average American firm.

_____ 2. Today's sales professional uses a "customer-oriented approach that employs truthful, nonmanipulative tactics to satisfy the long-term needs of both the customer and the selling firm."

_____ 3. In team selling, a sales practitioner seeks to build a mutually beneficial relationship with a customer on a regular basis over an extended period.

_____ 4. Approximately 60 percent of marketing graduates choose sales as their first marketing position.

_____ 5. Over-the-counter selling typically involves providing product information and arranging for completion of the sales transaction.

_____ 6. A salesman who is assigned to answer the phone and take orders or answer customers' questions is involved in outbound telemarketing.

_____ 7. Multimedia technology cannot be used for interactive sales training, order entry systems, or visual product demonstrations because they are to complex for its limited capacities.

_____ 8. The first step in order processing is to point out to the customer his or her need for the sales practitioner's product or service.

_____ 9. Most sales positions, even many of the most creative, involve a certain amount of order processing.

_____ 10. New products often require a lot of creative selling.

_____ 11. In many instances, missionary salesmen neither contact the actual (direct) users of the products they are selling nor do they take orders.

_____ 12. The first step in the selling process is making the approach to the prospective customer.

_____ 13. One of the most exciting things about prospecting is the high likelihood that the activity will offer an immediate payback.

_____ 14. Effective "precall planning" gives the sales practitioner valuable information about the prospect's purchasing habits, attitudes, activities, and opinions.

_____ 15. The seller's objective in a sales presentation is to talk about the good or service in terms that are meaningful to the buyer—explaining benefits, rather than technical specifications.

_____ 16. Objections raised by prospects in the selling process typically involve the product's features, its price, or services to be offered by the selling firm.

_____ 17.   Despite the fact that closing should be the natural conclusion of an effective sales presentation, a surprising number of sales practitioners find it difficult to actually ask for an order.

_____ 18.   The "If-I-can-show-you . . ." closing technique warns the prospect that a sales agreement should be concluded now because some important feature of the deal being offered, such as price or availability, will soon be changed.

_____ 19.   One of the problems with recruiting people to become sales practitioners is the low degree of job security offered by this kind of employment.

_____ 20.   A salesforce organized along product lines would have specialized salesforces for each major type of customer served.

_____ 21.   The concept of "span of control" refers to the number of sales representatives who report to the first level of sales management.

_____ 22.   According to Vroom's expectancy theory, motivation depends on the expectations an individual has of his or her ability to do the job—and very little else.

_____ 23.   A straight salary compensation plan gives management more control over how sales personnel allocate their efforts, but it reduces the incentive to expand sales.

_____ 24.   Compensating sales representatives by commission provides maximum selling incentive with ample reason to perform nonselling activities such as completing sales reports, delivering sales promotional materials, and normal account servicing.

_____ 25.   The process area of the work environment refers to the sales practitioner's technical ability; knowledge of the product, customer, and company, as well as selling skills.

Multiple Choice

Circle the letter of the word or phrase that best completes the sentence or best answers the question.

26.   The average firm's selling expenses (percentage of sales spent on personal selling activities) are likely to fall into which of the following ranges?
    a.   one up to three percent
    b.   three up to five percent
    c.   five up to ten percent
    d.   ten up to 15 percent
    e.   15 percent or more

27.   If, in a field selling situation, the sales practitioner is joined by specialists from other functional areas of the firm to assist with the sales process,
    a.   relationship selling is taking place.
    b.   it is an instance of team selling.
    c.   confusion can result because of all the points of view that have to be reconciled.
    d.   expectancy theory is being applied to the selling process.
    e.   a major accounts organization is probably in place.

28.   A sales practitioner whose job consists primarily of making sales calls on customers at their homes or places of business is involved in
    a.   creative sales.
    b.   over-the-counter sales.
    c.   field selling.
    d.   missionary work.
    e.   demand selling.

29. A selling approach conducted entirely over the telephone is most correctly known as
    a. field selling.
    b. under-the-counter selling.
    c. creative selling.
    d. order processing.
    e. telemarketing.

30. Today's sales practitioner should be most concerned with
    a. helping customers select the correct products for meeting their needs.
    b. selling whatever is available; after all, life must go on.
    c. generating the greatest possible number of commission dollars for his or her own welfare.
    d. being visible to upper management; after all, the goal is advancement within the firm.
    e. processing orders as quickly and efficiently as possible.

31. When a sales practitioner helps a customer identify his or her needs; points out those needs to the customer; and completes the order for the customer, that sales practitioner has
    a. engaged in order processing.
    b. completed a creative selling assignment.
    c. engaged in sales engineering.
    d. acted as a missionary to that customer.
    e. functioned as a "drummer" in the classic sense of the word.

32. Which of the following statements is true concerning the sales activity of prospecting?
    a. Previous customers of the company seldom make good prospects for new sales.
    b. Prospecting is easy; a good sales practitioner should never spend more than ten percent of his or her time prospecting.
    c. Prospecting can be very frustrating because there is no immediate payback from doing it.
    d. Once a good client base has been established, the sales practitioner can stop prospecting; sales will come from the referrals existing clients will provide.
    e. Advertising almost never serves as a useful vehicle for new customer prospecting.

33. The process of qualifying a sales prospect
    a. involves gathering relevant information about the prospect to make initial contact go more smoothly.
    b. is the task of making sure that the prospect really is a potential customer.
    c. is used less frequently by retail sales practitioners than it is by wholesalers' and manufacturers' sales representatives.
    d. involves making the initial contact with the prospect.
    e. is considered by many sales management experts to be the very essence of the sales process.

34. One important advantage of personal selling over most advertising is its ability to
    a. represent accurately the appearance of the product.
    b. describe and itemize the product's significant features.
    c. gain the customer's attention and develop interest.
    d. present a standardized treatment of the product to all prospects.
    e. actually demonstrate the product to the potential buyer.

35. The traditional approach to sales presentations pioneered by the National Cash Register Company during the late 1800's is
     a. the semi-prepared approach; the sales representative familiarizes him or herself only with basic product knowledge and expects natural selling talent to carry the presentation.
     b. the "never-take-no-for-an-answer" approach; the name of this approach really says it all.
     c. the professional approach; the sales practitioner approaches the prospect in a thoroughly professional manner, ready to deal with any questions and problems that individual has.
     d. the canned approach; a memorized sales talk is delivered to the prospect covering management's view of the significant points of the product.
     e. the basic approach; the sales professional deals with basics first, getting technical only when the prospect asks for a technical treatment of the product.

36. The key to a successful product demonstration is
     a. impact; the demonstration must be really impressive.
     b. planning; the demonstration must go off like it's supposed to or the effort is totally wasted.
     c. novelty; the prospect should be shown the product in a new and different way.
     d. effect; some practitioners say that the demonstration should sell the product all by itself.
     e. detail; the demonstration should show the product in every possible use or application.

37. The professional sales practitioner uses a prospect's objections
     a. as a device to abruptly end the sales presentation; it has been found that if a prospect is left to "stew" for a little while, they often exhibit heightened interest.
     b. as a lever to manipulate the prospect into buying what the salesman has to offer.
     c. as a cue for providing additional information to the prospect.
     d. to acquire additional information from the prospect about his or her background and history.
     e. as a basis for a different type of presentation, the "over-kill" presentation, which hammers objections down.

38. The moment of truth in selling is the
     a. approach; a good approach is everything.
     b. qualifying process; wasting time with unqualified prospects really reduces selling productivity.
     c. presentation; without a good presentation, you have no hope of gaining the customer's confidence.
     d. demonstration; as has been said so many times, "a demonstration is worth a thousand pictures."
     e. close; you will certainly never sell anything without eventually asking for the order.

39. When a sales practitioner asks a prospect, "Well, do you want the red Cadillac or the blue one?", he or she is using what kind of closing technique?
     a. the alternative-decision technique
     b. the If-I-can-show-you technique
     c. the standing-room-only technique
     d. silence; some people react positively to it
     e. an extra-inducement close

40. The successful sales practitioner seeks to ensure that today's customers will be future customers through effective
     a. handling of prospect objections; a convinced customer is a repeat customer.
     b. sales presentations; a customer well-sold is a repeat customer.
     c. use of closing techniques; a customer who believes it was all his or her own idea will come back again.
     d. follow-up; this postsales activity often determines whether a person will become a repeat customer.
     e. prospecting; a customer from the beginning is a customer for life.

41. The linking of the sales force with other elements of the internal and external environments of the firm by sales managers is a
    a. boundary-spanning role which they normally occupy.
    b. task which many sales managers avoid.
    c. new development in the field of organization theory.
    d. most unusual occurrence, not normally found in American business.
    e. unique phenomenon which occurs only in retail environments.

42. The initial step in building an effective sales force is
    a. organizing the sales practitioners in a format consistent with the firm's needs.
    b. training sales personnel in correct selling techniques.
    c. motivating sales personnel to persist in their selling efforts.
    d. compensating sales personnel fairly and equitably.
    e. recruiting and selecting a group of qualified personnel.

43. Which of the following is a true statement concerning selling as a profession?
    a. Advancement for salesmen seldom occurs laterally to a more responsible position in some other functional area of the firm.
    b. The earnings of successful sales practitioners are somewhat lower than those of successful people in other professions.
    c. Economic downturns affect personnel in sales less than they do people in most other employment areas.
    d. Sales practitioners seldom operate as "independent" business people but usually as part of a selling team.
    e. Sales practitioners derive satisfaction in their profession largely from their incomes and seldom from helping customers satisfy their wants and needs.

44. In the selection of sales personnel, which of the following is usually the last step before all information is analyzed and a hiring decision made?
    a. an in-depth interview
    b. a physical examination
    c. aptitude and intelligence testing
    d. reference checks
    e. filling out the application

45. A sales organization which markets large numbers of similar but separate products that are very technical or of a complex nature and are sold through different marketing channels would probably be organized
    a. geographically.
    b. along customer lines.
    c. using engineering specialties as a base.
    d. by product class.
    e. according to the sizes of the various customers of the firm.

46. The most common method(s) of compensating sales practitioners are
    a. straight commission, no salary.
    b. straight salary, no commission.
    c. a salary-plus-bonus plan.
    d. a salary-plus-commission program.
    e. (c) and (d), the proportion of firms using them being about the same.

47.   An internship program is often used
    a.   during the training of new sales personnel.
    b.   when sales managers make mistakes and have to be transferred.
    c.   in testing potential recruits for sales position.
    d.   to motivate sales personnel to higher achievement.
    e.   as an alternative to paying employees.

48.   Each aspect of sales performance for which a standard exists should be measured separately. This helps to prevent
    a.   confusion on the part of the evaluated individual as to how the evaluation was conducted.
    b.   the halo effect in which the rating on one factor is carried over to other performance variables.
    c.   evaluation of the process of selling rather than the achievements of the sales operative.
    d.   personalities becoming the basis for evaluation, rather than performance.
    e.   the bad news being transmitted back to the sales employee through unauthorized channels.

49.   Motivation of sales personnel
    a.   is not a complex process because of the simplicity of the work.
    b.   seldom appeals to ego needs, peer acceptance, or recognition.
    c.   usually takes the form of debriefings, information sharing, and financial and psychological acceptance.
    d.   requires tight supervision and constant monitoring of their work.
    e.   requires little feedback from management—the sales force is usually well aware of how well or badly it's doing.

50.   The compensation plan giving management the greatest control over how sales personnel allocate their efforts but least incentive to expand sales is
    a.   the straight commission plan.
    b.   a salary plus bonus plan.
    c.   the commission with bonus plan.
    d.   a straight salary plan.
    e.   salary with commissions.

Name _____   Instructor _____

Section _____   Date _____

Applying Marketing Concepts

During your last semester in school, you go to your school's placement office and sign up to interview with firms seeking people with your qualifications. You are surprised to discover that there appear to be quite a few positions available with local companies, primarily wholesalers, that call for sales skills but indicate that no outside work will be required. A number of other positions call for degrees in finance or marketing, and show that "business development" is the area for which personnel are being sought. A little investigation reveals that the accounting firms and financial institutions listing these positions are among the most aggressive in the area, seeking new commercial accounts in an active fashion. You sign up for several of these interviews, and are somewhat surprised when you are told that a number of these companies have specified that a person must have had certain courses before they can even be interviewed. Either because of good planning or dumb luck, it happens that you have taken all the required courses, and interview with a number of these firms. They all require a seemingly endless stream of paperwork. First, there is the placement office form to fill out, then each company seems to want you to fill out a "personal data sheet," and finally there is the interview. You wonder who the people who are interviewing you are. They seem to know the company and its products quite well, and indicate that if you were to be chosen to fill an open position, you would be working for them. After your third interview in two days, you decide to go somewhere quiet and think about this whole process. It seems very detailed and confusing.

1. The positions with local wholesalers calling for selling skills but no outside work are probably
   a. missionary sales positions.
   b. positions as sales trainers.
   c. over-the-counter sales positions.
   d. creative selling positions.
   e. field sales positions.

2. The positions with the accounting firms and financial institutions are most likely
   a. portfolio analysts' positions.
   b. openings for staff accountants in the auditing division.
   c. related to sector analysis or loan profitability.
   d. field sales positions in the commercial accounts area.
   e. missionary sales positions designed to build public image.

3. If the interviewing process is considered to be a sales opportunity for the companies interviewing (selling the idea of working for them), then their requirement that you have a degree in a particular major and/or have taken particular courses would be part of the
   a. prospecting and qualifying process.
   b. approach to the prospect.
   c. presentation of company advantages.
   d. preapproach planning.
   e. followup step in sales.

4.   If one of the firms with whom you have interviewed is interested in you, what do you suppose will happen next?
     a.   You will be asked to report to a doctor's office for a physical examination.
     b.   You will be called in for a second interview.
     c.   The company will make you take a battery of placement tests.
     d.   You will be hired immediately.

5.   The people with whom you had your first interview are probably
     a.   professional interviewers who do this sort of thing all the time.
     b.   people who occupy the same position you would and have been told to find a successor so they can be transferred.
     c.   sales managers for the companies in the local area, doing part of their job.
     d.   representatives of your college filling in for people who work for the interviewing companies.
     e.   staff people from the interviewing companies who have nothing better to do.

You have gone to your favorite record store to buy a new CD by your favorite musical group. A helpful clerk has assisted you to find the CD you want and you are in the process of walking to the cash register to pay for them. On the way, the clerk stops at a display of CD storage boxes and asks if you have a problem storing your tunes neatly and conveniently. Though you say you've never had a problem—your old shoe box works just fine—he shows you how this particular box has little partitions in it which separate the CDs and can even be locked to keep out the curious and lightfingered.

6.   The clerk's demonstration of the storage box is an example of
     a.   order processing.
     b.   creative selling.
     c.   telemarketing.
     d.   closing.
     e.   prospecting.

7.   The clerk's assistance to you in finding the CD that meets your needs and ringing up the sale is an example of
     a.   order processing.
     b.   creative selling.
     c.   missionary selling.
     d.   passive selling.
     e.   qualifying.

8.   The position occupied by this sales clerk would be classified as
     a.   field selling.
     b.   missionary selling.
     c.   telemarketing.
     d.   over-the-counter sales.
     e.   merchandising.

The sales force at DeRussy, Sandarto and Company, a major distributor of business equipment—copying machines, communications equipment, computer peripherals, and the like—is divided into three groups: the consumer products group, the major accounts group, and the industrial products group. Sales representatives in the consumer products group are paid a base salary plus ten percent of their gross sales after they have met a minimum sales volume requirement for the month. The requirement is set on a month-by-month basis.

The industrial sales force is also salaried, but they receive an additional payment each month based on the new account activity they generate. The amount is based on the number of new accounts each sales representative opens weighted by management's estimate of the ultimate volume each account will generate. The amount the sales representative sold the account in opening does not matter.

The members of the major accounts group are not thought of as sales representatives. They number among themselves work design specialists, process engineers, graphic designers, and even a group of repair technicians. A delegation from DeRussy, Sandarto and Company will often visit one of the major accounts as a group, each member prepared to deal with customer interaction in his or her own specialty. They try to develop the customers' confidence in their ability to solve his or her firm's problems better than anyone else.

9. The sales force at DeRussy, Sandarto and Company is organized along
   a. product lines.
   b. customer lines.
   c. geographical lines.
   d. a combination of geographical and customer lines.
   e. a combination of product and geographical lines.

10. Sales representatives in the consumer products group are compensated on a
    a. straight salary basis.
    b. salary plus commission basis.
    c. salary plus bonus basis.
    d. straight commission basis.
    e. basis no one understands.

11. Sales representatives in the industrial products group are paid
    a. a straight commission.
    b. salary plus commission.
    c. straight salary.
    d. salary plus bonus based on new business.
    e. commission plus bonus.

Name   _____   Instructor   _____

Section   _____   Date   _____

Experiential Exercises

1. In this exercise, you will experience the sales process from the sales professional's point of view. (Your instructor may decide to conduct this exercise in class as a role-playing exercise, so be prepared to participate should the need develop.)

   The product you are to sell is called *Copymatic*. Like its predecessor, *Vegamatic*, *Copymatic* is a full-featured product in a compact package. It makes perfect copies, in color, of any document laid on its top platform, operates from three "D" size flashlight batteries (alkaline recommended) which last for up to 3,000 copies, and its compact size of 8.5 by 11.0 by 1.5 inches (almost exactly the size of your study guide—happy coincidence!) makes it quite portable. The device costs $395 complete, and is warranted against all failures for one full year from date of purchase. It can copy on any piece of paper, has no moving parts, requires no ink, and is disposable after it has produced a guaranteed minimum of 20,000 copies. (The design life of a *Copymatic* is actually 25,000 copies.)

   a. From among your friends, acquaintances, and business contacts, create a prospect list. Qualify each prospect on the basis of need for *Copymatic* and ability to pay.

   b. Devise an approach strategy to use in bringing *Copymatic* to the attention of qualified prospects. What kinds of preapproach planning do you intend to do? How will the approach be made?

c. Write (using a separate piece of paper, if necessary) a sales presentation for *Copymatic*. As a part of your presentation, demonstrate *Copymatic's* many remarkable properties.

d. How would you handle the objection: "Yes, it's a great little machine, but I really don't need one."

e. *Copymatics* are sold only for cash. Create a close that minimizes the difficulties of asking for "cash on the barrelhead" but at the same time asks for the order.

f.   Create a follow-up program to keep *Copymatic* owners happy.

2.   Personal selling is an interpersonal activity, conducted on a face-to-face basis. As such, it implies human relationships with all of the variability that the species can produce.

Operators of retail stores whose employees have face-to-face contact with the general public are well aware of the problems associated with customer-employee interaction. Because of high employee turnover and a low level of prior preparation, such employees are often ill-suited for direct contact with the man-off-the-street. Attitude, dress, mannerisms, and even such things as vocal accents all affect the promotional process in a face-to-face situation.

a.   Make a list of five do's and five don'ts for the employees of a small retail store such as a fast-food restaurant that would help minimize face-to-face promotional problems between customer and employee.

DO	**DON'T**

1.

DO	**DON'T**

2.

3.

4.

5.

b. List three things that you would do to motivate employees in that same fast-food restaurant. These motivational tools can be used weekly, monthly, quarterly, or with whatever frequency you think will work best.

Motivational Tool	How Will it Help?
1.	
2.	
3.	

3. A prospect's objections can actually help sell the product. Name a consumer product; list an objection a customer might have to buying it; give possible answers to the objections; and tell how this process may have helped sell the product.

Example:

Product: A new automobile

Objection: "I can't say I'm crazy about the color of this car."

Answer: "This is only one of many colors available; here, let's look at the color chart for this model."

How it helped: The objection was really a request for additional information about color availability. The customer needs to know about all of the colors that are available.

Your Turn at bat —

Product:

Objection:

Answer:

How it helped:

Name _____   Instructor _____

Section _____   Date _____

Computer Applications

Review the discussion of the workload method used to determine the required number of sales professionals in your text. Then use menu item 16 to solve each of the following problems.

1. Melvin Taylor is vice-president for sales of National Auto Supply. He has classed his firm's 6,000 commercial accounts into three groups. There are 800 firms in class A, 2,120 in class B, and 3,080 in class C. He would like to have his sales personnel call on each class A account at least 26 times a year, each class B account 20 times, and each class C account 15 times. Each sales call on a class A or B account should last 25 minutes, but a call on a class C account should be over in 12 minutes. Each of Mel's sales professionals works a 40 hour week 48 weeks a year. Fifty percent of selling time is spent calling on established accounts, thirty percent on travel, and twenty percent on non-selling activities. How many sales staff should National Auto Supply have?

2. Elaine Morel is a Baton Rouge-based manufacturer's agent in the business forms business. She has 2,900 established customers, of whom 500 are classed type A, 650 type B, and the remaining 1,750, type C. Each type A account is contacted once a month and a sales call lasts one hour. Type B accounts are contacted once every two months for 40 minutes per call. The less profitable type C accounts receive four calls per year for 35 minutes each. There are unplanned or "fill-in" calls that add another five percent to the total. Ms.

Morel's average sales representative works a 40 hour week for 46 weeks a year. Sixty percent of their time is spent working established accounts, with the remainder being equally divided among calls on new prospects, travel, and nonselling activities. How many sales practitioners are needed to cover Ms. Morel's market?

3. SunFun Swimming Pool Supply Company, a wholesaling operation out of International Falls, Minnesota, currently serves retail accounts all over the midwest. Fifteen percent of the firm's accounts are type A, another 25 percent are type B, and the remainder are type C. Type A accounts receive a weekly sales call lasting 35 minutes; type B accounts are called on every other week for 25 minutes; and type C accounts are visited every month for 20 minutes apiece. The nature of the pool supply business in the upper midwest is such that 20 percent must be added to the total for unplanned calls on customers. Each SunFun sales representative works 48 weeks per year (many pools become ice-skating rinks for a very substantial portion of the year, and SunFun sells those lines, too) for an average of 40 hours each week. About 45 percent of each sales rep's time is spent on established accounts, with 25 percent spent on calling on new prospects, 20 percent traveling, and ten percent on non-selling activities. At present, the company has 2,200 active accounts.

a. How many sales representatives does SunFun need?

b. If sales calls on type C accounts are increased from 12 to 24 per year, what impact will this have on the number of sales representatives needed?

c. Mr. Gunnar Sjoblom, sales manager for SunFun, thinks he needs to make a reallocation of his sales force's time to contact more potential accounts. He is considering reducing the amount of time spent by each sales professional to 35 percent of total time on the job. How would this change affect the number of sales representatives needed?

Crossword Puzzle for Chapter 18

CROSS CLUES

A seller's promotional presentation conducted on a person-to-person basis with the buyer

Personal selling task where the buyer needs help solving problem in analytical decision making

Face-to-face sales presentations made at a prospective customer's home or place of business

Personal selling in which customers come to the seller's place of business

Level of expected sales or profits for a product, etc., against which real results are compared

Sales approach using a memorized sales talk to ensure uniform coverage of major selling points

Indirect type of selling in which specialized salespeople promote good will for the firm

DOWN CLUES

2. Establishment of a sustained seller-buyer relationship
3. Promotion using the telephone on an outbound basis by salespeople or an inbound basis by customers
4. Fixed compensation payments made periodically to an employee
6. Identifying and pointing out customer needs and completing orders at wholesale/retail
7. Use of specialists from other functional areas to help sell a product
10. Stage of the personal selling process where the sales rep asks the customer to make a purchase
12. Salesperson's initial contact with a prospective customer

WORD LIST:

APPROACH
CANNED
CLOSING
CREATIVE
FIELDSELLING
MISSIONARY
ORDERPROCESSING

OVERTHECOUNTER
PERSONALSELLING
RELATIONSHIPSELLING
SALESQUOTA
SALARY
TELEMARKETING
TEAMSELLING

Chapter 18 Solutions

Key Concepts

1.	n	6.	w	11.	l	16.	x	21.	f
2.	q	7.	t	12.	h	17.	m	22.	v
3.	j	8.	i	13.	b	18.	d	23.	k
4.	s	9.	g	14.	p	19.	a	24.	u
5.	r	10.	e	15.	c	20.	o	25.	y

Self Quiz

1.	F	11.	T	21.	T	31.	a	41.	a
2.	T	12.	F	22.	F	32.	c	42.	e
3.	F	13.	F	23.	T	33.	b	43.	c
4.	T	14.	T	24.	F	34.	e	44.	b
5.	T	15.	T	25.	F	35.	d	45.	d
6.	F	16.	T	26.	d	36.	b	46.	e
7.	F	17.	T	27.	b	37.	c	47.	a
8.	F	18.	F	28.	c	38.	e	48.	b
9.	T	19.	F	29.	e	39.	a	49.	c
10.	T	20.	F	30.	a	40.	d	50.	d

Applying Marketing Concepts

1.	c	6.	b	11.	d
2.	d	7.	a	12.	c
3.	a	8.	d	13.	d
4.	b	9.	a		
5.	c	10.	b		

Computer Applications

1. Class A accounts: 800 x 26 contacts x 25 minutes each
    Class B accounts: 2,120 x 20 contacts x 25 minutes each
    Class C accounts: 3,080 x 15 contacts x 12 minutes each

    Class A: 520,000 minutes (or 650 minutes per client)
    Class B: 1,060,000 minutes (or 500 minutes per client)
    Class C: 554,400 minutes (or 180 minutes per client)

    Total time required: 2,134,400 minutes or 25,573.33 hours

    Hours available for sales calls per sales practitioner:
    48 weeks x 40 hours x .50 = 960

    Number of sales practitioners required:
    25,573.33 hrs./960 hrs. per pract. = 37.06 = 38

2. Class A accounts: 500 x 12 contacts x 1   hour
    Class B accounts: 650 x 6 contacts x 2/3 hour
    Class C accounts: 1,750 x 4 contacts x 7/12 hour

    Class A: 6000   hours
    Class B: 2600   hours
    Class C: 4083.33 hours

    Time required: 12,683.33 hours
    Plus fill-in calls: 634.1665 hours
    Total time needed: 13,317.5 hours

    Hours available for sales calls per sales practitioner:
    40 hrs. x 46 weeks x .60 = 1,104 hours

    Number of practitioners needed: 13,317.5/1,104 = 12.06 = 13

3. a. Class A accounts: 2,200 x .15 =   330 x 52 calls x 35 min
        Class B accounts: 2,200 x .25 =   550 x 26 calls x 25 min
        Class C accounts: 2,200 x .60 = 1,320 x 12 calls x 20 min

        Class A: 10,010 hours
        Class B: 5,958.33 hours
        Class C: 5,280 hours

        Total planned calling time = 21,248.33 hours plus unplanned calling time of 4,249.67 hours (21,248.33 x .20) = 25,498 hours

        Hours available for sales calls per practitioner:
        40 hrs. per week x 48 weeks x .45 = 864 hours

        Practitioners required: 25,498/864 = 29.51 = 30 people

b.   Increasing sales calls on type C accounts to 24 per year:

Class A: 10,010 hours
Class B: 5,958.33 hours
Class C: 10,560 hours

Total planned calling time = 26,528.33 hours plus unplanned calling time of 5,305.67 hours = 31,834 hours

Practitioners required: 31,834/864 = 36.84 = 37 people
The change increases the number of practitioners by 7.

c.   Hours of calling needed: 25,498 hours

Hours available per practitioner:
40 hours x 48 weeks x .35 = 672

25,498/672 = 37.94 = 38 people

Crossword Puzzle Solution

```
 1            2                                                3
 P  E  R  S  O  N  A  L  S  E  L  L  I  N  G                   T
    E                                                          E
    L                                                          L
    A     4                  5                                 E         6
    T     S                  C  R  E  A  T  I  V  E            M         O
    I     A            7                                       A         R
 8  O     A            T                                       R         D
 F  I  E  L  D  S  E  L  L  I  N  G                            K         E
    O     A            A                                       E         R
    N     R            M                                                 P
    S     Y            S                                                 R
    H           9               10                                       O
    I           O  V  E  R  T  H  E  C  O  U  N  T  E  R                 C
    P           L                L                  I                    E
    S     11                     12                 N                    S
    E     S  A  L  E  S  Q  U  O  T  A               G                   S
    L           I                S  A                                    I
    L     13                     I  P                                    N
    M  I  S  S  I  O  N  A  R  Y  I  P                                   G
 14 N           G                N  R
    M                           G  O
    I                              A
    N                              C
    G                              H
```

Name _____   Instructor _____

Section _____   Date _____

Cases for Part 6

1. *Servicios Tecnicos y Comercial por Empresas Pequenos de Cataluna, S.A.*

Servicios Tecnicos y Comercial por Empresas Pequenos de Cataluna (STECEPCA, for short), is a well-known financial planning firm headquartered in Barcelona. For the last 25 years, it has provided investment and portfolio planning services to small-to-medium size businesses all over Spain. Its promotional program has consisted of advertisements in the financial sections of the major regional newspapers, outlining the benefits of investment and portfolio planning for the smaller business and the advantages of working with a firm like STECEPCA.

Recently, responses to STECEPCA'as advertising have been on a decline, and the sales staff is wondering how they might better prospect for new clients. The newspaper ads had been quite successful in generating qualified leads. Part of this success was attributable to their placement in the financial section, but part also must be credited to the style of the ads, which made a direct appeal to senior executives of companies with funds to invest.

STECEPCA doesn't believe that the number of firms in need of its services has decreased, but the number of companies offering similar services has increased markedly. Some are national, like STECEPCA. Others, like Servicios Financieros de Madrid (SEFIM), serve only their province. None of the new firms have the expertise or experience of STECEPCA.

Question

Suggest several ways in which STECEPCA can generate more qualified prospects for its sales force to call on.

2. *O. Lee O'Leahy*, Inc.*

O. Lee O'Leahy, Inc., whose corporate offices are located in Geneva, Indiana, is one of America's premier producers of mountain-climbing boots. The firm makes not less than 27 different kinds of mountaineering footwear. Over the last five years, sales have leveled off but expenses have continued to increase.

Wally Ballou, promotions manager for the firm, is in a quandary. He feels that the way promotions are budgeted may affect sales. Until now, the amount available for promotion was a percentage of the prior quarter's sales.

*With fond apologies to the late Bob Elliot and not-so-late Ray Goulding.

Question

From Wally's point of view, what could O'Leahy do to help remedy this situation? What changes would your solution involve? Use numbers, if necessary, to illustrate your answer.

3. *Miller Major Appliance Corporation*

As the name implies, the Miller Corporation is a major producer of home appliances. The company's sales staff sells to wholesalers and distributors throughout the United States and Canada. Because of the nature of their selling job, they have traditionally been paid a straight salary. Miller is thinking about adding a new division which will sell direct to property developers—builders specializing in construction of condominiums, tract homes, and apartment complexes. This would be "package selling" in which Miller would furnish all the electrical appliances for the development: stoves, refrigerators, water heaters, dishwashers, garbage disposers, washing machines, clothes dryers, and heating and cooling systems. Some of these items would not be made by Miller but would be part of the package through arrangement with other manufacturers and would bear the Miller name. One consideration in establishing the new division is the sales force. Miller believes the creative type of sales practitioner is appropriate in this case.

Question:

What type of compensation plan might be most effective for the new division? Why?

4. *Central Shoe Company*

Central Shoe Company is a large manufacturer of shoes and related leather goods and is known as a leader in its industry. The firm's research and development department is particularly effective. Just over a year ago, Central first placed on the market a revolutionary type of shoe. Made of real leather, a special treatment made the product scuff and scratch proof, and it never had to be waxed or polished. For six months, Central had this segment of the market to itself, but within the last six months, several other firms have begun to market shoes with all the advantages of the Central shoe. Central's advertising program for the last year has centered on informing the public of the availability of the new shoes. Management now feels that the basic objective of its advertising should change.

Question:

What new objective for advertising should be established? Give some examples of ads that might be used to accomplish the new objective?

Name _____   Instructor _____

Section _____   Date _____

Creating a Marketing Plan:
Now Let's Get the Message Out: We're Here!

Introduction

Episode Six is designed to provide you with information which will let you complete Part III. D. of your marketing plan.

Episode Six

When we left our intrepid entrepreneurs, they were in the process of arranging for quarters into which to move their new business. It is now several weeks later, and most of the mechanics of set-up have been accomplished. The firm now has a business address, all of the appropriate licenses and permits, a stock of repair parts, a service area equipped with testing and repair equipment, and two well-equipped vans capable of doing field repairs or transporting equipment which can't be repaired in the field back to the service facility.

The problem now is to let people know that the firm exists, and that it is eager to provide the high-quality service its owners have made as their objective. The three partners have met to discuss the promotional means they're going to use to get their message across.

"Well, I think it's obvious that we need a display ad in the *Yellow Pages*," said Terry. "As I said before, there are all these repair firms which have listings, but only a very few ads. I think we need something to tell our target market we're out there to serve them."

"Good thought," replied Brian, "but the next edition of the *Yellow Pages* doesn't come out for four months. What are we going to do in the meantime? I propose we advertise in the business section of the newspaper; just a small ad once a week, and we can offer a free "preventive maintenance check" as a get-acquainted deal."

"Now I know why you wanted those stickers with our name, address, and phone number printed on them," commented Laura, "you plan on sticking those on any piece of machinery we get our hands on!"

"And on any other logical surface that would give us a shot at being the first firm they think of when the office PC goes on the blink," laughed Brian. "Better than that. I propose that, for the time being, at least two of us act as a sales force and get out there dropping off business cards and stickers at every business whose door we can get through. How about it?"

"Real good," remarked Laura, "but I've been thinking; why just try to let these people know who we are. Why not generate cash flow as soon as possible by selling them maintenance contracts right off the bat. I've written up a little promotional piece that we can drop off along with our business cards when we call on people. See, it tells them a little about the three of us—let's face it, we've got pretty good credentials and if we don't toot our own horn who's going to toot it for us—along with some of the costs of having computers repaired versus what we planned to charge for complete maintenance contracts. I think we can generate some business that way. I've even had the back page printed with some important computer facts that will let them spot problems they can correct without calling us. That may keep them from throwing the brochure away."

"Super job!" was Terry's comment, "and though it may be a little bit off the track, let me volunteer to do something which may seem a little strange but I think will do us a world of good. I'm going to hire my niece—she's your cousin Erin, Brian—to come over on Saturday mornings and work on the grass and shrubs around this building. Have you noticed what dumps most of our competitors' facilities are? I don't see any reason why we shouldn't have a good looking place. And I think we should spend time keeping the inside neat, too."

"Not off the track at all, Ter," said Laura, "people do react to the appearance of a place, and we have to expect our customers to come by here to drop off and pick up the equipment we haven't gone and gotten from them. They might as well get a good impression of us from our store as well as from our work. Besides, this isn't a bad neighborhood for a commercial street. We might as well get along with our neighbors, too. I know Erin loves to work in the yard. Maybe we can get her to plant some of those flowering shrubs she put in around your aunt's house."

Guidelines:

Examine the suggestions the partners have made and use them and your own ideas to complete Part. III. D. of the marketing plan.

Solutions to Cases for Part 6

1. Servicios Tecnicos y Comercial pro Empresas Pequenos de Cataluna, S.A.

There is not sufficient information in the case to absolutely sure, but it is likely that STECEPCA is suffering from the influx of competition into its industry. STECEPCA needs a new promotional approach to combat this competition. In most countries, firms like these are prohibited by law from advertising much more than what is known as "tombstone" information about their financial offerings—just the facts and only the facts, without projection. STECEPCA must find a new way to promote itself. Their newspaper advertising probably should be continued. To discontinue it would remove them from the day-to-day awareness or potential of it by their most likely market segment. There are, however, alternative approaches which can be tried.

One alternative promotional approach which STECEPCA can probably use to good effect is direct mailings to selected, well-known firms not now among their clients. A brochure featuring the qualifications of STECEPCA's personnel and the services they can provide and featuring a return card or coupon which can be used to request specific information has proven effective for a number of firms in this field. Of course, this assumes that STECEPCA can acquire the names of the firms' decision-makers and direct their mailings to these people. Another device which has been quite effective in this regard is the offering of free investment seminars (by invitation) to decision-makers who are pre-qualified by mailings or particulars they provide on requests for additional product information.

Ultimately, the goal of the basic advertising and sales promotional activities done by this firm is to put qualified investors in contact with sales practitioners who can serve their needs and generate revenues for the firm through sales commissions. Creative prospecting and qualifying are necessary to bring these prospective investors in touch with sales professionals who can fulfill their needs.

2. O. Lee O'Leahy, Inc.

If sales have leveled off, the percentage-of-sales method of allocating promotional dollars will yield a constant dollar promotional budget. The implied objective of the firm is to increase its sales continually. The firm should analyze the market potential and the current nature of the competition to see if such an objective is realistic. If it is (in terms of market potential), then several alternative allocation methods are available.

The most useful budget allocation method is probably the task-objective method. Setting a sales objective and then budgeting to reach that objective is the most logical way to approach a problem of this sort.

3. Miller Major Appliance Corporation

The sales force assigned to selling the development packages would undoubtedly have to be quite creative to tie developers to a total need contract for all their appliances. The lead time from contact to sale, however, will undoubtedly be of some considerable duration, so that a plan which features a basic salary every month plus a commission or bonus when a sale is made seems most appropriate.

4. Central Shoe Company

This case should lead you to think about the product life cycle and its influence on the promotional program of the firm. This product is moving (rather rapidly) from the introduction stage into the growth stage. It is now time to shift the emphasis of the promotional program from informative advertising to persuasive product advertising. Until now, Central has properly attempted to tell people about the existence of its product, since it was the only game in town. Now, consumers must be convinced of the advantages of the Central product over the products of other makers. The specific goal served by such advertising would be to build consumer preference for Central over other brands.

Solutions for Creating a Marketing Plan

Episode Six

In this episode, Brian, Terry, and Laura reveal a rather complex but fairly well thought out promotional plan. They will be using *Yellow Pages* advertising and newspaper advertising, sales promotional stickers and business cards, personal selling, and even public relations to develop a positive image for their firm. It might be very interesting to attempt to explicitly differentiate among the various forms of promotion which the entrepreneurs plan to use. Are the stickers, for example, advertising or are they sales promotion? My view would be that they are a variety of point-of-purchase advertising, a sales promotion tool. When does personal selling end and sales promotion begin in those instances when one of the selling partners hands a prospect a promotional brochure? A discussion of "supportive literature" could be very beneficial at this point. And let us not forget the importance of the business card. Many of these are saved and filed on the chance that the person who gave it to the recipient will someday be needed in a professional capacity. For the small businessman they are almost literally worth their weight in gold.

A very fruitful discussion hinges on the idea of keeping the building clean, neat, and presentable, if only because so many service firms don't bother to do this. If neatness and attractiveness count in a retail environment, why is it that they seem not to at wholesale or for service firms? The answer, of course, is that they do. All other things being equal, a neat, tidy operation has the advantage over one which is kept in a less attractive state. Indeed, the neatness may be reflected in the firm's fire and liability insurance premiums because a neat area is usually a safe area.

Students should feel free to suggest alternative means of promotion which Latebri Industries could use. They should, however, be warned, should they suggest using radio or TV ads, that experience has taught us that using these media for this kind of service is generally ineffective for two reasons: (1) the ad is generally lost in the clutter of other advertising unless the service is needed right now, and (2) such advertising tends to create generic demand for the service, seldom specific demand for the services of a specific firm.

Part 7

Pricing Strategy

Price is the component of the marketing mix most universally affected by the legal environment. Antitrust legislation (see Chapter 3) provides the basic foundation for regulation of price, amplified by the Robinson-Patman Act that prohibits a broad range of price-discriminatory actions. At the state level, unfair-trade laws (also called Unfair Trade Practices Acts) also have an effect on price-setting.

Pricing objectives can be related to profitability, sales volume, meeting competition, and creating a prestige image for one's product or firm. Pricing objectives for not-for-profit organizations differ somewhat from those of for-profits. Elasticity of demand with respect to price is another factor which must be considered in the pricing of a product.

Price theory and cost provide the rational framework for pricing. Price theory is relatively seldom used in the setting of actual prices. Cost, on the other hand, are the most commonly used basis for setting prices today. The typical cost-plus approach to pricing attempts to set a price for the product which will recover the cost of producing and distributing it and allow for some margin of profit. Two methods of applying cost-plus pricing exist, the full-cost method and the incremental cost method.

Breakeven analysis is a technique which is often used to help marketing executives decide whether required sales levels to achieve profitability are a realistic goal. A modified breakeven model, which superimposes an estimated demand curve over the cost and revenue curves of the breakeven chart helps identify the range of feasible prices and provide a more realistic base for deciding on the price to actually ask in the marketplace.

The making of pricing decisions is a two-step process which involves the setting and administering of pricing structure. Alternative pricing strategies include a skimming strategy, a penetration pricing strategy, everyday low pricing, and a competitive strategy. Competitive conditions have a significant effect on which of these strategies is chosen by a particular firm.

There are numerous possibilities which influence price quotes, among them being a firm's costs and policies and discounts and allowances which may prevail in a particular industry. Shipping costs often represent a part of price, and it is important to know whether they will be paid by purchaser or vendor.

Pricing policies include psychological pricing, unit pricing, and flexible pricing. Price limits often relate the price/quality relationship in the consumer's mind.

Prices in the industrial market are often subject to negotiation. In large corporations, the necessity to set transfer prices when goods are transferred among profit centers of the same firm is a major decision problem.

Chapter 19

Price Determination

Chapter Outline

You may want to use the following outline as a guide in taking notes.

I. Chapter Overview—How Much Is a Product Worth?

II. Legal Constraints in Pricing

    A. Robinson-Patman Act

    B. Unfair-trade laws

    C. Fair-trade laws

III. The Role of Price in the Marketing Mix

IV. Pricing Objectives

    A. Profitability

    B. Volume

    C. Meeting competition

    D. Prestige

    E. Pricing objectives of not-for-profit organizations

V. How Prices Are Determined

VI. Price Determination in Economic Theory

    A. Cost and revenue curves

    B. The concept of elasticity in pricing strategy

    C. Practical problems of price theory

Name _____ Instructor _____

Section _____ Date _____

Key Concepts

The purpose of this section is to let you determine if you can match key concepts with their definitions. It is essential that you know the definitions of the concepts prior to applying the concepts in later exercises in this chapter.

From the list of lettered terms, select the one that best fits each of the numbered statements below. Write the letter of that choice in the space provided.

Key Terms

a. price
b. Robinson-Patman Act
c. unfair-trade laws
d. fair-trade laws
e. profit maximization
f. target return objectives
g. Profit Impact of Market
    Strategies (PIMS) Project
h. value pricing
i. customary prices

j. demand
k. supply
l. pure competition
m. monopolistic competition
n. oligopoly
o. monopoly
p. elasticity
q. cost-plus pricing
r. Breakeven analysis
s. Modified breakeven analysis

_____ 1. Point at which the additional revenue gained by increasing the price of a product equals the increase in total cost.
_____ 2. Practice of adding a percentage or specified dollar amount (markup) to the base cost of a product to cover unassigned costs and provide a profit.
_____ 3. Pricing technique used to determine the number of products that must be sold at a specified price in order to generate sufficient revenue to cover total cost.
_____ 4. Market structure involving only one seller of a product for which there are no close substitutes.
_____ 5. Pricing technique used to evaluate consumer demand by comparing the number of products that must be sold at a variety of prices in order to cover total cost.
_____ 6. Short-run or long-run pricing objective of achieving a specified return on either sales or investment.
_____ 7. Market structure involving relatively few sellers and barriers to new competitors due to high start-up costs.
_____ 8. Market structure involving a heterogeneous product and product differentiation among competing suppliers, allowing the marketer some control over price.
_____ 9. Measure of the responsiveness of purchasers and suppliers to a change in price.
_____ 10. Federal legislation prohibiting price discrimination that is not based on a cost differential; this law also prohibits selling at an unreasonably low price to eliminate competition.
_____ 11. State law requiring sellers to maintain minimum prices for comparable merchandise.

_____ 12.   Market structure characterized by homogeneous products for which there are so many buyers and sellers that none has a significant influence on price.

_____ 13.   Exchange value of a good or service.

_____ 14.   Schedule of the amounts of a firm's product that consumers will purchase at different prices during a specified time period.

_____ 15.   Schedule of the amounts of a product or service that a firm will offer for sale at different prices during a specified time period.

_____ 16.   Major research study that discovered a strong positive relationship between a firm's market share and its return on investment.

_____ 17.   Statutes enacted in most states that permitted manufacturers to stipulate a minimum retail price for a product.

_____ 18.   Pricing strategy based on the traditional prices that customers expect to pay for certain products.

_____ 19.   Pricing strategy emphasizing benefits derived from a product in comparison to the price and quality levels of competing offerings.

Name   _____   Instructor   _____

Section   _____   Date   _____

Self Quiz

You should use these objectives to test your understanding of the chapter material. You can check your answers with those provided at the end of the chapter.

While these questions cover most of the chapter topics, they are not intended to be the same as the test questions your instructor may use in an examination. A good understanding of all aspects of the course material is essential to good performance on any examination.

True/False

Write "T" for True and "F" for False for each of the following statements.

_____   1.   The Robinson-Patman Act extends the power of the federal government into the international sphere by prohibiting price discrimination in international trade.

_____   2.   The price of an item is what it can be exchanged for in the marketplace.

_____   3.   The basic argument behind fair-trade laws is that a product's image, which is implicit in its price, is a property right of the manufacturer who should have the right to protect it.

_____   4.   The Robinson-Patman Act is sometimes called the "Anti-P & G Act," because it was designed to curb pricing abuses by large consumer-goods manufacturers like Proctor and Gamble.

_____   5.   The Robinson-Patman Act absolutely prohibits price discrimination in sales to wholesalers, retailers, and other producers.

_____   6.   Unfair-trade laws are federal laws requiring sellers to set prices at cost plus some modest markup.

_____   7.   The Miller-Tydings Resale Price Maintenance Act of 1937 exempted interstate fair-trade contracts from compliance with anti-trust requirements.

_____   8.   Price serves as a means of regulating economic activity; employment of any or all of the factors of production depends on the price each factor receives.

_____   9.   In classical economic theory, maximizing gains and minimizing losses is assumed to be a basic objective of the firm.

_____   10.   Target return pricing objectives are designed to generate a "fair" profit as judged by management, stockholders, and the public.

_____   11.   Many firms set a minimum acceptable sales level and then seek to maximize profits subject to the sales constraint in the belief that increased profits are more important than increased sales in the long run.

_____   12.   The amount of profits a firm makes may be computed from the equation: Profits = Price times Quantity Sold minus Expenses.

_____   13.   If a firm raises its prices ten percent and sales decline by 11 percent, the firm's revenues will increase.

_____   14.   In marginal analysis, profit maximization is achieved when the addition to total revenue caused by selling one more unit equals the increase in total cost caused by producing that unit.

_____   15.   Value pricing is typically used for goods and services that are less expensive than premium brands.

_____ 16.   Economic theory assumes that all businesses strive to maximize sales; the truth is that many of them seek to maximize profits, perceived to be a more realizable goal.

_____ 17.   PIMS data reveals that firms with a 40 percent or greater share earn an average of 32 percent on investment, while those with a less than ten percent share earn an average of only 13 percent.

_____ 18.   The PIMS study revealed that two of the most important factors influencing profitability were markup percentages and market location.

_____ 19.   The net result of a "meeting competition" pricing objective is a de-emphasis of price and a stronger focus on nonprice competition.

_____ 20.   Segmentation strategies seeking to obtain small shares of larger markets rather than those seeking to gain larger shares of small markets might be the most successful if PIMS data is correct.

_____ 21.   The fact that Joy perfume is advertised as "the costliest perfume in the world" indicates that its maker is seeking to achieve a prestige pricing objective.

_____ 22.   Some not-for-profit organizations attempt to recover only the actual cost of operating their unit.

_____ 23.   Pure competition is a market structure with large numbers of buyers and sellers of heterogeneous products in which product differentiation exists, allowing the marketer some control over prices.

_____ 24.   The price set for a product or service in the marketplace must be sufficient to cover the variable cost involved in producing and marketing it.

_____ 25.   The elasticity of demand is the percentage change in the price of a product or service divided by the percentage change in the quantity of the product or service that is demanded.

Multiple Choice

Circle the letter of the word or phrase that best completes the sentence or best answers the question.

26.   The law, typical of Depression-era legislation, which was inspired by price competition from developing grocery store chains and prohibits price discrimination in sales to wholesalers, retailers, and other producers is
a.   the Clayton Act.
b.   the Miller-Tydings Act.
c.   the Robinson-Patman Act.
d.   the Consumer Goods Pricing Act.
e.   the McGuire-Keogh Act.

27.   A defense may be made against a charge of violating the price discrimination provisions of the Robinson-Patman Act if it can be shown that
a.   another firm violated the Act in the same fashion and wasn't caught.
b.   price differentials were used to meet competitors' prices and were justified by cost savings.
c.   competitors engage in similar behavior on a regular basis.
d.   nobody in the firm is competent to understand the meaning of the law.
e.   the company has been doing this sort of thing for years.

28.   A firm using value pricing for a product might promote that product using a slogan such as:
a.   "Great performance at a reasonable price."
b.   "Be the envy of your friends."
c.   "Among the most expensive wines in the world."
d.   "The highest quality available."
e.   "The resort hotel of incomparable service."

29. Which of the following is a volume pricing objective?
   a. seeking a 20 percent annual rate of return on investment
   b. matching the prices of the established industry price leader
   c. establishing relatively high prices to develop and maintain an image of quality and exclusiveness
   d. seeking to capture and retain a specific market share
   e. attempting to assure a specific dollar profit in the current year

30. Marginal analysis is the approach used to determine the price to set when a firm's pricing objective is
   a. maximizing sales volume.
   b. maximum profit.
   c. meeting competition.
   d. creating prestige.
   e. market leadership.

31. The net result of the pricing objective of meeting competition is
   a. emphasis of the price element of the marketing mix.
   b. a more complex analytical process when prices are set.
   c. maximization of profits at the expense of image creation.
   d. creating an image of quality and exclusiveness.
   e. de-emphasis of the price element of the marketing mix and a stronger focus on nonprice competition.

32. Which of the following would be more likely to be a pricing objective of a not-for-profit organization than of a for-profit one?
   a. meeting competitors' prices
   b. achieving a target return on investment
   c. generating a specific dollar sales volume
   d. seeking to discourage consumption of a product
   e. maximizing sale volume

33. The producer of which of the following products most likely follows a prestige pricing policy?
   a. Baccarat crystal, "Crystal of Kings."
   b. Seiko watches, "Stylish, inexpensive timepieces."
   c. Budweiser beer, "The World's Most Popular Beer."
   d. Ken-l Ration for dogs, "Rover will love it."
   e. Coca-Cola, "The pause that refreshes."

34. One of the most significant studies of pricing strategies and objectives of the last twenty years was the PIMS project. For what does the acronym PIMS stand?
   a. Project to Investigate Marketing Scientifically
   b. Polish Institute of Marketing Studies
   c. Profit Impact of Marketing Strategies
   d. People Investigating Marketing Studiously
   e. Palmolive Investigation of Marketplace Situations

35. When a nonprofit organization follows a lower-than-average pricing policy or even offers a service free, it is probably following a strategy of
   a. cost recovery pricing.
   b. market suppression.
   c. profit maximization.
   d. seeking a target return on investment.
   e. providing market incentives.

36.   Retail prices that customers expect as a result of custom, tradition, and social habit are called
    a.   residual prices.
    b.   customary prices.
    c.   day-to-day prices.
    d.   unusual in today's market.
    e.   standard prices.

37.   A schedule of the amounts of a product or service that will be offered for sale at different prices during a specified time period is
    a.   a demand schedule.
    b.   competition in the marketplace.
    c.   a description of market structure
    d.   a supply schedule.
    e.   an equilibrium schedule.

38.   A market structure characterized by relatively few sellers, each of which may affect the market, though none of which may control it, is called
    a.   pure competition.
    b.   monopolistic competition.
    c.   oligopoly.
    d.   monopoly.
    e.   perfect competition.

39.   The market structure which is typical of most retailing and which features large numbers of sellers of heterogeneous and differentiated products, is
    a.   pure competition.
    b.   modified competition.
    c.   perfect competition.
    d.   oligopolistic competition.
    e.   monopolistic Competition.

40.   The average total cost of producing a product may be computed by
    a.   computing the change in total cost that results from producing an additional unit of output and dividing by total output.
    b.   determining the amounts of the costs that change with the level of production and dividing by gross revenue.
    c.   dividing the sum of total variable and fixed costs by the number of units produced.
    d.   dividing total revenue by the number of units sold to produce the revenue and subtracting variable cost.
    e.   determining the change in total revenue that results from selling one more unit of output.

41.   A condition of monopoly exists when
    a.   there is only one seller in a market and there is no close substitute for the product being sold.
    b.   sellers in the market are few but large and product is undifferentiated.
    c.   there are few buyers in a market, and sellers have to scramble to keep them supplied.
    d.   there are numerous buyers and sellers in the market but communication among them is imperfect.
    e.   buyers refuse to purchase what sellers have to offer.

42. Costs which remain stable regardless of the level of production achieved are called
    a. variable costs.
    b. fixed costs.
    c. average total costs.
    d. marginal costs.
    e. average revenue.

43. In the analysis of revenue and cost curves, profit maximization occurs when
    a. average total cost equals average revenue.
    b. marginal cost equals average revenue.
    c. average revenue equals average total cost.
    d. marginal cost equals marginal revenue.
    e. average total cost equals marginal cost.

44. The most popular method of setting prices today is
    a. marginal analysis pricing.
    b. cost-plus pricing.
    c. full-cost pricing.
    d. incremental-cost pricing.
    e. breakeven pricing.

45. The approach to pricing which uses only those costs directly attributable to a specific output in setting prices for that output is
    a. cost-plus pricing.
    b. customary pricing.
    c. full-cost pricing.
    d. breakeven pricing.
    e. incremental-cost pricing.

46. Modified breakeven analysis differs from traditional breakeven analysis in that
    a. breakeven occurs when total revenue equals marginal revenue, instead of when average revenue equals total cost.
    b. no consideration is given to the required profit when making the analysis.
    c. consideration is given to an evaluation of consumer demand as well as to considerations merely of prices and costs.
    d. breakeven no longer occurs when total profit equals total variable cost, but rather when total variable cost equals marginal revenue.
    e. calculations are made using computer programs, rather than manually.

47. Basic breakeven analysis
    a. identifies when a company's costs will exactly equal its revenues at some price for the product, assuming that costs can be assumed to be divisible into fixed and variable parts.
    b. is useless as a pricing tool because it is based on assumptions which are always untrue.
    c. has become less sophisticated in recent years because there has been a tendency to abandon it in favor of more useful tools.
    d. is an effective way of recognizing marketplace variables and preparing for them beforehand.
    e. is not described by any of the above choices.

48. Price elasticity of demand may be identified as
   a. the quantity change in demand for a product or service divided by the quantity change in its price.
   b. the quantity change in the price of a product or service divided by the quantity change in demand for it.
   c. the percentage change in the quantity of a product or service demanded divided by the percentage change in its price.
   d. the percentage change in the price of a product or service divided by the percentage change in the quantity of it which is demanded.
   e. the percentage change in the price of a product or service divided by the percentage change in the quantity of it which is supplied.

49. Demand for a product or service is considered to be elastic when the numerical value of the elasticity calculation is
   a. greater than one (>1.0).
   b. less than one. (<1.0)
   c. equal to one. (=1.0)
   d. greater than one-half (>0.5).
   e. less than one-half. (<0.5)

50. The Melvin Manufacturing Company makes metal castings for the plumbing industry. They are planning to introduce a new manhole cover assembly and are wondering how many units they'll have to sell to break even on the deal. Fixed costs to tool up to make this assembly have been $100,000. Variable costs for each unit produced will be $20. At a price of $45 per assembly, how many units must be sold to break even?
   a. 2,500
   b. 4,000
   c. 5,000
   d. 8,000
   e. 7,500

Name _____   Instructor _____

Section _____   Date _____

Applying Marketing Concepts

Southern Michigan Packing Company processes and sells canned fruit under the Southern Miss label. Noel Campbell, director of marketing for the packing company, was planning a speech to be delivered before the student marketing club at the local university. Noel knew the students would want to know about his company's marketing mix in general, but he knew that pricing was sure to be an exceptionally hot issue because of a big price-fixing case that had been getting a lot of publicity lately. He also knew that it would be difficult to explain the company's pricing policies since the firm did not aggressively use price to generate more sales. As one of three firms processing and selling canned fruit in a five-state area, Southern Michigan was satisfied with its third of the market and really didn't want to rock the boat unnecessarily. Prices were set at the beginning of the selling year, as the harvest was brought in. Those prices were then maintained till the next harvest, subject only to special promotional activities.

In general, prices were set by first estimating supply and demand for the company's products. Next, the cost of buying and canning the fruit was computed. Costs that could not be assigned to a particular fruit item were not included in the calculations. Once costs were determined, an amount sufficient to cover selling expenses and provide a reasonable profit was added to determine list price. Since the other two firms in the area used the same method of determining price, initial prices were usually quite close, and were often identical. Differences that existed in the early part of the season "ironed themselves out" by midyear.

_____ 1. Southern Michigan Packing Company's pricing objective would be classified as profit maximization.
_____ 2. The company would benefit from using modified break-even analysis.
_____ 3. Southern Michigan Packing is constrained by customary prices and thus cannot change prices from year to year.
_____ 4. The company's prices do not take into account demand for their products.
_____ 5. If Mr. Campbell were to apply modified breakeven analysis to his problem, he would have to use a method that assumes that variable cost would be a constant amount per unit.

6. Southern Michigan Packing Company's pricing objective is
   a. profit maximization.
   b. meeting competition.
   c. a target rate of return on investment.
   d. to maximize sales.
   e. to secure market share.

7. Mr. Campbell's talk is really about setting prices in a
   a. purely competitive market.
   b. monopolistically competitive market.
   c. oligopolistic market.
   d. monopsonistic market.
   e. market characterized by highly differentiated products.

8. The pricing mechanism which the company uses is
    a. the cost-plus approach.
    b. based on breakeven analysis.
    c. basically a modified breakeven process.
    d. based on analysis of demand elasticity.
    e. probably aimed at arriving at a customary price.

9. Mr. Campbell's method of determining costs for pricing purposes was to apply
    a. full costing.
    b. breakeven analysis.
    c. markup on selling price.
    d. incremental costing.
    e. differential costing.

10. If we had been told that the Southern Miss brand was strongly preferred over competing brands in two of the five states where it was sold, we could have concluded that, in those states, Southern Miss' market was probably
    a. purely competitive.
    b. monopolistically competitive.
    c. oligopolistic.
    d. poligopolistic.
    e. monopolistic.

Marcelin Plauché (pronounced ploe-shay) is in an enviable position. A graduate of the Ecole Polytechnique du Paris (civil engineering), Universität der Baukunst von München (architecture), and the Parsons School of Design (interior design), he is in such demand as both designer and contractor of private homes that he can literally name his own price. There are even reports of people hiring "hit" men to eliminate competitors for his services. Mr. Plauché realizes that popularity like his won't last forever and has stated in public that his fees are going to be high enough so that when things taper off he, his wife, and their twelve children will be able to live comfortably for many, many years.

The cost of a Plauché-built home is now about $300 per square foot. The average home built in the area costs around $50 per square foot. Though apoplectic with envy, other contractors continue to build and successfully sell houses because, even though they would love to be able to, not many people can afford a home that costs $300 per square foot.

11. Mr. Plauché is well aware that his work possesses an image of quality and exclusiveness that appeals to status-conscious people, and is pricing according to
    a. a prestige objective.
    b. a target return objective.
    c. a volume objective.
    d. an objective of meeting competition.
    e. an objective of maximizing sales.

12. The structure of the supply side of the home building market in Mr. Plauché's part of the country right now is probably
    a. purely competitive.
    b. monopolistically competitive.
    c. a monopoly.
    d. oligopolistic.
    e. monogamous.

13. If we assume that the actual cost of construction of a Plauché-built home is no greater than that of a home built by a "lesser" contractor and we take seriously his comments about "living comfortably for many, many years," we might conclude that his pricing objective would be
    a. profit maximization.
    b. target return on investment.
    c. meeting competition.
    d. securing market share.
    e. serving a selected market segment.

14. If Mr. Plauché collects money from his clients by submitting to them the invoices from his subcontractors and suppliers to which he adds sums for his own costs and efforts, then the pricing method he is using is
    a. breakeven pricing.
    b. incremental cost pricing.
    c. modified breakeven pricing.
    d. customary pricing.
    e. cost-plus pricing.

Name _____   Instructor _____

Section _____   Date _____

Experiential Exercises

1. This exercise allows you to obtain first-hand knowledge of the perceived importance of price by the marketing manager of a selected firm.

    Interview the marketing manager—whose title may be that of product manager, division manager, or general marketing manager—of a manufacturing, processing, or service firm to which you can gain access. Talk with this individual about the nature of the firm's marketing operation. When you have a good idea of the nature of the company's marketing operations, hand the manager four cards, each containing the name of a variable of the marketing mix: price, product, promotion, or distribution.

    a. Ask the marketing manager to rank the variables in order of importance to the product line that you have been discussing. List these variables in the spaces below.

        Ranking of Importance of Marketing Variables for:

        _____

        (Name of Product or Service)

        Ranked First:

        Ranked Second:

        Ranked third:

        Ranked fourth:

b. Ask the manager to explain why these variables have been ranked as they were. Why, for example, is the most important variable more important than the second-ranked variable? Try to get some measure of relative importance from the manager. How much more important is the first-ranked variable than the second, and so forth?

c. Compare the measures you gathered with those gathered by a classmate. Attempt to explain the similarities and the differences between the two sets of results.

2. A common price-setting technique among small retailers is "keystoning." Visit several retail establishments—stores such as independent hardware stores, small pharmacies, and home-owned spotting goods stores are suggested—and ask them about the use of "keystoning". (Warning: some may not know it or use it, but many do.)

   a. Outline the process of pricing by the "keystoning" method.

   b. What sort of pricing method is "keystoning?"

Name _____   Instructor _____

Section _____   Date _____

Computer Applications

Review the discussion of breakeven analysis in Chapter 19 of the text. Then use menu item 16 titled "Breakeven Analysis" to solve each of the following problems.

1. Pantothenic Products Company has been offered manufacturing and distribution rights to the Wainwright Walker, a therapeutic device which facilitates the healing of broken bones in the lower torso and legs. The current proprietor of the product, Bill Wainwright, has been unsuccessful in developing it and would be willing to sell out for only $20,000. Jan Sexton, the executive vice president of Pantothenic, believes that the product can successfully marketed at a price which will return $6.48 per unit to the company after all outside costs are paid. Examination of Wainwright's records indicates that variable cost of manufacture for the Walkers is $1.80 per unit. Fixed costs to Pantothenic to get under way with this product would be $56,000.

    a. What is the breakeven point in units?

    b. If Pantothenic wanted to recover the cost of acquiring rights to the walker during the first year of operations, what would the breakeven point be?

c. Pantothenic's president has mandated that every new product the company acquires must produce a $5,000 profit in the first year. How many units must the firm sell to break even if both acquisition costs and the mandated profit must be earned?

d. There is some question as to whether the variable costs that show on Wainwright's books are totally accurate. How would your answers to a, b, and c be affected if variable costs were twenty percent higher than expected?

2. Llewellen Welding and Fabrication Company of Aberswyth, Wales, builds sea-going barges widely used in the British-Irish and British-European transportation industry. Callan LLewellen, director of operations (and a fifth generation member of the firm) is working on its marketing plan for the next fiscal year. She has prepared the following estimates.

Fixed Costs	£1,092,000
Average Variable Cost per job	8,000

The table on the following page summarizes the company's capacity to handle jobs. Each line represents maximum capacity.

Price of Jobs	Number of Jobs
£ 20,000	48
40,000	32
60,000	21
80,000	16
100,000	12
160,000	10

a. Which average contract size would generate the most profit for the company?

b. In order to bid and win contracts over £90,000 additional equipment which would cost £160,000 must be obtained. How would the change in fixed costs affect the company's profitability?

Crossword Puzzle for Chapter 19

ACROSS CLUES

1. Pricing where a specified markup or percentage is added to base cost to arrive at final price
5. State law permitting a manufacturer to set a minimum retail price for a product
7. Exchange value of a good or service
11. Emphasizes benefits derived from a product compared to price and quality of competing offerings
12. Pricing based on traditional prices that customers expect to pay for certain products
13. Market structure with only one seller of a good or service that lacks close substitutes

DOWN CLUES

2. State law requiring retailers to maintain minimum prices for comparable merchandise
3. Pricing objective of achieving a specified return on either sales or investment
4. Amounts of a firm's product consumers will buy at different prices during a specified period
6. Type of competition involving a heterogeneous product and product differentiation among suppliers
7. Project that discovered a strong relationship between firm's market share and investment return
8. Measure of the responsiveness of purchasers and suppliers to a change in price
9. Market structure with relatively few sellers and high start-up costs as a barrier to entry
10. The amounts of product a firm will offer for sale at different prices during a stated period

WORD LIST:

COSTPLUS
CUSTOMARY
DEMAND
ELASTICITY
FAIRTRADELAW
MONOPOLY
MONOPOLISTIC

OLIGOPOLY
PIMS
PRICE
SUPPLY
TARGETRETURN
UNFAIRTRADELAW
VALUEPRICING

Chapter 19 Solutions

Key Concepts

1.	e	7.	n	13.	a	19.	h	
2.	q	8.	m	14.	j			
3.	r	9.	p	15.	k			
4.	o	10.	b	16.	g			
5.	s	11.	c	17.	d			
6.	f	12.	l	18.	i			

Self Quiz

1.	F	11.	F	21.	T	31.	e	41.	a
2.	T	12.	T	22.	T	32.	d	42.	b
3.	T	13.	F	23.	F	33.	a	43.	d
4.	F	14.	T	24.	F	34.	c	44.	b
5.	F	15.	T	25.	F	35.	e	45.	e
6.	F	16.	F	26.	c	36.	b	46.	c
7.	T	17.	T	27.	b	37.	d	47.	a
8.	T	18.	F	28.	a	38.	c	48.	c
9.	T	19.	T	29.	d	39.	e	49.	a
10.	T	20.	F	30.	b	40.	c	50.	b

Applying Marketing Concepts

1.	F	6.	b	11.	a
2.	T	7.	c	12.	b
3.	F	8.	a	13.	a
4.	T	9.	d	14.	e
5.	T	10.	b		

Computer Applications

1. a. Fixed Costs = $56,000; Variable Costs = $1.80;
        Selling Price = $6.48

    Contribution per unit = Price - Variable cost = $4.68

    Breakeven in Units = Fixed Costs/Contribution per Unit =
        $56,000/$4.68 = 11,966 units.

b.   Fixed Costs = $76,000; Variable Costs = $1.80;
     Selling Price = $6.48

     Per unit contribution = $4.68

     Breakeven in Units = $76,000/$4.68 = 16,240 units
              (16,239.316 Units)

c.   All prior costs remain the same, but $5,000 must be added to fixed costs.

     Breakeven point in units = $81,000/$4.68 = 17,308 Units
              (17,307.692)

d.   If variable costs were 20 percent higher ($1.80 x 1.20), contribution per unit would be only $4.32 ($6.48
     - $2.16), and the following would apply:

     for   a: $56,000/$4.32 = 12,963 units
           b: $76,000/$4.32 = 17,593 units
           c: $81,000/$4.32 = 18,750 units

2.   a.   Breakeven point in units = total fixed costs/contribution per unit (All monetary amounts in pounds
          sterling)

Price of Jobs	Number of Jobs	Breakeven Point	Profit
£ 20,000	48	91	(516,000)
40,000	32	35	(72,000)
60,000	21	21	0
80,000	16	15*	60,000
100,000	12	12	0
160,000	10	7*	428,000

*Both are actually slightly above the noted figure.

b.   New fixed costs = 1,252,000 (1,092,000 + 160,000)

Price of Jobs	Number of Jobs	Breakeven Point	Profit
£ 20,000	48	105	(loss)
40,000	32	40	(loss)
60,000	21	24	(loss)
80,000	16	18	(loss)
100,000	12	14	(loss)
160,000	10	8*	268,000

*A loss would be incurred at every contract price under 160,000. Profit at this level would be reduced
to 268,000.

Crossword Puzzle Solution

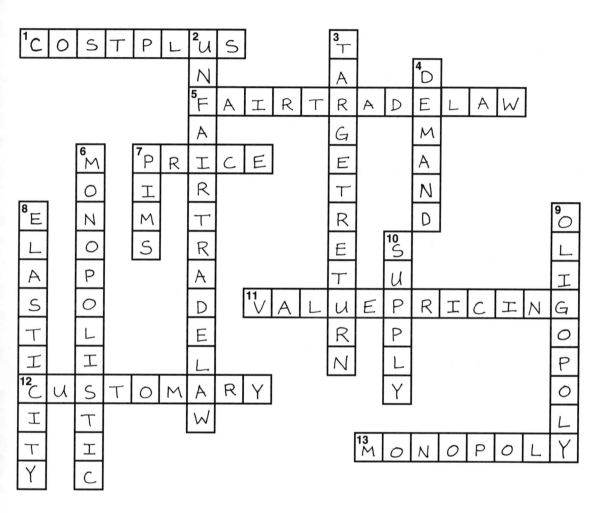

Chapter 20

Managing the Pricing Function

Chapter Outline

You may want to use the following outline as a guide in taking notes.

IV.   Pricing Policies

    A. Psychological pricing

    B. Price flexibility

    C. Product line pricing

    D. Promotional pricing

    E. Price-quality relationships

V.   Competitive Bidding and Negotiated Prices

VI.   The Transfer Pricing Dilemma

VII.   Setting and Managing Prices on a Global Basis

Name _____   Instructor _____

Section _____   Date _____

Key Concepts

The purpose of this section is to allow you to determine if you can match key concepts with their definitions. It is essential that you know the definitions of the concepts prior to applying the concepts in later exercises in this chapter.

From the list of lettered terms, select the one that best fits each of the numbered statements below. Write the letter of that choice in the space provided.

Key Terms

a. skimming price strategy
b. penetration pricing strategy
c. everyday low prices
d. competitive pricing strategy
e. list price
f. market price
g. cash discount
h. trade discount
i. quantity discount
j. trade-in
k. promotional allowance
l. rebate
m. FOB plant

n. freight absorption
o. uniform delivered price
p. zone pricing
q. basing point system
r. pricing policy
s. psychological pricing
t. odd pricing
u. unit pricing
v. price flexibility
w. product line pricing
x. promotional pricing
y. loss leader
z. Transfer price
aa. Profit center

_____ 1. Cost assessed when a product is moved from one profit center in a firm to another.
_____ 2. Price reduction granted for large-volume purchases.
_____ 3. "Free on Board" price quotation that does not include shipping charges, for which the buyer is responsible; also called FOB origin.
_____ 4. Pricing strategy involving the use of a price that is high relative to competitive offerings.
_____ 5. Pricing strategy involving the use of a relatively low entry price as compared with competitive offerings; based on the theory that this low initial price will help secure market acceptance.
_____ 6. Credit allowance given for a used item when a customer purchases a new item.
_____ 7. Advertising or sales promotional funds provided by a manufacturer to other channel members in an attempt to integrate promotional strategy within the channel.
_____ 8. Product offered to consumers at less than cost to attract them to retail stores in the hope that they will buy other merchandise at regular prices.
_____ 9. System for handling transportation costs used in some industries during the early twentieth century in which the buyer's costs included the factory price plus freight charges from the basing point city nearest the buyer.

_____ 10. System for handling transportation costs under which all buyers are quoted the same price, including transportation charges.

_____ 11. System for handling transportation costs under which the buyer may deduct shipping expenses from the cost of the product.

_____ 12. Practice of marketing different lines of merchandise at a limited number of prices.

_____ 13. Pricing policy permitting variable prices for goods and services.

_____ 14. Established price normally quoted to potential buyers.

_____ 15. Pricing policy based on the belief that certain prices or price ranges are more appealing to buyers than others.

_____ 16. General guidelines based on pricing objectives and intended for use in specific pricing decisions.

_____ 17. Price a consumer or marketing intermediary actually pays for a product or service after subtracting any discounts, allowances, or rebates from the list price.

_____ 18. Any part of an organization to which revenue and controllable costs can be assigned .

_____ 19. System for handling transportation costs under which the market is divided into geographic regions and a different price is set in each region.

_____ 20. Price reduction offered to a consumer, industrial user, or marketing intermediary in return for prompt payment of a bill.

_____ 21. Pricing policy in which prices are stated in terms of a recognized unit of measurement or a standard numerical count.

_____ 22. Pricing policy in which a lower-than-normal price is used as a temporary ingredient in a firm's marketing strategy.

_____ 23. Pricing strategy designed to de-emphasize price as a competitive variable by pricing a product at the general level of comparable offerings.

_____ 24. Refund for a portion of the purchase price, usually granted by the product's manufacturer.

_____ 25. Pricing policy based on the belief that a price ending with an odd number just under a round number is more appealing—for instance, $9.99 rather than $10.00.

_____ 26. Payment to a channel member or buyer for performing marketing functions; also known as a functional discount.

_____ 27. Pricing strategy involving the use of prices that are consistently lower than those of competitors.

Name _____   Instructor _____

Section _____   Date _____

Self Quiz

You should use these objective questions to test your understanding of the chapter material. You can check your answers with those provided at the end of the chapter.

While these questions cover most of the chapter topics, they are not intended to be the same as the test questions your instructor may use in an examination. A good understanding of all aspects of the course material is essential to good performance on any examination.

True/False

Write "T" for True and "F" for False for each of the following statements.

_____ 1. A "high-low" pricing strategy uses regular prices offset by frequent increases in specific prices.

_____ 2. Laser printers, television sets, digital watches, and pocket calculators were all introduced into the market using a skimming pricing strategy.

_____ 3. During the late growth and early maturity stages of the product life cycle, the price is typically raised because of the desire to control the size of the product's market.

_____ 4. One advantage of a skimming strategy is that it permits the marketer to control demand in the introductory stages of the product life cycle.

_____ 5. One of the forms of everyday low pricing involves manufacturers that seek to eliminate variations in wholesale prices often offered to retailers as part of trade promotion deals.

_____ 6. Penetration pricing is often called a "market-plus" approach to pricing because it is based on the premise that a higher-than-market price will attract buyers and move the brand from the "unknown" category to at least the brand recognition stage.

_____ 7. Since, in many instances, the firm intends to increase the price in the future, large numbers of consumer trial purchases are critical to the success of a penetration strategy.

_____ 8. Improvements in existing products seldom allow firms to introduce a skimming strategy where none existed before.

_____ 9. Price is not only a dramatic means of achieving a competitive advantage; it is also the easiest variable for competitors to match.

_____ 10. The basis on which most price structures is built is the list price—the rate normally quoted to potential buyers.

_____ 11. The typical marketer is unlikely to offer a combination of cash, trade, and volume discounts.

_____ 12. Trade discounts are justified on the grounds that large orders reduce selling expenses and may shift a portion of the product's marketing costs to the buyer.

_____ 13. If a trade discount were quoted as "35 percent, ten percent off list" to wholesalers, this would mean that wholesalers would pay the manufacturer of the good the list price less the 35 percent that they were to discount the list price to retailers, less another ten percent of the discounted price to compensate them for their costs, profits, and services.

_____ 14. A vendor who quotes a price of $5.00 per item on one to six units and $4.75 per item on seven to 12 units bought at the same time is offering a cumulative quantity discount.

_____ 15.   The major categories of allowances are price reductions and trade-offs.

_____ 16.   When "FOB origin" pricing is used, the buyer pays only the cost of loading the merchandise aboard the carrier selected by the seller.

_____ 17.   The method of quoting prices called "uniform delivered pricing" is sometimes also known as "postage-stamp pricing."

_____ 18.   The often-used term "FOB" is really an abbreviation for "Free of Bond."

_____ 19.   Both zone and uniform delivered pricing have the drawback that some customers, in the case of uniform delivered pricing those near the shipping point and in the case of zone pricing those near the inner boundary of the zone, will be paying "phantom freight."

_____ 20.   Originally, odd pricing was used as a cash-control device within the firm, forcing clerks to make change.

_____ 21.   Unit pricing—pricing goods in terms of some recognized unit of measure or by standard numerical count—has not improved the shopping habits of low-income consumers as originally envisioned.

_____ 22.   One-price policies characterize situations in which personal selling is employed, whereas variable pricing is used where mass selling is typical of transactions.

_____ 23.   Product-line pricing allows the shopper to pick a price range and then devote his or her attention to the other features of the product such as color, style, or material.

_____ 24.   Promotional pricing may be used recurrently or on a one-time only basis; in either case, it is considered to be a temporary ingredient in a firm's selling strategy.

_____ 25.   Many situations involving government and organizational procurement are characterized by set prices, particularly in cases of nonrecurring purchases like a weapons system for the Department of Defense.

Multiple Choice

Circle the letter of the word or phrase that best completes the sentence or best answers the question.

26.   Black Shield's strategy in pricing its Crown Jewel Connoisseur's Popcorn is characterized as a
   a.   skimming strategy.
   b.   penetration pricing strategy.
   c.   competitive strategy.
   d.   "market-plus" strategy.
   e.   functional strategy.

27.   Which of the following is one of the advantages of a penetration pricing strategy?
   a.   It allows the firm to quickly recover its research and development costs.
   b.   It is effective in segmenting the overall market on a price basis.
   c.   It allows a new product to reach the mass market quickly and capture a large share of it prior to entry by competitors.
   d.   It permits the marketer to control demand in the introductory stages of the product's life cycle and to adjust productive capacity to meet demand.
   e.   It largely negates the price variable in the marketing strategy.

28. When a skimming strategy is used, the product's price is typically reduced during the late growth and early maturity stages of the product life cycle because
    a. volume of production is sufficiently high to reduce the average per-unit cost of the product.
    b. competition has been effectively stifled and the product can now be allowed to sell at its "natural" price.
    c. the profits earned during the introductory and early growth stages of the cycle may be plowed into new productive technology, making lower prices possible.
    d. market.
    e. the product's proprietors have achieved their target objective and can now afford to take less "off the top" for contribution to profit and overhead.

29. Though the one chief disadvantage of a skimming pricing policy is its tendency to attract competition, it may still be used effectively for a long period of time if
    a. the firm marketing the product has patent rights over its design or can retain a proprietary ability to keep out competition (such as by keeping production methods a trade secret).
    b. research and development costs are small and the amounts to be recovered can be realized very early in the product life cycle.
    c. production facilities are developed so as to be able to satisfy all potential demand which may develop from whatever source.
    d. financial pressure can be brought to bear on potential competitors which will make them fearful of entering the market.
    e. inventories of goods are kept larger than any potential demand for the product which may develop.

30. When a penetration pricing strategy is used,
    a. prices are set at a level well above the prices of competing products.
    b. the price of the product is adjusted as necessary to keep it competitive with similar products in the market.
    c. the product is usually in the decline stage of its life cycle and price manipulation is a normal feature of this stage.
    d. it is almost necessary that there be no pre-existing competition; otherwise, the strategy won't work.
    e. products or services are priced noticeably lower than competing offerings.

31. A penetration pricing policy is likely to be used when
    a. few consumers are price-sensitive.
    b. there is some price-sensitivity among consumers.
    c. there is some price-sensitivity among suppliers.
    d. many consumers are highly price-sensitive.
    e. many suppliers are highly price-sensitive.

32. In industries where competitors' offerings are relatively homogeneous, a common pricing strategy is
    a. competitive pricing.
    b. skimming pricing.
    c. penetration pricing.
    d. pricing based solely on costs.
    e. market plus pricing.

33. Using a competitive pricing strategy
   a. is useful in segmenting the overall market on a price basis.
   b. conveys an image of distinction and appeal to buyers who are less sensitive to price.
   c. shifts the emphasis to nonprice competition in product, distribution, and promotional areas.
   d. is useful to introduce new products in industries where there are large numbers of competing brands.
   e. discourages competition, since the attractive financial returns associated with skimming are not usually present.

34. Which of the following most closely represents the list price of a product?
   a. the amount of money you and your next door neighbor's son both agree is fair to pay him to cut your lawn
   b. the amount of money you ask for when you decide to sell your 1986 Ford Taurus
   c. the manufacturer's "suggested retail price" on a new GE television set
   d. the advertised price of a home offered for sale by the owner in a classified newspaper advertisement
   e. the price you pay for an article after all discounts and allowances are subtracted from the original price

35. Reductions in price offered to consumers, industrial users, or channel members for prompt payment of a bill are known as
   a. trade discounts.
   b. cash discounts.
   c. quantity discounts.
   d. cutback discounts.
   e. "off price" discounts.

36. If the payment terms on an invoice are shown as 3/10, net 45, then
   a. the full amount must be paid within ten days and legal action will be taken after 45.
   b. the full amount is due in 45 days but if you pay the invoice in ten days you can deduct three percent from the total.
   c. three percent of the invoice must be paid in ten days, and the rest in 45 days.
   d. ten percent of the amount due must be paid in three days, with the rest due at the end of 45 days.
   e. three-tenths of the amount billed is due in 45 days.

37. Trade discounts are also known as
   a. cash discounts.
   b. seasonal discounts.
   c. incremental discounts.
   d. functional discounts.
   e. quantity discounts.

38. If a trade discount of 50 percent, 15 percent off list were offered to a wholesaler by a manufacturer, then the wholesaler would pay which of the following prices for a good whose usual retail price to the consumer was $100?
   a. $32.50
   b. $35.00
   c. $37.50
   d. $41.00
   e. $42.50

39. A discount that depends only on the number of units or dollar value of product bought in a single transaction is a
    a. noncumulative quantity discount.
    b. cumulative quantity discount.
    c. promotional discount.
    d. cash discount.
    e. market status discount.

40. Allowances are similar to discounts in that they are
    a. justifiable on the grounds that larger customers deserve to pay less per unit for the materials they buy.
    b. based on the operating expenses of each level in the channel of distribution.
    c. deductions from the prices purchasers must pay.
    d. the rates normally quoted to potential buyers.
    e. used uniformly across the consumer and industrial segments of the market.

41. Trade-ins that are used in the sale of consumer durables such as automobiles are examples of
    a. trade discounts.
    b. rebates.
    c. market pricing.
    d. allowances.
    e. variable pricing.

42. When a seller quotes all potential buyers the same price for goods, transportation included, regardless of where the potential purchasers are located, that seller is using
    a. FOB plant pricing.
    b. freight absorption pricing.
    c. zone pricing.
    d. all-for-one pricing.
    e. uniform delivered pricing.

43. Uniform delivered pricing is also known as
    a. postage-stamp pricing.
    b. pricing to the market.
    c. zone pricing.
    d. basing point pricing.
    e. standard industry pricing.

44. Pittsburgh-plus pricing was
    a. a variety of zone pricing once used in the meatpacking industry.
    b. a type of FOB origin—freight allowed pricing typical in the fresh produce (fruits, vegetables, and like goods) industry.
    c. widely used by manufacturers of parts for automobiles during the 1960's and 1970's.
    d. the once-standard method of quoting prices in the steel industry in the United States.
    e. a method of determining how much it would cost to ship anything to Pittsburgh.

45. When a retailer prices merchandise in terms of some standard unit of measure (ounce, liter, pound, gram), that retailer is using
     a. promotional pricing.
     b. unit pricing.
     c. odd pricing.
     d. psychological pricing.
     e. average-cost pricing.

46. The use of a one-price policy by a seller
     a. facilitates mass selling where the customer does not expect to haggle over the price.
     b. creates the possibility of haggling with the seller over the price of every item in the store.
     c. can often be recognized by the preponderance of prices ending in 5, 8, or 9.
     d. is quite rare in retailing, where flexible pricing is the rule.
     e. may conflict with the provisions of the Robinson-Patman Act or retaliatory pricing by competitors.

47. When a retail firm prices goods below cost to attract customers whom it hopes will then buy other, regularly priced merchandise, the firm is using
     a. bait and pull pricing.
     b. bull and bear pricing.
     c. loss leader pricing.
     d. product-line pricing.
     e. multiple-unit pricing.

48. The concept of price limits basically says that
     a. people consciously limit their spending to goods which do not affect their consumption patterns.
     b. a firm may encounter legal opposition if the prices of its products exceed certain limits.
     c. the relationship between price and sales volume is limited to values greater than two.
     d. consumer have limits within which their product-quality perceptions vary directly with price.
     e. reasonable individuals expect to be able to limit spending to necessities and a few luxuries, even in bad times.

49. In the governmental and industrial markets, when there is only one supplier of a good or service or where extensive research and development work is called for by a contract,
     a. competitive bidding may nonetheless be required by law.
     b. negotiation is likely to be the basis on which the contract is awarded.
     c. an escalator clause is typically included in the contract to protect the buyer from price increases.
     d. transfer pricing may be used to reduce the process of contracting to a comprehensible level.
     e. specifications must be especially carefully written so that breach or abrogation of the contract will be easy to prove in court.

50. When a lower-than-normal price is used as a temporary ingredient in a firm's selling strategy,
     a. it is called predatory pricing.
     b. "market-up" pricing may result.
     c. pass-through pricing is the policy.
     d. "market-down" conditions may result.
     e. it is called promotional pricing.

Name _____   Instructor _____

Section _____   Date _____

Applying Marketing Concepts

Digital Synthesis Audio (DSA) manufactures a line of compact disk players that are distributed throughout the United States. Sold primarily through specialty outlets, DSA products are recognized as leaders in their field. Sales volume and profits have both increased dramatically over the last five years. DSA sells through its own sales force, but in those parts of the country where sales volume isn't large enough to justify maintaining a company sales representative, it uses electronics wholesalers .

DSA is a respected name in its industry. Retailers often feature in their advertising the fact that they carry the company's line . The company encourages this and gives dealers who advertise their DSA relationship price reductions on DSA products to help them pay their advertising costs. They also have a somewhat unusual approach to pricing for an electronics manufacturer. Prices on DSA products are the same, including transportation, to any dealer anywhere in the country.

The company's product line includes three types of CD players. The basic unit accepts and plays one CD at a time and sells in the $225 to $275 range, depending on special features. The "multi-change" models accept six CDs and play them as desired by the user. These units sell for $325 to $400. The top of the line "supercharge" models can handle up to twelve CDs and sell for $600 to $800. DSA publishes manufacturer's suggested retail prices (MSRP's) whose dollar amounts always end in a 98 (like $449.98) and encourages dealers to stick with that ending even if they discount the product off the MSRP. It is management's belief that the 98 ending helps sales.

_____ 1.   DSA's pricing policies encourage retailers to sell DSA products as loss leaders.
_____ 2.   Since DSA quotes the same price to all buyers of its products it is using a unit pricing policy.
_____ 3.   The company is encouraging retailers to use psychological pricing.
_____ 4.   If DSA were to institute a trade-in program, it would be encouraging retailers to sell the company's products at less than list price.
_____ 5.   By pricing its products in different ranges, the company is attempting to establish definite price/ quality relationships in the consumer's mind.

6. The discount which DSA gives wholesalers who sell to retailers is called a
   a.   cash discount.
   b.   trade discount.
   c.   quantity discount.
   d.   promotional discount.
   e.   rebate.

7. What kind of allowance does DSA currently grant its distributors?
    a. a rebate
    b. a trade-in
    c. a promotional allowance
    d. an allowance for returned goods
    e. a sales representative's field allowance.

8. DSA's geographic pricing policy is
    a. FOB plant.
    b. FOB plant—freight allowed.
    c. zone pricing.
    d. basing point pricing.
    e. uniform delivered pricing.

9. The company's general pricing policy is one of
    a. product line pricing.
    b. unit pricing.
    c. skimming pricing.
    d. penetration pricing.
    e. price fixing.

10. The firm encourages its retailers to engage in
    a. skimming pricing.
    b. penetration pricing.
    c. unit pricing.
    d. odd pricing.
    e. unusual pricing.

Fred Lee Motor Company is a multi-brand new car dealership in Stuttgart, Arkansas. The company sells two American, one German, and two Japanese makes. Advertising strongly suggests that potential new-car buyers "shop Fred Lee for best prices," but specific prices are never advertised and each retail customer bargains with the company for his or her own selling price on a car.

The company is also on the state's "bid list," so it periodically receives requests to bid on providing automobiles for the highway patrol, game and fish department, and other state agencies. These bid requests are carefully read, and if what is needed is clearly enough described, the company may enter a bid. Occasionally, the fleet manager may have to call Little Rock to find out exactly what is meant by certain wording in the request sent out by the state agency.

All cars sold by the Lee dealership are sold delivered in Stuttgart. If the buyer doesn't want to take delivery in Stuttgart, the company can make arrangements to have the car delivered to them by another dealer from his stock for the amount of money it would cost to ship the car from Stuttgart to that dealership.

When asked about his pricing policies, Mr. Lee said, "One thing we know is that we never want to be the cheapest dealer around nor do we want to be the highest priced. People don't like you to be either one of those things. We just want to sell cars at a reasonable price that people think represents good value for the money."

_____ 11.   Though all consumer prices are subject to negotiation at Lee's, the company's advertising suggests that their pricing strategy is a competitive one.

_____ 12.   When a supplier such as Lee's enters a bid on a state request for bids, they are really opening the process of negotiation to supply those vehicles.

13. Lee Motor Company's basic pricing policy appears to be a
     a. fixed-price policy.
     b. variable price policy.
     c. list price policy.
     d. product line policy.
     e. zone pricing policy.

14. When the fleet sale manager calls Little Rock to get additional information on bid requests, he is probably trying to clarify the bid request's product
     a. specifications.
     b. end-use.
     c. price limits.
     d. function.
     e. user name.

15. The geographical pricing policy the company uses for delivery of cars at locations away from Stuttgart is
     a. zone delivered pricing.
     b. freight absorption pricing.
     c. postage-stamp pricing.
     d. basing point pricing.
     e. FOB destination.

16. Mr. Lee's comments about not wanting to be too cheap nor too expensive suggest that he is aware of
     a. how fickle the consumer can really be.
     b. price limits.
     c. the uses of odd pricing.
     d. the essence of the automobile-buying experience.
     e. how difficult it is to make money.

Name _____   Instructor _____

Section _____   Date _____

Experiential Exercises

1. This exercise is designed to familiarize you with the psychological concept of price limits. You will visit various retail stores and investigate the range of prices for selected products.

   a. For each of the products listed below, determine the range of prices charged for that product in two stores.

		Price Range	
	Store Name	**Low**	**High**
1) Flowering Plants	#1 _____	_____	_____
	#2 _____	_____	_____
2) Women's suits	#1 _____	_____	_____
	#2 _____	_____	_____
3) 13 inch color TV sets	#1 _____	_____	_____
	#2 _____	_____	_____
4) 16 ounce curved claw nail hammers	#1 _____	_____	_____
	#2 _____	_____	_____
5) Personal Computers	#1 _____	_____	_____
	#2 _____	_____	_____

   b. Discuss the price ranges you have discovered with the manager of one of the stores you investigated. How do these price ranges relate to what you've read about price limits? How does the store manager feel about his prices and price limits?

2. This exercise is designed to give you a greater understanding of the discounting process in the industrial market.

Visit a local manufacturer or wholesaler. After identifying yourself as a college student, ask to speak with whomever is in charge of their "accounts payable" and their "accounts receivable" ledgers. This person may be the head of the bookkeeping department, or some other individual. Once contact has been made, request the following information:

a) What kinds of discounts do they grant and what are the terms on which these discounts are granted? (Don't be surprised if they're called something you haven't seen in your text. "Trade" terms often differ from academic ones.) Determine the types and terms of these discounts and enter below.

    1. Trade (functional):

       Terms:

    2. Quantity:

       Terms:

    3. Cash:

       Terms:

b. What are the types and the terms of the discounts they are offered by their suppliers? Determine the types and usual terms and enter below:

    1. Trade (functional):

Terms:

2. Quantity:

Terms:

3. Cash:

Terms:

c. Ask the person you're talking to if it is his/her company's policy to take cash discounts or to pay the invoice only when it's due.

The cost to a firm in terms of an equivalent rate of interest of granting a cash discount or of failing to take one when it's offered may be computed as follows:

Equivalent rate of interest = The stated percentage of the cash discount multiplied by 365 divided by the difference between the number of days when the invoice comes due less the last day to take the discount. Thus, if terms of 3/15, net 45 are offered, the equivalent rate of interest becomes

$$Ei = 3 \times \frac{365}{(45-15)} \quad \text{or } 36.5\%$$

Determine the cost to the company of *granting* or *not taking* cash discounts.

Name _____   Instructor _____

Section _____   Date _____

Computer Applications

Review the description of the expected net profit (ENP) approach to competitive bidding in Chapter 20 of the text. Then use menu item 6 titled "Competitive Bidding" to solve problems 1 and 2.

1. Underwood Construction Company has received a request for bids from the City of Camden, New Jersey, for the design and construction of a new water purification plant. Underwood's estimating department has concluded that the cost to complete the project will be $1,920,000. Miller McDermott, Underwood's president, has prepared two bids based on this estimate, a low bid of $2,320,000 and a high bid of $3,040,000. McDermott estimates that there is a 40 percent chance that the higher bid will be successful and a 55 percent chance of winning the contract with the lower bid.

    a. Which of the two bids would provide the higher expected net profit?

    b. If new information, such as the decision by a major Underwood competitor not to bid, increased the probability of acceptance of the high bid to 60 percent and that of the low bid to 70 percent, which bid now provides the higher expected net profit?

2. Tachikawa Kokugijutsu Kenkyujo, K.K. (TKK for short*) is an aeronautical engineering firm that special-
    izes in making and testing prototypes of sub-assemblies for new aircraft designs. They have been asked to
    bid on the fabrication and testing of the nose wheel retracting mechanism of the Mitsubishi A14M3 corpo-
    rate jet aircraft. It's a relatively small job, but Tomio Kobayashi, company president, would like to make
    ¥4,400,000 (about $22,000 US) on the job. He has estimated the cost of making and testing the assembly at
    ¥1,700,000 ($8,500 US).

    a. What is the probability of acceptance required to earn a net of ¥4,400,000 if Tomio submits a bid of
        ¥7,800,000?

    b. Suppose he decides to bid ¥9,800,000. What does the necessary probability of acceptance become?

        *Tachikawa Kokugijutsu Kenkyujo, K.K. translates as Tachikawa Aeronautical Research Institute, Inc.,
        in case you wondered.

Crossword Puzzle for Chapter 20

CROSS CLUES

With "pricing," policy of marketing different lines of merchandise at limited number of prices

Pricing strategy in which price is de-emphasized by pricing products the same as comparables

With "plant" or "origin," means price quoted does not include shipping charges

Pricing strategy involving use of low entry price compared to competition to gain acceptance

Established amount at which a good or service sells that is quoted to potential buyers

Pricing strategy involving the use of a high price relative to competitive offerings

Discount offered to a channel member or buyer for performing marketing functions

Refund of a portion of the purchase price, usually granted by the product's manufacturer

DOWN CLUES

1. Allowance of funds provided by a mfr. to other channel members to integrate promotional strategy
3. Price policy which permits variable prices for goods and services
4. Product offered to consumers at less than cost to attract them to store
5. Amount actually paid for a product after discounts, allowances, and rebates from list price
6. Cost assessed when product is moved from one profit center to another within the firm
7. Any part of an organization to which revenue and controllable costs can be assigned
8. Type of discount offered for prompt payment of a bill
9. Credit allowance given for a used item when a new item is purchased
12. Pricing policy based on the theory that a $9.99 price is more appealing than a $10.00 price

WORD LIST:

CASH
COMPETITIVE
FLEXIBILITY
FOB
LISTPRICE
LOSSLEADER
MARKETPRICE
ODD
PENETRATION

PRODUCTLINE
PROMOTIONAL
PROFITCENTER
REBATE
SKIMMING
TRADE
TRANSFERPRICE
TRADEIN

Chapter 20 Solutions

Key Concepts

1.	z	7.	k	13.	v	19.	o	25.	t
2.	i	8.	y	14.	e	20.	g	26.	h
3.	m	9.	q	15.	s	21.	u		
4.	a	10.	p	16.	r	22.	x		
5.	b	11.	n	17.	f	23.	d		
6.	j	12.	w	18.	aa	24.	l		

Self Quiz

1.	F	11.	F	21.	T	31.	d	41.	d
2.	T	12.	F	22.	F	32.	a	42.	e
3.	F	13.	T	23.	T	33.	c	43.	a
4.	T	14.	F	24.	T	34.	c	44.	d
5.	T	15.	F	25.	F	35.	b	45.	b
6.	F	16.	F	26.	a	36.	b	46.	a
7.	T	17.	T	27.	c	37.	d	47.	c
8.	F	18.	F	28.	d	38.	e	48.	d
9.	T	19.	T	29.	a	39.	a	49.	b
10.	T	20.	T	30.	e	40.	c	50.	e

Applying Marketing Concepts

1.	F	6.	b	11.	T	16.	b
2.	F	7.	c	12.	F		
3.	T	8.	e	13.	b		
4.	F	9.	a	14.	a		
5.	F	10.	d	15.	d		

Computer Applications

1. a.   ($2,320,000 - $1,920,000) x .55 = $220,000 ENP
         ($3,040,000 - $1,920,000) x .40 = $448,000 ENP
         The higher bid provides the higher expected net profit.

    b.   ($2,320,000 - $1,920,000) x .70 = $280,000 ENP
         ($3,040,000 - $1,920,000) x .60 = $672,000 ENP
         The new information makes the higher bid an even better choice to submit.

2. a.   (¥7,800,000 - ¥1,700,000)X = ¥4,400,000; X = ¥4,400,000/¥6,100,000
         72.13 percent or better

    b.   (¥9,900,000 - ¥1,700,000)X = ¥4,400,000; X = ¥4,400,000/¥8,200,000=
         54.32 percent or better

    Please note that these are what the probabilities of acceptance *would have to be* for Mr. Kobayashi to make his ¥4,400,000 on either of these bids. We do not know *what the probabilities actually are*. Thus, for TKK to net ¥4,400,000 on a bid of ¥7,800,000, the probability of acceptance would have to be 72.13% or better, and on the bid of ¥9,900,000, it would have to be 54.32% or better.

Crossword Puzzle Solution

Name _____ Instructor _____

Section _____ Date _____

Cases for Part 7

1. *Madame Gremillon's Creole Seasoning Mix*

In east central Louisiana south of the Red River and west of the Atchafalaya lies Avoyelles Parish.[1] The people there are Creoles (not Cajuns)[2] who have preserved their French language and customs with as little change as possible for the last 250 years. But like their Cajun cousins to the southwest, they are creative and have adapted much of their cuisine to use native ingredients.

Odile Passavant Gremillon is an exception to the comment that "all Creoles can cook" in only one respect: She can cook *better* than most Creoles, and has the a bunch of prizes won at Parish and State Fairs to prove it. For years, friends and local retailers have been urging Odile to sell her famous Creole Seasoning Mix commercially. Today she borrowed $35,000 from the Bank of Moreauville to produce and market her product. As a consequence, she will be facing competition from products already on the market in the local area. Madame Gremillon's Seasoning Mix can best be described as a combination of herbs, spices, and thickeners which, when added to the liquid of stews, soups, and other slow-cooked foods, gives them a delightful bouquet and flavor and adds to them a texture which would otherwise be lacking.

Question

What should Madame Gremillon's pricing objective be? Defend your position.

---

[1]Louisiana has no counties. As in France, its civil subdivisions are called Parishes.

[2]Creoles emigrated from France to Louisiana directly; most Creole families arrived before 1775, while the Cajuns (a corruption of the French *Acadien*, were forcibly ejected from what is now Nova Scotia somewhat later in the century. The Creoles (which term is itself a corruption of the Spanish *Criollo*, meaning a person of European stock born in the New World) landed in New Orleans and moved northward to settle in eastern Louisiana, while the Cajuns settled the southwestern part. There are vast differences in the two cultures, as there are vast differences in their cuisines. Where Cajun food tends to be spicy—heavy with red and black pepper flavor—Creole food relies more on seasoning—onion, garlic, bell pepper, celery, salt, and browned flour to define itself.

2. Liberty Chime and Bell Corporation

Ralph Bolt, director of market development for Liberty Chime and Bell Corporation, has been asked by Walt Hadband, the company president, to estimate demand after the firm implements a price level change.

Liberty markets carillon chimes and single-hung bells made of bronze all over the United States. Their products are used in churches, public buildings, and carillons. There are other manufacturers of similar products which can be used if Liberty's bells are unsatisfactory. Costs of labor and material have risen to the point where some adjustment must be made. Mr. Hadband has considered a ten percent price increase, but before announcing the change, he wants to know if sales will decline dramatically.

Question:

Can Mr. Bolt provide a reliable estimate of the demand change to Mr. Hadband? How should he go about estimating demand?

3. Gunnar Thorwaldsen, Free-lance Viking (A Saga of Tenth-Century Norway)

Gunnar Thorwaldsen, a journeyman knight and freelance yarl from up near Trondheim, has developed a revolutionary new ship which he thinks will revolutionize the manly art of Viking, that periodic quest for slaves and plunder every right-thinking tenth century Norseman deems it his right and obligation in which to engage.

His ship has a unique underwater hull shape which allows it to hold the sea in even the heaviest storms but still draw so little water that it can be grounded on a gradually sloping beach to allow the passengers to depart for a little light evening raiding and pillaging.

Thorwaldsen estimates that he can build his "Viking Special" for around 3000 kroner (or the equivalent). This includes both fixed and variable costs. Since Gunnar expects to sell his ships to the better class of Vikings, their materials and workmanship must be of the best quality, and the expected lifetime of each vessel (assuming it is not lost at sea, taken by pirates, or burnt by irate raidees) will be at least ten years.

The shape of the hull of Gunnar's ship is determined by a special soaking and caulking process which he himself developed and is done in secret. He fully expects it will be at least fifteen years before anyone else can figure out how he manages to create this secret configuration.

Question:

Should Gunnar adopt a skimming or a penetration pricing policy?

4. *Monkmeyer Drop Forging Company*

Ted Monkmeyer, president of Monkmeyer Drop Forging Company, feels that his firm has a problem. Distributors are treating the Monkmeyer line of specialty wrenches very casually, and don't seem to be making a very active effort to promote their sale. Jan Stockwell, Mr. Monkmeyer's new executive assistant, has suggested a course of action she thinks will go a long way toward solving the problem. Ms. Stockwell believes that Monkmeyer should raise its retail price, thereby increasing the amount of discount per item received by both retailers and wholesalers.

Gene Nolan, sales manager for Monkmeyer, is displeased with Jan's proposal. He favors the use of promotional allowances given for specific purposes. Mr. Nolan would use cooperative advertising and PMs.[1]

Questions:

a.   Discuss the advantages and disadvantages of each proposal.

b.   If you were the director of marketing for Monkmeyer Drop Forging, which of the two alternatives would you choose? Why?

---

[1]PMs, or "Push Monies" are payments made directly to sales clerks and wholesaler salespeople. They are usually figured as a certain percent of sales. They are sometimes called "spiffs".

5.   *Donald M. Landsdowne, Attorney at Law*

Donald M. Landsdowne is an attorney practicing in the State of North Carolina. Mr. Landsdowne specializes in personal injury cases in which he typically represents the plaintiff and is compensated for his services by receiving a percentage of whatever judgment his client receives from the court or he can negotiate with the defendant. Mr. Landsdowne is a very conscientious and thorough practitioner, and his services are considered to be among the best. He has traditionally charged 40 percent of any awards he was able to get for his clients as his fee.

In recent years, there has been an influx of attorneys into the legal profession, and sheer numbers have made the industry very competitive. Mr. Landsdowne has just learned that a number of his fellow attorneys have reduced their fees on personal injury cases to 35 percent, and some are even accepting thirty percent of the award. He is concerned about what to do. He knows that his reputation is well-established in this field of legal endeavor, and even with the increase in competition he hasn't noticed any diminishment of his caseload. He is concerned because he feels that if he reduces his fees he will be working for less than he is worth, and most of his cases come to him by referral (from people he has successfully represented in the past), anyway.

Question:

What should Mr. Landsdowne do?

Name   _____   Instructor   _____

Section   _____   Date   _____

Creating a Marketing Plan: How Much Is Too Much?
(And How Little Is Not Enough?)

The information contained in this episode will help you complete Parts III. A. and III. B. of your marketing plan for Latebri Industries. You may wish to review the material in Part Four of the text to refresh your memory before attempting to complete Part III. A..

Episode Seven

"OK," said Terry, "let me get this straight. We're going to offer 'minimum down-time' computer service aimed primarily at business users of PCs here in the New Essex area. We're going to be open 24 hours a day, and we'll repair any brand of PC that walks in the door. We're going to offer maintenance contracts on the machines, and we'll pick up and deliver equipment for servicing if desired. I see. That makes me happy. What about you, Brian?"

"I'm fine, too, Ter," Brian said, "I can see where I'm going to be spending a lot of time doing preventive maintenance for people who own those units with the built-in 'computer viruses.' You know, I'll bet we're one of the few service firms in town with people who know how to create the right diagnostics to track those little devils down. It should be fun!"

"Right, fellas," spoke up Laura, "but you know we've got to get down to brass tacks on price sooner or later. You guys have fun just going out there and playing around with all those different brands of machine, but if we don't make some money around here, it's not going to be long before we won't be able to pay the rent. Come look at these figures I've put together. They outline some price information I got my hands on." And so saying, she handed to Brian and Terry a copy of the information contained in Tables P7-1 and P7-2.

"Very interesting," muttered Terry, reading the charts he had been handed, "we've really got a wide range of prices here, don't we. It looks like the most common local hourly price is around 80 or 90 dollars and hour."

"Yes," replied Brian, "but there are ten firms charging only $75. I wonder if they know something we don't know—or maybe it's that we know something they don't—(laughing) like how to fix computers!"

"Well," smiled Laura, "I've run some figures and if they are right, we can make money according to our plans at any hourly rate equal to or greater than $75. That price would put us in a very competitive position as far as the other computer repair places are concerned."

Table P7-1: Typical IBM Personal Computer Component Service Prices

| Component | Value New | Price for the Average Service Repair | | | |
		Carry-in	Mail-in	On-site	Courier
CPU, 8 Meg, Keyboard	$3,000	$165	$145	$250	$200
EVGA Display	300	28	25	44	35
Hard Drive	300	75	65	116	93
Printer	600	40	35	65	50
Total	$4,200	$308	$270	$475	$378
Percentage of Original Cost		7.33	6.43	11.31	9.00

Table P7-2: New Essex Area Repair Price Data (From a Survey of 42 Firms)

Charge Per Hour	Number	Percentage Reporting
$150	4	9.5%
110	4	9.5
100	4	9.5
90	10	23.8
80	7	16.7
75	10	23.8
60	3	7.0

Mean per hour charge for repairs:	$91.19
Median per hour charge:	$90.00
Modal per hour charge:	$82.50

"Yes, that's true," answered Terry, "but it's still the next-to-the bottom price for the market. I think we're better than that. I think we should ask at least $80 per hour for our services, and there should be a one-hour minimum."

"I'll buy the one-hour minimum," spoke up Brian, "but the average I see in these figures is $91.00 and change per hour. Why don't we want to charge something like that?"

"Let's put that decision off for now," commented Laura, "if we offer maintenance contracts, you know, we're going to have to price them as well. How do you propose we do that?"

"I've got that one solved for you, Laura," responded Terry. "An article I read last night gave some actuarial figures and some prices for maintenance contracts and it said that maintenance contracts that sell cost approximately as much as a 'worst-case' repair."

"You mean a repair that involves the whole system?" asked Brian.

"Yes," answered Terry, "and it looks like that sort of call costs about ten percent, on average, of what a new system would cost. I think our maintenance contracts should be priced at around ten percent of the cost of a new system to the client."

Laura entered the conversation at this point to announce "Good thinking, Ter; I've seen that article and I think you're right. Let's work on that sort of price for maintenance contracts. Now let's get back to the per hour price for our standard repair service. What price do you think we should set? Let's vote on it."

Guidelines:

a.   Outline the company's product/service strategy in your planning notebook. Refer back to the information provided in the earlier parts of this exercise for items which may expand on what you learned in this part. Recognize how this strategy developed to serve the needs of the market and of our entrepreneurial trio.

b.   What sort of price structure do you favor for Latebri Industries? Should their hourly rate be $75, $80, $90 or some other amount per hour? This time, the decision is yours to make, but you should be able to justify it if called upon to do so.

Name: _____   Instructor: _____

Section: _____   Date: _____

Creating a Marketing Plan: So When Do We Start To Get Rich?"

Introduction

The material provided in this episode should allow you to complete section III. E. of your marketing plan.

Episode Eight

The three partners, having incorporated their business, have themselves each bought 20,000 shares of the authorized 80,000 shares of Subchapter S common stock for one dollar apiece. They have also secured a $90,000 bank loan at a rate of 9.5% to be repaid over five years in monthly installments of $1,890.90.

They have established that sales of $180,063 will allow them to break even. Pro Forma Income Statements for the first three years of operation have been prepared and are included in Table P8-1.

Table P8-1:
Pro Forma Income Statements for Years 1, 2, and 3 for Latebri Industries, Inc.

Year	One	Two	Three
Revenue	$ 66,568	$120,876	$144,147
Allowances	2,645	4,800	5,724
Net Sales	63,923	116,076	138,423
Cost of Services	24,105	24,675	24,920
Gross Margin	39,818	91,401	113,502
Operating Expenses	104,859	65,149	63,370
Marketing Expense*	14,359	30,031	32,389
Operating Income(Loss)	($ 79,401)	($ 3,779)	$ 17,743

*Includes Sales Commissions, Sales Staff Salaries, and Advertising.

The threesome, as sole employees of the firm, will have collected all the commissions and salaries paid by the firm during the first three years. Those amounts are summarized in Table P8-1.

Table P8-1:
Salaries and Commissions Paid, First Three Years, for Latebri Industries, Inc.

Year	One	Two	Three
Administrative Salaries	$30,000	$30,000	$30,000
Service Salaries	19,200	19,200	19,200
Sales Commissions	6,745	12,247	14,605
Sales Salaries	11,400	11,400	11,400
Total Amounts	$67,345	$72,847	$75,205

They are, of course, due any dividends which they may elect to pay themselves from profits earned in years three and subsequent years.

Guidelines:

Use this information to prepare Part III. E. of your marketing plan. Note that, since this is a startup business, projections have been made pro forma for a period of three years. Impact of the trio's efforts will be evidenced by the degree to which the projections and reality are similar.

Question:

Will it all have been worth it. Considering the future of the company, will the three partners have gotten out of it what they expected to, in your opinion? Remember, the psychic reward of entrepreneurship has some value.

Solutions to Cases for Part 7

1. **Madame Gremillon's Creole Seasoning Mix**
   Madame Gremillon can choose from four different pricing objectives: profitability, volume, meeting competition, and prestige. Let us examine Odile's situation before deciding on a preferred strategy. At the moment, the company is a cottage industry. There are no employees and total capital is $35,000. The product is a unique, "home-style" one which may well have an appeal only within a very limited radius of Mme. Gremillon's home. The potential competition, on the other hand, consists of people like McCormick and Spice Island as well as some of the regionals like the Zatarain, McIlhenny, and Chacere firms. No small potatoes, these. Odile has an advantage in the marketplace among people who like a certain flavor and texture to their food. She does not have any cost advantage over the competition. We must wonder what her motives for going into business are. Does she wish to make a great deal of money, or is she in it for a greater scope of recognition for her culinary skills? The selection of strategy depends on the interpretation of Mme. Gremillon's motives. The inference that many of you will make is that Mme. Gremillon's personal reputation will let her charge a prestige price. This is a logical inference, because her resource base doesn't really allow her to look at the other strategies too closely. We know that she does have an excellent local reputation, and there certainly is no obvious reason why she shouldn't play on it in the early going with her new company.

2. **Liberty Chime and Bell Corporation**
   Past experience can probably tell Ralph whether demand will decline precipitously if the price is raised. It is unlikely, however, that he will be able to tell by exactly how much it will decline. Predicting demand responses to price changes is not an exact science. The person changing the price does not really know if conditions are the same now as they were when the last price change was implemented. Inflation, changes in user tastes, and competitor reactions will all come into play in determining what will happen in the marketplace. If it is absolutely necessary to get more information than is on hand, a price expectation study could be conducted among known purchasers of carillon and other bells. It might even be feasible to change prices in a limited geographical area to see how bell buyers react to them.

3. **Gunnar Thorwaldsen, Freelance Viking**
   Gunnar would probably be better off entering the market with a penetration pricing policy. There are several reasons why this choice would be effective. First, his new ship does not immediately tell the potential user why he should buy it. Until one has ridden out an Arctic gale in one of these vessels one probably will not appreciate its seaholding capabilities. Gunnar's ship will ride and steer differently in a seaway than your standard Viking longship, and that will take some getting used to on the part of the rather conservative Norwegians. Even though the ships will be well-built and capable of lasting ten years, the rate of losses at sea, to pirates, and even to "irate raidees" should create a substantial replacement market once the product has gotten a "foot in the door" and becomes well known throughout Norsedom. All of these factors argue for a penetration price to induce potential buyers to give the product a try. The cost, by the way, is really rather modest. At current rates of exchange, it works out to be something less than $1,000 US, and while price levels in 10th century Norway were lower than is the case today, I expect that it's still a small enough amount so that even pricing at penetration levels, Gunnar certainly should be able to generate enough sales to buy himself a rather nice estate in relatively few years.

4. **Monkmeyer Drop Forging Company**
   a. This case really revolves around attempting to motivate marketing intermediaries by paying them more. Two approaches to this increase in payment are taken. The first suggests the raising of prices to increase the amount of trade or functional discount allowed the intermediaries. This approach has the advantage of not increasing the company's out-of-pocket expenses. The price increase at retail allows the interme-

diary to keep a greater dollar amount for every unit of product sold. It has two significant disadvantages, however: first, there is the risk that it will not motivate the distributor since the trade discount is considered to be his normal due for performing his distributional functions; secondly, that sales may decrease because of the higher price and the distributor receive the same or less money. It is not a sound business practice to attempt to get something for nothing, and this plan seems to be trying to do just that. The second plan provides promotional allowances for specific services provided, such as advertising and sales efforts by clerks. It would be necessary to monitor the performance of these specific services, a process which would cost some money. Thus, this approach creates two new costs, the cost of the services themselves and the cost of monitoring their performance. This approach tends to increase costs without impacting price, thus lowering profit margins for Monkmeyer. On the other hand, it does allow Monkmeyer to control the additional services offered by its distributors. It also provides a monetary incentive for helping Monkmeyer's market.

b.   Gene Nolan's suggestion seems to have the greater merit for the reasons stated in (a).

5.   Donald M. Landsdowne, Attorney at Law

It would appear that the prices of legal services are adjusting themselves to competitive conditions in the marketplace. The influx of new practitioners has, in effect, created an oversupply condition in which a new price schedule is appearing which reflects the relative desperation of the attorneys in the area. In the practice of law as in the selling of hardware, competitive conditions can be competitive, oligopolistic, monopolistic, or monopolistically competitive. One might suspect that Mr. Landsdowne, by virtue of his long experience and good track record, has developed for himself a monopolistically competitive position in the marketplace. He gets most of his cases on referral, which means he has a number of satisfied clients out there who recommend him to their friends when the need arises. When he is successful in a litigation or negotiation, his name appears in the newspaper, reminding people of who he is and what he does. In a situation like this, there doesn't seem to be any reason why Mr. Landsdowne should change his prices. I would recommend no change in his policies at present, but I would advise him to monitor carefully further developments in the marketplace so as to detect any additional information which might change this verdict.

Solutions for Creating a Marketing Plan

Episode Seven

a.   It should be well enough established by now that Latebri Industries intends to provide twenty-four hour a day, seven day a week PC service directed primarily at the business user of PCs that further elucidation would be unnecessary, but one can never be sure. This is, however, the first time the term "minimum down time" has been used to describe the firm's mission, and that may be significant in allowing students to differentiate between the uses of computers in the home and in business. Home users of computers do not usually view them as money-making tools which cost money when they are out of service, and hence will tolerate a certain amount of inconvenience and lost time getting their units repaired. If a business computer goes down, people cannot get their work done and the company loses money. There is a substantial situational difference here which can be explored at length if it desired to do so.

b.   The partners have any number of prices available to them. We know that $75 per hour is their bottom line minimum price below which they cannot go and achieve their stated objectives of volume and profitability. The data also shows that there is quite a lot of clustering at the price levels of $75, $80, and $90. As a new firm entering a fairly competitive market, it is probably unwise to try and adopt a skimming policy even though the quality of their product is ultimately going to be higher than that of the competition's. Their potential customers don't know that, and right now probably wouldn't care, anyway. A penetration pricing strategy would be the best choice in this case. My personal leanings are toward $80 per hour with a one-hour minimum. This places them 12.27 percent below the average price in the market and ten dollars below the median price, and still offers profit potential better than they have indicated they need in order to be satisfied. Their pricing of maintenance contracts will be in line with industry practice, and though it may be low when compared with the average of on-site repairs, must be discounted by the fact that the money is received up front and the repairs are made, if needed, somewhere down the road.

It is always well to remember that prices are not etched in stone. If Latebri's quality service develops for them a satisfactory volume of business, price can be adjusted upward or downward to satisfy the goals of the entrepreneurs. We might judge, from some of their discussions, that they really aren't in it just for the money, anyway, and that the desire for profit is the desire to put bread on the table as needed, but also to have a good time while doing it.

Episode Eight

Completing this section of the marketing plan completed the entire plan. The crucial question arising out of the projections of sales, costs, and revenues given in this section is meant to be "Will it be worth it?" On first blush, the income figures for these three fairly well-educated people may seem a little low: an average of $25,000 per year after three years of hard work—if it all works out! But there is more to it than may appear just in the raw figures. There is the equity, or sellout value in the company once it gets to be a going concern. There is the stream of profits which will just be starting to accrue at the end of that third year. There is the possibility of turning some of the day-to-day operations of the company over to hired employees and taking a little (or a lot) of time off. And, of course, there is the idea of working for yourself, rather than for someone else, which may itself be the motivation to start any small business. Some of your more dedicated students may attempt to project the income of this firm out for a longer period. If they do, advise them to pick a relatively conservative rate of growth, as was done in the model (20% per year). They may assume that gross margin will stabilize at about 80% of net sales, and total expenses at about 70% of net sales, quite possibly declining slightly as fixed costs become a somewhat smaller percentage of the total.

At the end of five years, if projections are fulfilled, this firm should be grossing in excess of $200,000 and earning a net profit of something in the neighborhood of $25,000 or more, after all expenses and salaries are paid. The question of the worth of that kind of return remains up in the air, and can only be answered in terms of the worth to the three entrepreneurs of being entrepreneurs. Somehow, I think they'll be happy with it.